ITALIAN CIVIL AND MILITARY AIRCRAFT
1930-1945

To my father, John H. Thompson

ITALIAN CIVIL AND MILITARY AIRCRAFT 1930-1945

By

JONATHAN W. THOMPSON

With Illustrations by the Author

1963

AERO PUBLISHERS, INC.

LOS ANGELES 26, CALIFORNIA

© AERO PUBLISHERS, INC. 1963

All rights reserved. This book, or parts thereof, must not be reproduced without permission of the publisher.

Library of Congress Catalog Card Number

63 — 17621

Printed and Published in the United States of America by Aero Publishers, Inc.

INTRODUCTION

In contrast to the wealth of material available on the aircraft of the other major powers of the Second World War, no book has presented a complete picture of the Italian machines of that fascinating period. Although some of the better-known Regia Aeronautica aircraft have received their share of attention, the majority have long been neglected. I hope that this book will remedy the situation and fill a gap in aviation literature.

At first I had intended to cover only those Italian military aircraft which actually participated in the conflict, but researches into their prewar backgrounds revealed so many interesting earlier aircraft that the period 1930-45 was finally selected. During the 1930's Italian aviation was at its peak; famous distance flights and international records made Italy one of the most prominent of air-minded nations. The creative imagination of her designers was matched by the initiative and daring of her airmen. Despite the apprehension attending the growth of Fascism, it was all too easy to admire Marshall Balbo's aerial fleet droning overhead toward the Chicago World's Fair in 1933. This impressive display came in an era when aviation was just beginning to prove itself a dependable instrument of transportation.

Notwithstanding this apparent lead, the Regia Aeronautica was surprisingly ineffective when war finally came. The reasons were primarily economic and political. In spite of her Fascist government, Italy was not aggressive to the degree that made Germany and Japan such dangerous threats. Her conquests in Africa and exploits in Spain were comparatively easy exercises that led her to believe, in June 1940, that Fascism was triumphant and little further effort was called for to secure the spoils of victory. When the war began to turn decidedly against Italy, the weaknesses of her war machine became apparent. The Italian economy was never strong enough to support the air force envisaged by Mussolini; in addition, Italy had to export badly needed aircraft in return for raw materials vital to production. This fact, rather than the supposed outdated design practices, accounted for the predominant use of wood in Italian aircraft. More important, engine development lagged seriously behind world standards, further hampering designers.

All these factors proved fortunate for the Allies, as an examination of mid-1943 Italian designs will make quite clear. Fighters like the FIAT G.56 and Macchi C.205V and bombers like the Cant Z.1018 gave away little to their Allied counterparts in terms of performance. Many other aircraft in this book, whether brilliant or mediocre in the final analysis, were of extremely imaginative and advanced concept. If this book helps to increase interest in Italian aircraft it will have served its purpose.

It is impossible to give enough credit to the many friends, associates, aviation historians, and collectors who have helped in the preparation of this book. I would like to thank particularly the following: Giorgio Apostolo, who provided many excellent photographs; Giorgio Bignozzi, who furnished drawings and photographs which were very helpful in the preparation of my own illustrations; Peter M. Bowers, whose giant file of aeronautica yielded a number of valuable photographs; John Caler, who very kindly made his vast collection of aviation books and periodicals available to me and who gave much encouragement during the initial stages of the book; C. J. D'Amato, who provided photographs; Hans J. Ebert, who provided information and photographs; Frederick G. Freeman, Jr., who furnished negatives from his collection; Heinz J. Nowarra, who provided photographs from his valuable aviation file; Giorgio Santocanale, who secured photographs for me; Peter Selinger, who provided photographs; Bruno Sermarini, whose invaluable assistance in unearthing a wealth of little-known information and many rare, previously-unpublished photographs cannot be overemphasized; Donald A. Tagg, who helped find numerous publications for my aeronautical library; John W. Underwood, who gave valuable advice and assistance in addition to several good photographs; and Giulio C. Valdonio, who furnished information and photographs. In addition, I wish to thank the public relations departments of AERFER (I.M.A.M.), S.A.I. Ambrosini, FIAT, and Aeronautica Macchi, as well as the Ministero della Difesa — Aeronautica and the Office of the Italian Air Attaché in Washington, the members of INTERCONAIR, the aviation and naval magazine, and Dr. Rosario Abate and Edizioni Aeronautica of Milan, Italy. Additional photographs were furnished by Air Mondial, Paris.

Jonathan W. Thompson

CONTENTS

AMBROSINI	7
BREDA	20
C.A.N.S.A.	45
CANT	52
CAPRONI	76
CAPRONI BERGAMASCHI	99
CAPRONI VIZZOLA	119
C.M.A.S.A.	123
C.N.A.	131
FIAT	134
MACCHI	175
MERIDIONALI	196
NARDI	214
PIAGGIO	218
REGGIANE	235
S.A.I.M.A.N.	248
SAVOIA-MARCHETTI	250
UMBRA	290
MISCELLANEOUS MANUFACTURERS	292
Appendices	
I — Notes on Conversion Factors	295
II — Aircraft Designations	295
III — Aircraft Engines	295
IV — Civil Registrations	297
V — Organization of the Regia Aeronautica	299
VI — Color Schemes, Camouflage, and Markings	299
Bibliography	304

AMBROSINI
Società Aeronautica Italiana Ing. A. Ambrosini & C.

In 1934 the Ambrosini industrial group absorbed the Società Aeronautica Italiana, located at Passignano, on Lake Trasimeno. Under the direction of Ing. Sergio Stefanutti, the company has specialized in the design and manufacture of high-performance light aircraft. The excellent postwar S.7 and Supersette (Super 7) trainers are direct developments of a series of sport, training, and fighter machines initiated in 1939 with the very advanced S.A.I 7. Prior to that, Ambrosini had devoted its efforts solely to civil aircraft.

S.A.I. 1
Built in 1935 for the Littorio Air Rally, the S.A.I. 1 two-seat biplane was powered by a 140 h.p. FIAT A.54 radial engine enclosed in an N.A.C.A. cowling. An interesting point was the upper wing center bracing, which incorporated transparent panels forming a vee-windscreen; separate screens were provided for each of the tandem open cockpits. Empty and loaded weights were 1342 lb. and 2046 lb.; at the latter figure the S.A.I. 1 achieved a maximum speed of 137 m.p.h. Cruising and landing speeds were respectively 121 m.p.h. and 53 m.p.h. Dimensions were: span 28 ft. 2 in., length 21 ft. 4 in., and height 8 ft. 2 in. Total wing area was 185 sq. ft.

S.A.I. 2
The S.A.I. 2, also designed for the 1935 Littorio rally, was in contrast a low-wing five-passenger cabin model. Two side-by-side seats were provided forward of the door, with accommodations for three passengers behind. Employing the same engine as the biplane, the S.A.I. 2 enjoyed an improved maximum speed of .149 m.p.h., in spite of the greater loaded weight of 2347 lb. Cruising speed was 127 m.p.h., although the landing speed did not increase. Weighing 1529 lb. empty, the S.A.I. 2 had a span of 33 ft. 5 in., a length of 23 ft. 3 in., and a height of 7 ft. 10 in. The wing area of 170 sq. ft. was only slightly less than that of the biplane, due to a substantial increase in the chord.

S.A.I. 2 S
Despite its similar designation, the S.A.I. 2 S bore only a general similarity to its 1935 predecessor. This four-seat cabin monoplane

The S.A.I. 1 two-seat sport biplane; note the screen built into the wing center bracing. (I-AZIR)

The S.A.I. 2's five-passenger cabin resulted in a bulky fuselage. (I-AMIR)

appeared in 1937 for the Italian Air Races, and was subsequently built in relatively large numbers. Several were still operating in Italy very recently. Powered by a 200 h.p. Alfa Romeo 115-I six-cylinder inverted in-line engine, the S.A.I. 2 S employed Handley-Page slots and flaps; some models were characterized by a tapering dorsal fin. Empty and loaded weights were 1958 lb. and 3124 lb. respectively. The S.A.I. 2 S reached a maximum speed of 155 m.p.h. and cruised at 134 m.p.h. Landing speed was 52 m.p.h. A range of 602 miles was possible; ceiling was 19,680 ft. Dimensions were: span 34 ft. 11 in., length 25 ft. 6 in., height 9 ft. 2 in., and wing area 193 sq. ft.

S.A.I. 3

Continuing the line of low-wing monoplanes was the S.A.I. 3, a two-seat light training and touring model of all-wood construction. Powered by either an 85 h.p. FIAT A.50 radial or a 130 h.p. Alfa Romeo 110 four-cylinder inverted in-line engine, the S.A.I. 3 had open cockpits, although all-enclosing canopies were fitted to some examples.

Using the FIAT engine, the S.A.I. 3 achieved a maximum speed of 124 m.p.h. and cruised at 105 m.p.h., landing speed being 60 m.p.h. Empty and loaded weights were 1210 lb. and 1738 lb. A ceiling of 13,120 ft. and a range of 385 miles were attainable. Dimensions included

Shown here is the extended dorsal fin fitted to some examples of the S.A.I. 2 S. (I-ELIS)

a span of 34 ft. 4 in., a length of 23 ft. 1 in., a height of 9 ft. 3 in., and a wing area of 150.6 sq. ft.

The higher-powered Alfa engine made a great improvement in the entire range of performance, as well as a slight increase in loaded weight to 1833 lb. Maximum speed became 143 m.p.h., cruising speed 121 m.p.h., and landing speed 58 m.p.h. Ceiling and range of the Alfa-powered model increased to 17,056 ft. and 422 miles respectively. Except for the greater length of 24 ft., dimensions remained as for the FIAT-equipped version.

With a German Bramo Sh 14 A4 radial of 160 h.p., the type became the S.A.I. 3 S. The only other modification was a slight reduction in chord, with a corresponding decrease in wing area. Although exact figures are not available, performance was improved.

S.A.I. 10

The last of the prewar Ambrosinis produced primarily for civil use was the parasol-wing S.A.I. 10 Grifone (Griffon), which could be fitted with either the horizontally-opposed

Above right, three views of an S.A.I. 2 S with postwar registration I-OZIR. Wheel spats were removed for competition. Below, the S.A.I. 3, an extremely graceful prewar two-seater. (I-AMBY)

The S.A.I. 3 S, fitted with a German Bramo Sh 14 A4 radial engine and open cockpits. (I-PIER)

C.N.A. D4 air-cooled engine of 60 h.p. or the much more powerful Bramo radial engine. Of fabric-covered wood and welded steel construction, the Grifone featured side-by-side seating and was intended mainly as a primary trainer. Span was 33 ft. 9½ in., length 21 ft. 4 in., height 6 ft. 10¾ in., and wing area 154 sq. ft. Empty weight was only 726 lb., while the fully loaded figure was 1210 lb. With the 60 h.p. engine, performance included a maximum speed of 100 m.p.h., a cruising speed of 90 m.p.h., a landing speed of 30 m.p.h., a range of 248 miles, and a service ceiling of 16,400 ft.

A version with an 85 h.p. FIAT A.50 engine weighed 880 lb. empty and 1353 lb. loaded. It had a maximum speed of 116 m.p.h., a cruising speed of 100 m.p.h., and a landing speed of 34

The S.A.I. 10 Grifone featured a parasol wing and side-by-side seating; this is the Bramo version.

The excellent aerodynamics of the S.A.I. 7 are well illustrated here. Finish was red overall. (I-AMBH)

m.p.h. An A.50-powered seaplane variant was also built.

S.A.I. 7

Certainly the most successful Ambrosini designs were the series of lightweight fighters developed from the S.A.I. 7 sport monoplane. This two-seat model was the first Ambrosini product with retractable landing gear; possessing exceptional lines, it achieved 251 m.p.h. with a Hirth H.M.508D eight-cylinder inverted air-cooled engine of only 280 h.p. Piloted by Giorgio Parodi, an S.A.I. 7 won the 1939 Raduno del Littorio (Littorio Air Rally), subsequently capturing the 100-km. (62.1-mile) closed circuit record for F.A.I. Category I at 244 m.p.h. The most striking feature of the design was the beautifully faired windscreen

The more orthodox two-seat fighter trainer version of the S.A.I. 7 was produced in 1941.

The postwar Ambrosini S.7 and Supersette were developments of the S.A.I. 7 (MM 52985)

originating forward of the engine cowling and extending in a continuous arc to the fin. Empty, the S.A.I. 7 weighed 1650 lb.; the normal loaded weight was 2640 lb., although a maximum of 3025 lb. was possible. Span was 29 ft. 5 in., length 23 ft. 9 in., height 7 ft., and wing area 141.4 sq. ft. The S.A.I. 7 could climb to 19,680 ft. in 14 minutes. Cruising range was 2020 miles.

Ing. Stefanutti was aware of the military potential of the basic design, and in 1941

S.A.I. 7

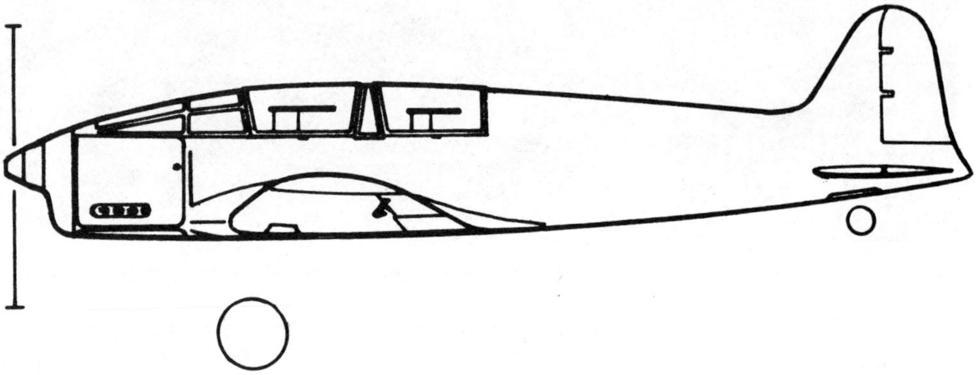

S.A.I. 7 TRAINER

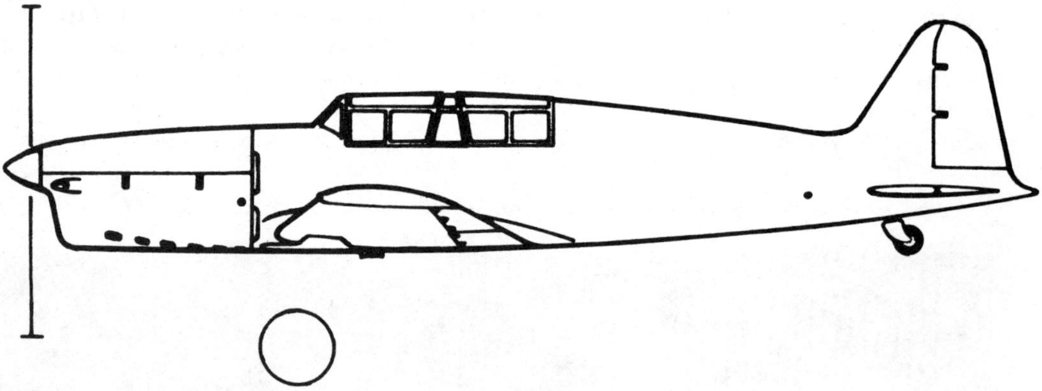

S.A.I. 107

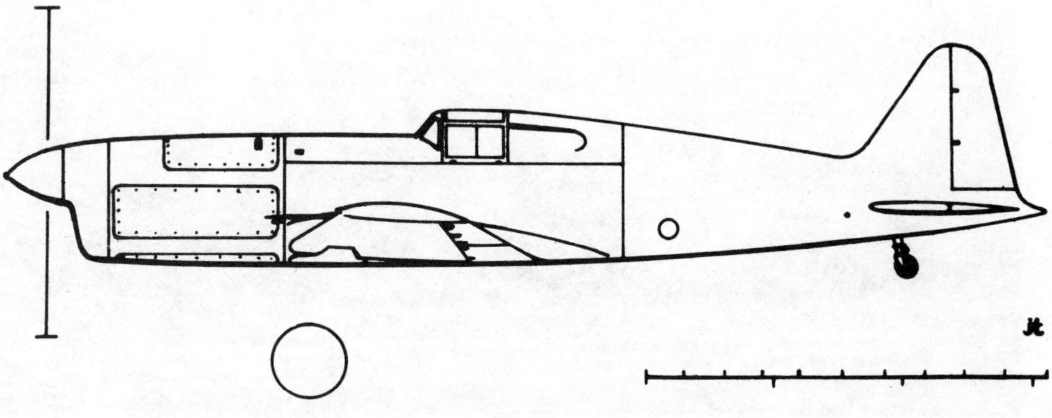

The S.A.I. 107 employed a 540 h.p. Isotta-Fraschini Gamma engine driving a two-bladed airscrew.

produced a two-seat fighter trainer. In most respects the trainer was similar to the sport model, except for the substitution of an Isotta-Fraschini Beta R.C.10 of 280 h.p. for the German Hirth engine. This lengthened the fuselage to 26 ft. 11 in. Span was also slightly increased to 29 ft. 6$^{1}/_{3}$ in. In addition, the fully streamlined windscreen was replaced by a

Above right, the prototype S.A.I. 207. Below, one of thirteen pre-production models. (MM 8431)

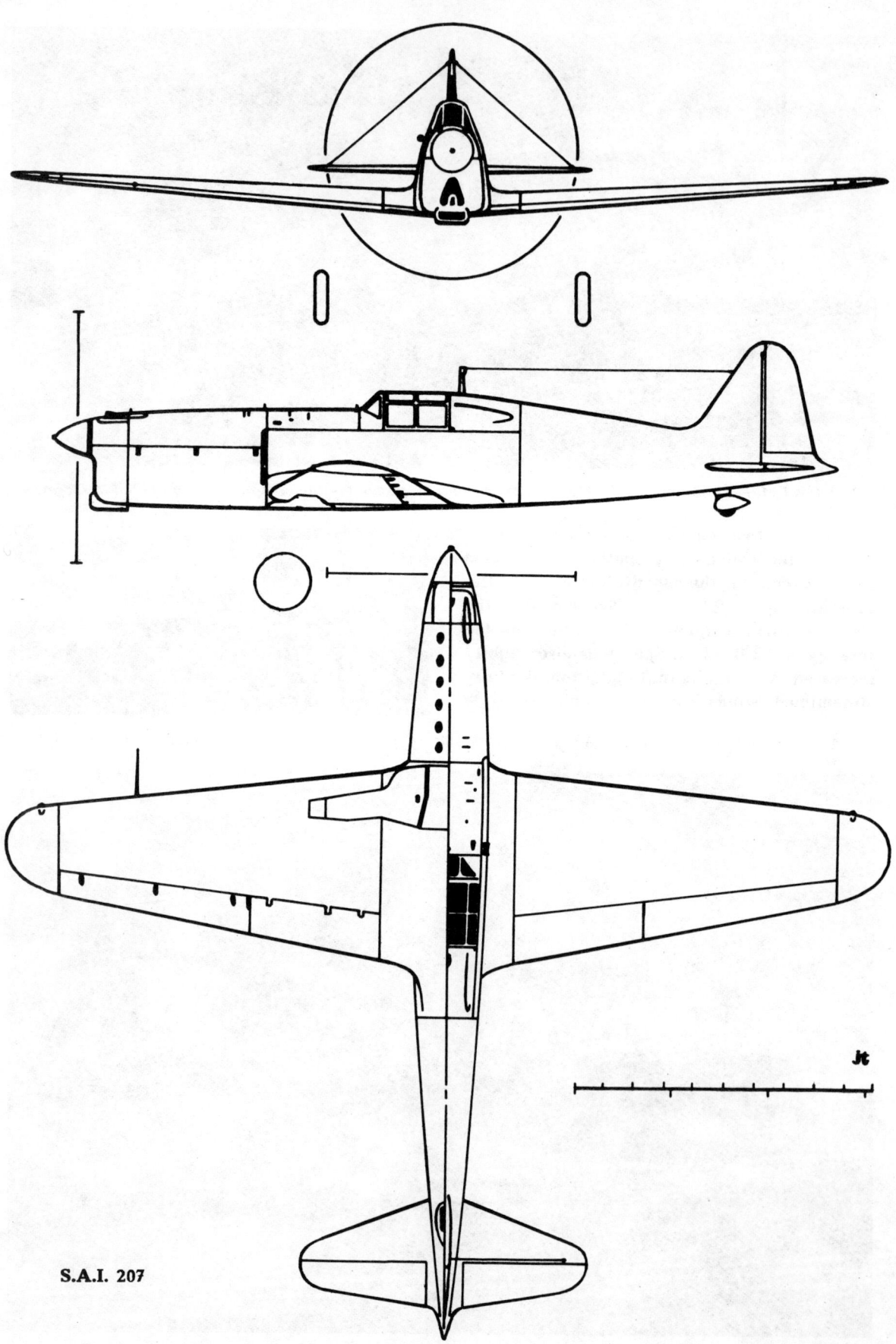

S.A.I. 207

normal cockpit canopy for pilot and pupil. Loaded weight was 3003 lb. The maximum speed was only slightly less than that of the original at 248 m.p.h. The war situation halted further development of the trainer, as combat aircraft received higher priority, but the design has been built in improved form since the war as the S.7 and Supersette.

S.A.I. 107

In view of the great need for combat aircraft by the Regia Aeronautica, the design was developed into the S.A.I. 107 experimental fighter in 1942. Intended only as a preliminary prototype, the S.A.I. 107 fitted a 540 h.p. Isotta-Fraschini Gamma engine driving a two-bladed airscrew. Fully loaded, this single-seat machine weighed only 2200 lb., and reached nearly 350 m.p.h. in trials held at the Guidonia research establishment. Maneuvrability proved to be excellent. Except for the length of 26 ft. $3^3/_4$ in., dimensions of the S.A.I. 107 were the same as those of the S.A.I. 7 trainer.

S.A.I. 207

The next step was the design of a fighter with full operational equipment. A further increase in power was needed to meet the operational requirements, and the resulting S.A.I. 207 used a 750 h.p. Isotta-Fraschini Delta R.C.40 inverted-vee engine. Aside from the engine change, and the fitting of a three-bladed airscrew, the main difference between the two fighters was the mounting of armament to the later model. The S.A.I. 207 carried two 20-mm. Mauser MG 151 cannon and two Breda-SAFAT 12.7-mm. machine guns. After tests, in which the fighter achieved 398 m.p.h. in level flight and nearly 600 m.p.h. in dives, 2000 examples were ordered by the Italian Air Ministry. However, only thirteen were actually built,

The S.A.I. 403 Dardo fighter achieved 403 m.p.h.

the remainder of the contract being diverted to the final development, the S.A.I. 403. Three S.A.I. 207's equipped the 3° Stormo C.T. at Ciampino and Cerveteri in July, 1943.

Dimensions of the S.A.I. 207 were: span 29 ft. $6^1/_3$ in., length 26 ft. $3^3/_4$ in., height 9 ft. 5 in., and wing area 149.6 sq. ft. Empty and loaded weights were 3858 and 5324 lb. respectively. Performance included a cruising speed of 304 m.p.h., a range of 528 miles, and a service ceiling of 39,370 ft. Climbing to 19,680 ft. required 7 min. 33 sec.

S.A.I. 403

Of all-wood construction like its predecessors, the S.A.I. 403 Dardo (Dart) featured numerous detail refinements intended to improve combat performance and to facilitate rapid production. The internal fuel and armament capacities were increased, and the resulting loaded weight of 5820 lb. called for an increase in wing area to 155.6 sq. ft. in order to maintain the standard of maneuvrability so important to the Italian airman. The vertical tail surface became larger and more angular, while such aerodynamic refinements as a fully-retractable tailwheel contributed to a minor gain in maximum speed of 5 m.p.h. over the S.A.I. 207. Various fuel and armament combinations were

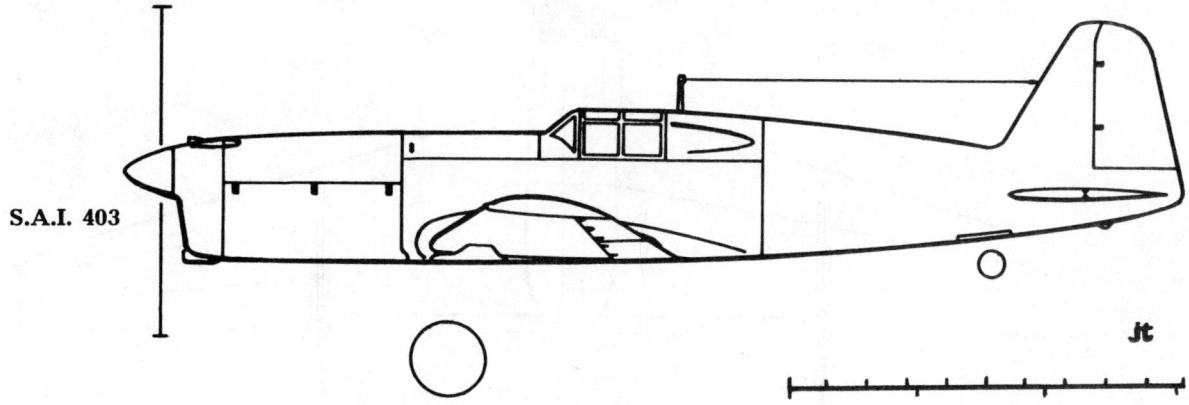

S.A.I. 403

tried in order to make the Dardo suitable for different roles. Armament ranged from the two 12.7-mm. machine guns of the light interceptor model to the two machine guns plus two 20-mm. wing cannon of the general purpose version. A third possibility intended for long-range duties employed only the wing cannon, plus two 42 U.S. gal. drop-tanks mounted beneath the wings. The interceptor, lightest of the three versions, weighed only 5459 lb. fully loaded.

3000 aircraft were ordered in January, 1943 to replace the S.A.I. 207 contracts, and production was to be undertaken by Caproni and Savoia-Marchetti in addition to the parent firm. However, this promising project came to an end with the Italian Armistice. Similar in concept to lightweight wooden fighters developed by other nations, the Ambrosini designs were the only fighters of the class which demonstrated both practicability and truly exceptional performance.

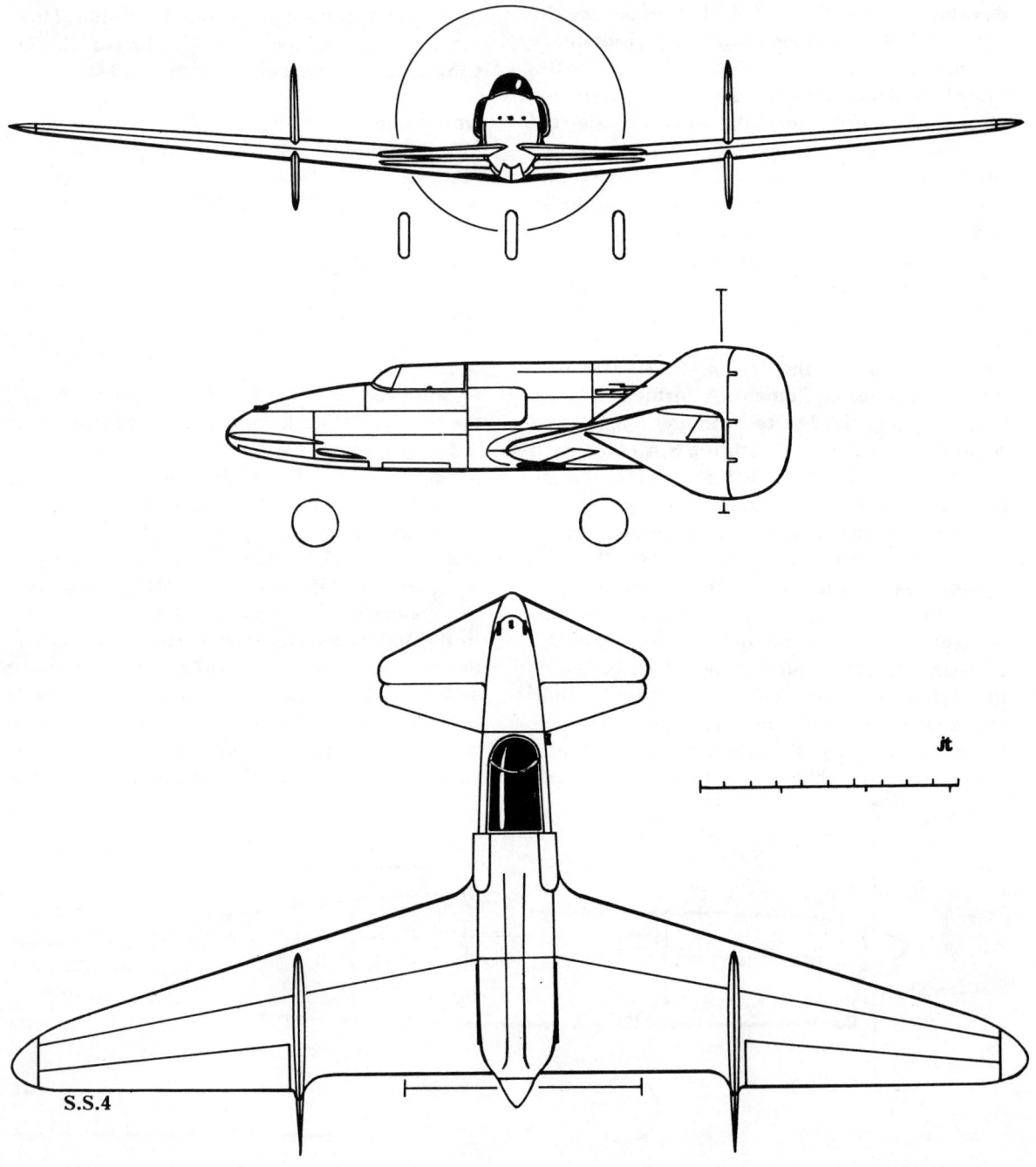

Above and below right, the S.S.4 canard interceptor, the sole example of which crashed in 1941.

The S.A.I. 403 had a span of 32 ft. 1³/₄ in., a length of 26 ft. 10³/₄ in., and a height of 9 ft. 6 in. Powered by the 750 h.p. Isotta-Fraschini Delta R.C.21/60 inverted-vee engine, the fighter achieved a maximum of 403 m.p.h. and cruised at 304 m.p.h. An altitude of 19,680 ft. could be reached in 6 min. 40 sec.; service ceiling was 39,810 ft. Range varied from 582 to 1164 miles, depending on the different fuel and armament arrangements.

S.S.4

A prewar design, the S.S.4 all-metal canard (tail-first) interceptor was the result of a totally different approach by Ambrosini's able designer. In 1938 Ing. Stefanutti had examined the flight characteristics of the unorthodox layout with the S.S.3 two-seat pusher monoplane, built at Guidonia by S.C.A. (Stabilimento Costruzioni Aeronautiche). The arrangement consisted of a fixed forward lifting surface with slotted elevator, and an aft-positioned cantilever wing incorporating normal ailerons and twin fins and rudders. The S.S.3, nicknamed Anitra (Duck), featured a fixed tricycle landing gear with steerable nosewheel. Power was supplied by a C.N.A. II bis flat-twin engine of 38 h.p. Numerous successful test flights demonstrated the efficiency of the arrangement, although performance was naturally limited by the low power available. Maximum speed was only 87 m.p.h., but the S.S.3 remained stable at a minimum speed of 34 m.p.h. Ceiling was 13,120 ft. Span was 41 ft. 11 in., length only 19 ft. 8 in., and height 6 ft. 7 in.

The canard layout offered many advantages for fighter aircraft, among them improved visibility, concentrated forward-firing arma-

ment, and the elimination of slipstream drag effects through the use of a pusher airscrew. Accordingly, Ing. Stefanutti developed the Ambrosini S.S.4 fighter, which flew for the first time in May, 1939. Handling qualities proved more than satisfactory in extensive tests at Guidonia during 1940-41, stability being particularly good. The steerable tricycle landing gear, fully retractable on the S.S.4, was a factor contributing to the excellent take-off and landing qualities. Unfortunately, the S.S.4 was destroyed in a landing accident caused by the failure of its 960 h.p. Isotta-Fraschini Asso XI R.C.40 engine. Although a further prototype was ordered immediately, the more easily developed wooden fighters were given priority, and the S.S.4 was finally abandoned in 1942.

Maximum speed had proved to be 355 m.p.h. Span was 40 ft. 5 in., length 22 ft. 1½ in., and height 8 ft. 1¾ in. The armament consisted of one 30-mm. cannon and two 20-mm. cannon, all mounted in the nose. Loaded weight was 5400 lb.

The Ambrosini S.S.4 canard design preceded that of the Kyushu J7W1 and Curtiss XP-55 fighter prototypes developed near the end of the war, as well as that of the Henschel Projekt 75, which was never built. In addition to its promise as an interceptor, the S.S.4 was considered suitable for the alternate role of dive bomber.

A.R.

The A.R. (Assalto Radioguidato) flying bomb was also conceived by Sergio Stefanutti, this time in cooperation with engineers Ermenegildo Preti and Stelio Frati. The Italian air arm had previously gained the distinction of being

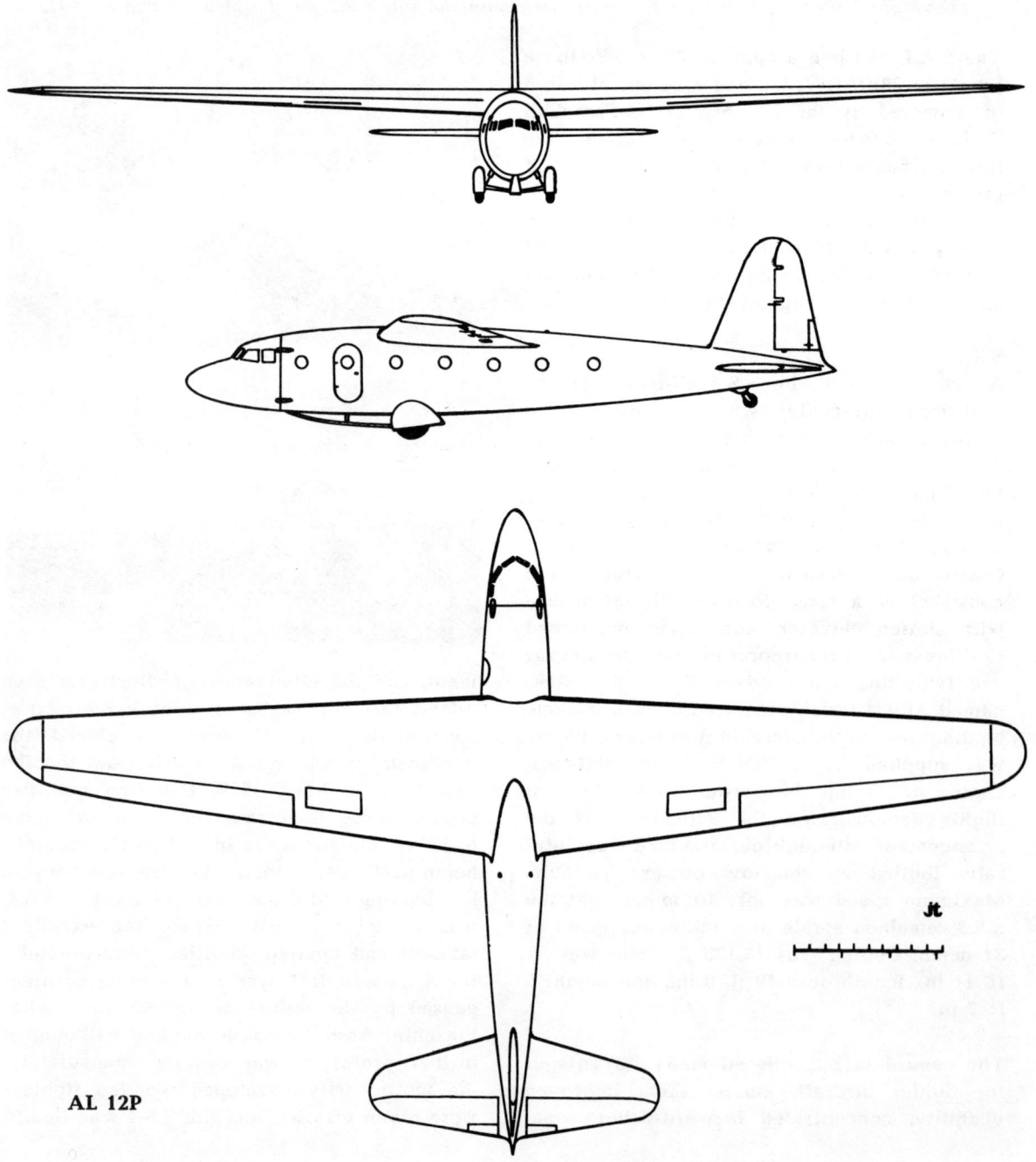

AL 12P

the first in the world to employ a radio-controlled flying bomb operationally, when, on August 13, 1942, it sent a much-modified SM.79 against a part of the British Fleet lying off the Algerian coast. Although unsuccessful, the attempt encouraged General Ferdinando Raffaelli, designer of the radio-control system, to urge the development of a cheap, expendable machine to fulfill the purpose more effectively.

The result was the A.R., a simple wooden mid-wing monoplane powered by a 1000 h.p. FIAT A.80 radial engine. The fuselage was of oval construction with plywood skin, and was to have contained two sealed-in 2200-lb. bombs. Wings and tail surfaces were angular and untapered. No flaps were required as landings were not anticipated. After experiments with take-off trolleys, a simple fixed undercarriage was employed which could be dropped after the bomb was airborne.

Flight tests began in June, 1943. Unlike the reaction-powered German V-weapons, the A.R. required a pilot for take-off. After radio control took over the guidance in flight, he bailed out. With a bomb load of 4400 lb. and a total weight of 13,200 lb., the A.R. was expected to have a maximum speed of 225 m.p.h. with undercarriage jettisoned. Five of the flying bombs were built at the Venegono plant in 1943 but none were ever used. The last four were destroyed before being tested. Wingspan was 55 ft. 9$^1/_2$ in., length 49 ft. 2$^1/_2$ in., and wing area 409 sq. ft. The empty weight was 7936 lb.

LOMBARDA AL 12P

Ambrosini also manufactured the AL 12P troop and cargo glider designed by Ing. Preti of

The A.R. bomb was an unsophisticated design.

Aeronautica Lombarda S.A. Constructed entirely of wood, the AL 12P possessed extremely clean contours. In addition to two normal doors, the fuselage featured a hinged forward section which swung to starboard to facilitate loading. Ten fully-equipped troops or a cargo up to a maximum of 3960 lb. could be carried. Air brakes were fitted above and below the wings just inboard of the ailerons. The AL 12P spanned 69 ft. 10$^1/_2$ in., was 45 ft. 1$^1/_8$ in. long, and had a wing area of 546 sq. ft. Empty weight was 3300 lb. and maximum weight 7260 lb.

A twin-engined variant, the P.512, was designed by Ambrosini and built after the war. Employing Alfa Romeo 115ter in-line engines of 225 h.p. each, the P.512 was essentially the same as the glider in other respects, although a modified landing gear was fitted.

Above right and below, the AL 12P troop and cargo glider designed by Lombarda and built by S.A.I.

BREDA
Società Italiana Ernesto Breda

The Breda group was one of the largest Italian aeronautical concerns. From its main offices in Milan it controlled a number of smaller companies engaged in the manufacture of all types of aircraft equipment and accessories, in addition to complete aircraft. Among the subsidiaries the most important was I.M.A.M. (Industrie Meccaniche e Aeronautiche Meridionali), covered in a separate section of this book. The main Breda works at Sesto San Giovanni (Milan) were supplemented by plants in Apaulia, Brescia, and Rome. Although Breda resumed aircraft manufacture after the Second World War with the Zappata-designed BZ.308 four-engined transport, activity was limited.

Breda began aircraft construction in 1917 with an order for 600 Caproni triplane bombers. After a short period of relative inactivity, during which only experimental work was undertaken, Breda started producing aircraft of its own design in 1922. Since that date Breda has built a large number of aircraft of all types, including pioneer work with all-metal cantilever monoplanes.

BREDA 15
Although designed in 1928, the Breda 15 was active throughout the 1930's in touring and sport flying. A light high-wing two-seat cabin monoplane, the Breda 15 was powered by a variety of engines in the 85 h.p. class, including the Cirrus III, Walter Venus, Argus As.8, D.H. Gipsy I and III, and Isotta-Fraschini units. Maximum speed was 112 m.p.h. at a loaded weight of 1540 lb. Span was 36 ft. 9 in., length 22 ft. 2 in.

A modified version, the Breda 15 S, featured a new elliptical wing and cleaner lines; the first example won the 1930 Giro Aereo d'Italia (Aerial Circuit of Italy) at an average speed of 94.4 m.p.h., piloted by Col. Paride Sacchi. Higher-powered engines were used, normal installations being the 115 h.p. Colombo S.63 six-cylinder in-line, Isotta-Fraschini 80T six-cylinder in-line, or Walter N.Z. radial engines.

BREDA 19
Produced in some numbers in 1932 for Regia Aeronautica training squadrons, the Breda 19 enjoyed a great success as an aerobatic machine for public demonstrations. It was a single-seat biplane powered by a 220 h.p. Alfa Romeo Lynx or a 240 h.p. Walter Castor radial engine. Empty and loaded weights were 1617 lb. and 1980 lb. The Breda 19 climbed to 16,400 ft. in 18 minutes and had a service ceiling of 22,960 ft. Maximum, cruising, and landing speeds were 130 m.p.h., 106 m.p.h., and 47 m.p.h. respectively. Dimensions included a span of 29 ft. 6 in., a length of 21 ft. 7$^{3}/_{4}$ in., a height of 8 ft. 6$^{3}/_{8}$ in., and a wing area of 269 sq. ft.

BREDA 25
Probably the most important training aircraft used in Italy during the 1930's, the Breda 25 and its numerous variants were instrumental in the instruction of over 10,000 pilots in the home country and the nations to which it was exported. These nations included Afghanistan,

Left, a Breda 15 with constant-chord wing. Right, the improved 15 S with elliptical wing. (I-AAUJ)

Above and below right, the single-seat Breda 19 aerobatic trainer was used in many flying shows.

China, Paraguay, and, ironically, Ethiopia, which was attacked and annexed by Italy in the campaign of 1935.

A very straightforward two-seat biplane design, the Breda 25 was normally powered by an Alfa Romeo D2 radial engine of 240 h.p., although various units were mounted. The Breda 25 was also built as a single-seat advanced trainer and as a twin-float seaplane, the 25 idro. Several of the latter were fitted with 240 h.p. Walter Castor radial engines; with this installation the maximum speed was 118 m.p.h., some 18 m.p.h. slower than that of the landplane.

Specifications of the normal two-seat landplane included empty and loaded weights of 1738 lb. and 2288 lb. Span was 32 ft. 9 in., length 25 ft. 7 in., height 9 ft. $3^{1}/_{3}$ in., and wing

Below left, a single-seat Breda 25 with Alfa D2 engine. Right, a two-seat model in Chinese markings.

ITALIAN CIVIL AND MILITARY AIRCRAFT

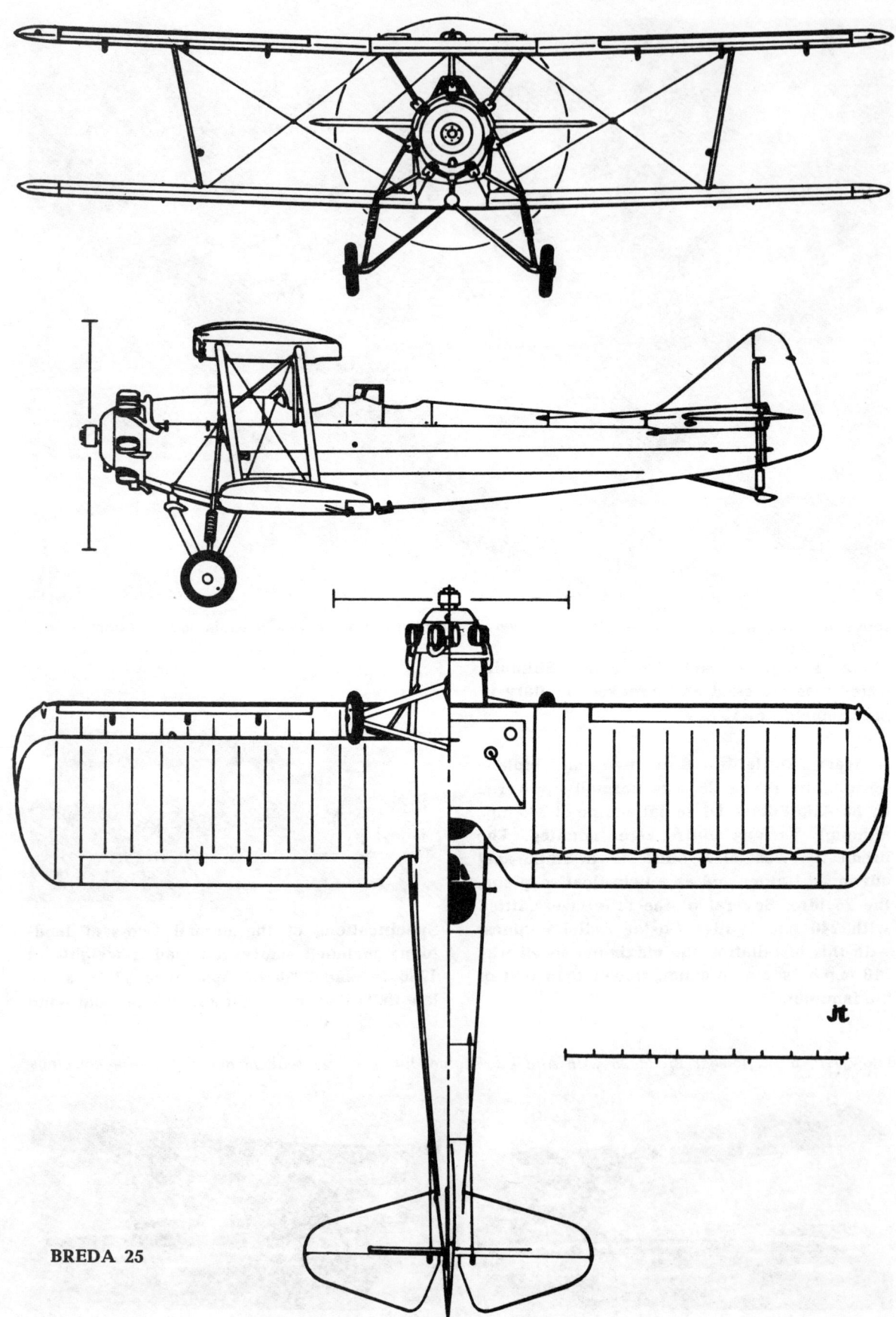

BREDA 25

A single-seat Breda 25 advanced trainer of the Regia Aeronautica. (MM 146)

SINGLE-SEAT BREDA 25

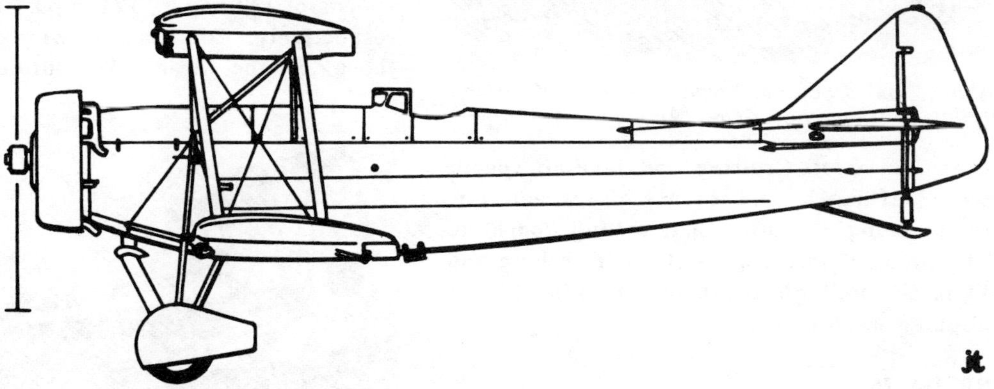

BREDA 25 IDRO

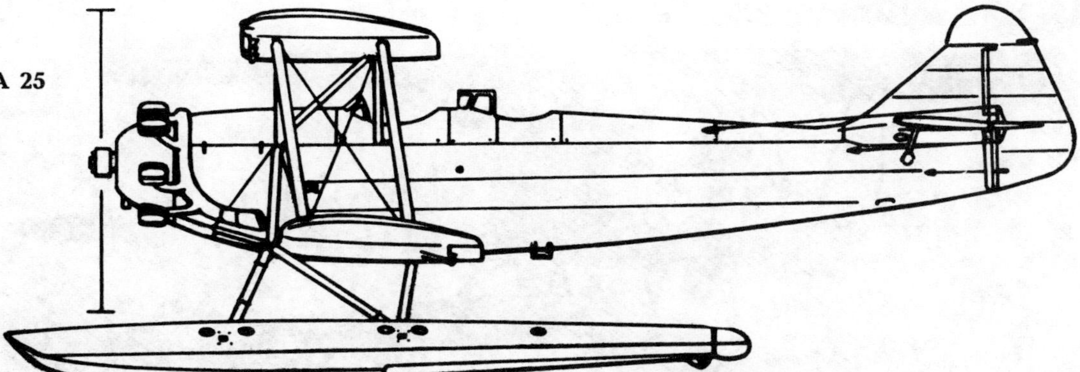

Above, top to bottom; Breda 25 idro (MM 50408), in-line version, and Regia Aeronautica trainer.

wing area and lower-powered Walter N.Z. radial engine, the Breda 26 was converted from the basic design for use as a primary trainer. The wingspan became 38 ft. and the total area 344.3 sq. ft. Length was 26 ft. 6 in. With 120 h.p. available, the maximum, cruising, and landing speeds were 93 m.p.h., 75 m.p.h., and 40 m.p.h. respectively. Range was 248 miles, service ceiling 14,100 ft. Empty and loaded weights were 1474 lb. and 2024 lb.

BREDA 28
The Breda 28 was a development of the same basic design for advanced instruction. The major change was the 370 h.p. Piaggio Stella VII Z (license-built Gnôme-Rhône K-7) radial engine. In addition, ailerons were incorporated in both upper and lower wings in contrast to the Breda 25, which employed them in the lower wings only. Minor refinements included improved engine cowling, an airscrew spinner, and an enlarged rudder like that of the 25 idro.

Performance of the Breda 28 was substantially higher, with maximum, cruising, and landing speeds of 149 m.p.h., 124 m.p.h., and 46 m.p.h. respectively. Dimensions were identical to those of the Breda 25, although weights

area 269 sq. ft. Cruising and landing speeds were 121 m.p.h. and 44 m.p.h. respectively, range being 310 miles and ceiling 24,600 ft. The Breda 25 idro was 29 ft. $10^{1}/_{4}$ in. long and 11 ft. $9^{3}/_{4}$ in. high. It cruised at 93 m.p.h. and alighted at 56 m.p.h.

BREDA 26
Similar to the Breda 25 except for its larger

Above right, a single-seat Breda 28. (I-ABFQ) Below, a Norwegian Breda 28 idro. (LN-EAD)

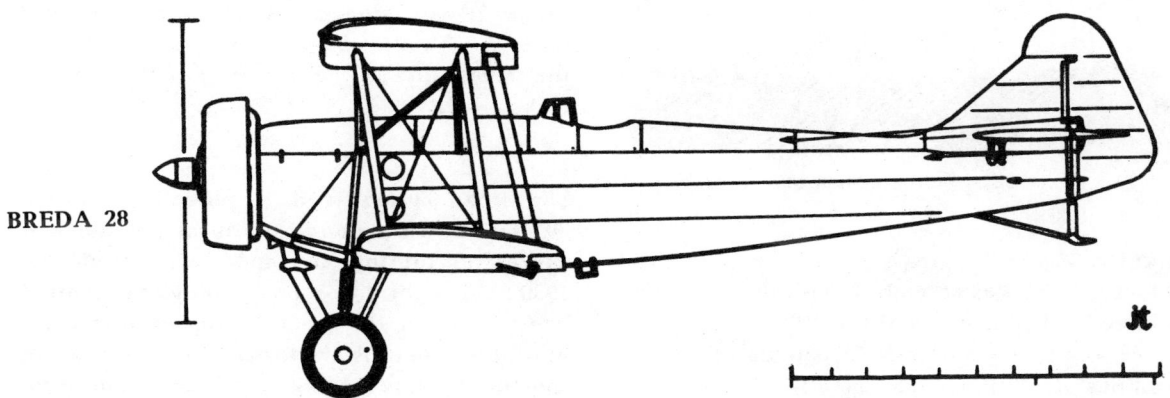

BREDA 28

increased to 2112 lb. empty and 2640 lb. loaded. As with its forerunner, the Breda 28 was also built in single-seat and seaplane versions.

BREDA 27

The Breda 27 was an externally-braced low-wing fighter with fixed landing gear, bearing a marked resemblance to the Boeing P-26. However, the Breda 27 was an entirely distinct design in spite of the many common features. If any design directly influenced it, the more likely candidate was the Travel Air Model R imported by Italy in the early 1930's. Powered by an Alfa Romeo Mercurius IV radial engine, the Breda 27 was produced in 1934 primarily for export. Armament was two 7.7-mm. Breda-SAFAT machine guns. The prototype Breda 27 had a two-bladed wood airscrew, short-chord cowling, and further-aft cockpit.

When the Chinese government invited Italy to send an Air Mission to replace an unofficial American group which had been withdrawn after complaints by the Japanese, a small number of Breda 27 fighters were supplied, equipping one Chinese squadron during 1935-38. Claimed performance included a maximum speed of 236 m.p.h., a landing speed of 62 m.p.h., and a ceiling of 29,520 ft. A time of 7 min. 30 sec. was given for a climb to 16,400 ft. Empty and loaded weights were 2772 lb. and 2938 lb. Dimensions were: span 31 ft. 1 in., length 24 ft. 11 in., height 11 ft. 2 in., and wing area 203 sq. ft.

Resemblance of the Breda 27 to the American Boeing P-26 was obvious but coincidental. (MM 218)

The Breda 32 trimotor commercial airliner.

BREDA 32

The Breda 32 was an eight to eleven-passenger commercial transport built in 1932. Employing three Pratt and Whitney Wasp-Junior radial engines of 320 h.p. each, the all-metal airliner spanned 87 ft. 6 in., was 54 ft. 11$^{3}/_{8}$ in. long and 13 ft. 7$^{1}/_{2}$ in. high. Wing area was 914.6 sq. ft. Empty the Breda 32 weighed 8360 lb.; with fuel and equipment weighing 2859 lb. and passengers and baggage of up to 2987 lb., the total loaded weight was 14,200 lb. Maximum speed was only 147 m.p.h., with cruising and landing figures of 131 m.p.h. and 58 m.p.h. A time of 52 minutes was claimed for a climb to 16,400 ft. in fully loaded condition; the service ceiling was 17,400 ft. The Breda 32 had a cruising range of 840 miles. A later model was built with FIAT radial engines. The Breda 32 was the basis for the larger Breda 46 bomber-transport of 1934.

BREDA 33

The Breda 33 and its developments, the Breda 39 and 42, were among the most popular and successful touring and sport aircraft of the 1930's. A light low-wing monoplane seating two in tandem, the Breda 33 appeared in 1931, scoring numerous victories and records in sporting events in the years that followed. Designed by Ing. Cesare Pallavicino, the Breda 33 was comparatively advanced for its time, featuring fully-faired landing gear and very clean lines with a minimum of external bracing.

The original model employed a 120 h.p. De Havilland Gipsy III four-cylinder in-line engine, providing a maximum speed of 143 m.p.h. The Breda 33 cruised at 124 m.p.h. and landed at 53 m.p.h. Empty weight was 946 lb.; loaded weight varied between 1606 lb. and 1826 lb. A climb to 13,120 ft. required 15 minutes; ceiling was 22,960 ft. Depending on the fuel load, range was 745—1120 miles. Dimensions were: span 30 ft. 10 in., length 22 ft. 3 in., height 6 ft. 7 in., and wing area 161.5

Above left, a Breda 33 (I-BIBI) clearing the wire in competition. Above right and below, the Breda 33 is shown with open cockpits and with canopies in place. (I-LARE)

The Breda 33 S was a single-seat model; note landing light on starboard wing above gear fairing.

sq. ft.

In 1931, a Breda 33 piloted by Ing. Ambrogio Colombo won the second Giro Aereo d'Italia at an average speed of 109.3 m.p.h. Another accomplishment of the type was a flight from London to Calcutta by the Italian aviator Robbiano. The distance of over 5000 miles was covered in seven stages during 1933. The

Above right, a Breda 39 at Tunis in 1935. (I-ACIE) Below, a Regia Aeronautica Breda 39. (MM 55827)

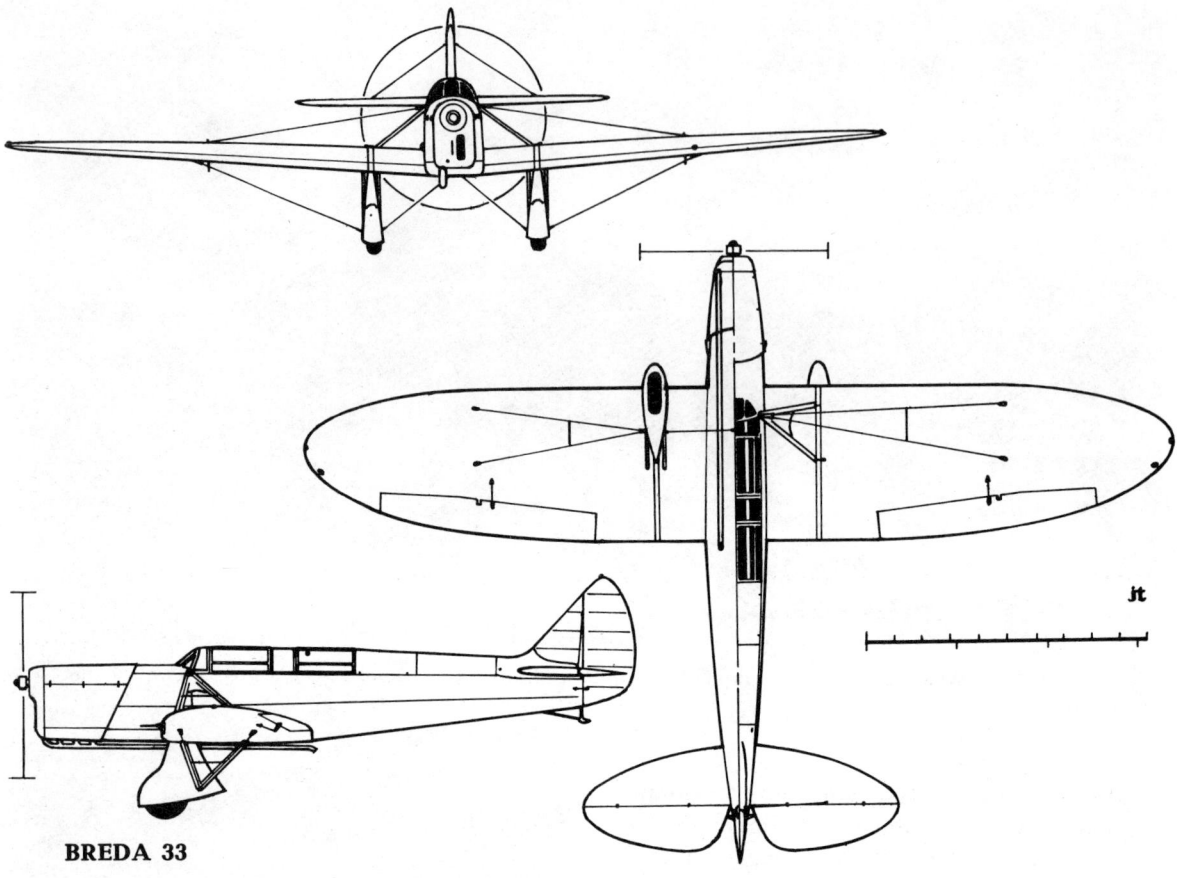

BREDA 33

following year Furio Niclot won the first Raduno del Littorio (Littorio Air Rally) with a Breda 33. The Mainichi Shimbun (a Japanese newspaper) imported one Breda 33 in 1932. A modified single-seat version was also built, designated Breda 33 S.

BREDA 39

A development of the design, the Breda 39, appeared in 1933. With a 140 h.p. Colombo S.63 six-cylinder in-line engine and greater dimensions, the Breda 39 was a considerably heavier model, scaling 1235 lb. empty. Slots and flaps were fitted; the former extended along the outer wing sections with an automatic control for high-incidence landings. This modification allowed a greatly reduced landing speed of 40 m.p.h. Normal loaded weight was 1852 lb., although the maximum was 2062 lb. Span was 34 ft. 2 in., length 24 ft. 5 in., height 9 ft. 8 in., and wing area 188.5 sq. ft. The Breda 39 was slower than its predecessor at 137 m.p.h. maximum, and required 21 minutes to reach 13,120 ft. Ceiling was 19,700 ft. and range 560 miles.

In spite of the apparent drop in performance, the Breda 39 was a more tractable machine; in 1934 the pilots Folonari and Malinverni completed a circuit of the Mediterranean Sea, starting and finishing at Turin. The Breda 39 S, seating three in tandem, was built in 1934.

BREDA 42

Developed from the Breda 39 for the 1934 Challenge de Tourisme International, the Breda 42 was distinguished by its N.A.C.A.-cowled radial engine, a 180 h.p. FIAT A.70 S. The leading-edge slots of the former model were replaced by Breda-Mazzini wing-valve slots. The Breda 42 weighed 1232 lb. empty and 2002 lb. with normal load. Dimensions included a span of 33 ft. 1 in., a length of 25 ft. 7 in., a height of 10 ft. 4 in., and a wing area of 170 sq. ft.

BREDA 44

Bearing a general similarity to the DeHavilland Dragon, the Breda 44 light transport was built in 1934. Like the Dragon, the Breda transport was a six-passenger twin-engine biplane; the

Above, a Breda 42 with postwar registration I-RANA. Below right can be seen the Breda-Mazzini wing-valve slots. This machine, I-OMBO, was photographed in Germany in 1934.

comparison was strengthened by the unstepped nose and the landing gear faired into the engine nacelles. Power was supplied by Walter Major-Six air-cooled in-line engines of 190 h.p. each. In addition to their limited use in Italy, a number of Breda 44 transports were exported to Paraguay during that country's war with Bolivia.

Maximum speed was 140 m.p.h., with cruising and landing speeds of 112 m.p.h. and 56 m.p.h. Other performance data included a cruising range of 335 miles and a service ceiling of 15,580 ft. Spanning 43 ft. 8 in., the Breda 44 was 33 ft. 11 in. long and 10 ft. 1 in. high; wing area was 387 sq. ft. The empty weight was 2970 lb. and the loaded figure 4774 lb. Alternate engine installations were 155 h.p. Colombo S.63 six-cylinder in-lines, giving a speed of only 115 m.p.h.; and 200 h.p. DeHavilland

Gipsy-Six inverted in-lines, providing 124 m.p.h.

BREDA 46

Basically a military adaptation of the Breda 32 transport, the Breda 46 was intended as a combination transport and bomber, carrying twelve troops and a normal bomb load of 2200 lb. Power was doubled by the use of

The Breda 44 was a twin-engined light transport bearing a general similarity to the D.H. Dragon.

Above and below right, the single-seat Breda 64 light reconnaissance bomber. (MM 250)

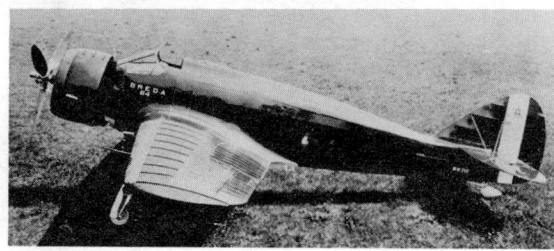

three Alfa Romeo Pegasus engines (license-built Bristol nine-cylinder radials) of 650 h.p. each, but this gain was necessary to provide an acceptable military performance at a loaded weight of 20,460 lb., up nearly 50 per cent from the Breda 32. Wing span and area were accordingly increased to 98 ft. 5 in. and 1119 sq. ft. respectively.

In addition to the accomodations for troops and bombs, the military equipment included four gun positions, two dorsal and two ventral. The forward upper position mounted one 7.7-mm. Breda-SAFAT machine gun, the rear post fitting either one 12.7-mm. gun or two 7.7-mm. guns. Below the fuselage the arrangement was the same, except that only one rear gun was employed. The internal bomb storage featured separate doors for 220-lb., 550-lb., and 1100-lb.

A two-seat Breda 64 with 1939-style camouflage and cockpit canopy like that adapted for the Breda 65.

bombs. When no troops were carried, the bomb load could be increased to 4400 lb.

Performance was much improved over that of the Breda 32, with a maximum speed of 196 m.p.h. at 16,400 ft. Cruising speed at 9840 ft. was 161 m.p.h.; landing speed was 68 m.p.h. The Breda 46 could climb to 16,400 ft. in 18 minutes, service ceiling being 25,360 ft. With a bomb load of only 2200 lb. and no troops aboard, the maximum range was 1242 miles; with double that load it was 683 miles. Except as mentioned, the dimensions of the Breda 46 were the same as for its transport predecessor. Empty weight was 12,100 lb.

The Breda 46 appeared in 1934, embracing the current Italian concept of tactical bomber-transports for colonial operations, but faster, sleeker bombers with retractable landing gear were beginning to change the accepted theories of bomber design. Consequently, Breda turned its efforts to the more advanced Breda 82 medium bomber and the smaller Breda 88 attack bomber.

BREDA 64

Forerunner of the well-known Breda 65, the Breda 64 was designed to fulfill the roles of fighter, light bomber, and reconnaissance plane. An all-metal low-wing monoplane with retractable landing gear, it was built in some numbers during 1933—34. The original model mounted a 700 h.p. Alfa Romeo Pegasus radial engine. Armament of the fighter version comprised four 7.7-mm. machine guns mounted in the wings; the two-seat reconnaissance model mounted an additional gun in the rear cockpit. Bomb loads ranging from twelve 8.8-lb. bombs to four 220-lb. bombs could be carried. A few examples of the Breda 64 featured an anti-turnover pylon above the windscreen, incorporating a rear-view mirror.

Performance was acceptable for the period, maximum speed being 224 m.p.h. Service ceiling of the fighter version was 26,240 ft. Varying with the load, cruising range was 560—932 miles. Following the accepted theory of Gen. Amedeo Meccozzi, the combination of roles was suitable to Italy's needs during the colonial conquests of the 1930's, but proved unsuccessful when the later Breda 65 met organized opposition in the Second World War. As late as 1939 at least 27 Breda 64's were still in service with the Regia Aeronautica, although the obsolete type was no longer in front-line use. In 1938 the Soviet Union bought two Breda 64's.

Dimensions were: span 39 ft. 8 in., length 31 ft. 6 in., height 10 ft. 11 in., and wing area 252.8 sq. ft. Empty weight was 3300 lb., while the maximum loaded figure was 5500 lb.

BREDA 65

A modernized version of the Breda 64 with an appreciable gain in performance, the Breda 65, first flown in 1935, nevertheless proved to be a disappointing machine in actual combat, and the problems experienced in North Africa by Italian squadrons equipped with the type were similar to those of the Fairey Battles over France in 1940. In both cases the bombers were too slow and unwieldy to protect themselves. Although faster than the larger Battle, the Breda 65 was a difficult machine to fly, and was generally ineffective throughout the North African campaign.

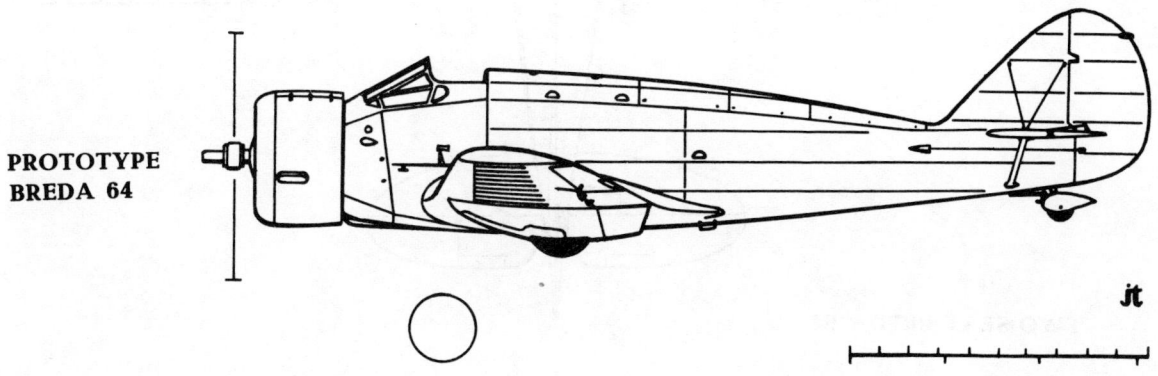

PROTOTYPE BREDA 64

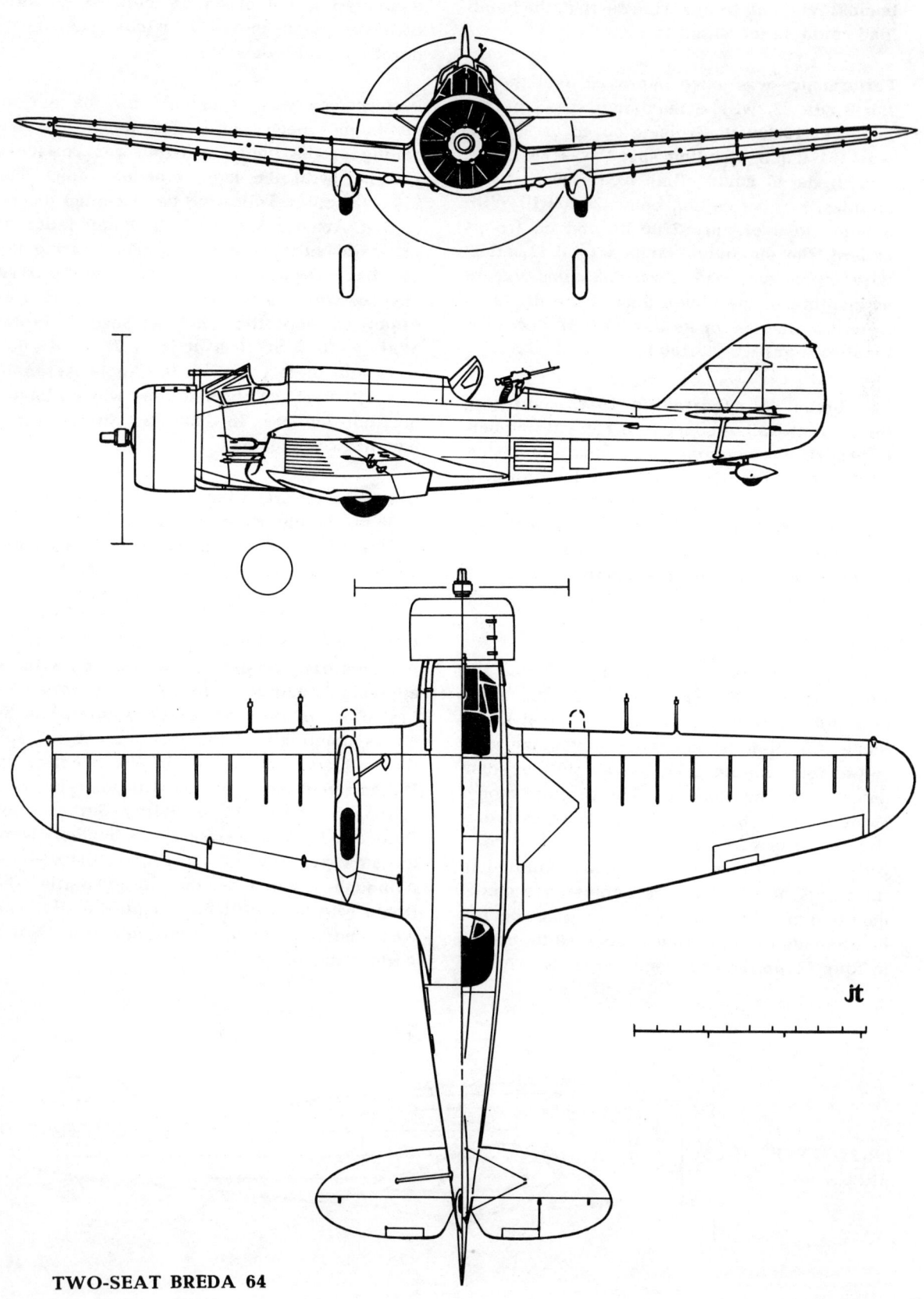

TWO-SEAT BREDA 64

A section of single-seat Breda 65 fighter bombers photographed in 1939.

Whereas the Breda 64 had an open cockpit, the pilot of the Breda 65 was provided a sliding canopy. This was usually left open, however, most Italian pilots preferring the classic arrangement. In fact, it was not until the latter stages of the war that this preferrence was overcome among Regia Aeronautica personnel. Originally fitted with the 1030 h.p. FIAT A.80 R.C.41 radial engine, the Breda 65 used the 900 h.p. Isotta-Fraschini K.14 (license-built Gnôme-Rhône 14 Krsd) radial engine on subsequent operational examples. A fuller fuselage and modified vertical tail surfaces were the most noticeable differences from the Breda 64. Again, the design was adapted for fighter, bomber and reconnaissance duties,

Above, a two-seat Breda 65bis reconnaissance bomber. A flexible machine gun was often fitted.

Above right, fifteen Breda 65 bis purchased by Iraq in 1938. Thirteen of these fitted the hydraulically-operated Breda L turret also shown on the Regia Aeronautica machine below.

This factory photograph of the prototype Breda 65 shows the machine on stands for landing gear retraction tests.

BREDA

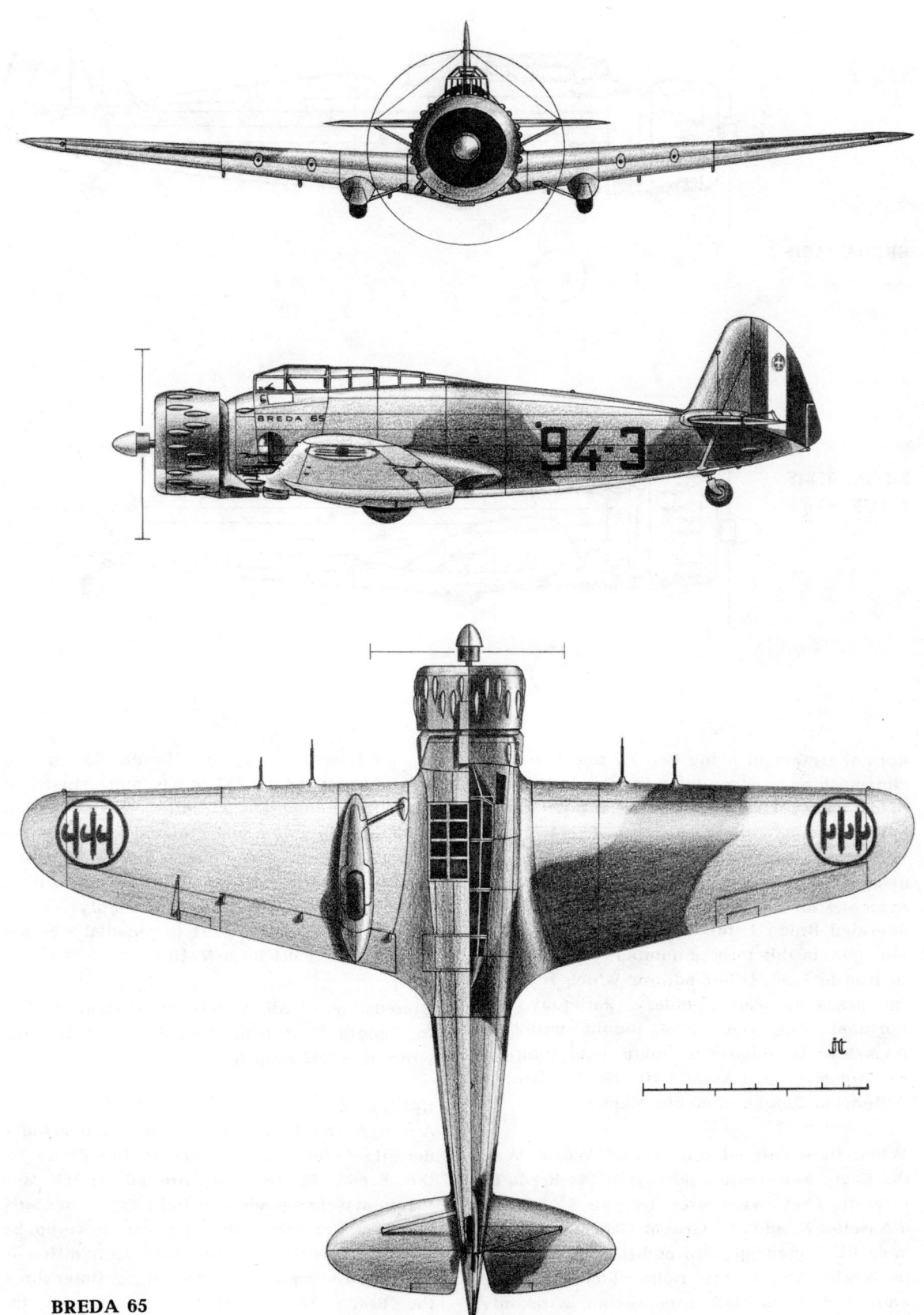

BREDA 65

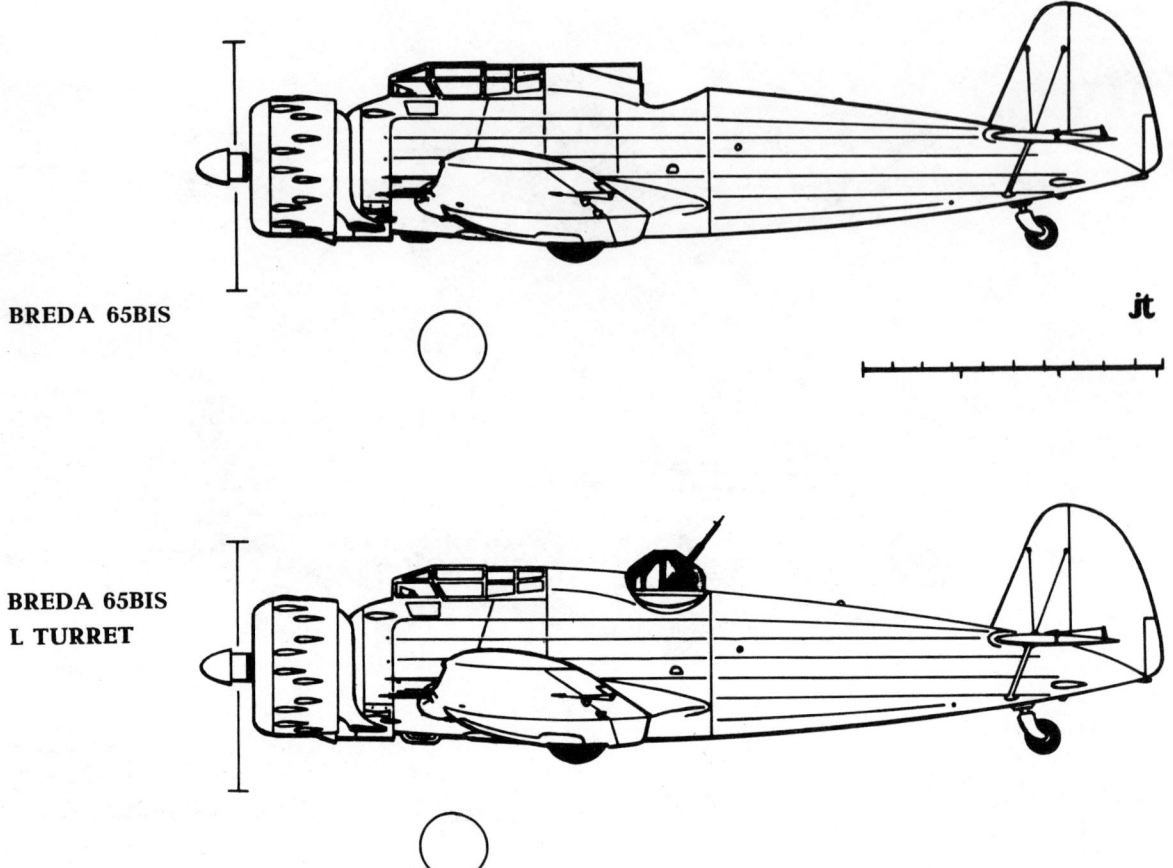

BREDA 65BIS

BREDA 65BIS L TURRET

normal armament being two 7.7 and two 12.7-mm. machine guns mounted in the wings. Bomb loads varied from 160 8.8-lb. anti-personnel bombs to one 2200-lb. weapon. The two-seat version, designated Breda 65bis, placed an observer-gunner in a rear cockpit; some examples of the 65bis had a hydraulically-operated Breda L turret containing one 12.7-mm. gun. In this form, a number were supplied to Iraq in 1938. Other nations which received the Breda 65 were Hungary, Paraguay, and Portugal. The type also fought with the Aviazione Legionaria in Spain, equipping the 65ª Squadriglia d'Assalto of the 35° Gruppo Autonomo Bombardamento Veloce.

When Italy entered the Second World War, the Regia Aeronautica possessed 154 Breda 65 aircraft. They were used by the 5° Stormo d'Assalto, 7° and 19° Gruppi Caccia, and 101ª and 102ª Squadriglie. In addition to their use in North Africa, the fighter-bombers were employed in the Balkan compaign, with only moderate success.

In single-seat form, the Breda 65 had a maximum speed of 267 m.p.h. and cruised at 230 m.p.h. Range was 342 miles, service ceiling 27,230 ft. Maximum and cruising speeds of the two-seat Breda 65bis were 255 m.p.h. and 227 m.p.h., range being doubled and ceiling dropping slightly to 25,290 ft. Empty weight of both versions was 5291 lb.; loaded weights ranged from 6504 lb. to 7716 lb.

Dimensions of all models were: span 39 ft. 8 in., length 31 ft. 6 in., height 10 ft. 6 in., and wing area 252.9 sq. ft.

BREDA 75

A larger shoulder-wing monoplane bearing a definite family resemblance to the Breda 65, the Breda 75 two-seat ground attack and reconnaissance plane was built experimentally in 1939. The sole prototype was powered by a 900 h.p. Isotta-Fraschini K.14. In addition to the raised wing position and larger dimensions, the Breda 75 was distinguished from the earlier models by a tall fixed landing gear

Two views of the Breda 75 ground attack and reconnaissance monoplane, built experimentally in 1939.

braced to the bottom of the fuselage, and by a number of observation windows beneath the wings.

Maximum and cruising speeds were 233 m.p.h. and 186 m.p.h., a range of 1056 miles being attainable with a payload of 3968 lb. Armament was two 12.7-mm. machine guns. Dimensions included a span of 51 ft. $2^{1}/_{8}$ in., a length of 37 ft. $0^{3}/_{4}$ in., and a height of 10 ft. 2 in.

BREDA 79
Designed in 1935, the Breda 79 S was a high-wing four-seat touring plane powered by a 200 h.p. Alfa Romeo 115 six-cylinder inverted in-line engine. Empty and loaded weights were 1694 lb. and 2684 lb. Dimensions were: span 38 ft., length 24 ft. 7 in., height 6 ft. $5^{1}/_{2}$ in., and wing area 193.7 sq. ft. Performance included a maximum speed of 155 m.p.h., a cruising speed of 137 m.p.h., a landing speed of 46

m.p.h., and a cruising range of 528 miles. The Breda 79 S climbed to altitudes of 3280 ft., 6560 ft., and 13,120 ft. in 3 min., 7 min. 30 sec., and 28 min. respectively.

BREDA 82
The Breda 82 medium bomber of 1937 was powered by two 1000 h.p. FIAT A.80 R.C.41 radial engines. A low-wing monoplane with retractable landing gear, the Breda 82 featured the then-popular but aerodynamically-inefficient "pigeon-chested" fuselage with forward gun turret above the bombardier's position.

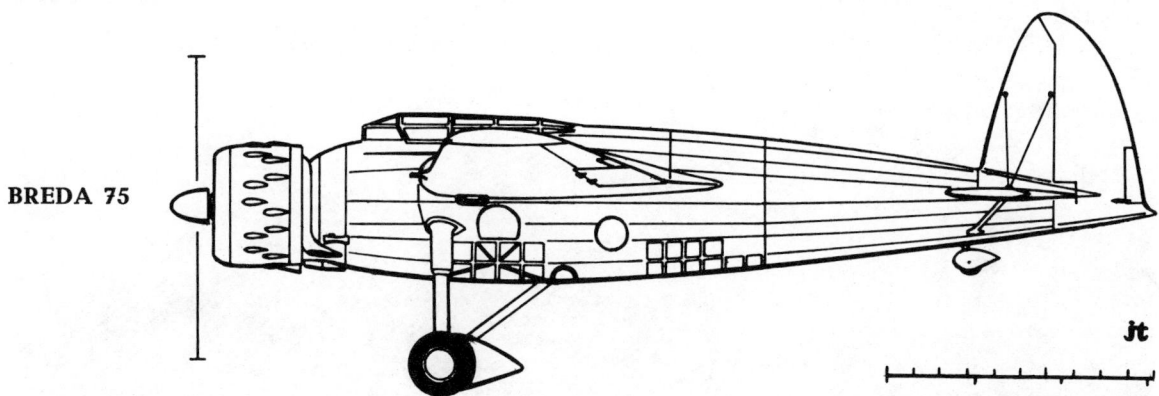

BREDA 75

The Breda 79 S touring monoplane. (I-ABFT)

Additional guns were located in dorsal and ventral turrets. The wing had split-flaps along the trailing edge. Dimensions were: span 68 ft. 11 in., length 45 ft. 11 in., and height 14 ft. 9 in. Performance included maximum and landing speeds of 264 m.p.h. and 81 m.p.h. respectively, and an absolute ceiling of 31,160 ft. The Breda 82 never went into production, as the FIAT A.80 proved to be unreliable and the Regia Aeronautica expressed preference for three-engined bombers.

BREDA 88
Probably the best-known Breda design, certainly the most highly publicized by the Mussolini government, was the Breda 88 twin-engine two-seat attack bomber designed in 1936. In spite of its considerable virtues the Breda 88 proved to be a wartime disappointment. The original model was an undeniably clean all-metal shoulder-wing monoplane, its excellent aerodynamics spoiled only by the bulk of its 900 h.p. Isotta-Fraschini K.14 radial engines. In December, 1937, the prototype Lince (Lynx) demonstrated its speed in establishing two F.A.I. records, carrying a 2205-lb. load 62.1 miles at 344.5 m.p.h. and 621 miles at 326.3 m.p.h. The pilot was Furio Niclot.

This model had a single fin and rudder, but later a more complicated braced twin fin-and-rudder arrangement was fitted to improve stability. The prototype had apparently been designed mainly for record purposes, since the necessary redesign to military standards resulted in a diminished performance, in spite of the slightly higher-rated 1000 h.p. Piaggio P.XI R.C.40's fitted. The speed of the production models was only 304 m.p.h. Assembly lines were established at both Breda and I.M.A.M., delivery beginning late in 1938.

Armament consisted of three nose-mounted 12.7-mm. Breda-SAFAT machine guns and a single 7.7-mm. gun in the rear cockpit. A Breda L turret was tried experimentally on the prototype. Payload was three 100-lb. bombs, three 220-lb. bombs, or two 550-lb. bombs. Maximum loaded weight was 14,881 lb. Cruising speed was 273 m.p.h., ceiling 26,240 ft., and range 1019 miles. Dimensions included a span of 51 ft. $2^{1}/_{8}$ in., a length of 35 ft. 5 in., a height of 10 ft. $2^{3}/_{4}$ in., and a wing area of 358.5 sq. ft. The Breda 88 climbed to 9840 ft. in 7 min. 30 sec. Production models which saw service with the 7° Gruppo in North Africa were extremely disappointing. Not only was performance inadequate, but numerous service problems arose and only 105 Lince bombers were completed before production was halted.

However, three examples of a further model, the Breda 88M, were produced in 1942—43 as dive bombers. Built at Cascina Costa, Varese, by the Agusta plant, this version mounted 840 h.p. FIAT A.74 R.C.38 radial engines, which

Above left and below, the Breda 82 medium bomber, which never went into production.

Above, the prototype Breda 88 with original tail assembly. Below, the same machine with twin fins.

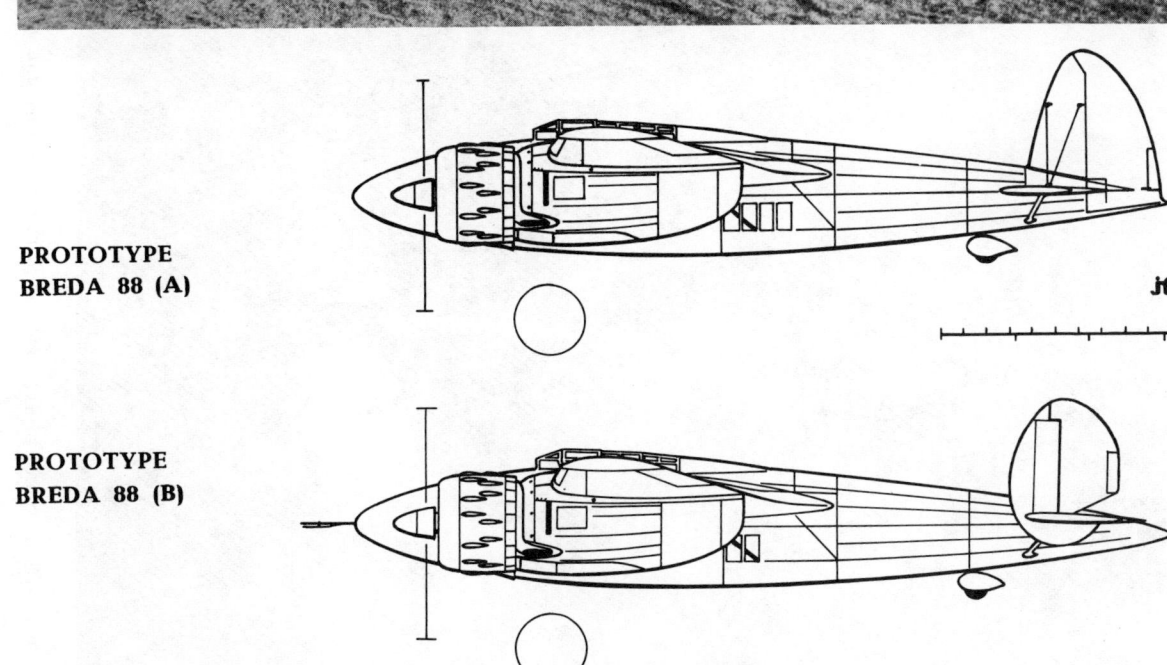

PROTOTYPE
BREDA 88 (A)

PROTOTYPE
BREDA 88 (B)

This striking view of the revised prototype shows the impressive lines of the Breda 88, which nevertheless proved to be a comparative failure.

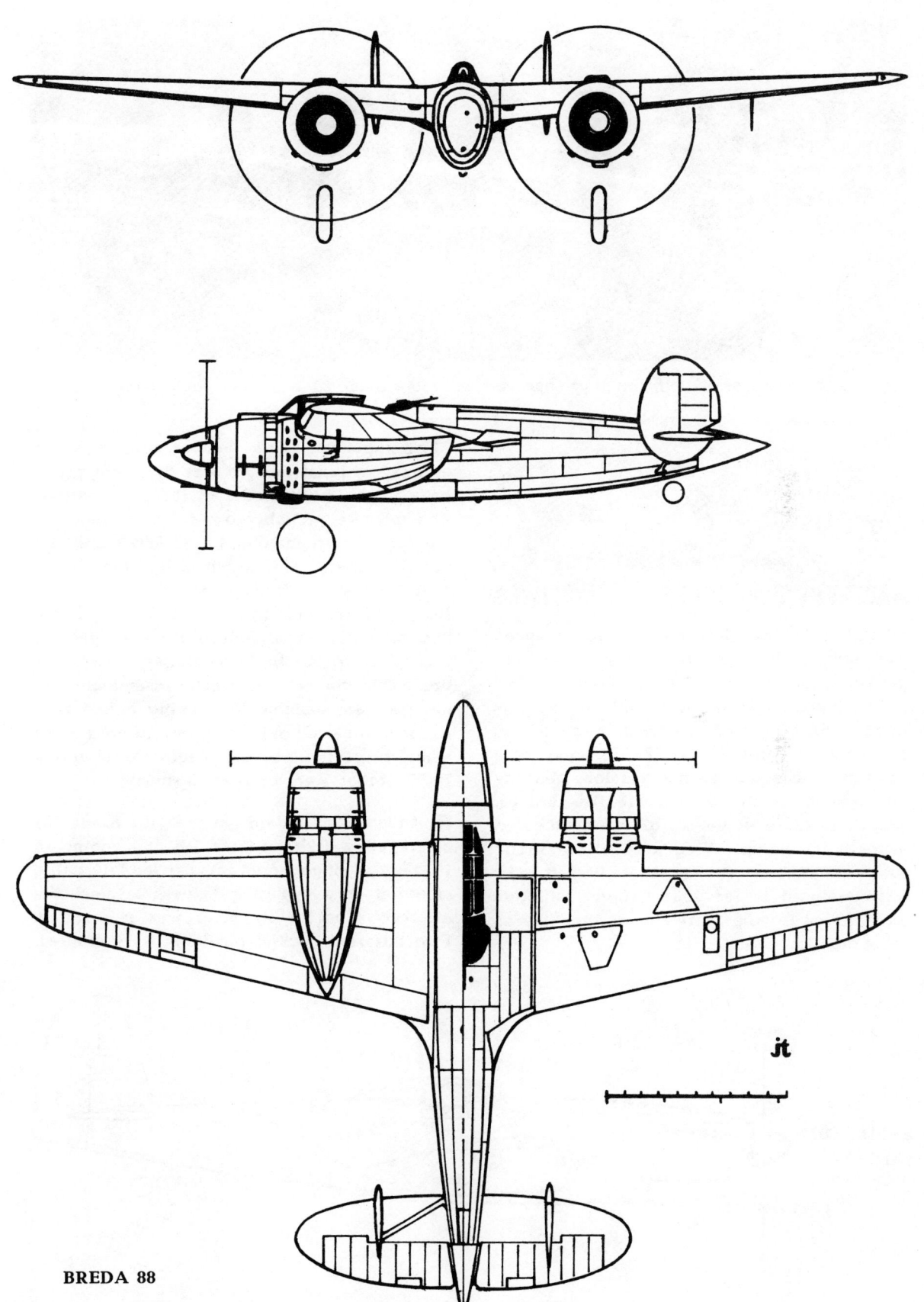

BREDA 88

Above and below left, the production version of the Breda 88. Note rear gun position.

proved to be insufficient as maximum speed was only 239 m.p.h. Nose armament was increased to four 12.7-mm. Breda-SAFAT machine guns, and the span and length grew to 58 ft. $0^{3}/_{4}$ in. and 37 ft. $10^{3}/_{4}$ in. respectively. The empty weight was 11,471 lb., some 1220 lb. higher than the earlier version, and the total loaded weight was 15,260 lb. Dive brakes, similar to those of the Ju 87, were mounted beneath the wings. Wing area of the Breda 88M was 425.2 sq. ft. The three aircraft built were assigned to the 103° Gruppo Tuffatori until seized by the Luftwaffe at the time of the Armistice.

BREDA 201

This single-seat dive bomber prototype, an entirely original design, was first thought to be a license-built model of the Ju 87 Stuka. The mistake probably owed its existence to the fact that a number of Ju 87B-1 and R-1 dive bombers did serve with the Regia Aeronautica, equipping the 96°, 97°, 101°, 102°, and 103° Gruppi Bombardieri a Tuffo. The nickname Picchiatello (Little Woodpecker) was given to the Ju 87 by Italian crews. The Breda 201 did bear a general resemblance to the German machine, employing a less pronounced inverted gull wing, but differed in all other respects. All the Regia Aeronautica Ju 87 Stukas were built in Germany.

First tested at Guidonia in 1941, the Breda 201 employed a Daimler-Benz DB 601 engine of 1050 h.p. A single bomb was carried internally, mounted on a swinging harness to clear the airscrew. The landing gear was retractable. Two different cockpit positions were studied,

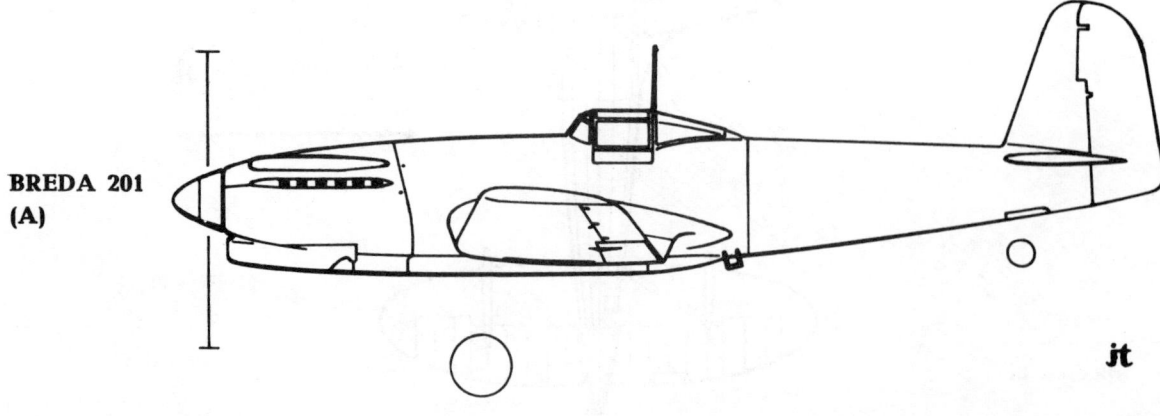

BREDA 201 (A)

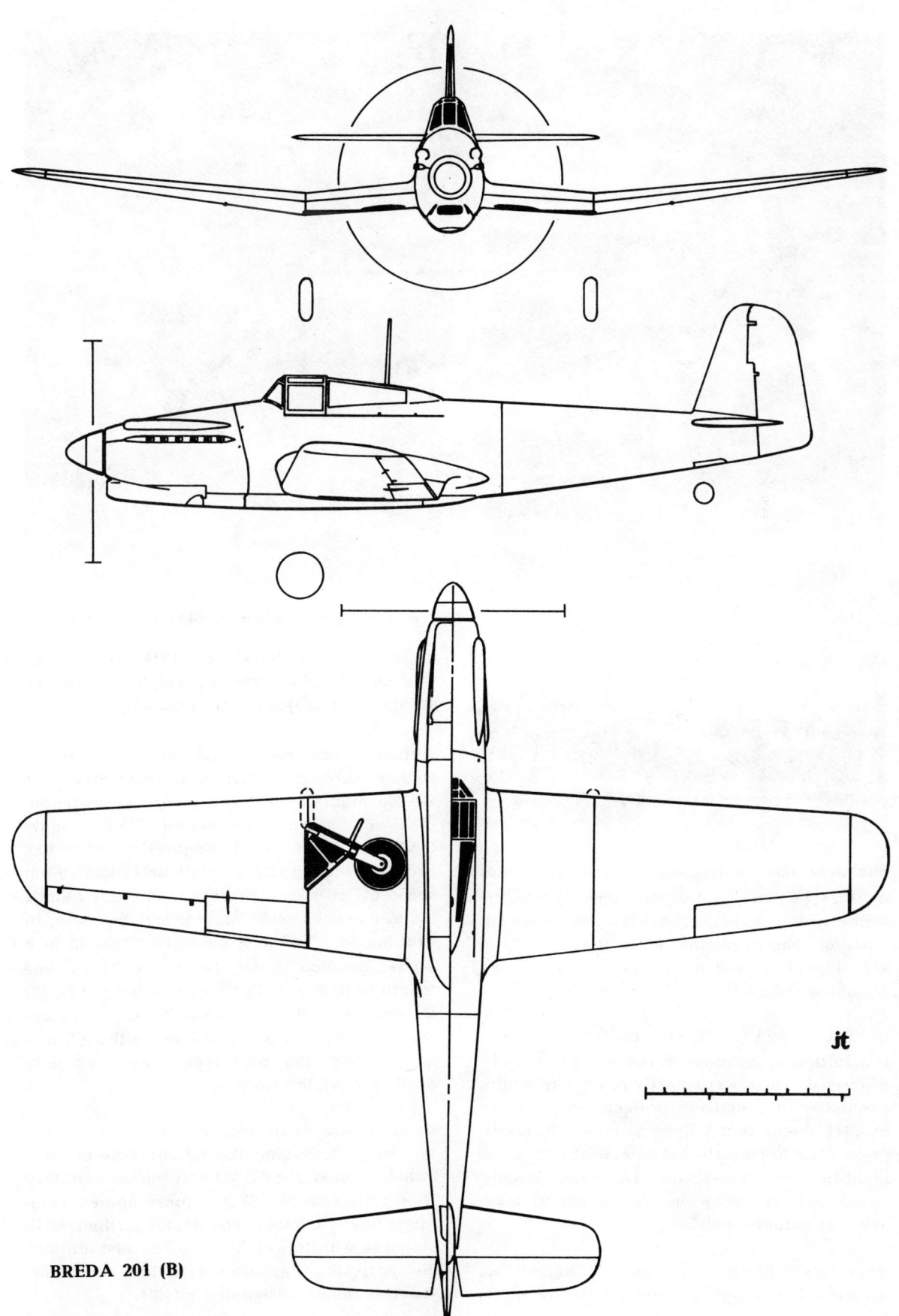

BREDA 201 (B)

Above, a Breda 201 mock-up with aft-positioned cockpit. Below, the prototype with cockpit moved forward.

one near the leading edge of the wing, and another behind the trailing edge. While the former offered better vision, the rearward position improved the aerodynamics. Span was 42 ft. 8 in. and length 36 ft. 6 in. Loaded weight was 8598 lb.

BREDA ZAPPATA PROJECTS

In addition to the major Breda designs already discussed, which were mostly of prewar origin, a number of promising projects were begun in 1941 under Ing. Filippo Zappata, formerly of the Cant organization. The Zappata projects, identified by the prefix BZ, were largely confined to the drawing boards, but at least one was actually built.

Zappata's first design was the BZ.301, an all-metal long-range medium bomber owing its basic layout to the Cant Z.1018. The BZ.302 was an all-metal twin-engined heavy fighter design. Both projects were abandoned.

Actually under construction at the time of the Italian surrender, but not completed, the BZ.303 night fighter was a very clean monoplane of mixed construction. Two Piaggio P.XV R.C.60/2V radial engines of 1450 h.p. each provided the BZ.303 with an estimated top speed of 360 m.p.h. No less than eight 20-mm. Mauser cannon were mounted in the nose, in addition to a 12.7-mm. defensive weapon in a dorsal position. Span was 67 ft. 11 in. and length 55 ft. $8^1/_2$ in. The loaded weight of 24,251 lb. and the estimated range of 962 miles are the only other details available, although it is known that the prototype was eventually destroyed by the Germans.

Zappata also projected several other aircraft for Breda, including the BZ.304 twin-engined attack bomber, the BZ.305 four-engined military transport, and the BZ.306 four-engined long-range heavy bomber. The BZ.308 airliner, built after the war, is well known. The last military design by Ing. Zappata was a light reconnaissance seaplane designated BZ.401.

C.A.N.S.A.
Costruzioni Aeronautiche Novaresi S.A. (FIAT)

C.A.N.S.A., located at Cameri, was one of the several FIAT subsidiaries, having been absorbed in 1939. Originally founded in 1913 as the Aeronautica Gabardini S.A., the company changed its title to C.A.N.S.A. in 1936. Early work included the series of Gabardini biplanes and the Lictor 90 and Lictor 130 lightplanes. The Lictor 90 was a low-wing cabin monoplane featuring side-by-side seating for two. Built in 1935 for the Littorio Air Rally, it was powered by an 85/90 h.p. FIAT A.50 radial engine. The Lictor 130 was the same design with a 130 h.p. D.H. Gipsy-Major four-cylinder inverted in-line engine.

With this background, the development of training aircraft for the Regia Aeronautica was a logical step. The types discussed below were all built primarily as trainers, except for the FC.20 reconnaissance and attack bomber.

C.5

The first C.A.N.S.A. design under FIAT ownership was the C.5 biplane, built in both single and two-seat versions, which flew for the first time in 1940. Intended for primary, advanced, and aerobatic training, the C.5 mounted a 100 h.p. FIAT A.50 radial engine. Of mixed construction, the single-seat biplane had empty and loaded weights of 1034 lb. and 1419 lb. It attained a maximum speed of 112 m.p.h. and landed at 48 m.p.h. Ceiling was 16,400 ft. and range 373 miles. Dimensions were: span 27 ft. 11 in., length 19 ft. 2 in., height 8 ft., and wing area 193.7 sq. ft.

The C.5B was a slightly heavier two-seat version weighing 1100 lb. empty and 1584 lb. loaded. Maximum speed dropped slightly to 109 m.p.h. Range and ceiling were respectively 292 miles and 13,120 ft. The C.5B/1, however, fitted a 130 h.p. Alfa Romeo 110-I in-line engine which boosted maximum speed to 124 m.p.h., range to 335 miles, and ceiling to 21,320 ft. The C.5B/1 climbed to 6560 ft. in 7 min. 40 sec., to 13,120 ft. in under 20 min., and landed

The C.5 single-seat training biplane. The two-seat C.5B was similar, changes being the addition of a second cockpit and a longer nose to maintain the center of gravity.

The C.5B/1 was a two-seater with a 130 h.p. Alfa engine in place of the FIAT radial. (MM 50850)

at 50 m.p.h. Length was 21 ft. 4¼ in. Most engines of the 90-150 h.p. class could be fitted if necessary or desirable.

C.6B

Making its appearance in 1942, the C.6B was a more advanced trainer with a 280 h.p. Isotta-Fraschini Beta R.C.10 engine and wings swept sharply back. Span and wing area were greater at 28 ft. 5 in. and 233.17 sq. ft. respectively. Of mixed metal and wood construction like the C.5, the C.6B weighed 2046 lb. empty and 2761 lb. loaded. Maximum speed was 162 m.p.h., ceiling 21,200 ft., and range 404 miles. The C.6B was a two-seater intended for advanced training and aerobatics.

The C.6B, nicknamed Falchetto (Little Falcon) after the CR.42 Falco fighter biplane. (MM 474)

Above, the C.4 trainer. (I-CANS) Below, the FC.12 with both military and civil markings. (I-TUFF)

C.4

In spite of its earlier type number, the C.4, also produced in 1942, was the last of the three trainer designs. It differed in being a low-wing monoplane. Built as both a trainer and a touring plane, the C.4 was powered by a 90 h.p. C.80 engine built by C.A.N.S.A. With a span of 39 ft. 9 in. and a wing area of 130.2 sq. ft., the C.4 achieved a speed of 134 m.p.h. and a range of 398 miles. Ceiling was 13,650 ft. Empty and loaded weights were 880 lb. and 1408 lb. respectively.

FC.12

Originally intended as a fighter and dive bomber trainer, the FC.12 was later projected as an operational light ground-attack machine. A tandem two-seat monoplane, the FC.12 was powered by a 600 h.p. FIAT A.30 R.A. in-line engine and featured underwing dive brakes and landing gear which retracted rearwards into wing fairings. The armament comprised five 12.7-mm. machine guns, two in the wings, two in the fuselage firing forward, and one swivel-mounted gun in the rear cockpit.

Performance included a maximum speed of 261 m.p.h., a range of 832 miles, and a ceiling of 25,350 ft. Dimensions included a span of 32 ft. 9¾ in., a length of 24 ft. 8 in., a height of 7 ft. 7 in., and a wing area of 213 sq. ft. Empty and loaded weights were 3960 lb. and 5115 lb.

The prototype FC.20 reconnaissance bomber was flown for the first time in 1941.

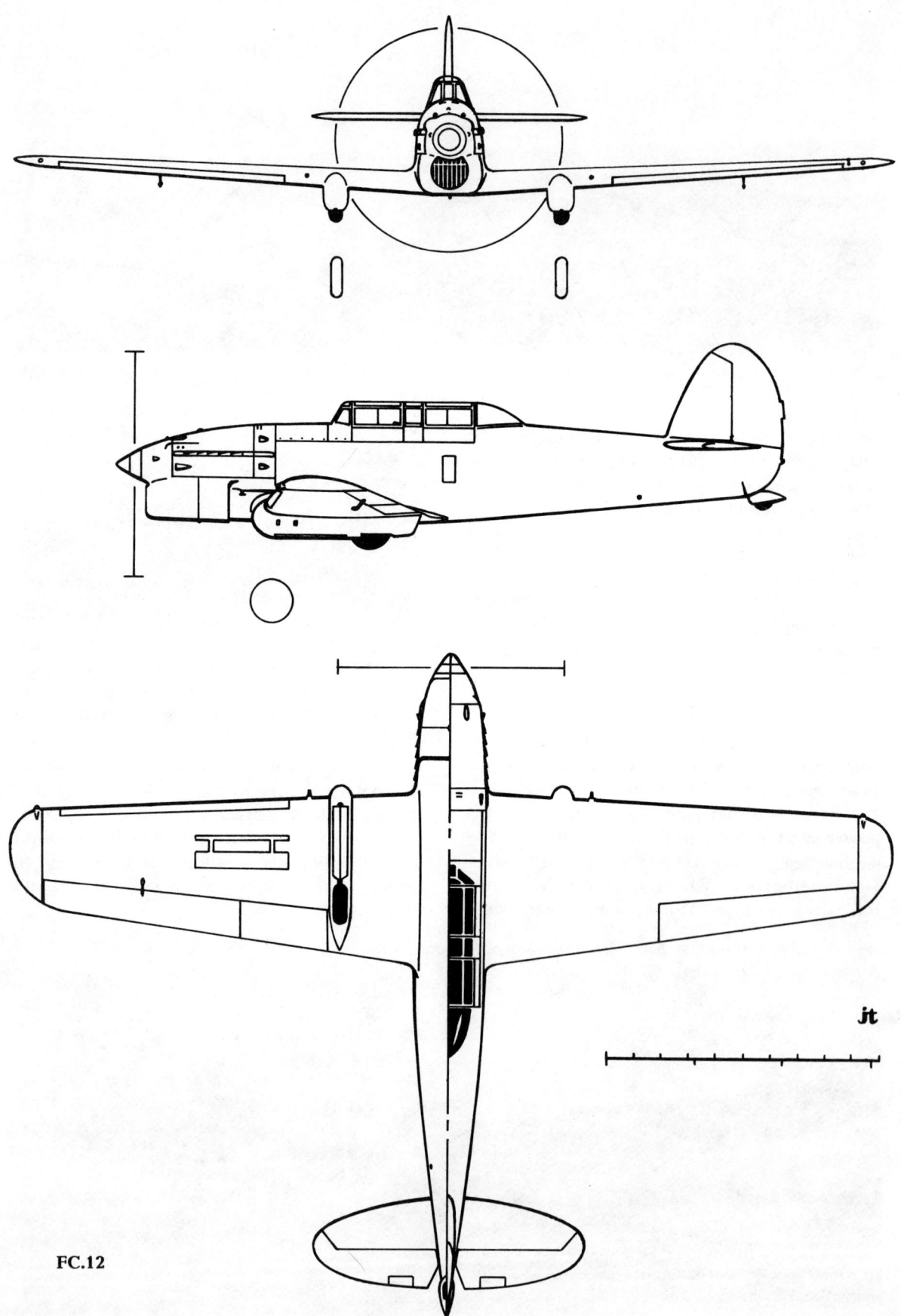

FC.12

The FC.20bis ground attack machine with 37-mm. nose cannon and dorsal turret. (MM 404)

The prototype FC.12 flew for the first time in 1940. Ten examples of the operational ground-attack model were built; it is unlikely that any saw actual combat.

FC.20

The first and only C.A.N.S.A. design planned from the outset as an operational military machine was the twin-engine FC.20. Flown for the first time in 1941 by C.A.N.S.A. test pilot Moroni, the prototype was a reconnaissance bomber powered by 840 h.p. FIAT A.74 R.C.38 radial engines. Wing area was 419.6 sq. ft. Performance of the FC.20 included a maximum speed of 292 m.p.h., a range of 807 miles, and a ceiling of 26,000 ft. However, it was decided to develop the basic design as a ground-attack machine, for which parallel studies had already been made.

The ground-attack version, the FC.20bis, appeared shortly after. In addition to a slight increase in wing area, the FC.20bis featured a shortened fuselage with the cockpit moved ahead of the wings and a 37-mm. Breda cannon mounted in the nose. Further armament consisted of a 12.7-mm. machine gun in a dorsal turret and two 12.7-mm. guns in the wing roots. A 54-mm. cannon was considered as a possible alternative to the 37-mm. weapon, but was never actually fitted. Two 352-lb. bombs could be carried beneath the wings outboard of the engine nacelles, and 126 4.4-lb. anti-personnel bombs could be housed internally. Loaded weight was 15,035 lb. Dimensions were: span 52 ft. 6 in., length 39 ft. 11 1/2 in., height 12 ft. 6 in., and wing area 430.4 sq. ft. Maximum and cruising speeds were 261 m.p.h. and 211 m.p.h.,

Nose cannon and wing root gun can be seen here.

range was 715 miles, and ceiling was 22,750 ft. The great similarity in appearance of the FC.20bis to the British Gloster F.9/37 escort fighter should be noted. Had both machines become operational, recognition problems would certainly have arisen. A further coincidence was the fact that liquid-cooled versions of both designs were also tested.

The FC.20ter, the third variant, reverted to the longer glazed nose and further-aft cockpit of the original reconnaissance model, but fitted 1000 h.p. FIAT A.80 R.C.41 radial engines. The final model, the FC.20quater, was an FC.20bis fitted with Daimler-Benz DB 601 liquid-cooled engines of 1250 h.p. each (built by FIAT as the R.A.1000). Tested in 1943, the FC.20quater substituted a Mauser Ikaria 37-mm. cannon for the Breda weapon, and two 20-mm. cannon for the 12.7-mm. wing guns. Loaded weight increased to 15,730 lb., speed to 311 m.p.h., and ceiling to 26,000 ft., although range dropped to 578 miles. Three FC.20bis equipped the 174[a] Squadriglia Ricognizione Strategica based at Cerveteri in July, 1943, but were never employed operationally.

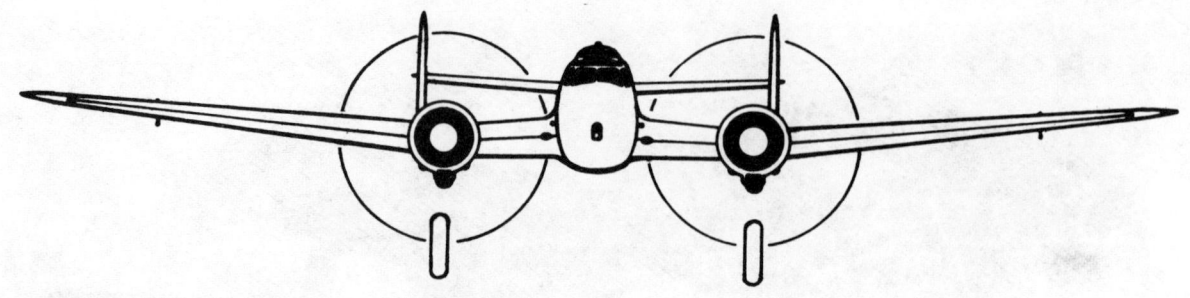
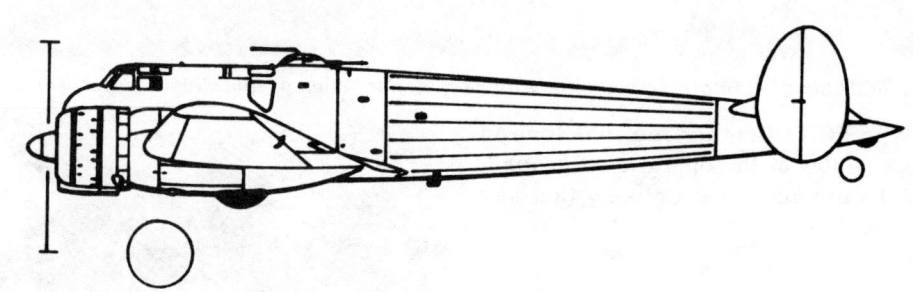

FC.20BIS

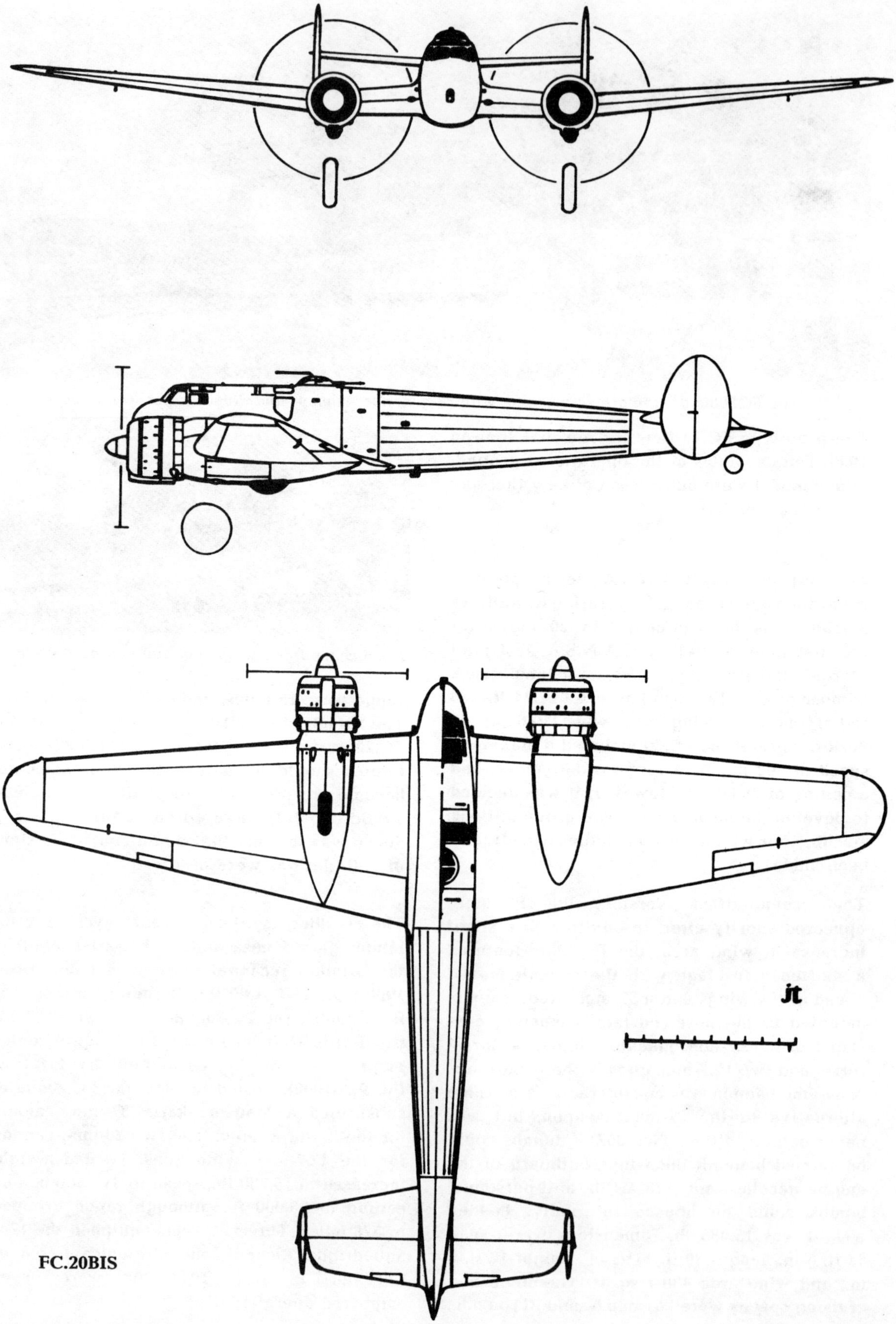

Above, the FC.20bis. (MM 404) Below, the same photograph retouched to depict the DB 601-powered FC.20quater, which was identical except for the engine change.

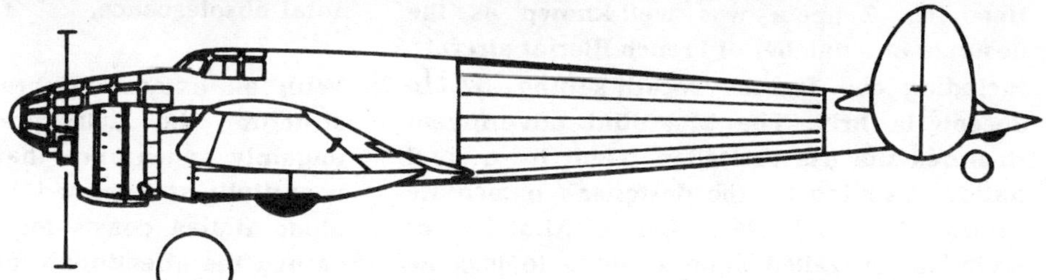

FC.20

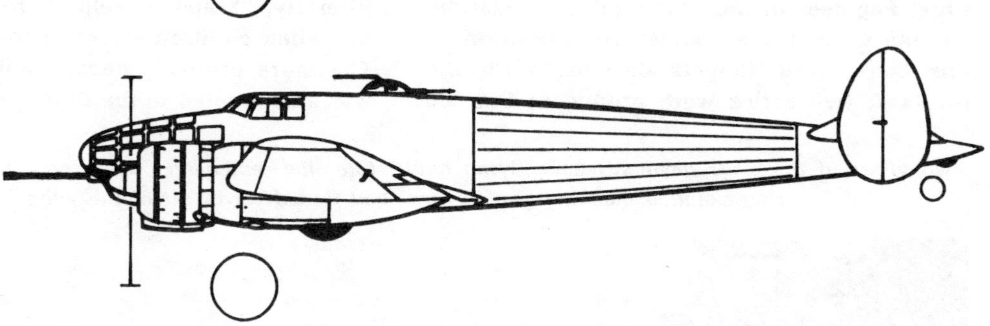

FC.20TER

FC.20QUATER

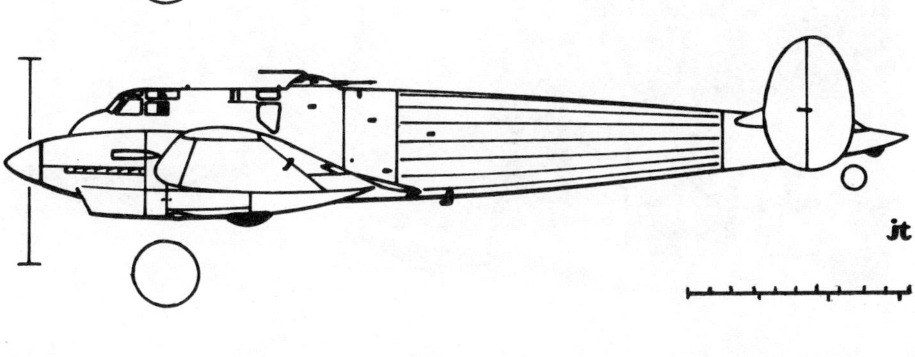

CANT
Cantieri Riuniti dell'Adriatico

The Cantieri Navali di Monfalcone, Trieste, was a firm of shipbuilders which entered the aircraft industry in 1923. Under the name Cantiere Navale Triestino, the company concentrated on water-based aircraft, building a number of flying boats and seaplanes for commercial and military use. Among the more notable of these were the Cant 6 bomber and Cant 6ter commercial transport, the Cant 10 light transport, the Cant 18 trainer, the Cant 22 commercial transport, and the Cant 25 fighter. A few landplanes were built, such as the Cant 23 commercial transport and the Cant 36 trainer, but it was not until the firm obtained the services of Ing. Filippo Zappata that a really varied program of successful aircraft was undertaken.

In 1931 the company reorganized under the name Cantieri Riuniti dell'Adriatico. At that time Ing. Zappata was well-known as the designer of a number of French Bleriot aircraft, including the famous record-setting BZ.110 Joseph le Brix. The Mussolini government deplored the use of Italian talent by a rival nation, insisting on the designer's immediate return. Marshall Italo Balbo, Minister of Aviation, prevailed upon Zappata to become Chief Engineer of the new Cant organization. All the Cant aircraft under consideration in this book were Zappata designs. With the prefix Z, two series were produced: the 500 series of water-based aircraft and the 1000 series of land-based aircraft.

Z.501

The Z.501 single-engined reconnaissance-bomber flying boat was the first project of the new staff. Built in 1934, the Z.501 immediately gained prestige for Italy with a non-stop seaplane distance record of 2560 miles from Monfalcone to Massawa, Eritrea, in October of the same year. In 1935, after the French had exceeded the distance, the Z.501 flew 3080 miles non-stop from Monfalcone to Berbera, British Somaliland, regaining the record. On both flights the pilot was Mario Stoppani, chief pilot for Cant. This was an auspicious start for the Z.501, which in 1936 began a long career of service with the Regia Aeronautica. The flying boat was still in limited use at the end of the Second World War, in spite of its total obsolescence.

With an extensively-braced wing and float structure, the Z.501 presented a somewhat ungainly appearance that contrasted with its beautifully-streamlined hull. A familiar sight along Italian coasts for ten years, the Z.501 earned the affectionate nickname Mammaiuto (literally, "Mamma, help!") from the reaction of Italian children seeing it for the first time. The more ordinary name Gabbiano (Seagull) was also applied to the flying boat. Employing

Two views of the Z.501 reconnaissance flying boat. Note the extensive wing and pontoon bracing, ring-mounted machine gun in bow, and dorsal turret aft of the wing.

A view of the record-breaking Z.501 reconnaissance flying boat, 1935.

a 900 h.p. Isotta-Fraschini Asso XI R2C 15 twelve-cylinder liquid-cooled engine mounted in the wing, the Z.501 was built almost entirely of wood, with fabric-covered wing and tail surfaces. The hull contained two gun positions, in the bow and aft of the wing; a third position was located in the engine nacelle above the wing. All three posts fitted single 7.7-mm. weapons. Bombs were carried under the wings in racks attached to the bracing struts. The load was normally two 550-lb. bombs, or four 352-lb., 220-lb., or 110-lb. bombs. Early models of the Z.501 employed two-bladed wooden airscrews, later replaced by the three-bladed metal type. The nose gun was omitted from some later models. Otherwise, the Z.501 underwent little change during its career.

In 1937-38 Rumania purchased a number of Z.501's to equip a coastal defense and naval cooperation group. Some of the Italian flying boats saw action in the Spanish Civil War.

When Italy entered the Second World War on June 10, 1940, the Z.501 equipped seventeen Squadriglie and four Sezioni, as follows: the 141a-148a, 171a, and 182a-189a Squadriglie da Ricognizione Marittima, and 1a, 3a-5a Sezioni Costiere; based on the Adriatic and Tyrrhenian Seas, Sardinia, Sicily, and smaller Italian islands. Of the 202 aircraft available, approximately 109 were in first-line operation. In spite of its long-range capabilities, the Z.501 was slow and vulnerable. Nevertheless, it served with the Regia Aeronautica until the Armistice, and continued with both the Allied Co-Belligerent Air Force and the Fascist Aviazione della RSI (Repubblica Sociale Italiana) until the end of fighting in Italy.

Performance of the Z.501 included a maximum speed of 171 m.p.h. at 8200 ft. and a cruising speed of 149 m.p.h. at 6560 ft. Climb to 13,120 ft. required 16 minutes. Normal cruising range with full military load was 621 miles, while maximum range was 1490 miles. Span was 73 ft. 10 in., length 46 ft. 11 in., height 14 ft. 6 in., and wing area 667.4 sq. ft. Empty the Z.501 weighed 8470 lb; with the normal load the weight was 13,090 lb., although the maximum figure was 15,510 lb.

Z.504

The Cant Z.504 was a single-engined, two-seat biplane flying boat built in 1935 as a naval fighter. Considerably smaller than the Z.501, it was quite similar in general appearance despite the biplane configuration and radial engine. The pilot sat just forward of the shoulder-mounted lower wing, with an observer's position behind incorporating one

The Z.504 two-seat catapult biplane. (MM 2406)

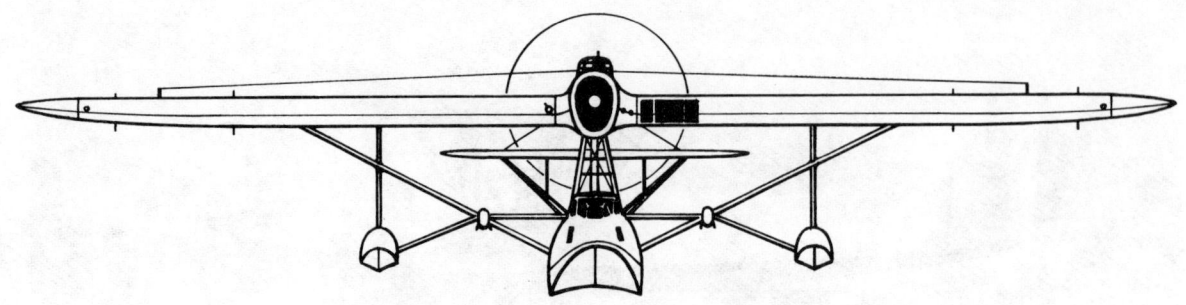
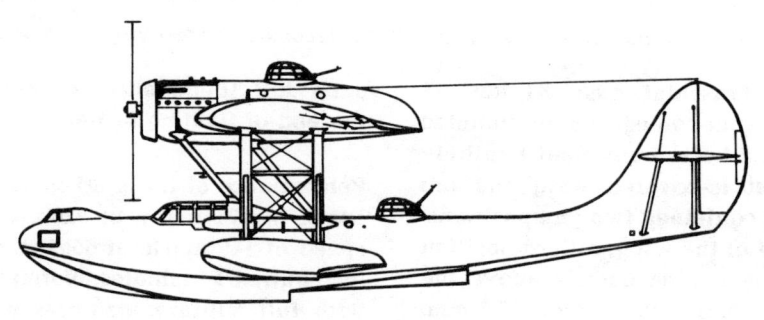
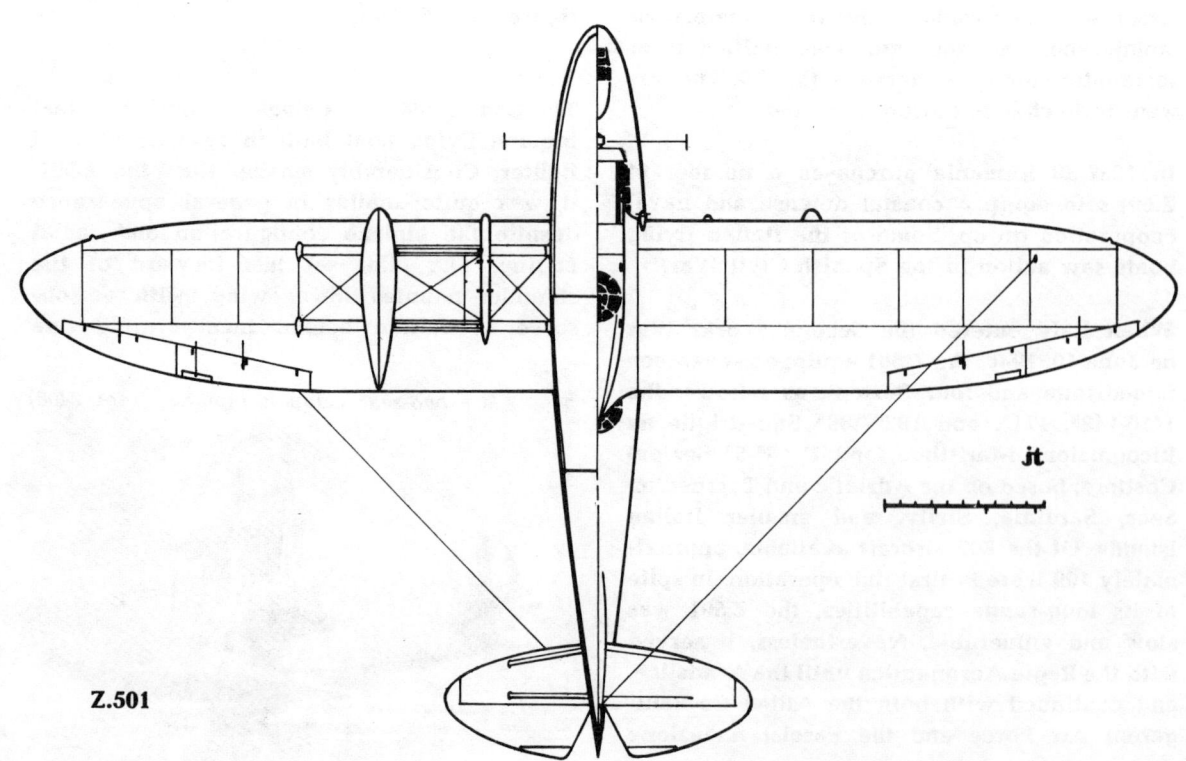

Z.501

Z.505. The tail was later changed to the familiar form used on subsequent Cant aircraft. (I-ZAPP)

7.7-mm. machine gun. The Z.504 was to have been catapult-launched from ships, but was not adopted by the Regia Marina. No further details are available.

Z.505

The forerunner of the well-known Z.506 series, the Z.505 three-engined twin-float seaplane was built in 1935 for mail service. It differed from the later series principally in the use of Isotta-Fraschini Asso XI R.C.15 in-line engines. As with nearly all Cant aircraft, construction was of wood, although metal floats were used. Except for a slightly inferior performance, the details and dimensions of the Z.505 closely matched those of the Z.506. Loaded weight was 28,207 lb. The Z.505 had a much greater dihedral than the Z.506.

Z.506

The most successful of Zappata's water-based designs, the Z.506 began a twenty-four-year career in 1935 as a twelve-passenger commercial seaplane. Initially, three 610 h.p. Piaggio Stella IX R.C. nine-cylinder radial engines were fitted, but later versions used 750 h.p. Alfa Romeo 126 R.C.34 radials. The Z.506A set a number of speed, altitude, and distance records for seaplanes during 1936-38. Among these records, mostly secured by Mario Stoppani, were speeds of 191.539 m.p.h., 198.700 m.p.h., and 200.118 m.p.h. over distances of 3105 miles, 1242 miles, and 621 miles, respectively. These records, achieved with the Alfa Romeo engines, exceeded those set earlier by a Z.506 equipped with 700 h.p. FIAT A.59 R.C. radial engines. The Z.506A reached an altitude of 25,623 ft. carrying a 4400-lb. payload, and 22,693 ft. carrying 11,000 lb. A distance record of 3345.225 miles over a closed circuit followed soon after.

Above right, a Z.506A adapted as a rescue plane. Left and right below, the Z.506A was employed commercially by Ala Littoria S.A. Note different paint schemes. (I-DUNA; I-GORO)

Above left, the prototype Z.506B. Right, a Z.506B with "anti-camouflage" diagonal wing stripes.

The Z.506A entered service with the Ala Littoria airline in 1936, powered by Piaggio engines. Sixteen aircraft were ordered during 1936-38. The Piaggio units were later replaced by Alfa Romeo 126 R.C.10 engines. The seaplane carried up to eighteen passengers at a cruising speed of 162 m.p.h. Maximum speed was 244 m.p.h., range 746 miles. Empty and loaded weights were 15,873 lb. and 23,147 lb. Dimensions were: span 86 ft. 11 in., length 62 ft. 1 in., height 22 ft. 2½ in., and wing area 936 sq. ft.

In 1937 the Z.506B continued the record-breaking activities of the design. The Z.506B was a military version featuring a ventral gondola, containing bombardier, bomb load, and rear-mounted defensive machine gun; and a semi-retractable dorsal turret. However, the military equipment was omitted from the record-breaking machine, which reached an altitude of 33,818 ft. with a 2200-lb. load. The same Z.506B flew 4362 miles non-stop from Cadiz to Caravelas. The record machine used 750 h.p. Alfa Romeo 127 R.C.55 engines and had a maximum speed of 242 m.p.h.

Thirty-two examples of the Z.506B Serie I were delivered to the Regia Aeronautica and Regia Marina in 1938. Given the name Airone (Heron), the reconnaissance-bomber could carry a 1764-lb. torpedo in the bomb bay, or a variety of bomb loads: one 1764-lb. bomb, two 1100-lb. bombs, two 551-lb. and three 110-lb. bombs, four 353-lb. and three 110-lb. bombs, nine 110-lb. or 220-lb. bombs, or sixteen 33-lb. or 44-lb. bombs. Armament comprised one 7.7-mm. Breda-SAFAT machine gun in the rear of the gondola, and one 12.7-mm. machine gun in the Breda M.1 upper turret. The pilot's cockpit, with tandem seating, was larger and higher than on the Z.506A.

A few Airones were used experimentally in the Spanish conflict, and thirty were ordered by Poland in 1938. Only one reached Poland before the German invasion; it was destroyed in the water by German fighters. The Regia Marina took over the remaining aircraft from the Polish contract. Italy possessed 95 Z.506B bombers in June 1940; of these, 61 were operational, equipping the 31° and 35° Stormi da Bombardimento Marittimo at Elmas and Brindisi, and the 147ª, 170ª, and 199ª Squadriglie da Ricognizione Marittima at Lero, Augusta, and Santa Giusta. During the war,

The Z.506B was a military model with dorsal turret, raised cockpit, and gondola for torpedo or bombs.

CANT

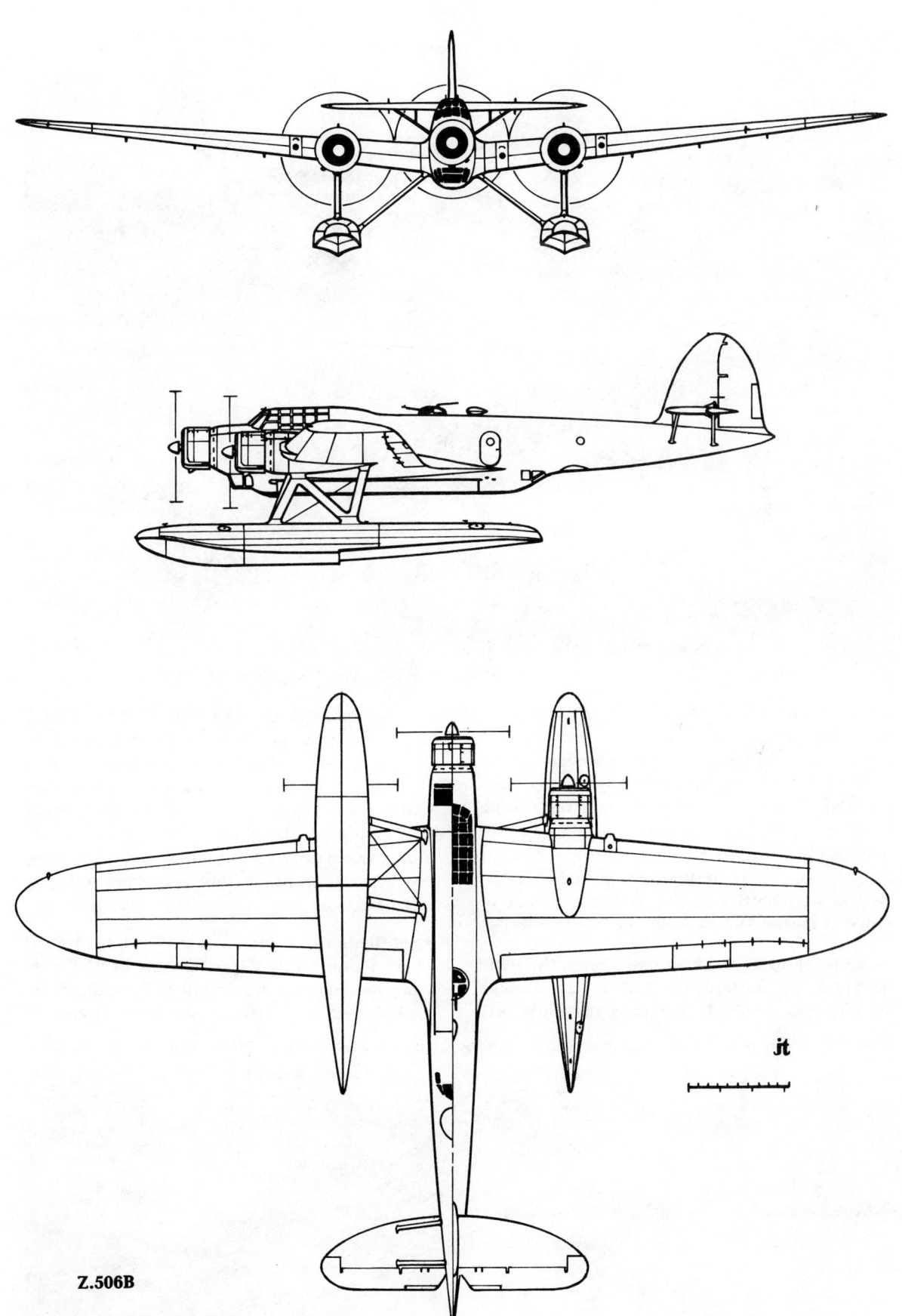

Z.506B

A Piaggio-built Z.506B being lowered into the water by the huge crane at Finale Ligure.

Airones were used for bombing and torpedo dropping, naval reconnaissance, rescue, and occasionally as troop and cargo transports for landing operations. Between 1940-42 Airones rescued 231 persons. After the war the rescue version (Z.506 S) continued Mediterranean operations with the 83°, 84°, and 85° Gruppi di Soccorso Aereo until 1959. In 1948 S.I.A.I. Savoia Marchetti had received a contract to convert 20 Z.506B's to Z.506 S specification.

In addition to the Monfalcone works, the plant at Finale Ligure built the Z.506B in a number of different versions, including the Serie XII, with bomb load increased from 2200 lb. to 2645 lb., waist gun positions incorporating two 7.7-mm. Breda-SAFAT machine guns, and a Caproni Lanciani Delta E turret with a 12.7-mm. Scotti gun in place of the Breda turret. Piaggio & C. also built the Z.506. Although the Aichi company secured the Japanese manufacturing license, it is unlikely that any were actually built in Japan.

Specifications of the Z.506B were: span 86 ft. 11 in., length 63 ft. $1^1/_2$ in., height 24 ft. $3^1/_3$ in., wing area 936 sq. ft., empty weight 18,298 lb., loaded weight 27,116 lb., maximum speed 227

The Z.506S was a rescue version converted directly from the Z.506B, and still in use as late as 1959.

CANT

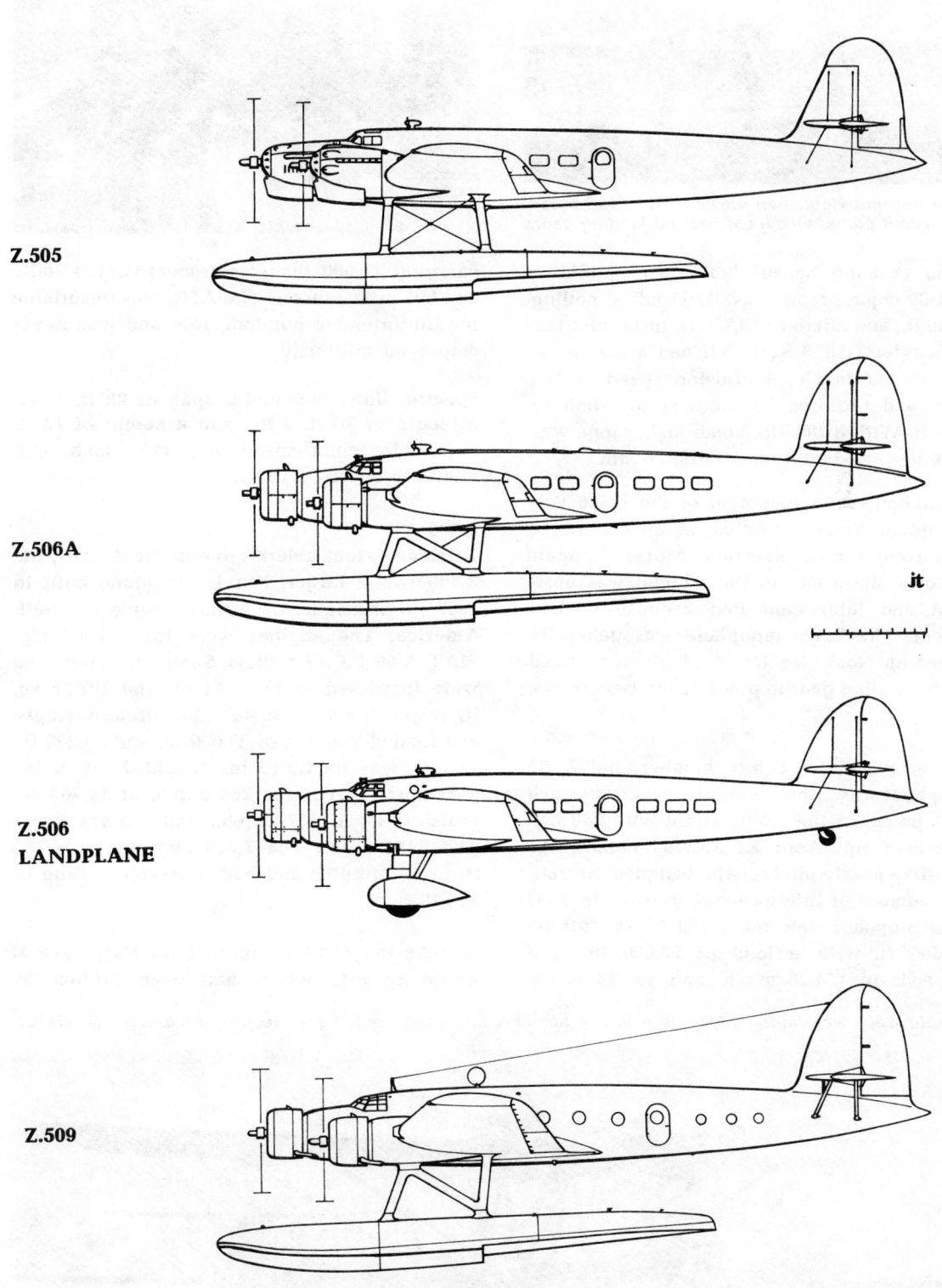

Z.505

Z.506A

Z.506 LANDPLANE

Z.509

Above left and right, two views of the land-based Z.506 record plane with fixed spatted landing gear.

m.p.h., cruising speed 202 m.p.h., alighting speed 80 m.p.h., range 1242-1705 miles, ceiling 26, 240 ft., and climb to 13,120 ft. in 14 minutes. The heavier Z.506B Serie XII had a maximum speed of 217 m.p.h., a cruising speed of 186 m.p.h., and required 20 minutes to climb to 13,120 ft. With a 2095-lb. bomb load, range was 1242 miles and endurance 6 hrs. 26 min.

A little-known development of the Z.506 was a landplane variant readied for an endurance flight from Elmas, Sardinia. Mario Stoppani was to be the pilot but the attempt was postponed and later cancelled because of bad weather. The Z.506 landplane was generally cleaned-up and lightened, featuring fixed spatted landing gear in place of the twin floats.

Z.508

Built in 1936 as a heavy bomber, the Z.508 flying boat was a three-engined, much enlarged development of the Z.501. Fitted with 840 h.p. Isotta-Fraschini Asso XI R.C.40 engines, the Z.508, like nearly all Zappata-designed aircraft, set a number of international records. In 1937 Mario Stoppani flew the Z.508 to an altitude of 6560 ft. with a load of 22,000 lb., and at speeds of 154.26 m.p.h. and 156.42 m.p.h. carrying 11,000 lb. over respective 1242-mile and 621-mile courses. The Z.508 was unsuitable for the intended bombing role and was never employed militarily.

Specifications included a span of 98 ft. 5 in., a length of 70 ft. 5 in., and a height of 18 ft. 7 in. Maximum speed was 196 m.p.h. and alighting speed 75 m.p.h.

Z.509

To some extent a derivative of the Z.506A, the Z.509 was a larger, heavier seaplane built in 1937 for transatlantic postal service to South America. The engines were three 1000 h.p. FIAT A.80 R.C.41 radials. Span and wing area were increased to 92 ft. 11 in. and 1075.8 sq. ft. respectively to sustain the greater empty and loaded weights of 22,000 lb. and 35,200 lb. Length was 62 ft. 10 in., height 24 ft. 8 in., Maximum speed was 264 m.p.h. at 14,760 ft., cruising speed 217 m.p.h., and normal range 2329-2484 miles. The Z.509 climbed to 14,760 ft. in 14 minutes and had a service ceiling of 26,240 ft.

In 1938 the Z.509 recaptured for Italy several speed records which had been broken by

The sole Z.508 was built in 1938 as a heavy bomber, but used only for record breaking. (I-VECC)

CANT

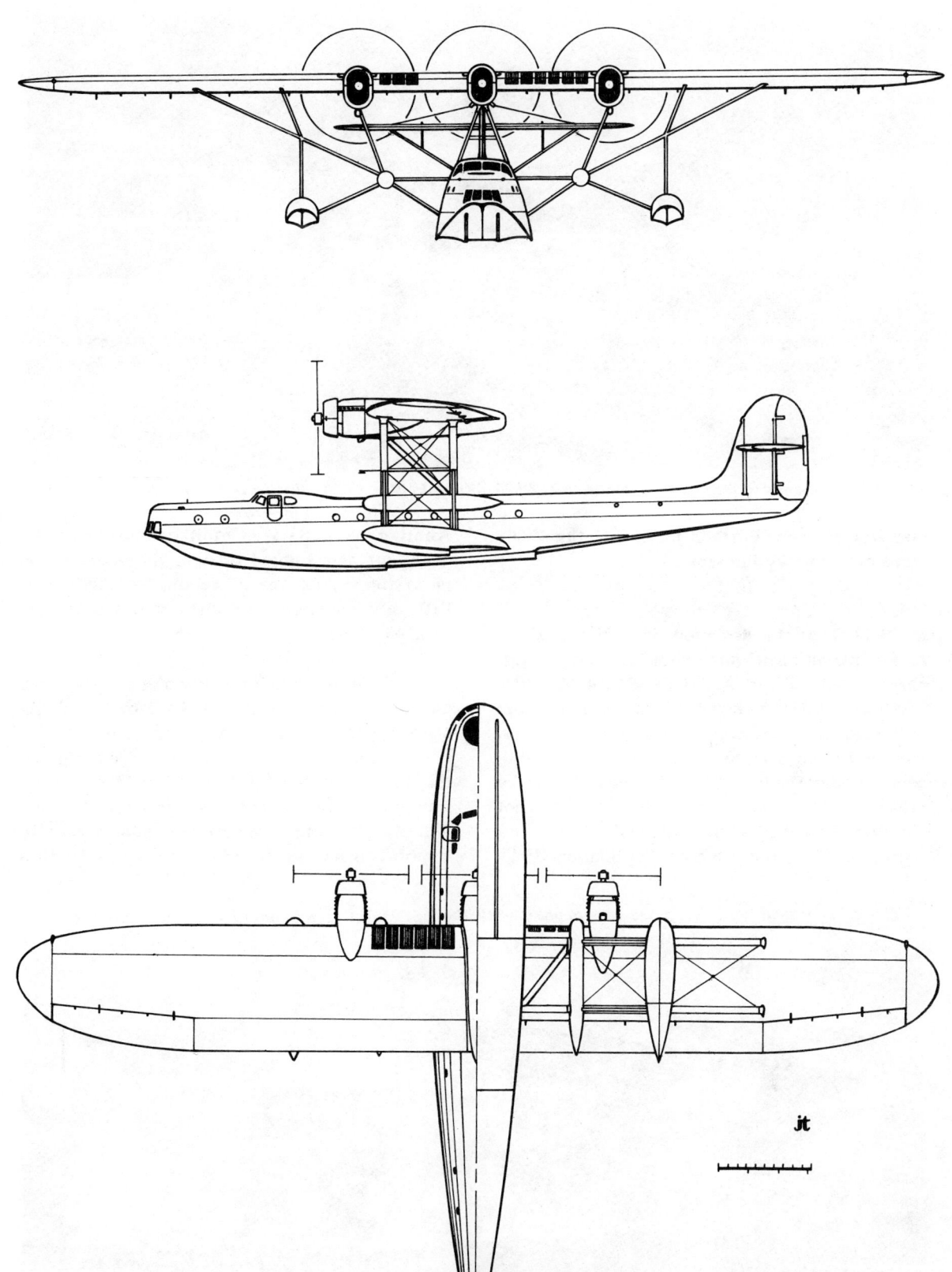

Z.508

Except for larger dimensions, the Z.509 differed little externally from the Z.506A.

German aircraft. Further plans for the Z.509 were cut short by the war.

Z.511

In 1939 Zappata designed the four-engined Z.511 transatlantic passenger airliner. Originally intended for Alitalia's South Atlantic route, the Z.511 featured a two-level fuselage with crew and passenger compartments above, and mail and freight holds below. Sleeping accommodations for sixteen persons were to be provided. However, the prototype was not completed until after the outbreak of the war, flying for the first time in September, 1943. Another example was built concurrently. An excellent and rugged design, the Z.511 could moor on waves nearly seven feet high with little adverse effect, and had a maximum range of 2796 miles.

An ambitious plan for raiding the New York harbor was under study in 1943 by the Regia Marina, using "Porcellini" man-guided torpedoes, already successfully employed against the British battleship Valiant at Alexandria. The two Z.511 seaplanes were to fly the Atlantic, taxying in under the radar screen to a point from which the manned torpedoes

The Z.511 transatlantic seaplane in company with the Z.515 light reconnaissance bomber seaplane.

CANT

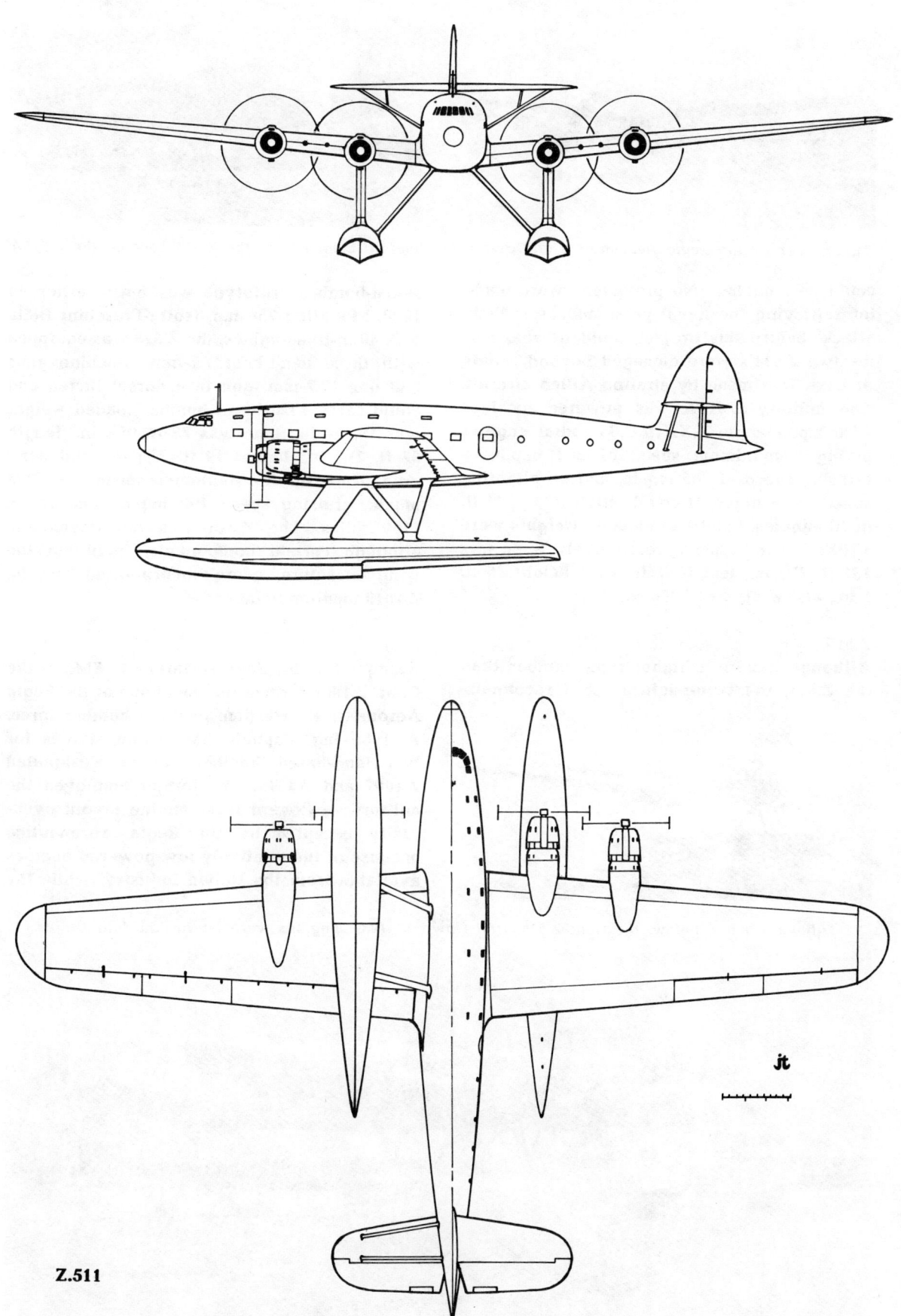

Z.511

Taken over by the Regia Aeronautica and given the standard camouflage, the Z.511 became the Z.511A.

could be launched. No provisions were made for retrieving the naval personnel after their attack. Before this project could be realized, the two Z.511's were damaged beyond repair at Lake Trasimeno by strafing Allied aircraft. The military Z.511A was powered by four 1500 h.p. Piaggio P.XII R.C.35 radial engines giving a maximum speed of 264 m.p.h., a cruising speed of 205 m.p.h., and an alighting speed of 84 m.p.h. It could climb to 13,120 ft. in 16 minutes. Empty and loaded weights were 45,012 lb. and 73,830 lb. respectively. Span was 131 ft. $2^1/_2$ in., length 93 ft. 6 in., height 36 ft. 1 in., and wing area 2098 sq. ft.

Z.515

Although it bore a higher type number than the Z.511, the twin-engined Z.515 reconnaissance-bomber prototype was built earlier, in 1938. Mounting 750 h.p. Isotta-Fraschini Delta R.C. 40 in-line engines, the Z.515 was equipped with three hand-held 7.7-mm. machine guns and one 12.7-mm. gun in a dorsal turret, and could carry 1320 lb. of bombs. Loaded weight was 18,700 lb. Span was 73 ft. $9^7/_8$ in., length 52 ft. $7^1/_2$ in., height 19 ft. $2^3/_4$ in., and wing area 679.2 sq. ft. Maximum speed was 238 m.p.h., cruising speed 190 m.p.h., and range 1180 miles. The Z.515 was not developed, although certain components, including the wing structure, were incorporated in the Z.1018 medium bomber.

Z.1007

Along with the Savoia-Marchetti SM.79, the Cant. Z.1007 formed the backbone of the Regia Aeronautica's wartime medium bomber force. In 1935 Ing. Zappata had begun studies for two land-based bombers to be designated Z.1007 and Z.1011. The former employed the militarily-awkward three-engine layout eventually accepted by the Regia Aeronautica because of the relatively low-powered engines available from the Italian industry, while the

Above left and below, the Cant Z.515, first flown in 1939. Engines were Isotta-Fraschini Deltas.

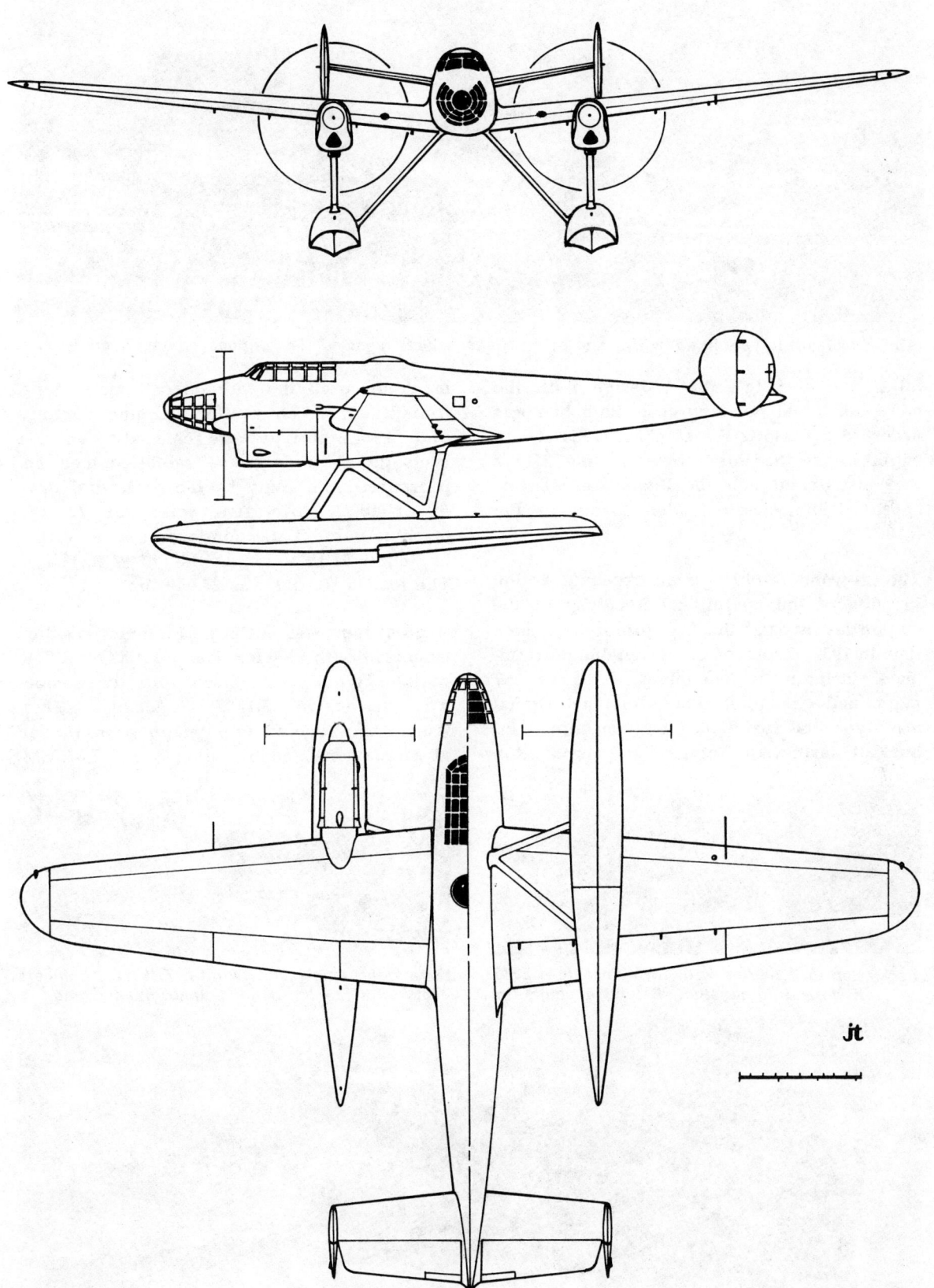

Z.515

The Z.1007 prototype fitted with annular cowlings, which replaced the original, conventional type.

latter was a twin-engined design with the more functional bombing nose. Both bombers used 840 h.p. Isotta-Fraschini Asso XI R.C.15 engines, but the total power of the Z.1011 was insufficient and the Regia Aeronautica approved the classic Italian layout of the Z.1007.

The all-wood Z.1007 was an excellent design in spite of the operational handicap of the engine layout, and the first prototype, which flew in 1937, displayed an acceptable performance, including a maximum speed of 267 m.p.h. and a range of 1740 miles. The original prototype had two-bladed wooden airscrews, but all further prototypes and production machines used the three-bladed metal type. In addition, the conventional engine cowlings of the first prototype were replaced by annular rings giving a deceptive radial-engined appearance, belied only by the horizontal rows of exhausts. Armament was four 7.7-mm. machine guns. Dimensions were: span 78 ft. 7 in., length 51 ft. 10 in., and height 17 ft. $1^{1}/_{4}$ in. The loaded weight was 27,000 lb.

A great improvement in performance resulted from tests with 1000 h.p. Piaggio P.XI bis R.C.40 radial engines. With these units the bomber was designated Z.1007bis Alcione (Kingfisher) and ordered into quantity production at Monfalcone and the Piaggio and I.M.A.M.

Above left, a Z.1007bis with twin fins. (MM 22365) Above right, single and twin-fin Z.1007bis bombers in formation together. Below, a single-fin Z.1007bis with the Mussolini Squadriglia insignia.

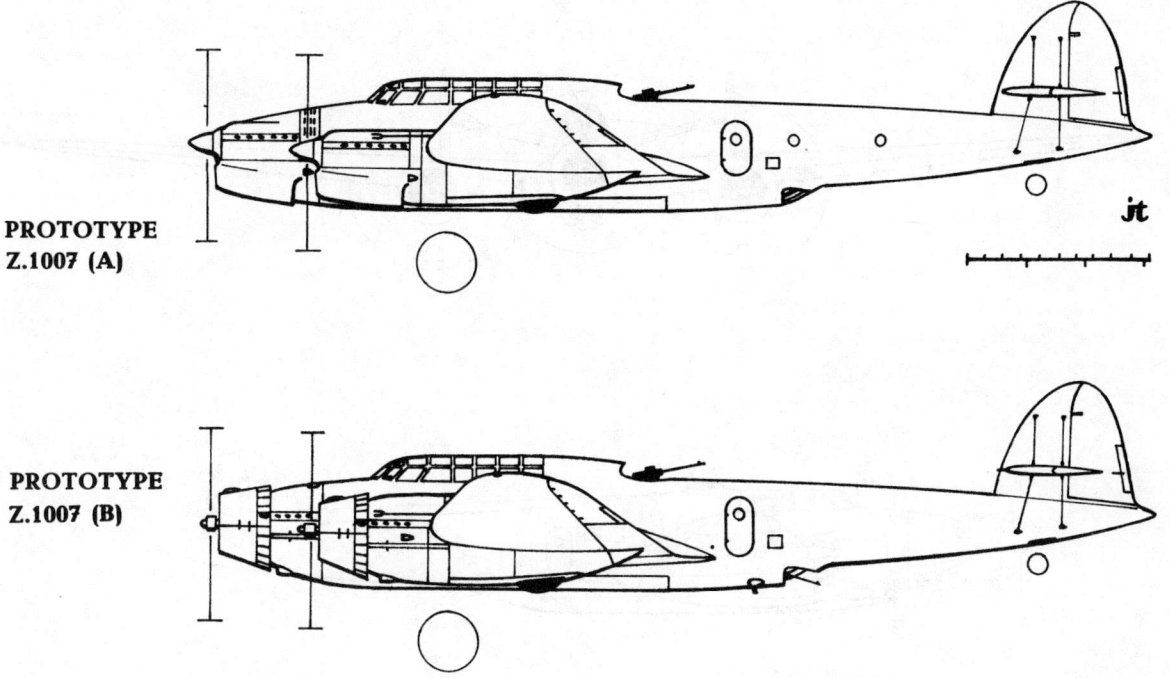

PROTOTYPE Z.1007 (A)

PROTOTYPE Z.1007 (B)

plants. The overall dimensions and weights were increased and 12.7-mm. machine guns replaced two of the four 7.7-mm. guns. The weight increase also necessitated a strengthened landing gear. The Z.1007bis was a very efficient bomber, with a maximum speed of 280 m.p.h. at 15,000 ft. and a possible bomb load of 4410 lb., although defensive armament was too light.

When Italy entered the war 87 Z.1007 and Z.1007bis bombers were available, of which 38 were operational. At that time the Z.1007 equipped the 16° and 47° Stormi da Bombardimento Terrestre at Vicenza and Ghedi, later serving with the 8°, 9°, 27°, 30°, and 35° Stormi B.T., the 41°, 50°, 51°, 87°, 90°, 95°, and 107° Gruppi B.T., and the 176ª and 264ª Squadriglie B.T., in Metropolitan Italy, Sicily, Sardinia, and Greece. It also was used briefly on the Russian front. Both single and twin fin Alciones served together in the same units,

A Z.1007bis with roundels and tail stripes of the Co-Belligerent Air Force. (MM 23408)

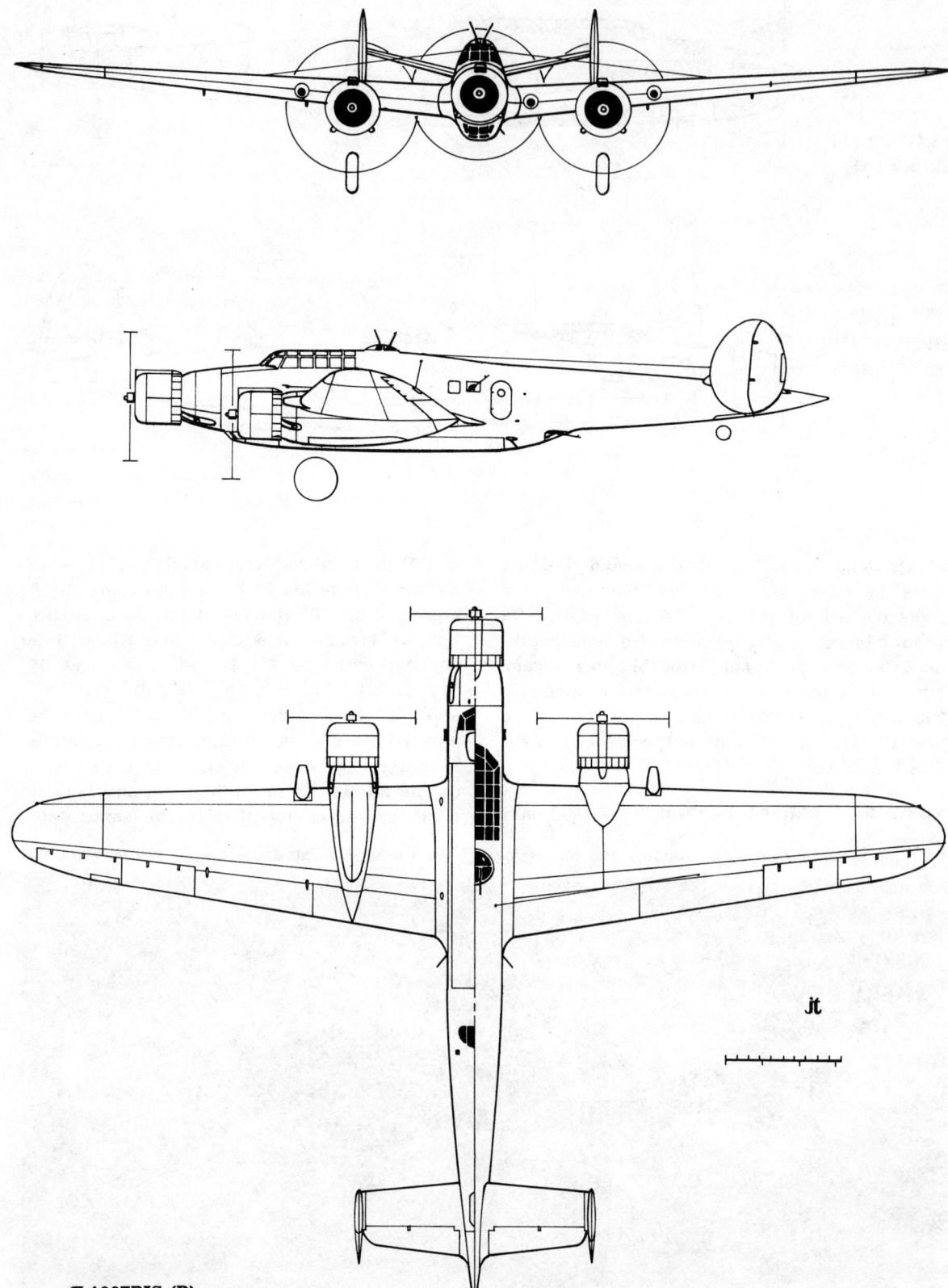

Z.1007BIS (B)

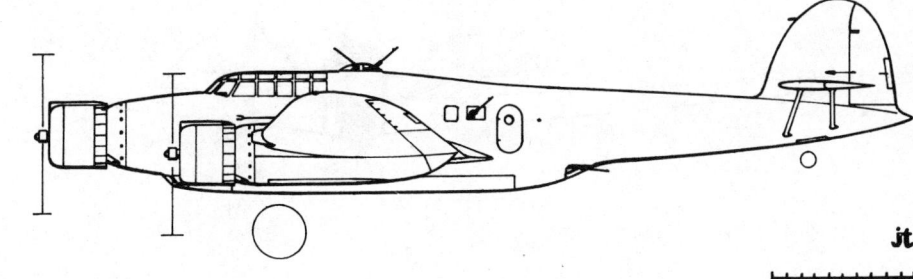

Z.1007BIS (A)

there being no distinction in designation or use. Individual crew preference and employment of rear-firing armament were the main factors involved.

In addition to the bombing role, the Z.1007 was employed for reconnaissance and anti-shipping attack, mounting two 1000-lb. torpedoes in the latter capacity. The four machine guns were located in ventral and lateral positions and in a dorsal turret. Dimensions of the Z.1007bis were: span 81 ft. $4^{1}/_{3}$ in., length 61 ft. $0^{1}/_{4}$ in., height 17 ft. $1^{1}/_{4}$ in., and wing area 936 sq. ft. Although the normal bomb load was 2600 lb., varying combinations were 56 26.4-lb. bombs, 32 33-lb. bombs, 20 44-lb. bombs, 18 110-lb. or 220-lb. bombs, four 550-lb. bombs, or two 1100-lb. bombs. Weights were 19,000 lb. empty, 28,211 lb. loaded. Range was 1242 miles, cruising speed 235 m.p.h., landing speed 84 m.p.h., and ceiling 26,500 ft.

The Free French Air Force operated one Z.1007bis for transport duties after it was captured in North Africa and refitted with three 1200 h.p. Pratt & Whitney Twin Wasp GR-1830 engines. The Z.1007ter was a version with 1100 h.p. Piaggio P.XIX radial engines and a reduced bomb load of 2200 lb. It achieved a maximum speed of 311 m.p.h. and a range of 1398 miles. Loaded weight was 29,073 lb. In other respects it was identical to the Z.1007bis.

Z.1010

Like the Ambrosini S.A.I. 2, the Cant Z.1010 was a five-passenger cabin monoplane built for the 1935 Littorio Air Rally. In contrast to the S.A.I. 2, the Cant design featured a high wing of elliptical planform and high aspect ratio. The power unit was a 130 h.p. DeHavilland Gipsy-Major. Performance included a maximum speed of 128 m.p.h., a cruising speed of 109 m.p.h., and a minimum speed of 40 m.p.h. using flaps. Service ceiling was 19,680 ft. Dimensions were: span 41 ft. 4 in., length 26 ft. $5^{1}/_{2}$ in., height 8 ft. 6 in., and wing area 172 sq. ft. Empty and loaded weights were 1320 lb. and 2200 lb.

Z.1011

Designed concurrently with the Z.1007, the twin-engine Z.1011 was initially highly favored by the Regia Aeronautica for medium bomber use. Five prototypes were built in 1935-36. Although the twin-engined layout offered a more satisfactory nose design for bombing operations than the classic three-engine arrangement, the 1680 h.p. offered by the two

The Cant Z.1010 was a five-passenger touring machine built in 1935 for the Littorio Air Rally. (I-ABLB)

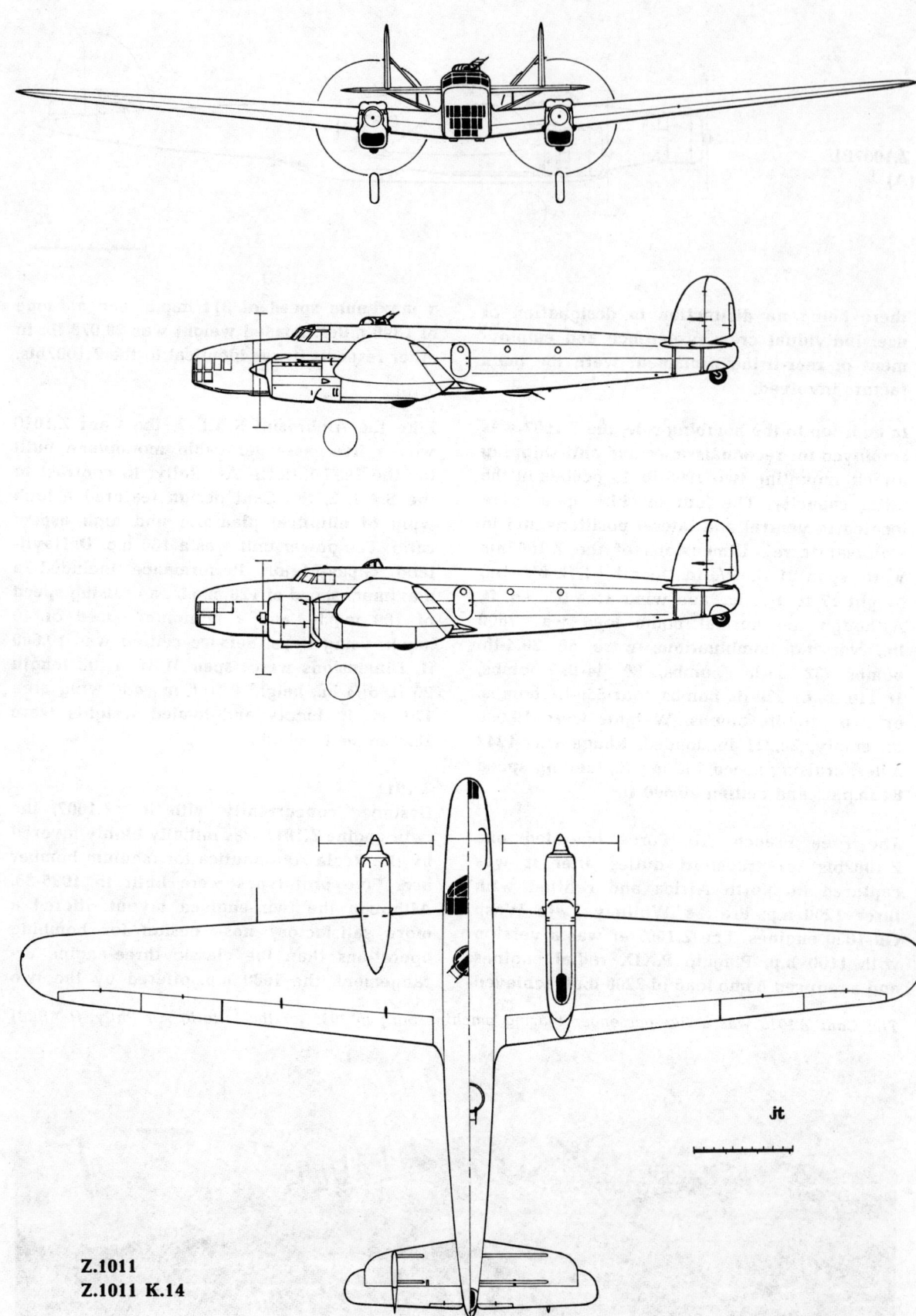

Z.1011
Z.1011 K.14

A view of the Asso-powered Z.1011, showing dorsal and ventral gun turrets.

Isotta-Fraschini Asso XI R.C.15 engines fell far short of the power required for satisfactory performance, in spite of the relatively light empty weight of 12,540 lb. The five prototypes were eventually used as personnel transports for high-ranking officials. At least one Z.1011 was fitted with 800 h.p. Isotta-Fraschini K.14 radial engines.

Like most other Cant aircraft, the Z.1011 was of wood structure with plywood skin. Compared to other members of the Zappata family, however, it was notably angular and ungraceful. Armament consisted of five machine guns, two each in dorsal and ventral turrets aft of the wings, and one hand-held gun in the nose. Performance included a maximum speed of 230 m.p.h. at 14,760 ft., a cruising speed of 193 m.p.h., a landing speed of 78 m.p.h., a range of 1242 miles, and a ceiling of 26,240 ft. The Z.1011 could climb to 9840 ft. in 11 min. 42 sec., and to 16,400 ft. in 19 minutes.

Span was 92 ft., length 55 ft. 9 in., height 17 ft. $2^{5}/_{8}$ in., and wing area 860.8 sq. ft.

Z.1012

First displayed at the Belgrade Exposition in June 1938, and subsequently used by Col. Vincenzio Coppola, Italian Air Attaché in Washington, the Z.1012 was a light 4/6 passenger transport powered by three Alfa Romeo 110-I four-cylinder engines of 120 h.p. each. Alternatively, Alfa Romeo 115 six-cylinder 170 h.p. engines were fitted. With the four-cylinder engines, performance included a maximum speed of 174 m.p.h., a cruising speed of 149 m.p.h., and a landing speed of 68 m.p.h. Range was 807 miles and ceiling 16,400 ft.

Performance with the six-cylinder 170 h.p. engines was much improved, with corresponding speeds of 199 m.p.h., 162 m.p.h., and 74 m.p.h. Range and ceiling were 621 miles and

This rear view of the Isotta-Fraschini K.14-powered Z.1011 emphasizes its angular lines.

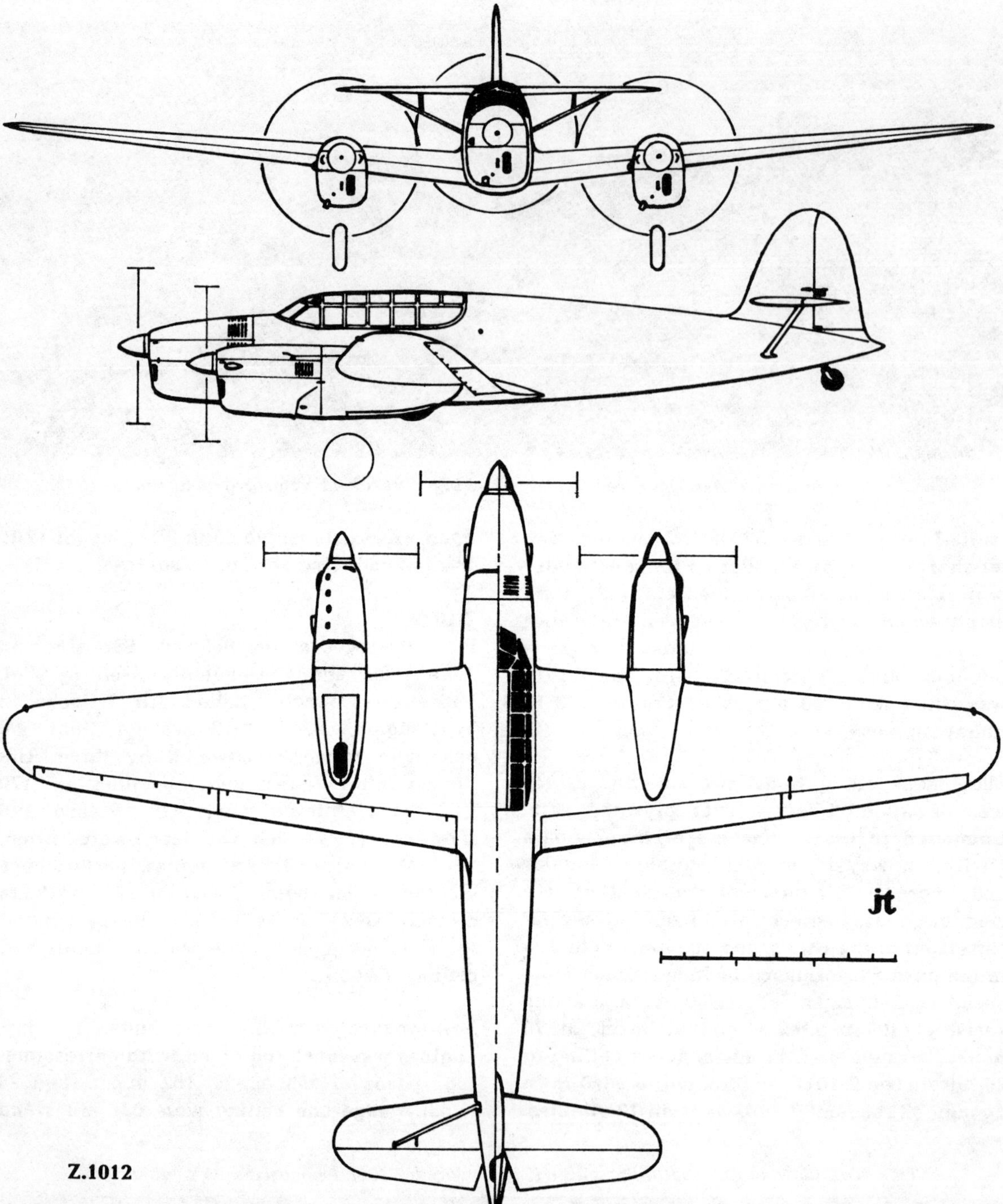

Z.1012

Below, the Z.1012 used by Col. Coppola, Italian Air Attaché in Washington. (MM 367)

19,680 ft. Climb to 6560 ft. required only 10 minutes, compared to 14 minutes for the Z.1012 with the four-cylinder 120 h.p. engines. Dimensions of both models were: span 49 ft. 2$^1/_2$ in., length 32 ft. 9$^1/_2$ in., height 11 ft. 10$^7/_8$ in., and wing area 269 sq. ft. Empty and loaded weights with the 120 h.p. engines were 4290 lb. and 6050 lb. respectively, increasing to 5060 lb. and 6820 lb. with the more powerful power plants.

A Z.1012 fitted with four-cylinder 120 h.p. Alfa Romeo 110-I in-line engines.

Z.1015

A modification of the Z.1007 incorporating 1500 h.p. Piaggio P.XII R.C.35 radial engines, the Z.1015 made its appearance in 1939 as a long-distance mail plane, although definitely intended as an improved bomber prototype. The civil version set a record of 347.97 m.p.h. at an altitude of 14,760 ft., but the military development saw no operational use during the war. Details were as for the Z.1007bis, except for the length of 59 ft. 6 in., the loaded weight of 29,988 lb., and the maximum range of 1864 miles. There is no record of the armament fitted.

Z.1018

The last design by Ing. Zappata before he left Cant for the Breda organization was the Z.1018 twin-engined medium bomber, probably the best bomber actually built in Italy during the war. Although the first six examples were built of wood, the production Z.1018 contrasted with all its Cant forebears by employing all-metal construction. A number of different prototypes were built, incorporating 1500 h.p. Piaggio P.XII R.C.35, 1400 h.p. Piaggio P.XV R.C.45, and 1400 h.p. Alfa Romeo 135 R.C.32 radial engines, as well as one fitted with 1475 h.p. FIAT R.A.1050 R.C.58 Tifone (Typhoon) liquid-cooled engines, which were license-built DB 605A-1 units. The first prototype, employing four-bladed airscrews and twin fins and rudders, flew in 1940. Subsequent changes, in addition to the variety of engines tested, included three-bladed airscrews, a cockpit moved from behind the wing leading edge to a position ahead of the engines, and a single fin-and-rudder assembly.

The prototype Z.1018 bore little resemblance to the later production machines.

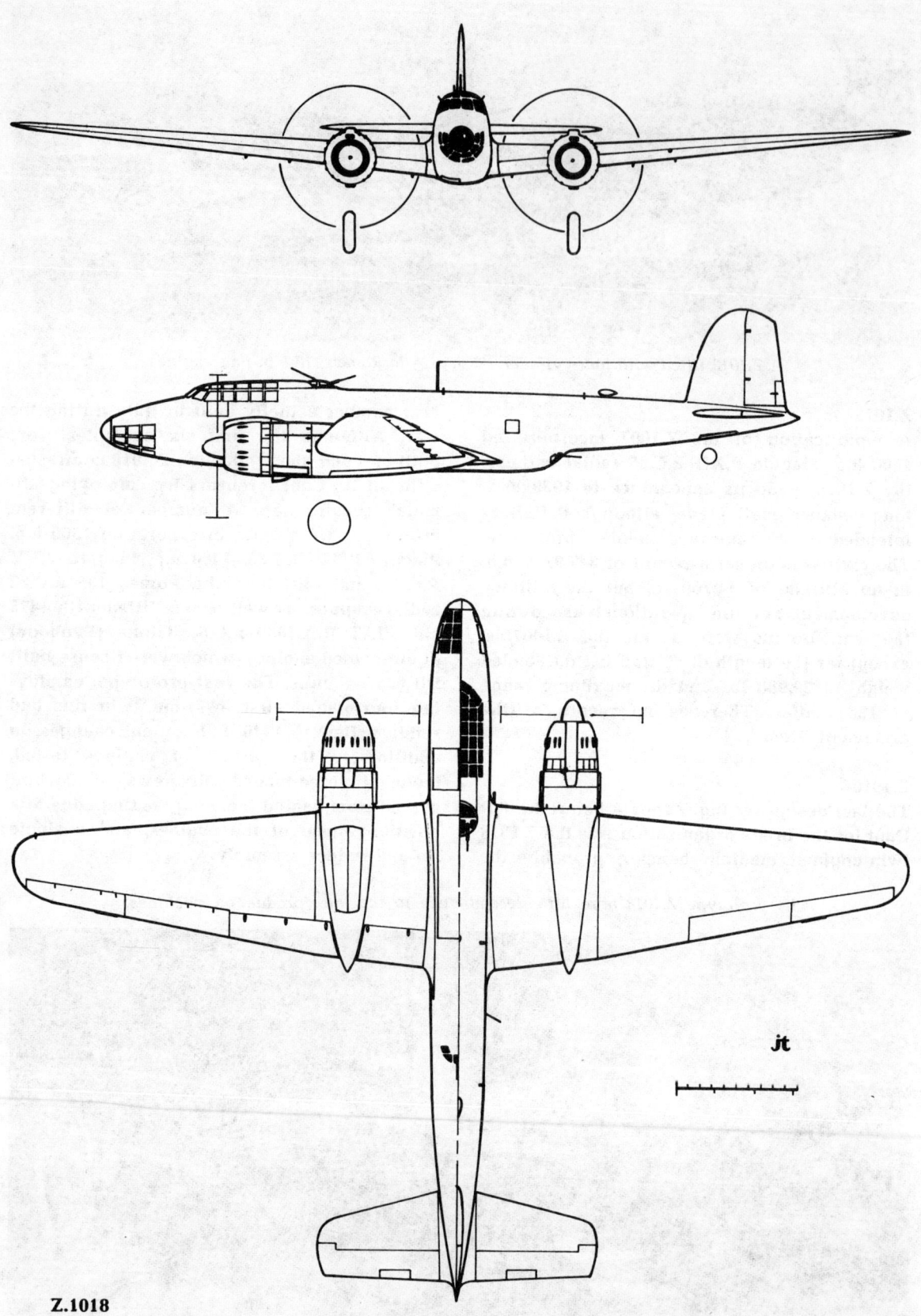

Z.1018

The Z.1018 was the best bomber designed in Italy during the war, but it came too late to be of use.

So exceptional was the performance of the Z.1018 that 300 production machines were ordered in 1941, to be powered by 1320 h.p. Piaggio P.XII R.C.35 or 1350 h.p. Alfa Romeo 135 R.C.32 Tornado engines, both eighteen-cylinder radials. Given the name Leone (Lion), the Z.1018 carried a maximum bomb load of six 550-lb. bombs and defended itself with one 12.7-mm. machine gun in a dorsal Caproni Lanciani Delta F turret, one 12.7-mm. gun in a ventral position, and two 7.7-mm. guns firing from hatches in the sides of the fuselage. An offensive forward-firing 12.7-mm. weapon was mounted in the starboard wing near the root.

By early 1943 a few Z.1018 bombers reached the Regia Aeronautica, equipping the 101° Gruppo of the 47° Stormo Bombardimento Terrestre, which was already operating Z.1007 bis Alciones. However, the Leone saw little action, the Italian surrender coming only a short time later.

Maximum speed was 323 m.p.h., range 700-1367 miles, and service ceiling 23,785 ft. The Z.1018 climbed to 6560 ft. in 3 min. 10 sec. Span was 73 ft. $9^{3}/_{4}$ in., length 57 ft. 9 in., height 19 ft. $11^{1}/_{2}$ in., and wing area 679.2 sq. ft.

Projected but never built were two additional variants, a heavy day fighter with seven 20-mm. MG 151 cannon in the nose and three 12.7-mm. defensive machine guns, and a night fighter with German Lichtenstein SN 2 radar mounted in the nose. Estimated maximum speed of both models was 385 m.p.h. The 1250 h.p. FIAT A.83 R.C.24 eighteen-cylinder radial engine was also considered for installation on the Z.1018.

The Cant Z.1018 was the first Italian bomber with performance and armament comparable to the best German and Allied types, and it was unfortunate for the Regia Aeronautica that the production models began to appear too late in the conflict to have any noticeable effect on the outcome.

The production Z.1018 featured lengthened nose, single fin, Piaggio P.XII or Alfa Romeo 135 engines.

CAPRONI
Società Italiana Caproni

The huge Caproni organization, founded in 1908 by Count Gianni Caproni, was very well-known during the First World War for its large biplane and triplane bombers and rivalled only by FIAT in the number and diversity of its products. The various Caproni subsidiaries built more than one hundred distinct types of aircraft, many of them outstanding, during the period between the two World Wars, securing a position at the forefront of Italian aviation. Nevertheless, only a few modern Caproni designs were in service with the Regia Aeronautica when Italy entered the Second World War, and these aircraft were not noted for their performance or efficiency. This curious decline, similar to that of the American Curtiss firm during the war, cannot be attributed to any one major cause. Rather it was the result of numerous factors, including uninspired design, poor production standards, and overly diversified industrial interests.

Like Breda, Caproni produced all types of aircraft equipment and components, of which the most famous were probably the Isotta-Fraschini engines. The main airframe works, originally known as the Società per lo Sviluppo dell'Aviazione in Italia, were located at Taliedo, Milan. The other members of the family were Cantieri Aeronautici Bergamaschi (later Caproni Aeronautica Bergamasca) at Ponte San Pietro, Bergamo; Caproni Vizzola S.A. at Vizzola Ticino, Varese; C.N.A. (Compagnia Nazionale Aeronautica) at Littorio, Rome; Aeronautica Predappio S.A. at Predappio; Officine Meccaniche Reggiane S.A. at Reggio Emilia; and Società Anonima Industrie Meccaniche Aeronautiche Navali (SAIMAN) at Lido di Roma. Except for Aeronautica Predappio, which built only a few training aircraft, each of the associated firms is covered in a separate section of this book. Of all the Caproni interests, only Bergamaschi and Reggiane produced modern aircraft in any real quantity.

CA 73

Still in service with the Regia Aeronautica bomber squadrons as late as 1933, the Ca 73 was designed by Ing. Rodolfo Verduzio in 1924. An unequal-span biplane, the Ca 73 was built in both commercial and military forms. The original Ca 73 was a civil transport powered by two 500 h.p. Isotta-Fraschini Asso twelve-cylinder water-cooled vee engines, mounted in tandem between the wings. Empty weight was 7480 lb. Carrying ten passengers, a crew

The Ca 73ter (or Ca 82) was an elderly bomber still in service with the Regia Aeronautica in 1933.

Left, the Ca 73bis commercial airliner. (I-BAUP) Right, the Ca 80 S ambulance version.

of two, plus fuel, oil, mail and baggage, the Ca 73 weighed 11,880 lb. Maximum speed was 112 m.p.h., landing speed 44 m.p.h., and endurance 3 hours. Dimensions were: span 82 ft., length 49 ft. 6 in., height 18 ft. $4^{3}/_{4}$ in., and wing area 1539.2 sq. ft. The shorter upper wing, without dihedral, spanned 59 ft. Ailerons were fitted to the lower wing only. The biplane tail spanned 20 ft. 6 in.

The Ca 73bis was a nearly identical commercial transport with two 400 h.p. Lorraine-Dietrich engines. The Ca 73ter (also designated the Ca 82) was a bomber variant employing Asso engines. Dimensions of the Ca 73ter matched those of the transport, but the empty and loaded weights increased to 5071 lb. and 12,566 lb. Two machine gun positions were located in the nose and amidships; the bomb load was 2200 lb. In addition, a greater fuel load was carried, permitting an endurance of 6 hours. Maximum and landing speeds were 122 m.p.h. and 50 m.p.h.

Further developments were the Ca 80 (two 400 h.p. Jupiter radials) and the Ca 88 and Ca 89 (or Ca 73 quater) with fuselage modifications including a retractable ventral turret. All these types were reclassified under the common designation Ca 74 to avoid confusion. The Ca 73 and its derivations were standard equipment of Regia Aeronautica bomber units, seeing wide use until 1934.

CA 90

The largest aeroplane in the world at the time of its appearance (1929), the Ca 90 was a six-engined biplane designed as a heavy bomber. The huge machine was constructed of welded steel tubing, fabric-covered throughout except for the forward fuselage, which was clad in corrugated sheet duralumin. The engines were 1000 h.p. Isotta-Fraschini Asso eighteen-cylinder W-type water-cooled units mounted in tandem pairs above the fuselage and on each lower wing. The three tractor engines drove two-bladed airscrews, while the pusher units drove four-bladed airscrews. The lower wing, featuring a marked dihedral, was some 38 ft. 4 in. longer than the straight upper wing. The four main wheels of the landing gear were six feet in diameter. All the components of the Ca 90 were rigorously tested at the Instituto di Costruzioni Aeronautiche del Politecnico

The Ca 90 was the largest aeroplane in the world in 1929; longer lower wing was Caproni trademark.

The extremely long wings of the Ca 95 heavy bomber are apparent in this view.

di Milano (Milan Polytechnic Institute). The Ca 90 was also known as the Ca 6000 (6 x 1000 h.p.).

With approximate empty and loaded weights of 33,070 lb. and 66,140 lb., the Ca 90 had no difficulty in establishing load, altitude, and endurance records, carrying a 22,000 lb. load to 10,684 ft. and remaining aloft with that load for 3 hrs. 31 min. Armament was seven machine guns. The bomb load of 17,640 lb. could be made up of 220-lb., 550-lb., 1100-lb., and 1760-lb. bombs in various quantities. Performance included maximum and landing speeds of 127 m.p.h. and 56 m.p.h., a ceiling of 14,764 ft., and an endurance of 7 hours. Dimensions were: span 114 ft. 6 in. (upper wing), 152 ft. 10 in. (lower wing), length 88 ft. 4²/₃ in., height 35 ft. 5 in., and wing area 5346.4 sq. ft.

The German Dornier Do X twelve-engined flying boat, also built in 1929, was 4 ft. 7 in. greater in span and had a maximum loaded weight of 123,200 lb., but the Ca 90 remained the largest landplane until the completion of the Russian Tupolev ANT-20 "Maxim Gorky" in 1934.

CA 95

The Ca 95 was a three-engined four-man bomber with shoulder wing and fixed spatted landing gear. Powered by the 1000 h.p. Isotta-Fraschini Asso engines, the monoplane featured dorsal and ventral turrets and weighed 7480 lb. empty and 12,540 lb. loaded. Performance included maximum, cruising, and landing speeds of 155 m.p.h., 130 m.p.h., and 56 m.p.h. respectively, and a range of 1863 miles. Dimensions were: span 135 ft. 11¹/₂ in., length

Powered by a single 500 h.p. Jupiter radial, this reconnaissance version of the Ca 97 featured a dorsal machine gun position aft of the wing.

72 ft. 3 in., height 18 ft. 9$^{1}/_{8}$ in., and wing area 251.8 sq. ft.

CA 97

Probably the earliest Caproni type which was in general use during the mid-1930's was the Ca 97 six-passenger high-wing monoplane. Adaptable to a multitude of civil and military uses, the Ca 97 was unusual in that it could be fitted with one, two, or three engines with a total output in the region of 400 h.p., although the single-engined version was the most common. A 1927 design, the Ca 97 originally employed three 130 h.p. Lorraine-Dietrich five-cylinder radial engines. Later models were equipped as light transports, ambulances, military trainers, day bombers, and reconnaissance aircraft, the last-named type being fitted with a dorsal turret aft of the wing. The Ca 97 equipped several reconnaissance squadrons of the Regia Aeronautica in 1930-33.

Dimensions common to most models of the Ca 97 were: span 52 ft. 4$^{3}/_{8}$ in., length 35 ft. 1$^{2}/_{3}$ in., height 11 ft., and wing area 430.5 sq. ft. Empty weight varied from 2200 lb. to 3300 lb. depending on the role, while the loaded figure was between 4400 lb. and 5500 lb. The slowest model was the three-engined transport at 93 m.p.h.; in reconnaissance form with a 500 h.p. Jupiter engine the Ca 97 achieved 140 m.p.h.

The trimotor version of the Ca 97, with 130 h.p. Lorraine-Dietrich five-cylinder radial engines.

Landing speed was 50-68 m.p.h., range 497-621 miles, and service ceiling between 10,496 ft. and 24,272 ft. Because of the multiplicity of engine and duty combinations, it is impossible to specify exact figures for each type within the space available.

The Ca 97 Idro fitted a 500 h.p. Jupiter radial engine and twin duralumin floats. Empty and loaded weights of the seaplane were 4070 lb. and 6270 lb. respectively. Maximum speed was 137 m.p.h. and service ceiling 16,400 ft.

CA 100

Built under license from DeHavilland, the all-wood, fabric-covered Ca 100 was based generally on the D.H. Moth, although differing in detail design. Dating from 1929, the tandem two-seat light biplane was still in frequent use during the Second World War, having been produced in large numbers for civil flying clubs throughout Italy. The original model

The Ca 100 was based on the D.H. Moth, but differed considerably in detail. (I-ABMT)

ITALIAN CIVIL AND MILITARY AIRCRAFT

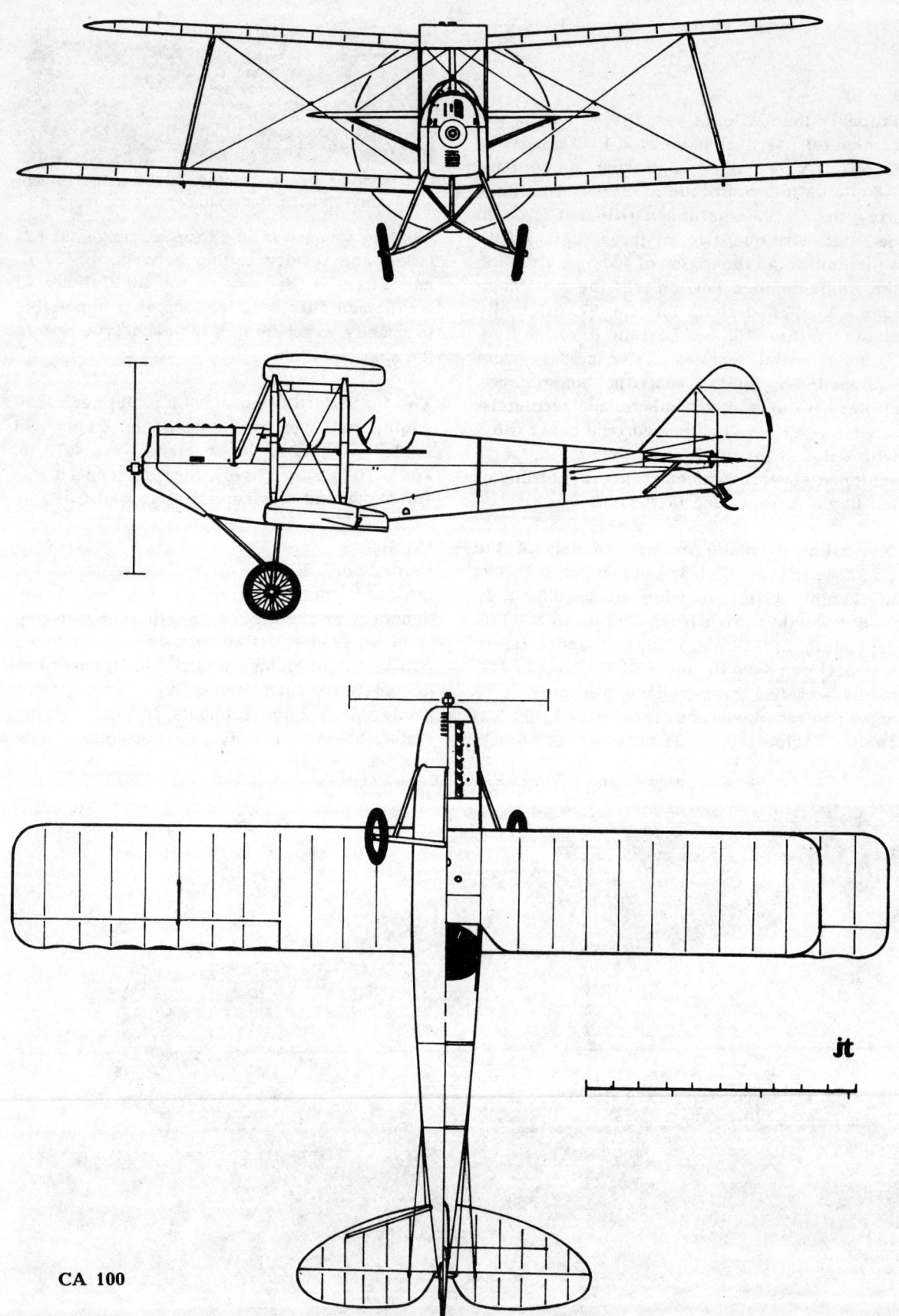

CA 100

A Ca 100 idro with steep Italian hillside as a backdrop.

was powered by a D.H. Gipsy four-cylinder in-line engine of 85 h.p., although various other units, such as the 90 h.p. Blackburn Cirrus Minor, were fitted. Several Ca 100's are still flying today, including a twin-float Ca 100 Idro amphibian. In 1931, a Ca 100 Idro established an altitude record of 17,462.7 ft. for seaplanes of Category I, flown by Pilots Antonini and Trevisan. Empty and loaded weights of the Idro model were 1144 lb. and 1639 lb. The Ca 100 was also known as the Caproncino (Little Caproni).

The Ca 100 landplane achieved maximum and cruising speeds of 102 m.p.h. and 87 m.p.h., landing at 40 m.p.h. A range of 435 miles and a ceiling of 13,120 ft. could be reached. Climbing to 3280 ft. required 7 min. 40 sec.; to 8200 ft., 23 min. 18 sec. Empty and loaded weights were respectively 882 lb. and 1498 lb. Dimensions included spans of 27 ft. 5 in. (upper wing) and 32 ft. 10 in. (lower wing), a length of 23 ft. 11 in., and a height of 9 ft. Total wing area was 262.5 sq. ft.

A special bombing trainer was built in early 1934, fitted with a 130 h.p. radial engine. It could carry four small bombs and had a maximum speed of 124 m.p.h.

When an Italian Air Mission was established in Peru in 1935, a ten-year agreement was signed between Caproni and the Peruvian government for the supply of aircraft and the construction of a factory, completed in 1937. Initially a number of Ca 100 trainers were supplied from Italy; a further twelve machines were built at the Peruvian factory, but production costs were abnormally high. At least one Ca 100 was supplied to Portugal in 1933.

CA 101

The Ca 101 was essentially an enlarged Ca 97 which appeared in 1927 as a commercial transport, powered by three Alfa Romeo-built 200 h.p. Armstrong-Siddeley Lynx radial engines. Specifications of this model included a span of 65 ft., a length of 44 ft. 8 in., a height of 12 ft. 6 in., and a wing area of 592 sq. ft. The empty and loaded weights were 4730 lb. and 7920 lb. Maximum speed was 121 m.p.h. and ceiling 13,120 ft.

Relatively large numbers of the Ca 101 saw

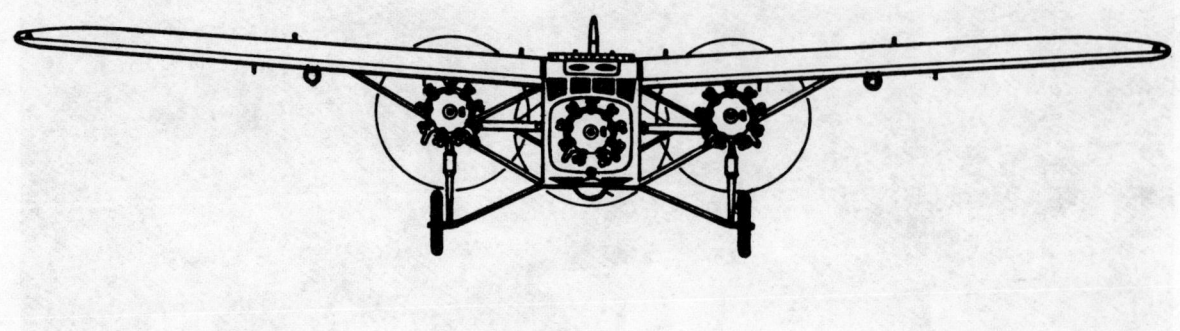

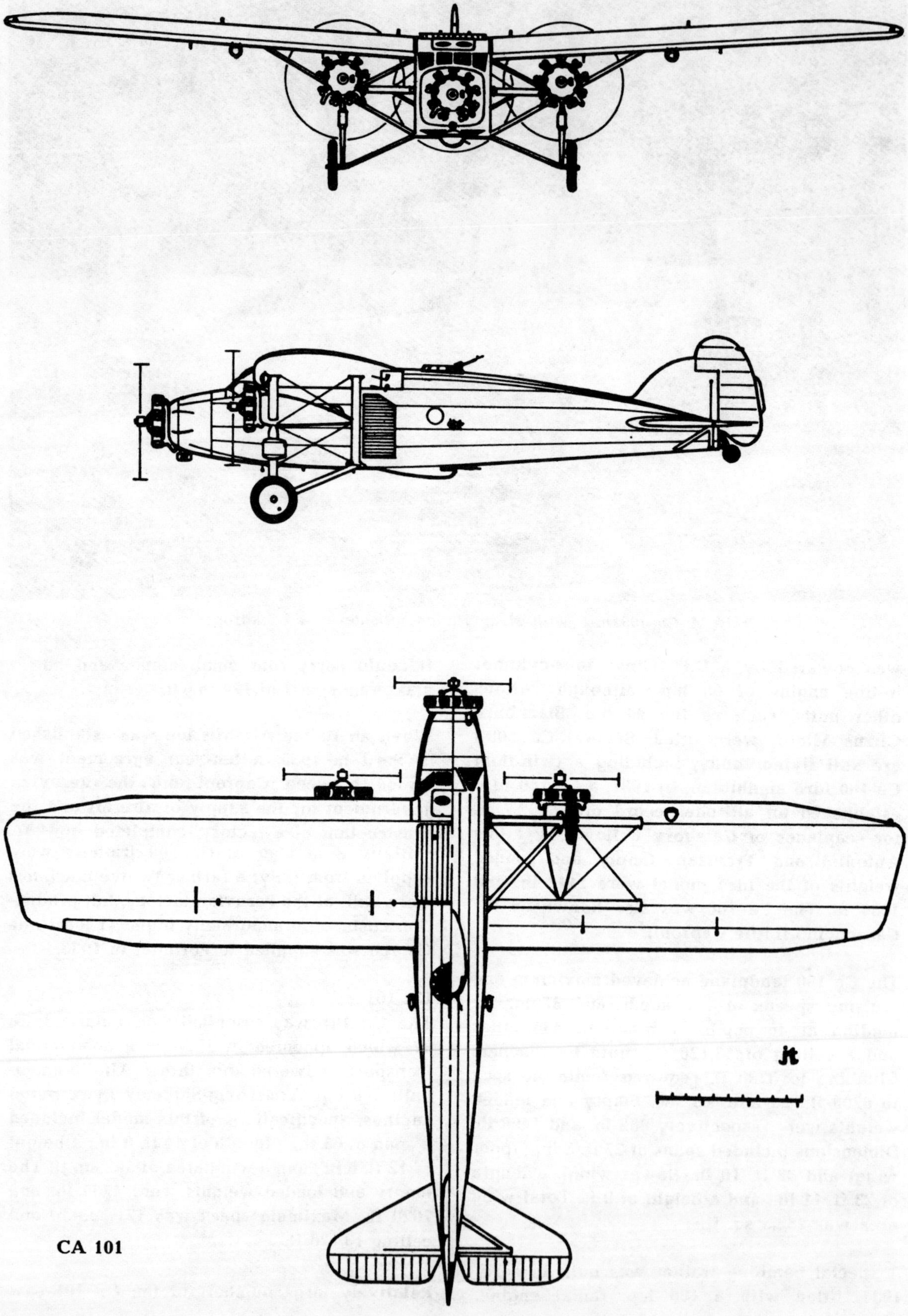

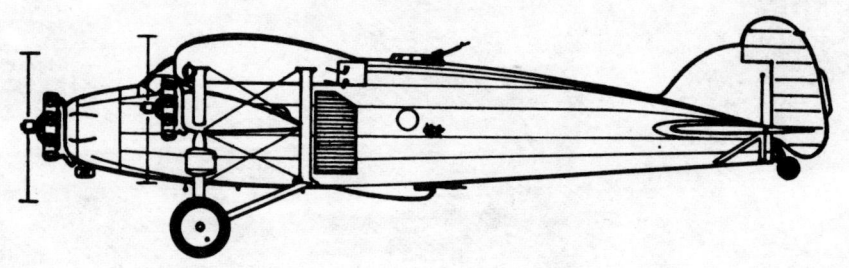

CA 101

A Ca 101 colonial monoplane fitted with three Alfa Romeo D2 radials.

extensive service during Italy's conquests in Africa, particularly with La Disperata squadron during the Ethiopian campaign, and some remained in use during the Second World War, despite their total obsolescence. A slab-sided high-wing monoplane with a generous interior, the Ca 101 was well suited to the colonial administration uses to which it was first put. As a bomber, powered by three 370 h.p. Piaggio Stella VII radial engines, it fitted four bomb racks and three machine guns, one in a dorsal turret and two firing through the floor. The military Ca 101's equipped night bomber squadrons of the Regia Aeronautica, as well as the colonial units. Engines fitted to the colonial versions were three 240 h.p. Walter Castor or three 270 h.p. Alfa Romeo Dux radials. In service with the well-publicized La Disperata squadron, commanded by Count Galeazzo Ciano, the Ca 101 was flown by Bruno, Vittorio, and Vito Mussolini, sons and nephew respectively of Il Duce. A civil accomplishment of the Ca 101 was Mario de Bernardi's 1933 non-stop flight from Rome to Moscow, carrying six passengers. Paraguay purchased a few Ca 101's in 1933.

Of fabric-covered welded steel tube construction, the Ca 101 weighed 7577 lb. empty and 11,317 lb. fully loaded, its complement including radio, camera, and stretchers, in addition to the armament, Span was 64 ft. $6^{1}/_{2}$ in., length 47 ft. $1^{1}/_{2}$ in., height 12 ft. 9 in., and wing area 664 sq. ft. The performance included maximum, cruising, and landing speeds of 155 m.p.h., 127 m.p.h., and 59 m.p.h. respectively, a range of 621 miles, and a service ceiling of 19,680 ft. Climb to 3280 ft. took 3 min. 15 sec;

The Ca 101 was used with considerable success in A.O.I. (Italian East Africa). Note dorsal machine gun.

A development of the Ca 101, the Ca 105 had single engine, fixed-pitch metal airscrew, round wingtips.

to 9840 ft., 12 min. 31 sec.; and to 16,400 ft., 37 min. 32 sec.

CA 102

The Ca 102 was essentially similar to the Ca 101 except for the substitution of two 500 h.p. Bristol Jupiter engines for the three lower-powered units. Like the Ca 101, it was built in both military and commercial versions, but not in large numbers.

The Ca 102 quater had four engines in tandem pairs; it was used by the 62ª Sperimèntale Bombardieri Pesanti (Experimental Heavy Bomber Units).

CA 111

A single-engined long-range reconnaissance development of the Ca 101, the Ca 111 origi-nally fitted a 750 h.p. FIAT twelve-cylinder vee engine and featured a larger wing of 75 ft. 5 in. span, the wing area becoming 914.6 sq. ft. In this early form performance was low, with a maximum speed of 134 m.p.h. and a service ceiling of 19,680 ft. Weights were 6600 lb. empty and 9900 lb. loaded.

In 1934 the Ca 111 reverted to a wing only slightly longer than that of the Ca 101, but of higher aspect ratio, giving a marginally smaller area of 661.7 sq. ft. This model employed an 830 h.p. Isotta-Fraschini Asso 750 R.C. eighteen-cylinder water-cooled engine and weighed 7700 lb. empty and 12,100 lb. loaded. Maximum speed became 180 m.p.h., cruising speed 158 m.p.h., landing speed 61 m.p.h., range 807 miles, and service ceiling 21,976 ft. The Ca 111 climbed to 3280 ft. in 5 min. 22 sec. and

The Ca 111 was a single-engined long-range reconnaissance monoplane also developed from the Ca 101. Above, two views of the land version. Below, the Ca 111 idro, a twin-float adaptation.

Above, the prototype Ca 113, with large wheel spats. Below right, a two-seat Ca 113 trainer.

to 9840 ft. in 14 min. 32 sec. Either three-bladed or four-bladed wooden airscrews were fitted. When the Italian Air Mission aided China in 1935, a number of Ca 111's equipped as bombers were among the aircraft supplied.

The Ca 111 idro was built concurrently and differed little from the land version other than in the adoption of twin floats. Weights increased to 8140 lb. empty and 12,540 lb. loaded, and maximum speed dropped to 174 m.p.h. Service ceiling was also slightly diminished at 21,320 ft. The range of the seaplane was only 621 miles. Some Ca 111 idro transports were sent to Peru in 1936 in addition to a few land-based models, nicknamed Panchos by the Peruvians. The landplane was also used by the Regia Aeronautica in Ethiopia and was still in service, although primarily as a trainer, in 1940. The Ca 112 was a strategic reconnaissance version employed in Ethiopia.

CA 113

A development of the Alfa Romeo Lynx-powered Ca 109 trainer, the Ca 113 biplane first appeared in 1931 as a tandem two-seat advanced trainer with a 240 h.p. Walter Castor radial engine. Featuring dual controls, it was also used as an aerobatic trainer and stunt plane. Later the Ca 113 employed the 370 h.p. Piaggio Stella VII C.35 radial engine, achieving 155 m.p.h. Landing speed was 50 m.p.h., range 186 miles, and ceiling 24,000 ft. The Ca 113 climbed to 3280 ft. in 1 min. 30 sec., to 9840 ft. in 5 min. 40 sec., and to 16,400 ft. in 11 min. 15 sec.

Italian pilots Mario de Bernardi and Tito Falconi flew Ca 113's in exhibitions in the United States during the 1930's. In 1931 De Bernardi won the aerobatic trophy at the Cleveland Air Races. Falconi set a record of 3 hrs. 6 min. for a flight from St. Louis to Chicago on August 23, 1933. On April 11, 1934, Renato Donati set a world altitude record of 47,352 ft. in a specially-modified Ca 113 employing a supercharged Alfa Romeo-built Bristol Pegasus radial engine of 530 h.p., a four-bladed airscrew, a pressurized suit designed by Prof. Amedeo Herlitzka, and greatly-lengthened wings spanning 46 ft. 5 in.

The following year Countess Carina Negrone set the women's record at an altitude of 39,402 ft. in the same Ca 113. The record machine was referred to as a "Ca 114" to publicize that fighter project.

Dimensions of the standard model were: span 34 ft. 5 in., length 23 ft. 11 in., height 8 ft. 11 in., and wing area 290.5 sq. ft. Weights were 1870 lb. empty and 2420 lb. fully loaded.

CA 114

Designed in 1933, the Ca 114 fighter biplane was built in both single and two-seat versions. In spite of a performance which compared favorably with contemporary biplanes such as the FIAT CR.32, the Ca 114 was not adopted by the Regia Aeronautica, and only a few were sold to the Peruvian government. The power unit was a 420 h.p. Bristol Mercury nine-cylinder radial with a Townend ring cowling and a three-bladed airscrew; empty and loaded weights were 2882 lb. and 3652 lb.

Due to its light weight the Ca 114 enjoyed a higher rate of climb than the CR.32, reaching 3280 ft. in 1 min. 10 sec., 9840 ft. in 4 min., and 19,680 ft. in 8 min. 30 sec. Maximum speed at 16,400 ft. was 220 m.p.h., cruising and landing speeds being 143 m.p.h. and 62 m.p.h. respectively. The Ca 114 had a range of 373 miles and a ceiling of 31,160 ft. Dimensions included a span of 34 ft. 5 in., a length of 25 ft. $2^{1}/_{2}$ in., a height of 8 ft. 4 in., and a wing area of 276.5 sq. ft. Armament consisted of two forward-firing 7.7-mm. machine guns, supplemented by a rear-firing gun on the two-seat model.

CA 123

In 1934 Caproni designed an airliner in the DC-2/DC-3 class, a low-wing twin-engined transport with retractable landing gear. Powered by 870 h.p. Gnome-Rhone K-14 radial engines, the transport was designated Ca 123. With a crew of pilot, co-pilot, and radio operator, a fuel load of 530 gal., and 28 passengers, the Ca 123 weighed 19,404 lb. Performance was good compared to contemporary world practice, with a maximum speed of 211 m.p.h. at 6790 ft., and a cruising speed of 168 m.p.h. The landing speed was 68 m.p.h. The Ca 123 had a service ceiling of 24,700 ft. and a range of 932 miles. Climbing performance included times of 4 min. 12 sec. to 3280 ft., 8 min. 13 sec. to 6560 ft., and 32 min. 29 sec. to 16,400 ft.

This performance, although omitting the factor of dependability at which the DC-3 excelled, was only marginally inferior to that of the Douglas transport, except in the respect of range. Because of the shorter airline distances on the Italian peninsula, range was understandably sacrificed in favor of a greater payload. However, the Ca 123 was never purchased by any major air carrier; the Italian lines relied almost exclusively on the Cant seaplanes and Savoia-Marchetti land-based transports.

The Ca 123 weighed 11,686 lb. empty. It spanned 91 ft. $4^{1}/_{2}$ in., was 59 ft. 8 in. long, and 19 ft. 8 in. high; wing area was 986.4 sq. ft.

CA 124

Little definite information is available concerning the Ca 124 reconnaissance bomber. Although designed about 1933, this single-engined twin-float seaplane received little publicity until details were issued several years later as a part of the general propaganda

The Ca 125 featured excessively full fuselage contours, contrasting with the graceful elliptical wings.

Above, the Ca 125 landplane. (3364) Right, the Ca 125 idro, with twin duralumin floats.

scheme. Such releases often indicated that a design had become obsolete, and as the Ca 124 was never adopted by the Regia Marina, it is probable that the project was dropped after initial tests, in favor of the later three-engined Cant Z.506B.

The fuselage and wings were metal-covered with fabric-covered movable control surfaces. The engine was a 900 h.p. Isotta-Fraschini Asso XI R.C. 15 water-cooled vee unit, giving maximum, cruising, and alighting speeds of 202 m.p.h., 164 m.p.h., and 68 m.p.h. respectively. Bombs were stored within the oval-section, semi-monocoque fuselage below the cantilever mid-wing. Alternatively, a single torpedo could be carried below the fuselage. Dimensions included a span of 62 ft., a length of 45 ft. 3 in., and a height of 15 ft.

CA 125

A portly little tandem two-seat touring biplane designated Ca 125 appeared in 1933, powered by a Colombo S.63 in-line engine of 125 h.p. In spite of the fat fuselage contours, necessitated by the engine mounting and the interior accommodations of the biplane, the Ca 125 possessed extremely efficient elliptical wings. Forward vision was severely limited; since the Colombo engine was not inverted, a high position had to be adopted to obtain the proper thrust line. The Ca 125 featured wheel fairings, and ailerons on the lower wing only. It weighed 1195 lb. empty and 1789 lb. fully loaded.

Performance included a maximum speed of 143 m.p.h. and a landing speed of 37 m.p.h. Ceiling was 18,040 ft. and range 621 miles. Dimensions were: span 29 ft. $0^1/_8$ in., length 23 ft. $9^1/_3$ in., and height 8 ft. $0^3/_8$ in.

Essentially similar to the Ca 125 landplane except for the adoption of twin floats, a seaplane version, designated Ca 125 Idro, was also built.

CA 132

Employing the basic wing structure, tail group, and retractable landing gear of the Ca 123, the Ca 132 was a slightly smaller, but heavier, twenty-passenger commercial transport with the traditional Italian three-engined layout. The 610 h.p. Piaggio Stella X R.C. radials offered a total output greater than that of the Ca 123's two Gnôme-Rhônes, but only the cruising speed was improved, to 183 m.p.h. The maximum speed was 205 m.p.h. at 13,120 ft., ceiling 20,000 ft., range 932 miles, and lading speed 68 m.p.h. Empty, the Ca 132 weighed 13,200 lb.; fully loaded, the figure was 20,900 lb. Span was 85 ft. 3 in., length 54 ft. 2 in., height 16 ft. $2^1/_2$ in., and wing area 914.6 sq. ft.

CA 133

When Ing. Rodolfo Verduzio rejoined Caproni in 1934, he immediately began projects aimed at improving the existing Caproni range of aircraft. A development of the basic Ca 101 design, designated Ca 131, was still further improved under Verduzio, emerging as the Ca 133. Three Piaggio Stella P.VII C.16 radial engines of 460 h.p. each were chosen to power the modernized transport, and both sixteen-passenger commercial and military bomber and troop transport versions were built. Despite the obsolete configuration, which really dated back even further than the Ca 101 to the Fokker and Ford trimotors, the Ca 133 was a functional and reasonably efficient design which saw considerable service during the late 1930's and early war years. The civil version served with Ala Littoria, while the military model functioned long and well in the Italian colonies, notably A.O.I. (Africa Orientale Italiana, or Italian East Africa).

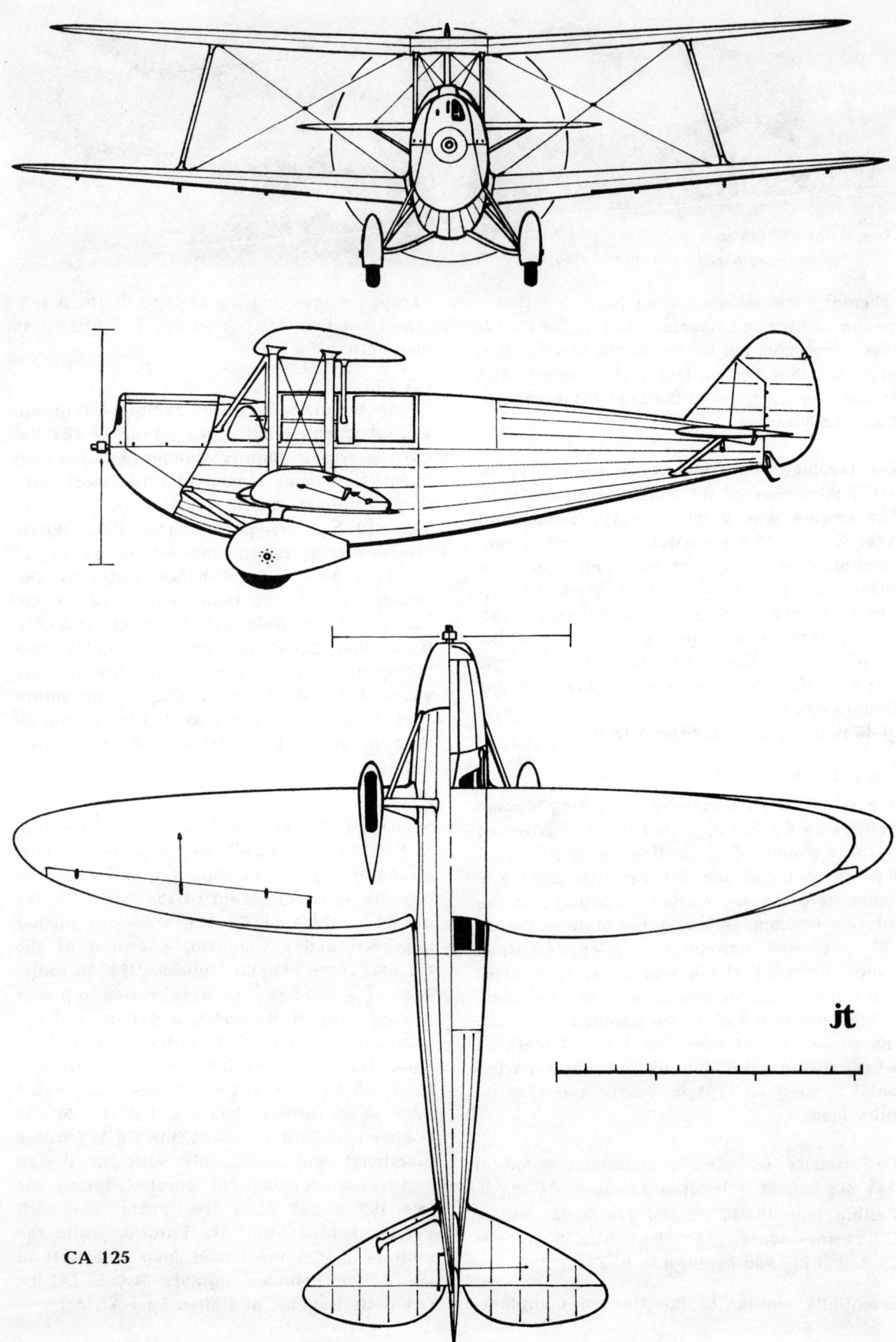

CA 125

The Ca 133 was a modernized, cleaned-up version of the Ca 101.

Although the basic airframe remained the same, the Ca 133 was considerably improved over the Ca 101 by the higher-powered engines, and by such refinements as N.A.C.A. cowlings, smoothly faired engine nacelles and landing gear, flaps, and revised tail surfaces. The Ca 133 was of welded steel construction with mixed metal and fabric covering. Retaining the dorsal turret and ventral gun positions, the military Ca 133 also mounted a lateral machine gun firing from the door on the port side of the fuselage, bringing the total armament to four 7.7-mm. guns. Two 550-lb. bombs or one 1100-lb. bomb could be carried beneath the fuselage. A larger number of smaller bombs were occasionally carried: six 220-lb., 110-lb., or 44-lb. bombs, or fifteen 33-lb. or 27-lb. bombs. As a military transport the Ca 133 carried up to eighteen fully-equipped troops.

In 1939 the Regia Aeronautica possessed 259 Ca 133 aircraft, of which 183 were bombers in service in A.O.I. Performance was adequate only for colonial use against limited opposition, and by the outbreak of the Second World War the Ca 133 had limited military value. The Capronis were destroyed in large numbers during the North African conflict, usually on the ground. Maximum speed was only 166 m.p.h., cruising speed 144 m.p.h., and landing speed 63 m.p.h. The cruising range was 838 miles and the service ceiling 18,050 ft. Dimensions were: span 69 ft. 8 in., length 50 ft. 4 in.,

The Ca 134 reconnaissance biplane. Not apparent in this view is the biplane tail.

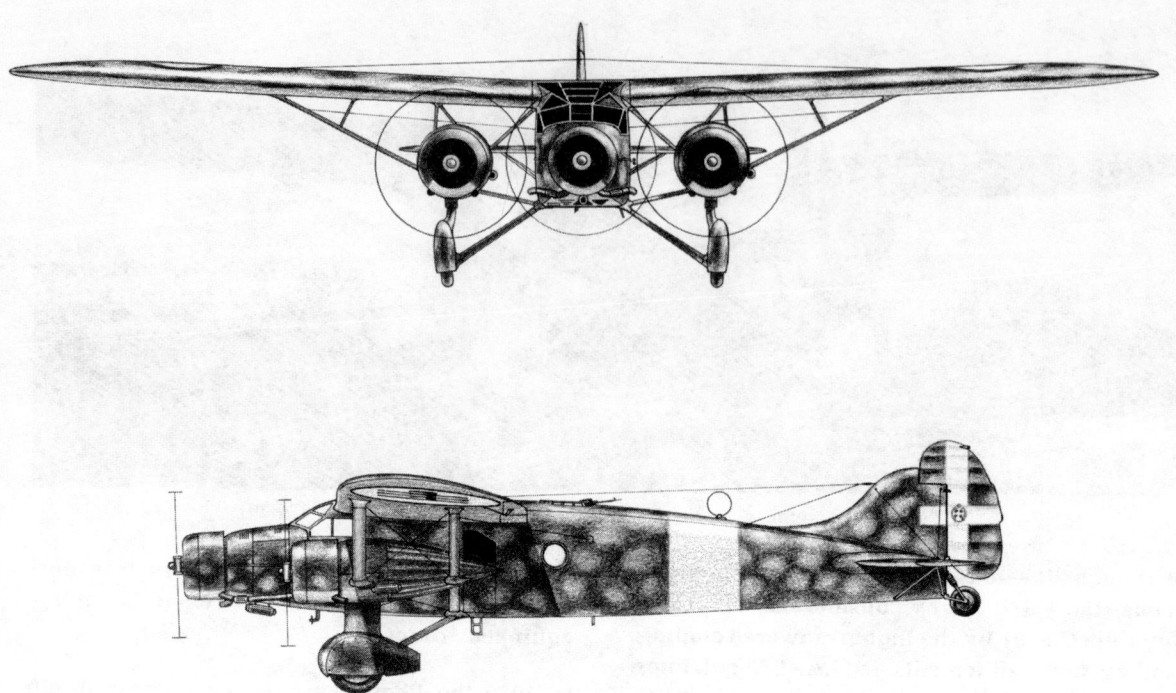

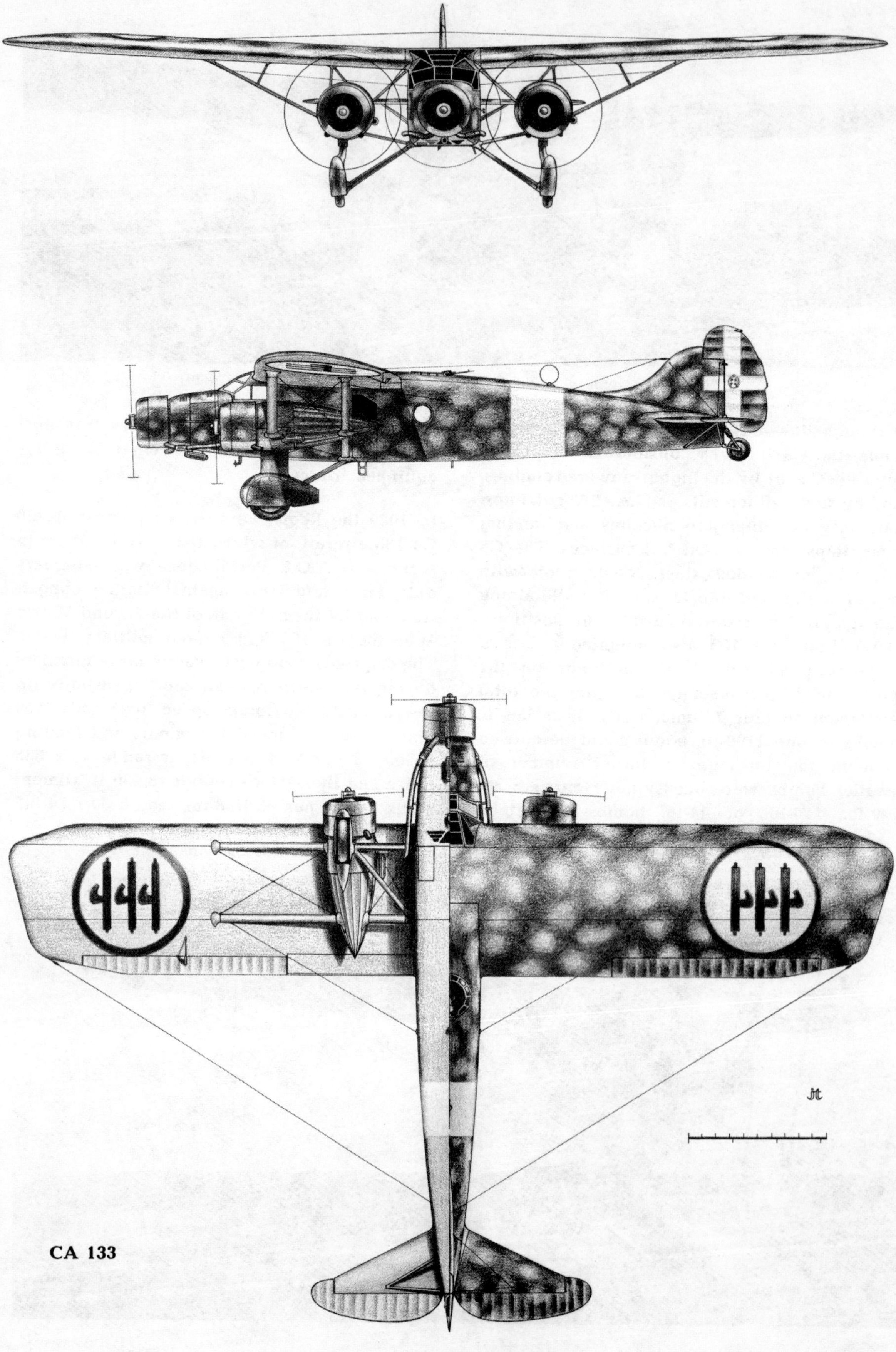

CA 133

CAPRONI

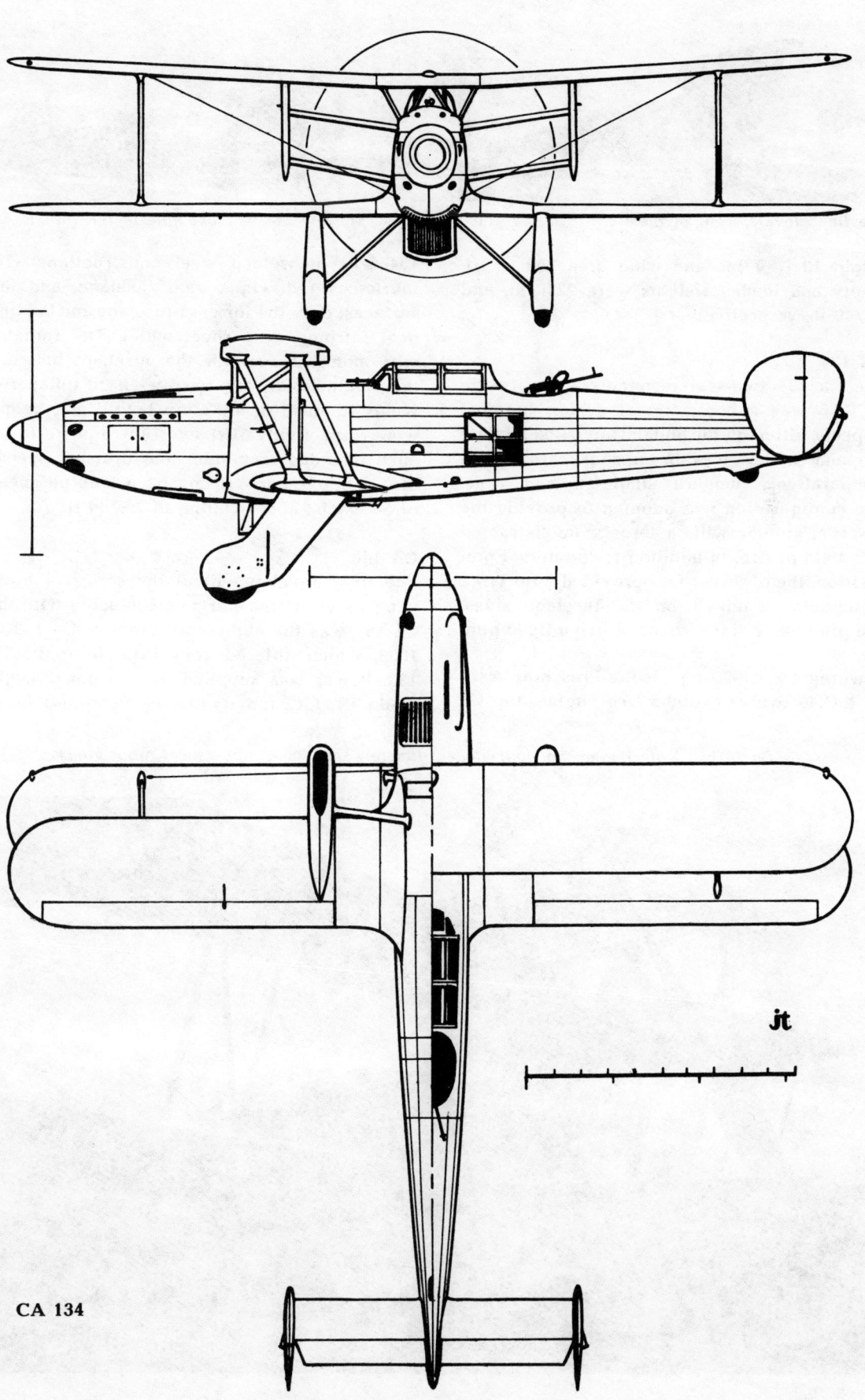

CA 134

The final development of the Ca 101 series, the Ca 148. At right, a postwar example of the Italian AF.

height 13 ft. 1 in., and wing area 700 sq. ft. Empty and loaded weights were 9240 lb. and 14,740 lb. respectively.

CA 134

The Ca 134 two-seat reconnaissance biplane of 1936 was a conventional design in most respects, although the biplane tail with endplate fins and rudders was an unusual feature on a comparatively modern single-engined type. The configuration was adopted to provide the observer/gunner with a largely unobstructed rear field of fire. In addition to the dorsal gun position, the observer was provided with large rectangular windows on the fuselage sides. The pilot had a single forward-firing fixed gun.

Powered by a 900 h.p. Isotta-Fraschini Asso XI R.C.40 twelve-cylinder vee engine, the Ca 134 was of welded steel construction, with fabric-covered wings, rear fuselage, and tail surfaces; only the forward fuselage and landing gear fairings were sheet metal. The radiator was mounted beneath the fuselage between the landing gear. The narrow-chord untapered wings spanned 31 ft. 2 in.; length and height were respectively 31 ft. and 10 ft. 6 in. Performance included maximum and cruising speeds of 242 m.p.h. and 218 m.p.h., a landing speed of 56 m.p.h., and a ceiling of 26,240 ft.

CA 148

The final development of the series of high-wing trimotor transports commencing with the Ca 101 was the eighteen-passenger Ca 148 of 1938, which differed very little from the Ca 133. Power was supplied by 460 h.p. Piaggio Stella VII R.C. radials driving Piaggio-d'Asca-

The Ca 161bis. Note the special four-bladed airscrew and long, high-aspect-ratio wings.

Left, a Ca 164 captured by U.S. forces in Sicily and painted in USAAF markings, including serial. Right, a Ca 164 with postwar registration I-COME.

nio variable-pitch airscrews. The only important modifications were confined to the fuselage. The pilots' cabin was moved forward approximately three feet from its former position just ahead of the wing, and the loading door beneath the port wing was moved behind the trailing edge. Aside from these changes, which were made to increase the capacity of the fuselage, and a strengthened undercarriage to cope with the increased loaded weight of 10,956 lb., the characteristics of the Ca 148 were the same as for the Ca 133. Intended for operation in East Africa, only a small number of transports were built, a few serving with the postwar Italian Air Force. One example, owned by the Aero Club d'Italia, was still flying as late as 1956.

CA 161

In order to retain the world altitude record for Italy, a special high altitude research team, the Reparto Alta Quota di Guidonia, was organized at the Test Center in June, 1934, under Col. Mario Pezzi. A specially modified version of the Ca 113 was developed by Ing. Verduzio for high altitude attempts, receiving the designation Ca 161. The Ca 161 was a single-seat biplane with greatly elongated wings, reduced weight, and a special Piaggio P.XI R.C.100 engine driving a four-bladed airscrew. The record, which had passed successively to France and England in 1936, was regained for Italy by Col. Pezzi in May, 1937, when he reached 51,361 ft. in the Ca 161. For this flight he wore a pressurized suit with a helmet resembling the deep-sea diving type.

A further modification of the biplane, the Ca 161bis, was readied for the next conquest, which took place on October 22, 1938. On this occasion Col. Pezzi achieved an altitude of 56,046 ft. to set a record for propeller-driven aircraft that stands even today, due to the concentration on jet-propelled and rocket aircraft since the war. Not content merely with the absolute record, the Reparto Alta Quota prepared a float version, designated Ca 161 Idro N.S., which gained the seaplane record at 44,429 ft. on September 25, 1939, piloted by Ten. Col. Nicola di Mauro.

The Ca 161bis had a wingspan of 46 ft. 9 in., giving a total wing area of 382 sq. ft. Length was 27 ft. $0^{3}/_{4}$ in., height 11 ft. $5^{3}/_{4}$ in. The Piaggio P.XI R.C. 100 fourteen-cylinder engine developed 700 h.p., allowing the biplane to climb to 16,400 ft. in 8 min. 40 sec., to 32,800 ft. in 14 min. 30 sec., and to 52,480 ft. in 26 minutes.

CA 164

The Ca 164 was a two-seat training biplane of conventional design and construction. The fuselage and tail surfaces were of welded steel tubular structure with fabric covering; the wooden wings were also fabric-covered. Power was furnished by a 185 h.p. Alfa Romeo 115-I in-line engine, giving maximum, cruising, and landing speeds of 144 m.p.h., 114 m.p.h., and 56 m.p.h., respectively. Cruising range was 329 miles and service ceiling 13,776 ft. Weights were 1870 lb. empty and 2596 lb. loaded. Dimensions included a span of 30 ft. $10^{7}/_{8}$ in., a length of 22 ft. $11^{5}/_{8}$ in., a height of 9 ft. 10 in., and a wing area of 252.5 sq. ft. The Ca 164 was a product of the Predappio works.

Built in limited numbers as both a touring and training plane, the Ca 164 did not see widespread use. Although described as a military trainer during the early war years, it is unlikely that it was standard equipment of any training squadron. Surprisingly, one Ca 164 was used for short-range reconnaissance, liaison, and messenger work in Croatia in 1942. Along with a companion Nardi FN.305, it was based at Grobnico, not far from the Italian border. A few Ca 164's still remained after the war, seeing occasional use.

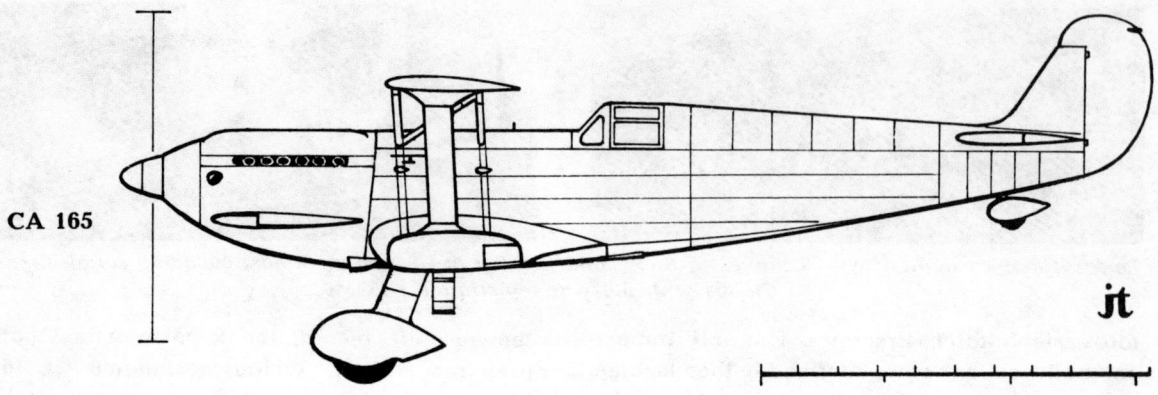

CA 165

CA 165
Sharing basic components with the Ca 134 reconnaissance biplane, the Ca 165 single-seat fighter was an anachronism which appeared in numerous publications during the Second World War but never entered service with the Regia Aeronautica. It was powered by a 900 h.p. Isotta-Fraschini Asso L.121 R.C.40 twelve-cylinder engine. Although the wings were nearly identical in structure to those of the Ca 134, they were unstaggered, necessitating a different bracing arrangement. The N-struts of the reconnaissance plane were replaced by single faired I outer struts on the fighter. The prototype Ca 165 had a "solid" fairing from the cockpit back to the fin, while the later versions had all-transparent canopies. Two 7.7-mm. machine guns mere mounted in the cowl firing through the airscrew disc.

Performance included a maximum speed of 280 m.p.h. at 16,400 ft., with cruising and landing speeds of 235 m.p.h. and 68 m.p.h. respectively. Service ceiling was 32,800 ft. Dimensions were: span 30 ft. $6^{1}/_{4}$ in., length 26 ft. $6^{7}/_{8}$ in., and height 8 ft. $4^{1}/_{2}$ in.

CA 183
The Ca 183bis high-altitude interceptor fighter, to be powered by a German Daimler Benz DB 605 in-line engine of 1250 h.p. and a 700 h.p. FIAT A.30 radial engine within the fuselage driving a Campini compressor, was under construction in 1943 but never completed. The compressor was expected to furnish a boost of 60 m.p.h. over the speed attainable with the piston engine, and was similar to the unit which powered the Campini N.1. The fuselage featured a carburettor air intake behind the cockpit and three cooling ducts on the sides and bottom.

Estimated maximum speed and range were 460 m.p.h. and 1242 miles respectively. The very heavy armament was to have comprised five 20-mm. cannon, four in the wings outboard of the airscrew disc, and one firing through the hub of the two three-bladed contrarotating airscrews. Fully-loaded design weight was 16,538 lb.

CA 225
The Ca 225 was an interesting design for a two-seat attack bomber which never passed the project stage. Two 1250 h.p. Isotta-Fraschini Zeta R.C.42 X-type engines were to provide a maximum speed of 395 m.p.h. and a range of 1242 miles. Armament was to have been four forward-firing 20-mm. cannon and two 12.7-mm. defensive machine guns. Specifications included a span of 48 ft. $6^{2}/_{3}$ in., a length of 43 ft. $5^{2}/_{3}$ 'n., and a loaded weight of 12,560 lb.

CA 602
Built at the Aeronautica Predappio works, the Ca 602 was a two-seat light trainer. Powered by a 150 h.p. Alfa Romeo 115-I in-line engine, the biplane had a maximum speed of 171 m.p.h. and a landing speed of 62 m.p.h. It climbed to 13,120 ft. in 14 minutes and had a ceiling of 22,960 ft. Range was 373 miles, or endurance 2 hrs. 30 min. Empty and loaded weights were 1034 lb. and 1606 lb. Dimensions were: span 29 ft. 6 in., length 21 ft. 8 in., height 8 ft. 4 in., and wing area 172 sq. ft.

CA 603
The Ca 603 was a single-seat aerobatic version of the Ca 602. Powered by the same engine, it featured a reduced wing area and generally strengthened structure, with interconnected ailerons on upper and lower wings. Empty and

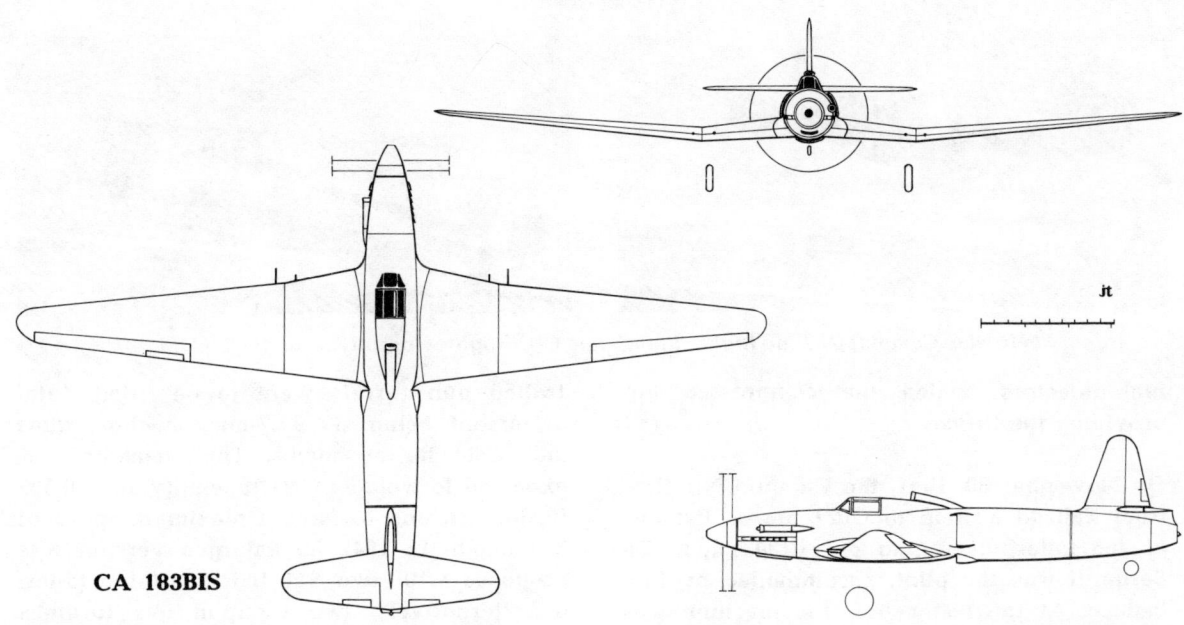

CA 183BIS

loaded weights were 1540 lb. and 1914 lb. Maximum speed was 174 m.p.h., landing speed 65 m.p.h.; climb to 13,120 ft. required 13 minutes. Ceiling was 23,620 ft. Dimensions included a span of 24 ft. 7 in., a length of 21 ft. 4 in., a height of 8 ft. 7 in., and a wing area of 140 sq. ft.

CAMPINI

Much heralded during the early war years as the world's first jet-propelled aeroplane, the Caproni Campini was actually an extremely inefficient design which flew a year after the secret but far more promising German Heinkel He 178 had made its first flight, and fourteen months after the debut of the He 176 rocket plane. Nevertheless, the Caproni Campini merited close attention as one of the first reaction-powered aircraft.

In 1931 Ing. Secondo Campini had founded the firm S. Campini per Velivoli e Natanti a Reazione, to study the prospects of reaction propulsion. During the next eight years he conducted numerous experiments before constructing an actual aircraft power unit. The Caproni N.1, often inaccurately referred to as the C.C.2, was built at Caproni Taliedo in early 1940, flying for the first time on August 28 with Mario de Bernardi at the controls. The N.1 was a two-seat all-metal monoplane with a 900 h.p. Isotta-Fraschini radial engine mounted within the fuselage, driving a variable-pitch, ducted-fan compressor. A ring of

Although preceded by several Heinkel aircraft in the reaction propulsion field, the Caproni Campini received great publicity in 1940. Shown here next to an Italian P-51, the Campini still exists in Milan.

Left, the Campini N.1 in flight. Right, the CH.1 fighter prototype of 1935. (MM 237)

fuel injectors heated the compressed air, providing the thrust.

On November 30, 1941, the Campini N.1 flew from Taliedo airfield to Guidonia, a distance of 168 miles, averaging only 130 m.p.h. De Bernardi was the pilot, accompanied by Ing. Pedace. At the test center the machine was evaluated for eight months, but the limited promise of the design led to the discontinuation of flight trials. Signor Campini continued to develop the propulsion system to augment the performance of piston-engined combat aircraft such as the Re 2005 and the projected Ca 183bis, but it was never actually used in a completed airframe.

Campini proposed a number of further jet-propelled designs during the war, but his enthusiasm was not shared by the Regia Aeronautica. The first proposal was for a twin-engined high-altitude bomber with DB 605 engines in the fuselage turning wing turbines by remote drive. Two remote-controlled gun turrets were to be fitted, total armament being six 12.7-mm. machine guns and 2200 lb. of bombs. This machine was expected to weigh 14,991 lb. empty and 30,533 lb. loaded, and to have a maximum speed of 373 m.p.h. In 1942 an enlarged version was proposed with two Rel 103 R.C.50-I engines, or alternatively two Campini gas turbines (supposed to develop 3500 e.h.p. at 19,680 ft.), and a bomb load of 3300 lb. Also projected was a twin-jet fighter resembling the British Gloster Meteor, incorporating four 12.7-mm. machine guns and two 20-mm. cannon in the nose. Loaded weight was to be 7165 lb. and maximum speed 503 m.p.h. None of these plans were given much consideration, and no detail design was undertaken.

The Caproni Campini N.1 had a span of 52 ft., a length of 43 ft., and a wing area of 387.4 sq. ft. Empty and loaded weights were 8024 lb. and 9250 lb. An afterburner effect was used to increase the maximum speed from 205 m.p.h. to 233 m.p.h. at 9800 ft. Maximum altitude

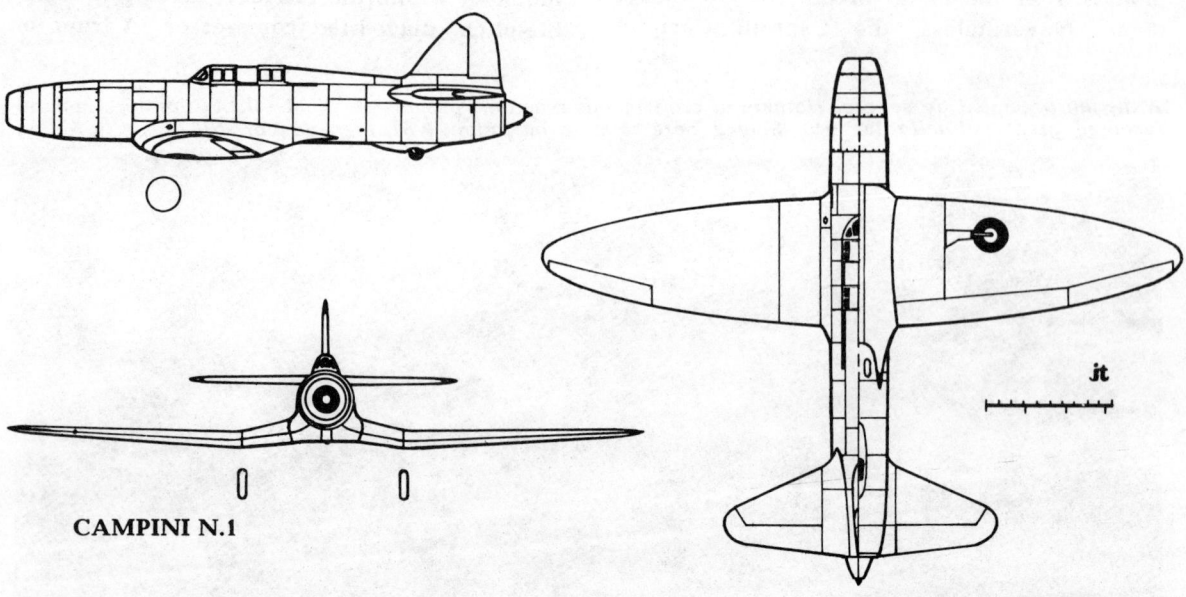

CAMPINI N.1

attained during flight tests was 13,120 ft., although this did not constitute the absolute ceiling. The Campini N.1 is still stored in the Museo della Scienza e della Tecnica at Milan.

CH.1

The CH.1 was a private-venture single-seat fighter produced in 1935. A very small biplane powered by a 780 h.p. Gnôme-Rhône 14 Kfs radial enngine, the CH.1 weighed 3300 lb empty, 4620 lb. loaded, and fitted two forward-firing machine guns. Claimed maximum speed was 273 m.p.h. at 15,580 ft., with a cruising speed of 236 m.p.h. The climbing performance claimed for the CH.1 seems optimistic and theoretical, with times of one, two, three, and four minutes to altitudes of 3280 ft., 6560 ft., 9840 ft., and 13,120 ft. respectively; 19,840 ft was supposed to have been attainable in six minutes. Dimensions were. span 28 ft. 2^1/$_2$ in., length 23 ft. 5^1/$_2$ in., height 9 ft. 6 in., and wing area 204.4 sq. ft.

STIPA

Ordered by Gen. Luigi Crocco, technical director of the Air Ministry, the Caproni Stipa was built in 1932 to test the theories of Ing. Luigi Stipa regarding the thrust effect of a venturi-tube fuselage. The barrel-like two-seat machine, mounting a 120 h.p. D.H. Gipsy III engine within the mounth of the tube, made a number of successful flights at Taliedo and Guidonia, but did not possess outstanding performance, even considering the low power. It was estimated that the fuselage contributed 37 per cent of the total lift of the machine. The Stipa achieved a maximum speed of 81 m.p.h. and landed at 42 m.p.h. Ceiling was 12,136 ft. Empty and loaded weights were 1320 lb. and 1760 lb. Dimensions included a span of 46 ft.

The Caproni Stipa was perhaps the least graceful aeroplane ever built. Maximum speed was 81 m.p.h.

10 in., a length of 19 ft. 4 in., a height of 9 ft. 10 in., and a wing area of 204 sq. ft.

The French firm Les Mureaux (Les Ateliers de Constructions du Nord de la France et des Mureaux) acquired the French license for the Stipa patents in 1935. It was intended to build a twin-engined version for the French government, but the plans never reached fruition. It is interesting to compare the Caproni Stipa with the more recent annular-wing aircraft experiments.

TRICAP

Another experimental machine outside the normal Caproni production scheme was the "Sauro 1", or Tricap, so named from a project initiated by Col. (Dott. Ing.) Emmanuele Trigona and built by the Caproni firm at Taliedo. First flown in 1933, the Tricap featured an inverted gull wing of great efficiency, offering high speeds, stability, and excellent handling compared to contemporary aircraft. Tests at Guidonia were extremely favorable. The Tricap was a very clean two-seat touring

The Tricap featured inverted gull wings, smoothly faired landing gear, and semi-open cockpits. (MM 196)

monoplane powered by a 130 h.p. Farina T.58 five-cylinder radial engine and featuring smoothly-faired fixed landing gear. Empty and loaded weights were 1056 lb. and 1852 lb. respectively. Span was 37 ft. $4^{2}/_{3}$ in., length 19 ft. $0^{2}/_{3}$ in., and height 7 ft. $2^{1}/_{2}$ in. Maximum speed was 140 m.p.h., ceiling 19,680 ft., and endurance 6 hours.

Following the success of the Tricap, Ing. Trigona worked on a fighter design incorporating some of the same features. It was eventually abandoned in 1943.

TM.2

The TM.2 cargo glider, designed by Ing. Del Proposto, made its first flight in the spring of 1943. During early trials the prototype was damaged when the towing cable came off, putting the glider into a low-level spin which ended fatally for the pilot. The TM.2 was repaired, but further tests were abandoned at the time of the Armistice. After the war Caproni planned to install two engines in the wings, but the project was never realized. Of all-wood construction with plywood and fabric covering, the glider featured four large doors on the fuselage sides, giving access to the cargo compartments. Empty and loaded weights were approximately 4400 lb. and 8800 lb. Span was 74 ft. $9^{1}/_{2}$ in., length 42 ft. 6 in., and wing area 495 sq. ft. Like the Campini N.1, the TM.2 is still stored at the Milan museum.

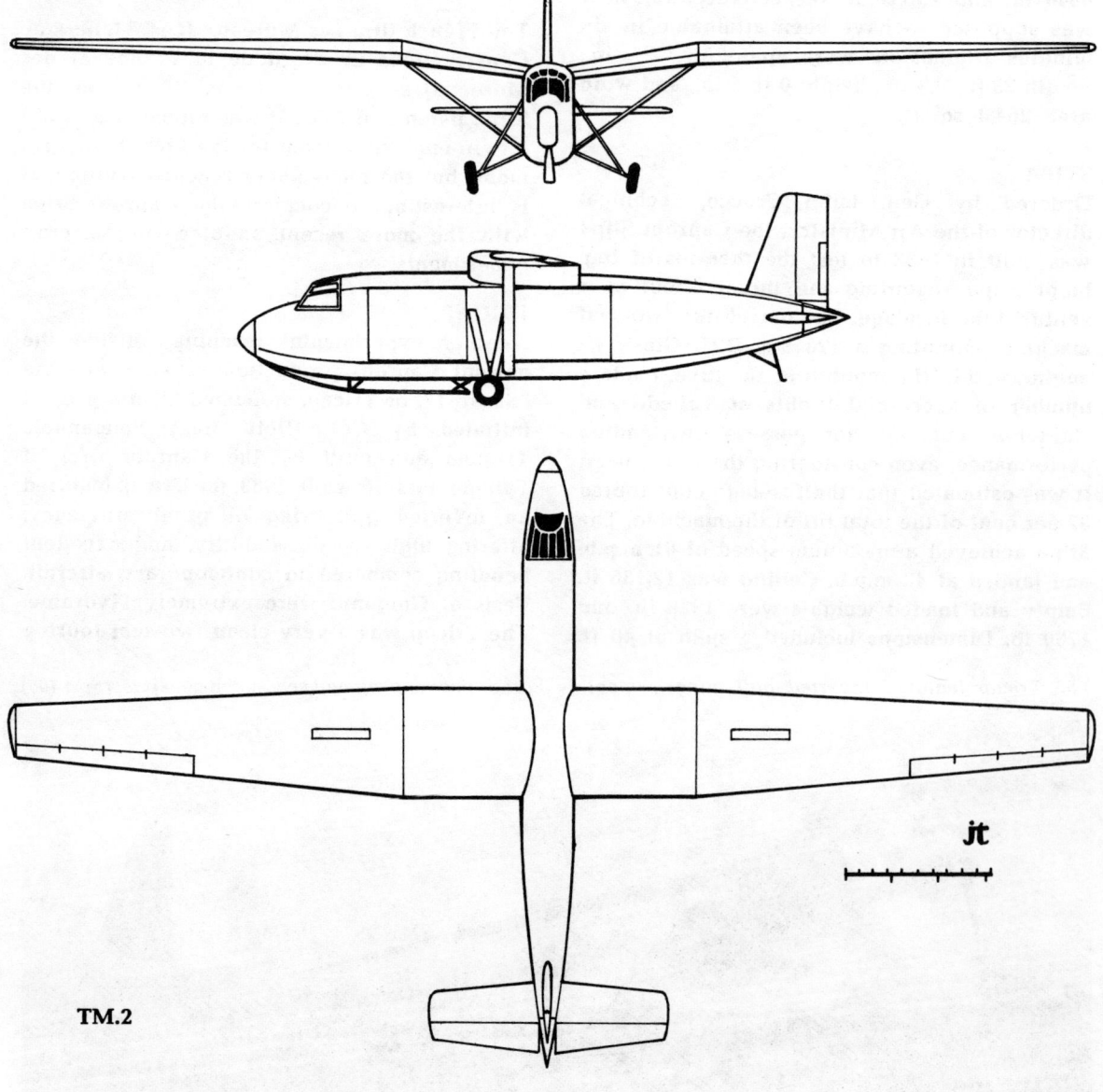

TM.2

CAPRONI BERGAMASCHI
Caproni Aeronautica Bergamasca

Founded in 1927 at Ponte San Pietro, Bergamo, the Cantieri Aeronautici Bergamaschi built only a few training biplanes before it was absorbed by Caproni in 1931. In 1933, Ing. Cesare Pallavicino, formerly with Breda, became Chief Engineer. Under his direction the company, renamed Caproni Aeronautica Bergamasca, embarked on a completely modernized program. Although a subsidiary, the Bergamo plant produced more advanced aircraft than the main works at Taliedo, and subsequently became the only Caproni company other than Reggiane to manufacture modern aircraft in any quantity during the Second World War.

PL.3
The first Bergamaschi design under Caproni ownership was the PL.3 long-range two-seat monoplane built in 1934 to compete in the London-Melbourne race for the MacRobertson Trophy. Powered by a 700 h.p. FIAT A.59 (license-built Pratt & Whitney Hornet) nine-cylinder radial engine enclosed in an N.A.C.A. cowling and driving a controllable-pitch two-bladed airscrew, the PL.3 featured side-by-side seating, retractable landing gear, and a fuel capacity of 550 gal. The very clean monoplane had a top speed of 224 m.p.h. at 11,152 ft. and a range of 1925 miles. The PL.3 climbed to 3280 ft. in 3 min. 15 sec., to 6560 ft. in 7 min. 15 sec., and to 13,120 ft. in 17 min. 30 sec. Dimensions were: span 39 ft., length 29 ft. 8 in., height 9 ft. 1 in., and wing area 258 sq. ft. Empty and loaded weights were 3740 lb. and 7700 lb.

PS.1
A contemporary of the PL.3, the PS.1 four-seat cabin monoplane was designed for the 1934 Challenge de Tourisme International. Featuring dual controls and retractable landing gear, the PS.1 was powered by a 190/205 h.p. FIAT A.70 S radial engine in an N.A.C.A. cowling. Empty and loaded weights were 1452 lb. and 2376 lb. Performance included maximum, cruising, and landing speeds of 162 m.p.h., 143 m.p.h., and 37 m.p.h. respectively. Range was 500 miles and ceiling 21,320 ft., while a climb to 13,120 ft. required 26 minutes. Dimensions were: span 34 ft. $11^7/_8$ in., length 23 ft. 7 in., height 7 ft., and wing area 188.8 sq. ft.

AP.1
Originally designed in 1934 as a low-wing single-seat fighter, the AP.1 was later developed into a two-seat reconnaissance and attack plane when it became outmoded for the fighter role. A 600 h.p. Piaggio IX R.C. nine-cylinder radial engine was fitted to the original version, giving a maximum speed of only 196 m.p.h. at 14,760 ft. One of the few Bergamaschi designs with fixed landing gear, the AP.1 fighter mounted two machine guns in the gear fairings and a third in the fuselage. Bombs could be carried in the fuselage and under the wings. Empty and loaded weights were 3520 lb. and 5126 lb. Landing speed was 62 m.p.h. and ceiling 24,000 ft. The fighter climbed to 13,120 ft. in 10 min. 23 sec. Dimensions included a span of 39 ft. 4 in., a length of 29 ft $4^1/_2$ in., a height of 9 ft. 3 in., and a wing area of 258.2 sq. ft.

The two-seat light reconnaissance bomber employed a 650 h.p. Alfa Romeo 126 R.C. 34 radial. Although empty and loaded weights

Left, the PS.1 four-passenger monoplane built in 1934 for the Challenge de Tourisme International. (I-MELO) Right, the PL.3 intended for the MacRobertson race. Registration I-TALY is significant.

The original AP.1 prototype, built as a single-seat fighter. (MM 242)

increased to 4070 lb. and 6050 lb. respectively, performance was improved. Principal changes, other than in the type of engine used, were the provision of a second seat for the observer/gunner, an increased wing area, and small wheel spats in place of the large landing gear fairings. In later operational use, the spats were customarily omitted. Skis were fitted to at least one example. The armament comprised two forward-firing machine guns in the wing leading edges and a third hand-held gun in the rear cockpit. Up to 880 lb. of bombs could be carried.

Maximum speed of the AP.1 reconnaissance bomber was 242 m.p.h. at 13,120 ft.; the machine climbed to that altitude in 7 min. 50 sec. Ceiling was 26,240 ft. and range 932 miles. Dimensions were: span 42 ft. $8^1/_8$ in., length 32 ft. 3 in., height 11 ft. 10 in., and wing area 290.5 sq. ft.

Thirty-four AP.1's were included in the 1939 strength of the Regia Aeronautica; they were still described as fighters although they were already obsolete even in the reconnaissance role. No AP.1 aircraft saw action in the Second

Left, a line-up of AP.1 reconnaissance aircraft. Above, a ski-equipped model. Below, a standard reconnaissance AP.1. Note mirror, gun barrel clip.

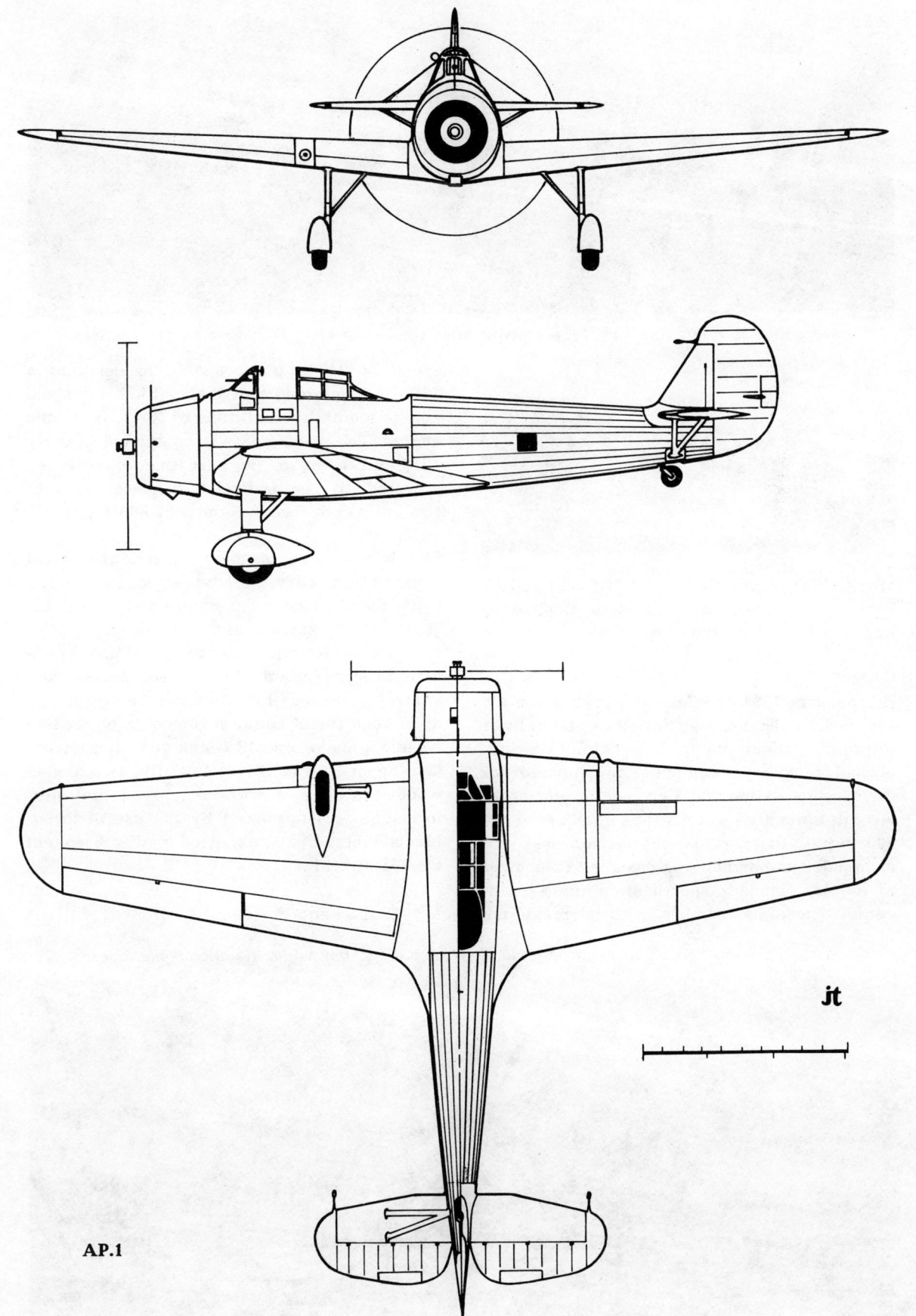

CAPRONI BERGAMASCHI

AP.1

Above and below left, the Ca 135 prototype after the fitting of three-bladed metal airscrews.

World War. A few fighters were supplied to Paraguay in 1935, and four were shipped to El Salvador in exchange for coffee.

CA 135

Designed in 1934 at Ponte San Pietro, the Ca 135 medium bomber was initially to be built at Caproni's Taliedo plant, but eventually Bergamaschi took over complete development of the design. Although Caproni Bergamaschi aircraft normally received type numbers in the 300 series, the Ca 135 designation was not changed. The bomber was designed in answer to an Air Ministry specification for a twin-engined medium bomber with a maximum speed of 240 m.p.h., capable of carrying a 2650-lb. bomb load a distance of 621 miles and able to maintain an altitude of 16,400 ft. on one engine. The prototype was completed in early 1935 and flown for the first time on April 1st, powered by Isotta-Fraschini Asso XI R.C. twelve-cylinder vee engines of 800 h.p. each.

The wings were of mixed metal and wood construction, covered with wood and fabric, while the fuselage was composed of a stressed-skin forward section and a wood and fabric-covered welded steel rear section. Three Breda turrets were mounted in nose, dorsal, and ventral positions, the latter two being retractable. Each turret could accomodate either two 7.7-mm. guns or one 12.7-mm. gun. Retractable landing gear was fitted. Initially, two-bladed wooden airscrews were employed, but performance was improved by the use of three-bladed metal airscrews, fitted to all subsequent Ca 135 aircraft.

In 1936 the Regia Aeronautica ordered fourteen

A Ca 135 Tipo Spagna in Regia Aeronautica camouflage but without national markings.

examples under the designation Tipo Spagna, but no Ca 135's were actually used in the Spanish conflict. This version was also referred to as the Ca 135 Asso. Power was slightly raised by the use of 836 h.p. Asso XI R.C.40 engines, but the Tipo Spagna weighed 18,500 lb. loaded (compared to 16,225 lb. for the prototype), and maximum speed dropped from to 248 m.p.h. to only 227 m.p.h. In addition, the service ceiling and climbing performance were diminished, although the increased fuel capacity improved the range to 992 miles. Cruising speed of the Tipo Spagna was 193 m.p.h., the landing speed being 81 m.p.h. The Spagna reached 6560 ft. in 8 min. 36 sec., 13,120 ft. in 16 min. 45 sec., and 16,400 ft. in 21 min. 54 sec.

During the same year the Peruvian government ordered six machines fitted with 815 h.p. Asso XI R.C.45 engines, and later received a total of 32 bombers designated Tipo Peru, these being distinguished by their modified gun positions, cleaner engine cowlings, and Asso XI R.C.40 engines of 900 h.p. each. These fought against Ecuador during the short campaign in 1941. One other Ca 135 with Asso engines was the Ca 135 Raid built for the Brazilian pilot De Barros. On this example, power was raised to 986 h.p. per engine, and fuel capacity increased, all-up weight being 21,000 lb. Attempting to fly from Rome to Brazil in 1937, De Barros disappeared over the West African desert.

A Ca 135 with Hispano-Suiza 12 Y 21 engines of 910 h.p. was proposed, but this arrangement did not pass the design stage. It was considered only as a possible alternative to the Assos. All of the early Asso-engined variants had been seriously underpowered; to remedy this

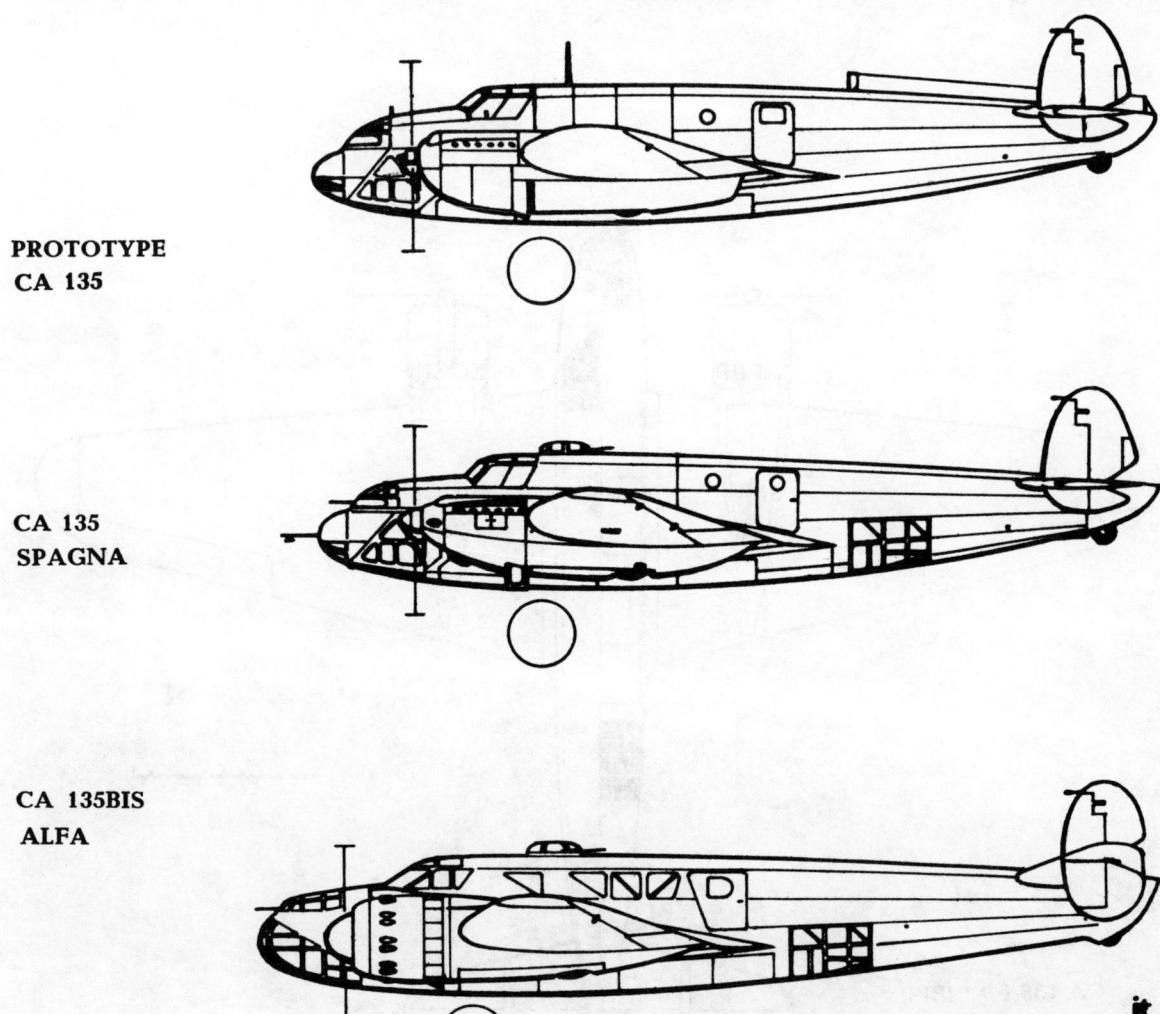

PROTOTYPE CA 135

CA 135 SPAGNA

CA 135BIS ALFA

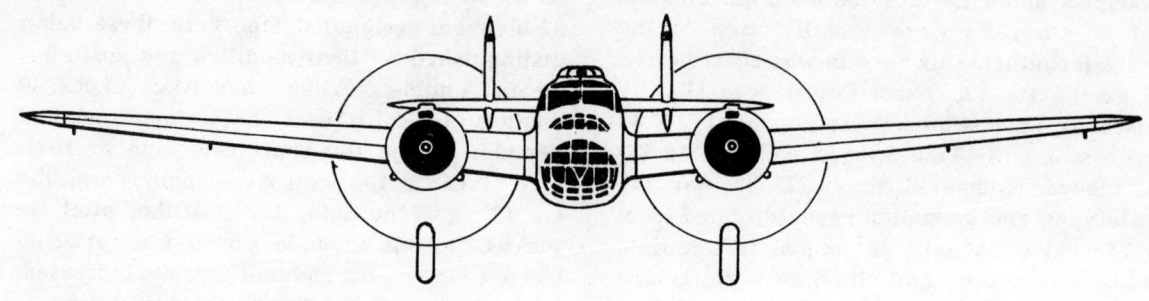

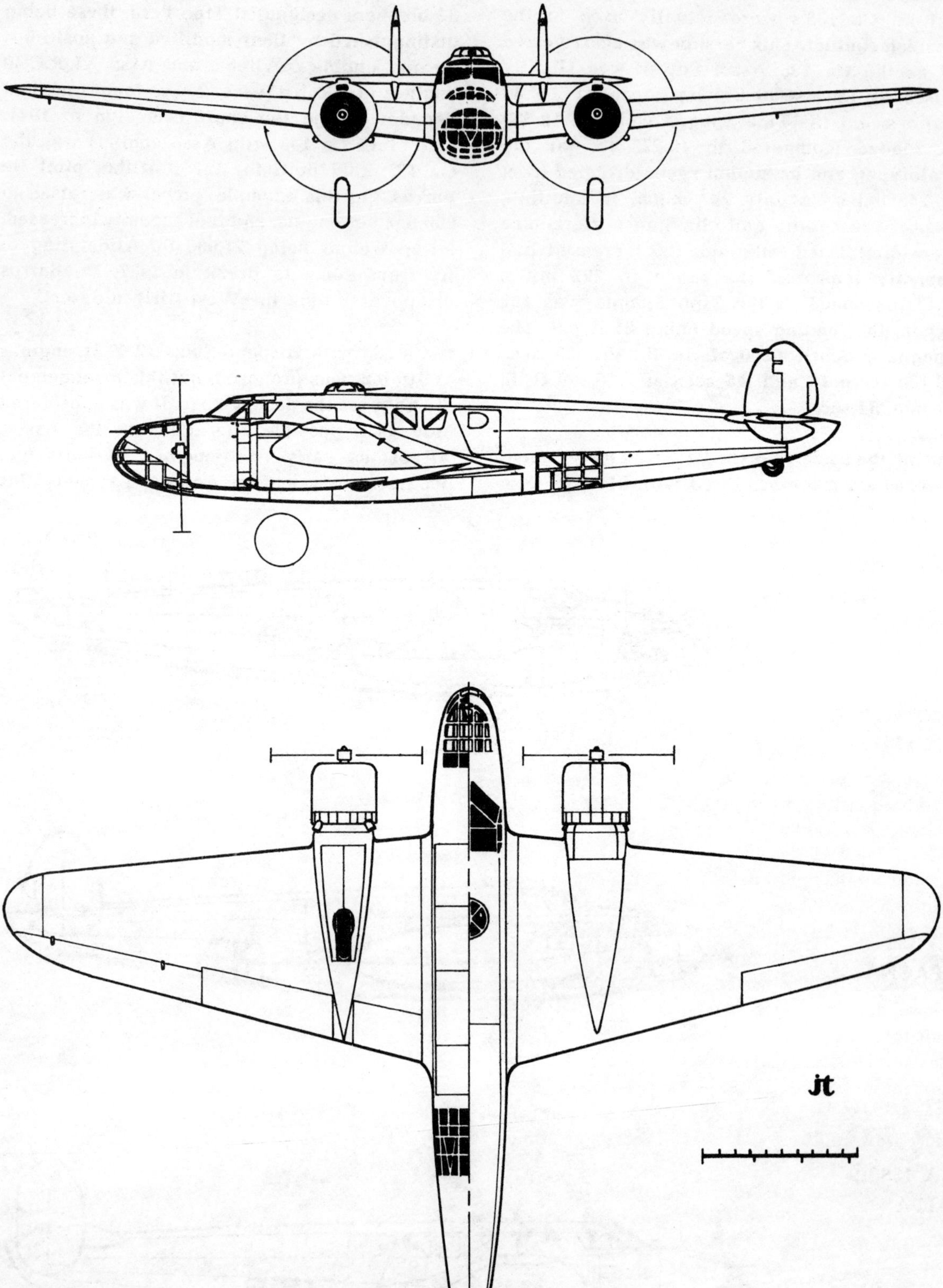

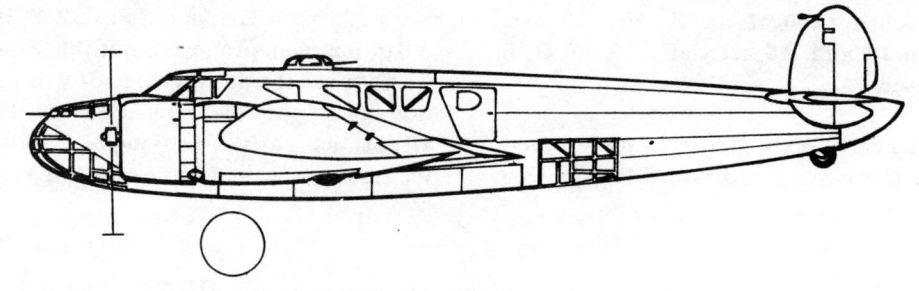

CA 135/P.XI (BIS)

Ca 135 with 1000 h.p. FIAT A.80 R.C.41 radials.

shortcoming, both the eighteen-cylinder FIAT A.80 R.C.41 and fourteen-cylinder Piaggio P.XI R.C.40 radials were installed in Tipo Spagna airframes early in 1938. Both engines offered 1000 h.p., but the FIAT unit proved unreliable and did not improve performance as much as expected. The few FIAT-powered Ca 135's were turned over to the Regia Aeronautica bombing schools and eventually dismantled. The Piaggio version, however, proved to be very successful and possessed the highest performance of any of the Ca 135 series. Designated Ca 135/P.XI, the variant featured a new, cleaner nose section and Mercier engine cowlings like those on the Cant Z.1007bis. A new Caproni Lanciani dorsal turret was also fitted. The Ca 135/P.XI was evaluated by the Japanese Army Air Force in May 1938, along with the FIAT BR.20. In spite of the good performance of the Caproni bomber, the BR.20 was chosen to equip the JAAF medium bombing units until their own Mitsubishi Ki-21 became available.

As the Regia Aeronautica preferred the three-engined Cant Z.1007bis and Savoia Marchetti SM.79 to twin-engined types, the Ca 135/P.XI became purely an export machine and about 100 were supplied to the Hungarian Air Force. These aircraft were attached to the German Luftflotte IV and served successfully against Russia. The last Ca 135/P.XI was retained by the factory and fitted with 1400 h.p. Alfa Romeo 135 R.C.32 Tornado radial engines, very large spinners, and a dihedral tailplane. Maximum speed exceeded 300 m.p.h., but the Ca 135 design was not developed further. In spite of the great publicity given the bomber by Italy in the late 1930's, only about 150 were built and none ever equipped operational units of the Regia Aeronautica.

The Ca 135/P.XI weighed 13,340 lb. empty and 21,050 lb. fully loaded, accommodating 3520 lb. of bombs and three 12.7-mm. machine guns. The span of 61 ft. 8 in., the wing area of 645.6 sq. ft., and the height of 11 ft. 2 in. were common to all models of the Ca 135, although the Ca 135/P.XI was some 2 ft. $2^1/_2$ in. longer than previous models at 47 ft. 2 in. Performance included a maximum speed of 273 m.p.h. at 15,750 ft., a cruising speed of 217 m.p.h., and a landing speed of 80 m.p.h. Range varied from 745-1242 miles, and service ceiling was 21,300 ft. The Ca 135/P.XI climbed to 13,120 ft. in 11 min. 36 sec. and to 16,400 ft. in 17 min. 24 sec. The various radial-engined versions of the Ca 135 were often referred to as the Ca 135bis.

BOREA

The Borea (North Wind) twin-engined light transport was the forerunner of a long line of transport, reconnaissance, and bombing aircraft that comprised the bulk of Bergamaschi's production immediately before and during the Second World War. Intended for short-distance runs linking the major airline routes, the six-passenger low-wing Borea employed two 185/200 h.p. Walter Major six-cylinder in-line air-cooled engines. The cockpit seated the two crew members side by side with dual controls; immediately behind was the passenger cabin with two rows of three seats. Notable were the extremely large windows. The baggage compartment was located between the cabin and the tail. Fixed landing gear were faired into the engine nacelles. Empty and loaded weights were 3740 lb. and 5720 lb.

The last Ca 135bis was re-engined with 1400 h.p. Alfa Romeo 135 R.C.32 Tornado radials. Very large spinners and dihedral tailplane were also tried.

The Bergamaschi Borea was the first of a long line of twin-engined transports and reconnaissance planes.

Sometimes known as the Ca 308, the Borea served in limited numbers with Ala Littoria. Performance included a maximum speed of 155 m.p.h. at 1985 ft., a cruising speed of 140 m.p.h., and a landing speed of 51 m.p.h. with flaps. Initial rate of climb was 846 ft. per minute, with a service ceiling of 17,712 ft. An altitude of 4920 ft. could be maintained on one engine. The Borea had a span of 53 ft. 1½ in., a length of 42 ft. 3 in., a height of 10 ft. 8 in., and a wing area of 416.5 sq. ft.

CA 309

The first important development of the Borea was the Ca 309 Ghibli (Desert Wind) general purpose colonial monoplane, powered by two 185/200 h.p. Alfa Romeo 115-I or II six-cylinder in-line engines. Essentially similar to the Borea, the Ghibli was distinguished by a further-aft cockpit and a lengthened bombing nose with transparent panels. Making its appearance in 1936, the Ghibli, like the Borea, was of mixed construction, with plywood-covered wooden wing and fabric-covered and alloy-panelled welded steel tube fuselage. The prototype weighed 3850 lb. empty and 5940 lb.

Left, a Ca 309 Ghibli taking off in rally competition. (I-LIBS) Below, a Ca 309 Serie V of the Regia Aeronautica. (MM 12390)

CAPRONI BERGAMASCHI

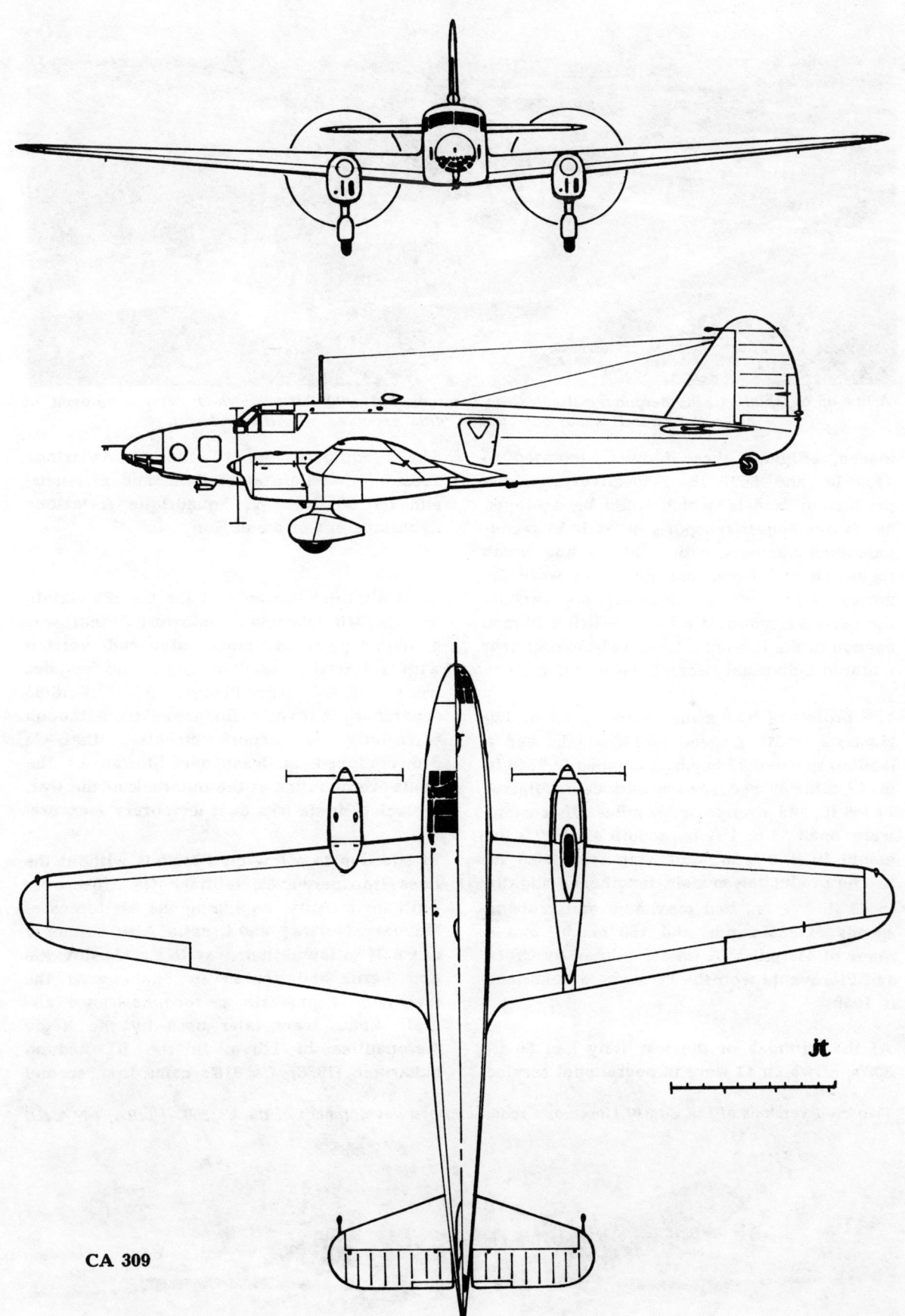

CA 309

A line-up of Ghiblis at the Bergamo airfield. Note the radiating wing stripes, which were employed to make the aircraft stand out against wide expanses of African desert.

loaded, although these figures increased to 4409 lb. and 6607 lb. respectively on the production models, which could be equipped as six-passenger transports or as light reconnaissance bombers with cameras and bomb racks. Three 7.7-mm. machine guns were the normal armament. A close-support version, the Serie VI, mounted a forward-firing 20-mm. cannon in the fuselage. The fixed landing gear featured individual streamlined wheel spats.

The prototype had a maximum speed of 159 m.p.h., a cruising speed of 137 m.p.h., and a landing speed of 52 m.p.h. It climbed to 9840 ft. in 17 min. 30 sec., had a service ceiling of 14,760 ft., and a range of 962 miles. Dimensions were: span 53 ft. 1½ in., length 42 ft. 7½ in., height 10 ft. 8½ in., and wing area 416.5 sq. ft. The production models, lengthened slightly to 43 ft. 7¼ in., had maximum and cruising speeds of 155 m.p.h. and 130 m.p.h., and a range of 417 miles. A Ca 309 piloted by Croce and Fioravante won the IV Raduno Sahariana in 1939.

At the outbreak of the war Italy had 69 Ca 309's, of which 42 were in operational service. These equipped the 1° and 2° Aviazione Presidio Coloniale at Mellaha and El Adem, and the 26ª and 99ª Squadriglie Aviazione Sahariana at Cufra and Hon.

CA 310

A parallel development of the Ca 309 Ghibli, the Ca 310 Libeccio (Southwest Wind) was a higher-powered, more advanced version with retractable landing gear. The engines were 430/470 h.p. Piaggio P.VII C.16/35 supercharged seven-cylinder radials. Although essentially an export machine, the Ca 310 equipped at least one Stormo of the Regia Aeronautica at the outbreak of the war, replacing Breda 65's as a temporary measure.

In addition to a few civil models without the nose transparencies, military Ca 310's were built in quantity, equipping the air forces of Hungary, Norway, and Croatia. Also, a number of Ca 310's found their way to Czechoslovakia and Peru, and served in Spain with the Aviazione Legionaria as reconnaissance aircraft. Some were later used by the Regia Aeronautica in Libya. In the III Raduno Sahariana (1938), Ca 310's came first, second

Two civil versions of the Ca 310 Libeccio, a radial-engined development of the Ca 309. (I-LIRA; I-MANU)

Above and right, the military version of the Ca 310 Libeccio featured extra nose transparencies and dorsal turret, plus two guns in wing roots.

and third, piloted by Ivo de Vittembeschi, Umberto Maddalena, and Giorgio Parodi.

The Ca 310 was structurally and dimensionally very similar to the Ca 309. The fuselage was slightly shorter at 40 ft. 0¼ in. Empty and loaded weights were 6730 lb. and 10,250 lb. Although a number of Libeccios were built without armament, the standard array was three 7.7-mm. machine guns, one flexible dorsal gun and two fixed forward-firing guns in the wing roots. Bomb load was 880 lb. Maximum speed was 218-227 m.p.h. depending on the engines and equipment, with a cruising speed of 177-196 m.p.h., and a landing speed of 65 m.p.h. The Ca 310 had a ceiling of 22,960 ft. and a range of 745-1025 miles. It climbed to 6560 ft. in 6 min. 40 sec., to 13,120 ft. in 12 min. 23 sec., and to 16,400 ft. in 15 min. 32 sec.

Additional models of the Libeccio were the twin-float Ca 310 idro and the Ca 310bis, which was the prototype of the Ca 311 production machine, featuring an all-transparent, unstepped nose similar to that of the Bristol Blenheim I.

CA 311

The Ca 311 was powered by Piaggio P.VII C.35 engines up-rated to 500 h.p. for take-off and featured the nose section of the experimental Ca 310bis. Armament comprised three 7.7-mm. guns, one in a dorsal Caproni Lanciani turret, one in the port wing root firing forward, and one firing aft through a ventral hatch. An 880 lb. bomb load was stored internally. The Ca 311 weighed 8020 lb. empty and 11,062 lb. loaded. Maximum and cruising speeds were 217 m.p.h. and 186 m.p.h., and range was 800-

Above left, the Ca 310bis, prototype for the Ca 311 Above right, a Ca 311 reconnaissance bomber. Below, the Ca 311M, similar except for the adoption of a stepped windscreen.

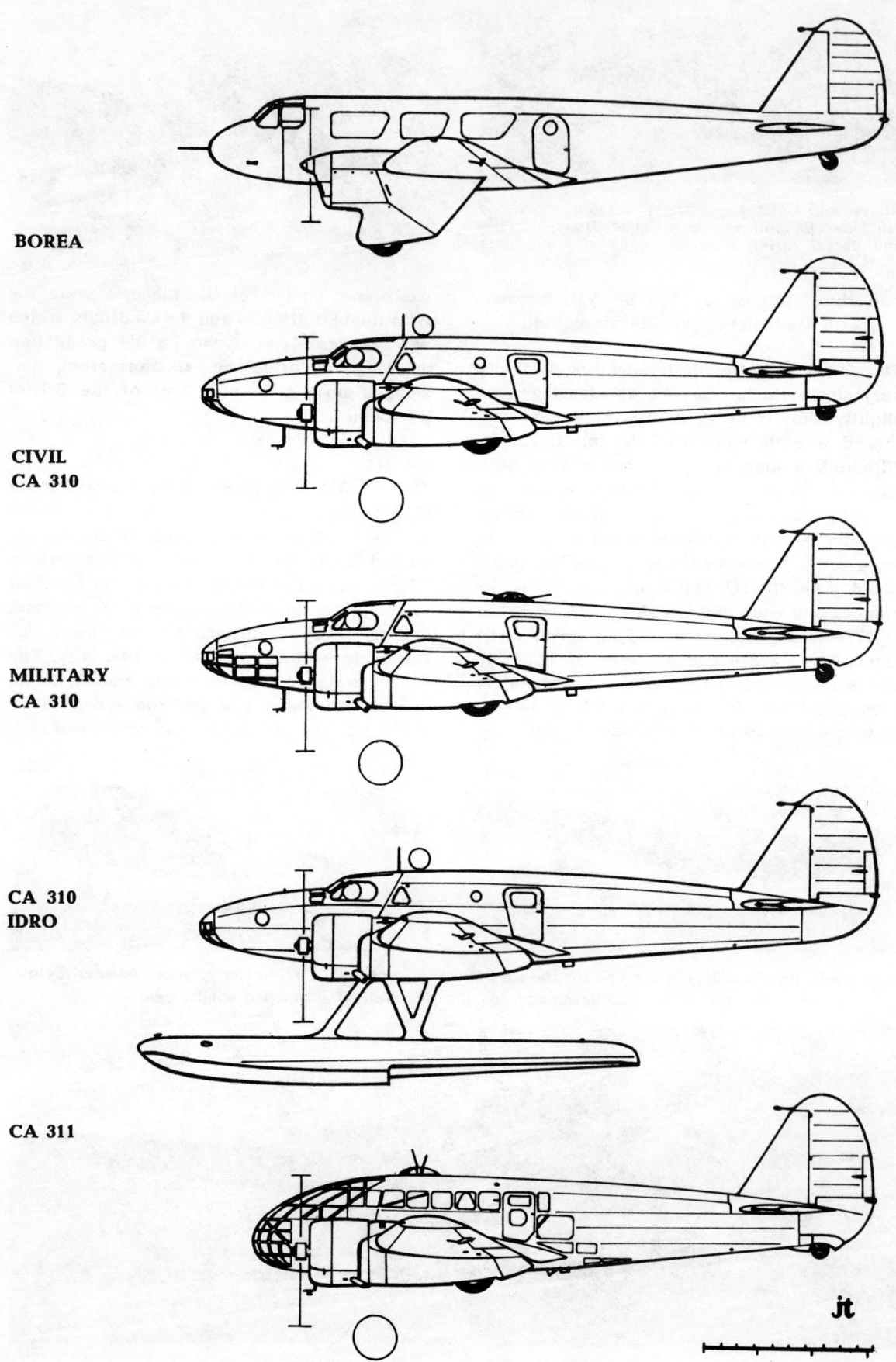

CAPRONI BERGAMASCHI

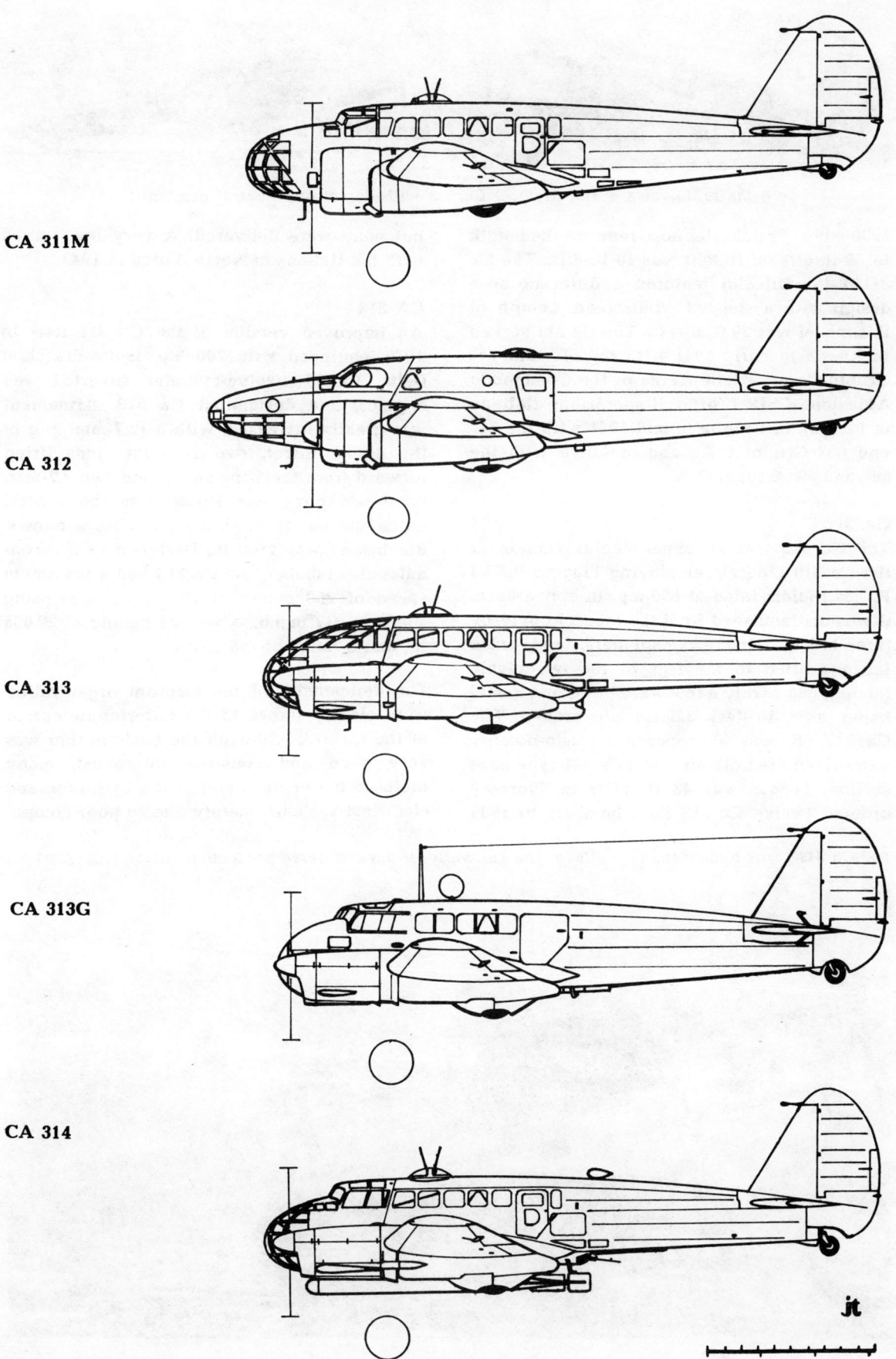

CA 311M

CA 312

CA 313

CA 313G

CA 314

Left, the prototype Ca 313. Right, a Ca 313 with dorsal and ventral gun positions.

1200 miles. The shorter nose reduced the length to 38 ft. 6$^{1}/_{8}$ in. Height was 10 ft. 6 in. The Ca 311M (Modificato) featured a different nose design with a stepped windscreen. Length of this model was 39 ft. 8$^{1}/_{2}$ in. The Ca 311 served in Russia in early 1941 with the 61° and 71° Gruppi Osservazione Aerea of the Commando Aviazione CSIR (Corpo di spedizione Italiano in Russia), in Croatia in mid-1941 with the 61° and 63° Gruppi O.A., and in Libya with the 68° and 69° Gruppi O.A.

CA 312

The Ca 312 was an experimental version of the Ca 310 Libeccio employing Piaggio P.XVI R.C.35 radials rated at 650 h.p. In appearance, it was distinguished from the Libeccio only by three-bladed airscrews, spinners, and extra fairings fitted to the legs of the retractable landing gear. Only a few were built, one model being used to test Balerio air brakes. The Ca 312 I.S. was a proposed torpedo-bomber variant with twin floats and a Ca 311-type nose section. Length was 43 ft. 11$^{1}/_{2}$ in. Norway ordered twelve Ca 312 light bombers in 1939 but none were delivered. A very few served with the Italians in North Africa in 1942.

CA 313

An improved version of the Ca 311 flew in 1940, equipped with 700 h.p. Isotta-Fraschini Delta R.C.35 twelve-cylinder inverted vee engines, and designated Ca 313. Armament was greatly increased, with a 12.7-mm. gun in the dorsal turret, two 12.7-mm. guns firing forward from the wing roots, and two 7.7-mm. hand-held guns, one firing from the ventral hatch and one through the aft cabin windows. Bomb load was 1100 lb. Designed as a reconnaissance bomber, the Ca 313 had a maximum speed of 268 m.p.h. at 16,400 ft., a cruising speed of 217 m.p.h., a service ceiling of 29,035 ft., and a range of 795 miles.

The deficiencies of the Caproni organization were clearly shown in the unfortunate career of the Ca 313. Although the basic design was very good and construction robust, many faults in the engines and in the hydraulic and electrical systems, mainly due to poor compo-

The Ca 313G was a crew trainer built for the Luftwaffe; it never entered production. Below, Ca 313G V3.

Above and right, the Ca 314 reconnaissance bomber. Torpedo-carrying version was Ca 314-RA.

nent inspection, caused a number of failures, fires, and accidents during the Ca 313's operational history. The Swedish government ordered 90 of the type in 1940, but only 82 succeeded in reaching southern Sweden after a flight from Italy via Germany. Of those which actually arrived, many had suffered a failure of one engine and numerous other breakdowns. During the five years that they were operated by the Flygvapnet (Swedish Air Force), Ca 313's experienced further malfunctions resulting in the death of 44 Swedish airmen, certainly an unenviable record. Yet the Ca 313 possessed good flying characteristics and a rugged construction capable of absorbing considerable damage. In Sweden, the Ca 313 was known variously as the B 16 (bomber), S 16 (reconnaissance), T 16 (torpedo bomber), and Tp 16 (transport).

At the same time, the Ca 313 was slowly entering Italian service, eventually equipping the 13°, 15°, 19°, and 41° Stormi, as well as serving with the CSIR in Russia. The same problems which plagued the type in Sweden manifested themselves, to a lesser extent, in Regia Aeronautica service; these were further compounded by lack of materiel, spares, and armament, causing infrequent delivery.

Dimensions of the Ca 313 were the same as for the Ca 311. Empty and loaded weights were 9832 lb. and 13,477 lb. The Ca 313G was an experimental modification for training and liaison, built as a Luftwaffe project. At least three were built, although the Ca 313G was never placed in production. A version to have been built in Germany under license was designated Ca 315. Ten Ca 313's were ordered for the postwar Italian Air Force in 1947.

CA 314

The most advanced of the series, the Ca 314, was a more heavily armed development of the Ca 313. Employing the same Delta engines, the Ca 314 was built at Ponte San Pietro, Taliedo, and Castellamare di Stabia, commencing in 1941. Featuring a nose similar to that of the Ca 311M, the Ca 314 had slightly shorter wings (span 52 ft. $11^{7}/_{8}$ in.). A number of different models were built, including the Ca 314-SC (Scorta) for convoy escort duties, the Ca 314-RA (Ricognizione-Aerosiluranti) reconnaissance torpedo bomber which carried a 450-mm. (17.7-in.) torpedo under the fuselage, and the Ca 314-C (Combattimento) with two extra 12.7-mm. guns in the wing roots. Normal armament and bomb load were the same as those of the Ca 313. Maximum speed was 253 m.p.h. at 16,400 ft., cruising speed 237 m.p.h., range 665 miles, and ceiling 27,070 ft. The empty and loaded weights were 10,443 lb. and 14, 776 lb.

The Ca 314 equipped the 5° and 63° Gruppi Osservazione Aerea, the 32° Gruppo Bombardimento Terrestre, and the 30° and 43° Gruppi Combattimenti, as well as the 20° and 21° Stormi O.A. of the Aviazione per il Regio Esercito (Italian Army).

CA 315

A proposed training and liaison variant of the Ca 313/314, the Ca 315 was to have been manufactured in Germany. After testing prototypes at Rechlin, the Luftwaffe ordered 1000 machines, but none were ever delivered.

CA 316

The Ca 316 was a twin-float seaplane for reconnaissance duties with the Regia Marina (Italian Navy). Intended to replace the Ro 43 biplanes, the Ca 316 was to have been catapult-launched from warships of the R.M. Powered by two 450 h.p. Piaggio P.VII C.16 radial engines, only a few prototypes were completed.

Performance included a maximum speed of 204 m.p.h., a cruising speed of 186 m.p.h., a service ceiling of 19,680 ft., and a range of 994

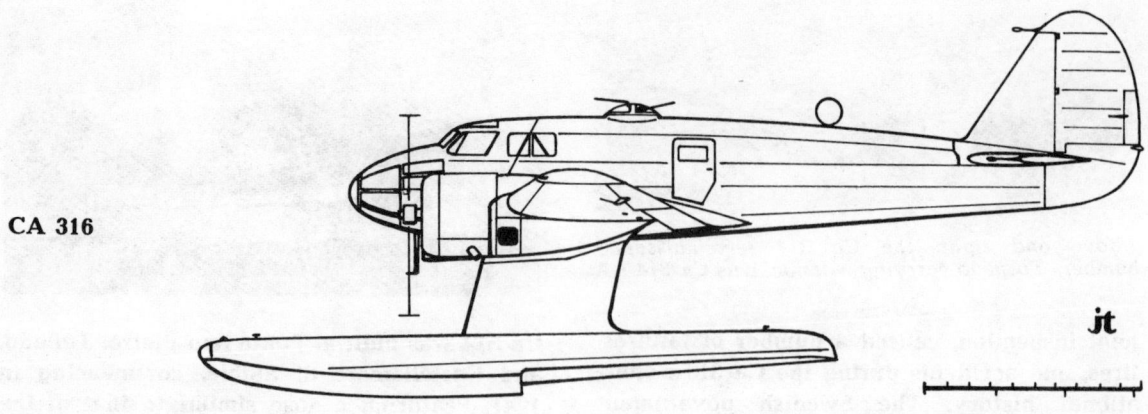

CA 316

The Ca 316 naval reconnaissance seaplane.

miles. Span was 52 ft. 2 in., length 42 ft. 3½ in., height 16 ft. 9 in., and wing area 409 sq. ft. Armament consisted of a 12.7-mm. machine gun in the port wing root and a 7.7-mm. gun in a Lanciani dorsal turret; 880 lb. of bombs or a single torpedo made up the offensive load. The first prototype flew in August, 1940. 500 h.p. P.VII C.35 radials were proposed for production machines, which in the event never materialized, priority having been given to the Ca 313 and Ca 314.

CA 325
The Ca 325 was a development of the Ca 135 to have been powered by 1450 h.p. eighteen-cylinder Isotta-Fraschini Asso L.180 I.R.C.C.45 radial engines. Studied in 1939, the Ca 325 was built in mock-up form only.

CA 330
The Ca 330 was a 1939 design for a twin-engined light reconnaissance bomber which also halted at the mock-up stage. As no orders were placed for the Ca 330 by the Air Ministry, work was transferred to the Ca 331 project.

CA 331
The first Bergamaschi machine with all-metal stressed-skin structure, the Ca 331 Raffica (Squall) flew for the first time on August 31, 1940. Designed as a twin-engined light reconnaissance bomber, the prototype achieved a maximum speed of 300 m.p.h. at 16,750 ft. and demonstrated excellent handling qualities in tests at Guidonia. The engines were Isotta-Fraschini Delta R.C.40 in-line air-cooled units of only 770 h.p. each.

Although the Regia Aeronautica did not express immediate interest, a visiting German

The prototype Ca 331A, first flown in 1940, had beautiful fuselage contours.

The Ca 331A was the first Bergamaschi design with all-metal stressed-skin structure.

technical group was highly impressed, and the prototype was tested at Rechlin in 1942 with production for the Luftwaffe in mind. However, aluminum shortages thwarted these plans. The original reconnaissance bomber version, the Ca 331A, was tested with three 12.7-mm. SAFAT machine guns, two in the wing roots and one in a Caproni Lanciani dorsal turret, plus a 7.7-mm. gun in a retractable ventral turret. A 2200 lb. bomb load could be carried.

Second thoughts by the Regia Aeronautica led to the adoption of the design in three-seat night fighter form, with the designation Ca 331B. The streamlined transparent nose of the Ca 331A (rather like that of the Heinkel He 111P & H series) gave way to a stepped, "solid" nose mounting six 12.7-mm. SAFAT machine guns. 840 h.p. Delta IV engines were mounted. By September 1943, the Ca 331B was almost ready for mass production, with components to be manufactured at Ponte San Pietro, Reggio Emilia, and Trento. The two existing prototypes of the Ca 331B were dismantled by the Germans and production plans dropped after the Italian surrender.

The night fighter was tested with various forward-firing armament, including two 12.7-mm. machine guns and four 20-mm. Mauser cannon, or six of the lighter Ikaria 20-mm. cannon, in a ventral bulge. Defensive armament was two 12.7-mm. machine guns in dorsal and ventral positions. The bomb bay could house 2200 lb. of small bombs, one 1100 lb. bomb, or a 137-gal. auxilliary fuel tank. Two underwing tanks or 220 lb. bombs could also be carried. Studies for the mounting of a ventral 37-mm. cannon were made, and 1475 h.p. FIAT R.A.1050 R.C.58 (DB 605A-1) engines were considered for installation. With these units, estimated maximum speed was in the region of 400 m.p.h.

Performance of the Delta IV-powered Ca 331B included a maximum speed of 314 m.p.h. at

Above and below, the Ca 331B night fighter featured a revised nose with up to six 20-mm. cannon.

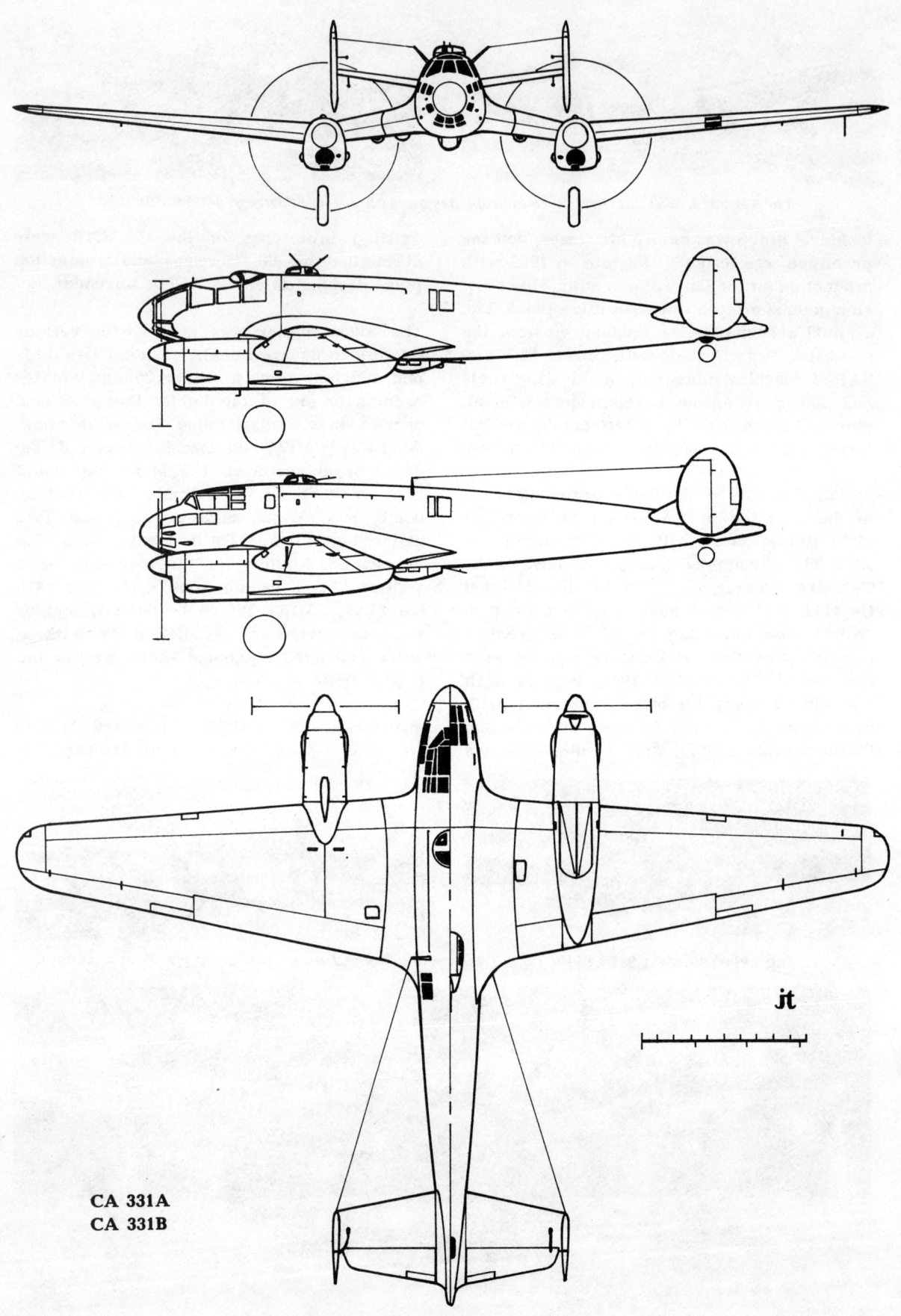

CA 331A
CA 331B

The Ca 335, or S.A.B.C.A. S. 47, was to have been built in quantity by the Belgian firm.

17,400 ft., a cruising speed of 280 m.p.h., a range of 994 miles, and a service ceiling of 26,550 ft. Climbing time to 13,120 ft. was 9 min. 35 sec. Weights were 10,140 lb. empty and 14,992 lb. loaded. The Ca 331B had a span of 53 ft. 9¾ in., a length of 38 ft. 6½ in., a height of 10 ft. 6¼ in., and a wing area of 414.4 sq. ft.

CA 335

Originally powered by a radial engine and designated Ca 335 Maestrale (Mistral), this two-seat fighter/reconnaissance monoplane was designed in 1938 at Ponte San Pietro, but after the construction of the first prototype in 1939, the manufacturing license was sold to S.A.B.C.A. (Société Anonyme Belge de Constructions Aeronautiques) of Brussels, Belgium. Powered by an 860 h.p. Hispano-Suiza 12 Ycrs twelve-cylinder vee liquid-cooled engine and designated S.47, the Belgian version was to have been built in quantity, but this was prevented by the overwhelming German invasion. Armament comprised one 20-mm. cannon firing through the airscrew hub, two 7.7-mm. Browning machine guns in the wings, and one flexible hand-held gun in the rear cockpit. Empty weight was 4950 lb. and loaded weight varied from 6545 lb. (fighter) and 7128 lb. (reconnaissance) to 7370 lb. for attack.

Performance included a maximum speed of 311 m.p.h. at 13,780 ft., a service ceiling of 32,800 ft., and a range of 978 miles, or a duration of 2 hrs. (fighter) to 4 hrs. 30 min. (reconnaissance). The S.47 fighter climbed to 6560 ft. in 3 min. 30 sec., to 13,120 ft. in 7 min. 20 sec., and to 19,680 ft. in 12 min. 20 sec. Dimensions were: span 43 ft. 3 in., length 34 ft. 9 in., height 10 ft. 6 in., and wing area 254 sq. ft.

The Ca 355 dive bomber was a smaller development of the Ca 335 with an Isotta-Fraschini Delta engine.

CA 350

The Ca 350 was a projected all-metal two-seat interceptor fighter to be powered by a 1250 h.p. Isotta-Fraschini Zeta R.C.42 twenty-four-cylinder X air-cooled engine. Dating from 1939, the design was expected to weigh 9700 lb. fully loaded and to achieve 403 m.p.h. However, the project was abandoned and construction halted. Span was 43 ft. $7^{1}/_{4}$ in.

CA 355

Flown for the first time in January, 1941, the Ca 355 was a smaller dive bomber development of the Ca 335/S.47. Of mixed construction, the sole Ca 355 prototype employed an 850 h.p. Isotta-Fraschini Delta IV twelve-cylinder air-cooled engine and a rearward-retracting landing gear based on that of the Curtiss P-40. Split dive brakes were fitted to the trailing edges of the wings and a swinging bomb harness guided a single 1100-lb. weapon. In spite of successful trials, the Ca 355 did not receive any production orders. No defensive armament was fitted to the prototype. Empty and loaded weights were 4356 lb. and 7810 lb. Span was 42 ft. 6 in., length 32 ft. 7 in., and height 10 ft. 4 in. Performance included a maximum speed of 302 m.p.h. and a cruising speed of 236 m.p.h.

CA 365

The Ca 365 was development of the Ca 135 projected with two 1250 h.p. Isotta-Fraschini Zeta R.C.42 twenty-four-cylinder X engines, but it did not progress past the drawing board.

CA 370

The Ca 370 was a further development of the Ca 331 which also halted at the design stage. Again twenty-four cylinder Zetas were the intended power units. The Ca 370 had an estimated maximum speed of 383 m.p.h.

CA 380

A twin-engined, twin-boom, high-altitude two-seat fighter bomber designed in answer to the DeHavilland Mosquito, the Ca 380 Corsaro (Corsair) was partially completed at the time of the Armistice but never flew. The pilot and radio operator were seated back to back in the starboard boom, with fuel and equipment in the port boom. The Ca 380 was to have been powered by 1475 h.p. Daimler Benz DB 605 engines, although 1550 h.p. DB 603 units were contemplated as later production replacements. Armament was four 20-mm. Mauser cannon in a pod under the wing center section and two 12.7-mm. SAFAT machine guns in the wings outboard of the airscrew discs. Estimated performance was: maximum speed 400 m.p.h. at 23,525 ft., maximum continuous cruising speed 311 m.p.h., range 1336-1616 miles, service ceiling 34,450 ft., and climb to 19,680 ft. in 7 min. 9 sec. Loaded weight was 16,383 lb. Dimensions included a span of 52 ft. 6 in., a length of 39 ft. $0^{1}/_{2}$ in., a height (in horizontal attitude) of 12 ft. 6 in., and a wing area of 432.7 sq. ft.

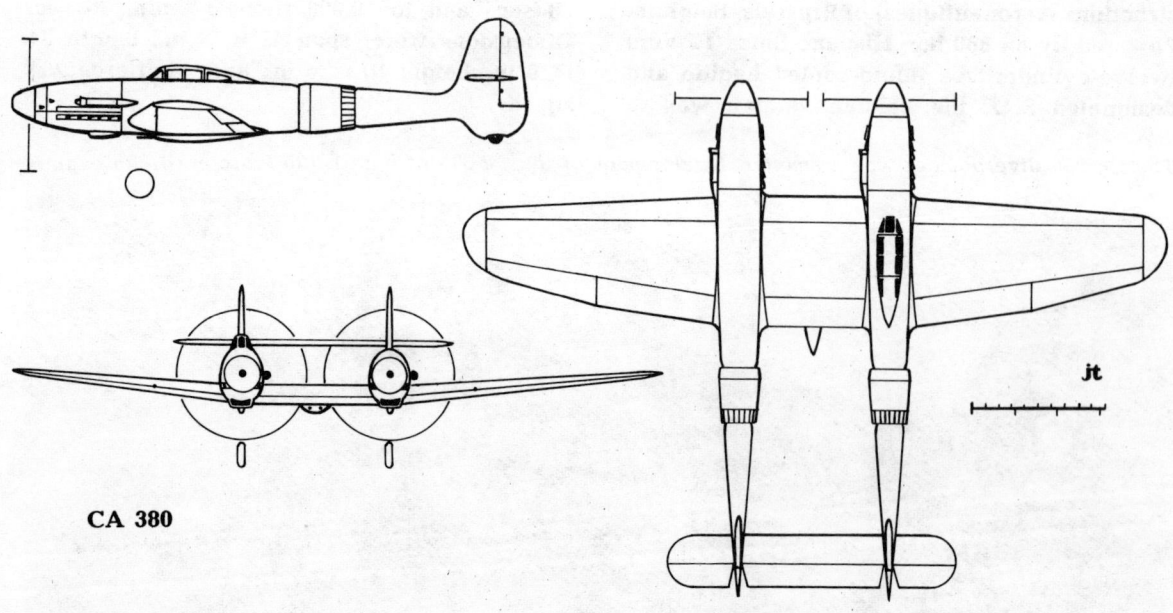

CA 380

CAPRONI VIZZOLA
Caproni Vizzola S.A.

Originally the Scuola di Aviazione Caproni, one of the earliest Italian flying schools, Caproni Vizzola S.A. of Vizzola Ticino, Varese, was modernized and expanded in the mid-1930's and began the manufacture of various aircraft components. Caproni Vizzola modified a number of Ca 101 and Ca 133 transports for colonial service, and carried out sub-contract work on the Breda 65. In 1937 the firm began original work in its own design office under Ing. Fabrizi.

F.4

Developed in 1938 in parallel with the similar radial-engined F.5, the Caproni Vizzola F.4 low-wing single-seat fighter was originally to have employed a 960 h.p. Isotta-Fraschini Asso 121 R.C. 40 twelve-cylinder vee engine, but the decision was made instead to incorporate an 1175 h.p. Daimler Benz DB 601A twelve-cylinder engine, delaying flight trials until 1940. The F.4 successfully completed these tests, demonstrating excellent maneuvrability, but was dropped in favor of the more advanced DB 605-powered F.6.

The F.4 was of mixed construction, with plywood-covered two-spar wooden wing and welded steel tube fuselage covered with duralumin skin. Inward-retracting landing gear was fitted. Armament comprised two forward-firing 12.7-mm. Breda-SAFAT machine guns mounted in the fuselage sides above the wing roots. Empty and loaded weights were 5428 lb. and 6614 lb. respectively. Performance included a maximum speed of 342 m.p.h. at 12,500 ft., a cruising speed of 304 m.p.h., a range of 466 miles, and a service ceiling of 32,800 ft. Dimensions were: span 37 ft. $0^7/_8$ in., length 29 ft. $2^1/_3$ in., height 9 ft. $6^1/_8$ in., and wing area 189.5 sq. ft.

F.5

The F.5, although designed concurrently, actually preceded the F.4 in flight tests by well over a year; it had an almost identical airframe mounting an 870 h.p. FIAT A.74 R.C.38 fourteen-cylinder radial engine. The F.5 was one of the new generation of Italian fighter monoplanes appearing in the late 1930's which included the FIAT G.50, Macchi C.200, Meridi-

The F.5 single-seat fighter, fourteen of which served as night fighters in defense of Rome. (MM 413)

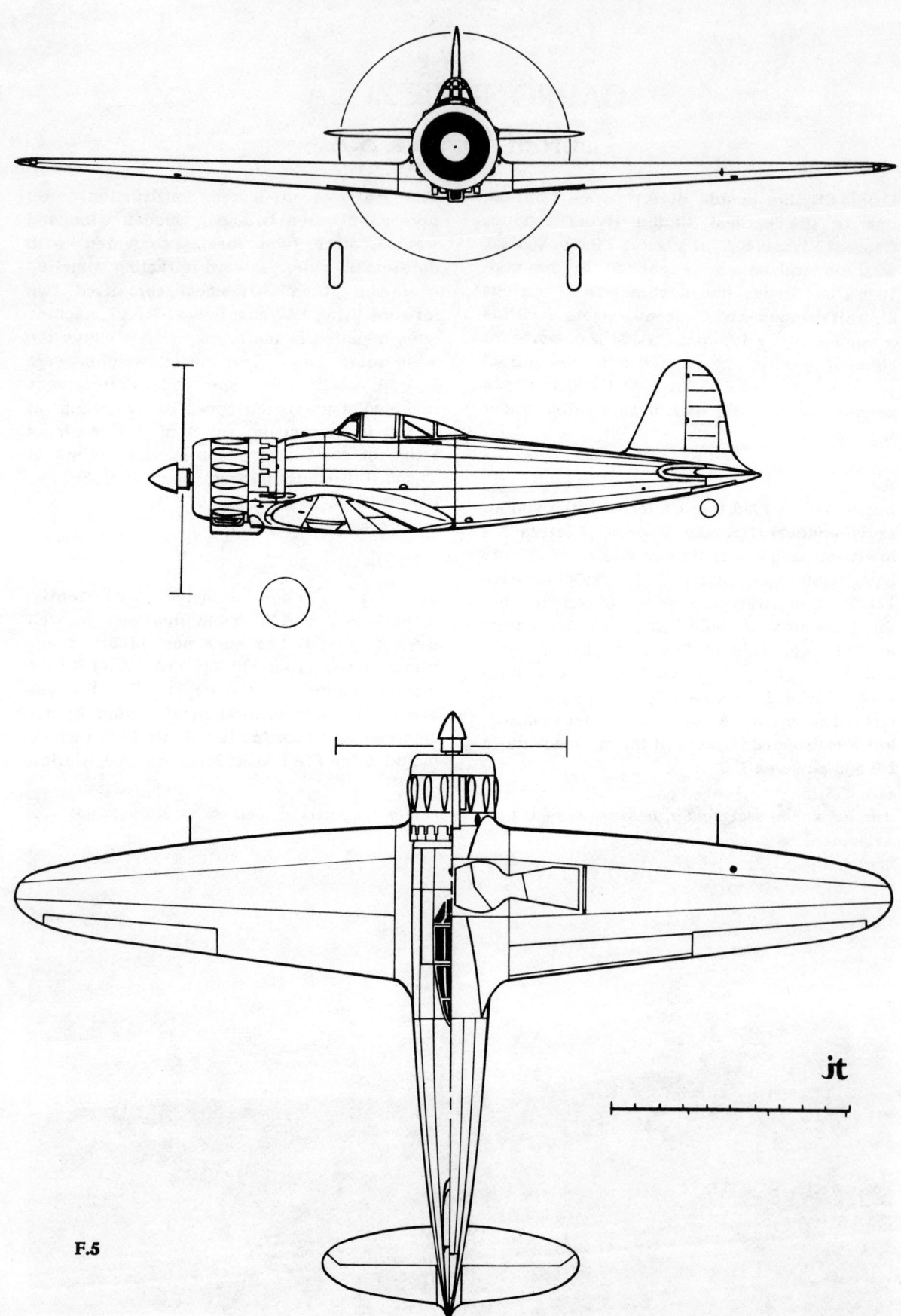

F.5

Left, the F.4 with DB 601A engine. Above, the prototype F.5, flown for the first time in early 1939.

onali Ro 51, Reggiane Re 2000, and Aeronautica Umbra T.18. All of these aircraft were powered by the same FIAT A.74 radial engine except the Re 2000 and T.18, which employed Piaggio and FIAT A.80 units, respectively. The Caproni Vizzola F.5 competed in 1939 trials with the G.50 and MC.200, and fourteen pre-production aircraft were ordered by the Air Ministry.

These differed from the prototype in having a revised cockpit canopy, extra fuel tank, non-retractable tailwheel, and enlarged fin and rudder. The pre-production examples were assigned to the 51° Stormo of the 8a Brigata Caccia Terrestre (land-based fighters), and given the task of defending the Rome area at night, along with the standard FIAT CR.42's and G.50's.

The F.5 featured a variable-incidence tailplane and ailerons which drooped automatically, assisting the flaps, on landing approaches. Armament was identical to that of the F.4. Empty and loaded weights were 4078 lb. and 5181 lb. Dimensions were: span 37 ft. 0⁷/₈ in., length 25 ft. 11 in., height 9 ft. 10 in., and wing area 189.5 sq. ft. Performance included a maximum speed of 317 m.p.h. at 9840 ft., a cruising speed of 292 m.p.h., a range of 373-621 miles, and a service ceiling of 31,170 ft. The F.5 could climb to 21,325 ft. in 6 min. 30 sec.

Two unrealized projects incorporating different engines were the F.5bis, with an 1175 h.p. Alfa Romeo R.A.1000 R.C.44-1a (license-built DB 601A-1) Monsonie (Monsoon) liquid-cooled unit, and the F.5 Gamma, a one or two-seat advanced trainer powered by a 540 h.p. Isotta-Fraschini Gamma R.C.35 IS air-cooled engine. The single-seat F.5 Gamma, mounting one 7.7-mm. Breda-SAFAT machine gun, had an estimated maximum speed of 254 m.p.h.

Above right and below, the F.6M, powered by a 1475 h.p. DB 605A liquid-cooled engine. (MM 481)

F.6

The first F.6 was created by mounting a 1475 h.p. Daimler Benz DB 605A in one of the pre-production F.5 airframes. Further prototypes featured all-metal construction, however, and were designated F.6M (metallico). The license-built version of the DB 605A, the FIAT R.A.1050 R.C.58 Tifone, was to have powered subsequent production machines. Armament was four 12.7-mm. Breda-SAFAT machine guns. Performance included a maximum speed of 353 m.p.h. at 16,400 ft., a cruising speed of 296 m.p.h., a range of 590 miles, and a service ceiling of 34,450 ft. The F.6M could climb to 19,685 ft. in 5 min. 30 sec. Dimensions included a span of 37 ft. $0^7/_8$ in., a length of 30 ft. $0^1/_4$ in., a height of 9 ft. $10^2/_3$ in., and a wing area of 189.5 sq. ft.

The twenty-four cylinder 1150 h.p. Isotta-Fraschini Zeta R.C.35 X-type unit was also proposed for the fighter, but development troubles delayed the actual installation of the engine until mid-1943, by which time it was designated Zeta R.C.25/60. Fitted with a Wright-type two-speed supercharger, it produced 1250 h.p. Although the Zeta-powered F.6MZ completed flight tests satisfactorily, the Armistice brought an end to the program. The F.6MZ mounted two 12.7-mm. and two 7.7-mm. machine guns, and weighed 7382 lb. empty and 9022 lb. fully loaded. Maximum and cruising speeds were 404 m.p.h. and 367 m.p.h. respectively; range was 851 miles and service ceiling 26,240 ft. Dimensions included a span of 38 ft. $9^1/_3$ in., a length of 29 ft. $6^3/_4$ in., a height of 9 ft. $10^2/_3$ in., and a wing area of 198.6 sq. ft.

F.7

The F.7 was an extensively revised and lightened development of the F.6 which was to have employed the 1175 h.p. Alfa Romeo R.C.44-1a Monsonie engine. With a much smaller fuselage, the F.7 was designed to accommodate one 20-mm. Mauser MG 151 cannon and two 12.7-mm. Breda-SAFAT machine guns. It was expected to attain a maximum speed of 373 m.p.h. at 18,370 ft. and a range of 777 miles, and to climb to 13,120 ft. in 3 min. 40 sec. The design had not progressed past the planning stage by September, 1943.

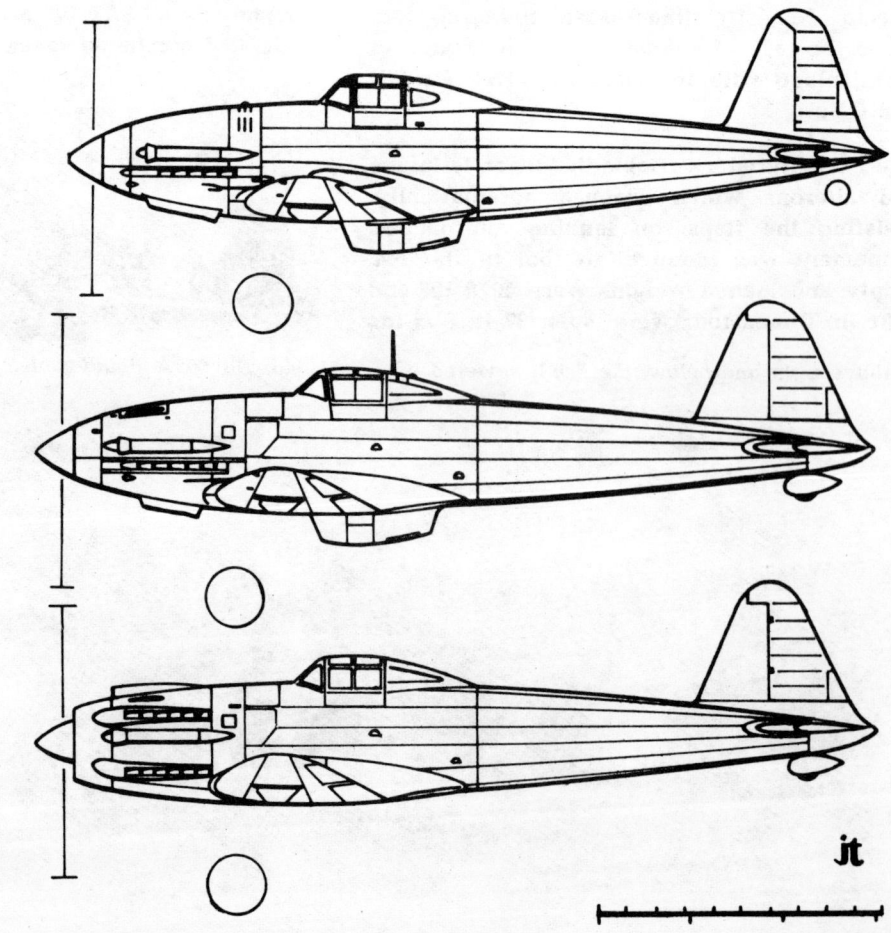

F.4

F.6M

F.6MZ

C.M.A.S.A.
Costruzioni Meccaniche Aeronautiche S.A. (FIAT)

C.M.A.S.A., which became a subsidiary of FIAT in 1929, was founded in 1922 at the ex-Gallinari works at Marina di Pisa, under the name Società di Costruzioni Meccaniche di Pisa. Originally concerned with the manufacture of Dornier aircraft under license, the firm built a number of Do E, Do F, Dolfin, and Wal machines, customers being the navies of Netherlands and Spain, the Soviet Air Force, and the Argentine, Yugoslav, and Chilean Naval Air Forces. In 1930 the company changed its name to Costruzioni Meccaniche Aeronautiche S.A. (FIAT), and built a few FIAT CR.20 Idro fighter seaplanes. C.M.A.S.A. became a specialist constructor for the organization, modifying standard FIAT products for alternate uses, although it built several designs of its own conception. In 1932 C.M.A.S.A. built the CR. Asso, a modification of the standard Rosatelli-designed fighter, incorporating a 450 h.p. Isotta-Fraschini Asso engine.

MF.4

The MF.4 (MF = Marina FIAT) was a two/three-seat reconnaissance flying boat flown for the first time in 1933. Powered by a 600 h.p. Piaggio Stella IX R radial engine mounted ahead of the wing, the MF.4 showed much Dornier influence, including the characteristic sponsons. With empty and loaded weights of 4035 lb. and 6052 lb. respectively, the MF.4 featured gun positions in the bow and amidships. The few remaining available details are: wing area 441.2 sq. ft., maximum speed 137 m.p.h., ceiling 18,370 ft., and endurance 6 hrs. 45 min.

MF.5

A twin-engined, all-metal, ten-passenger commercial flying boat developed from the Wal, the MF.5 also flew in 1933, powered by 700/750 h.p. FIAT A.24 R twelve-cylinder liquid-cooled vee engines. Again employing the familiar Dornier-type sponsons, the MF.5 was in effect a sesquiplane. Empty and loaded weights were 10,391 lb. and 16,280 lb. Performance included a maximum speed of 141 m.p.h., a cruising speed of 118 m.p.h., and an alighting speed of 61 m.p.h. Range was 497-621 miles, and ceiling 16,400 ft. The MF.5 climbed to 6560 ft. in 10 min. 3 sec., to 9840 ft. in 19 min. 30 sec., and to 13,120 ft. in 35 min. 10 sec. Dimensions included a span of 76 ft., a length of 59 ft. 10 in., a height of 18 ft. 10 in., and a wing area of 1038.4 sq. ft.

Above, the MF.4 and MF.5 (Wal) flying boats. Below, the MF.6 seaplane and MF.10 flying boat.

MF.6

The MF.6 two-seat catapult reconnaissance seaplane of 1934 was a biplane featuring a single main float and auxilliary wing floats, and employing a Piaggio-built Jupiter VI radial engine of 575 h.p. The MF.6 weighed 3267 lb. empty and 5060 lb. fully loaded. It had a maximum speed of 161 m.p.h., an alighting speed of 57 m.p.h., a range of 745-807 miles, and could climb to its ceiling of 16,400 ft. in 26 minutes. Dimensions were: span 36 ft. 5 in., length 30 ft. 6 in., height 11 ft. 8 in., and wing area 370 sq. ft. A single rear gun was fitted. With a 700 h.p. Hornet radial, the MF.6 had a maximum speed of 180 m.p.h. at 6560 ft.; it climbed to 16,400 ft. in 12 min.

MF.10

Powered by a 600 h.p. FIAT A.30 RA engine driving a pusher airscrew, the MF.10 light reconnaissance flying boat was intended to be catapulted from warships. First flown in 1935, the MF.10 biplane featured open pilot's and observer's cockpits ahead of the wings. Maximum and alighting speeds were 171 m.p.h. and 61 m.p.h.; range was 795 miles, and ceiling 24,600 ft. The MF.10 climbed to 6560 ft. in 5 minutes, and to 16,400 ft. in 16 minutes. Dimensions were: span 38 ft. 4 in., length 30 ft. 8 in., height 10 ft. 7 in., and wing area 382 sq. ft. Empty and loaded weights were 3410 lb. and 5203 lb.

G.8

Designed by Ing. Giuseppe Gabrielli, the G.8 was a two-seat touring and training biplane produced in 1934. Featuring Warren-type wing bracing and a 135 h.p. FIAT A.54 seven-cylinder radial engine in a Townend ring cowling, the G.8 had tandem open cockpits with dual controls. It weighed 1232 lb. empty and 1842 lb. loaded. Maximum, cruising, and landing speeds were 132 m.p.h., 114 m.p.h., and 52 m.p.h. respectively. Ceiling was 17,056 ft. and range 575-807 miles. The G.8 climbed to 6560 ft. in 5 min. 14 sec., and to 9840 ft. in 17 min. 41 sec. Dimensions were: span 28 ft. 9 in., length 22 ft. 11 in., height 8 ft. 2 in., and wing area 203.7 sq. ft.

A few G.8 trainers were used by the Regia Aeronautica. At least one privately-owned

Above left, a surviving G.8 trainer. Right, a prewar Regia Aeronautica example. The original G.8, built in 1934, is shown below. Note typical FIAT Warren wing-bracing.

example remained in flying condition as late as 1956.

B.G.A.
Bearing a great similarity to its close relative the FIAT BR.20, the B.G.A. was an experimental prototype twin-engined bomber with retractable landing gear, built at C.M.A.S.A. in 1936. Although classed as a heavy bomber at the time, it would have been in the medium bomber category had it been developed up to the outbreak of the Second World War. The B.G.A. was a mid-wing monoplane powered by 1050 h.p. FIAT A.80 R.C.41 radial engines.

The forward section of the fuselage was of all-metal monocoque construction, while the rear part was of fabric-covered welded steel tubing. The cantilever wings featured slotted flaps, and automatic leading-edge slots extending along the outboard sections. Defensive armament was fitted in a nose turret above the bombardier's position, and in dorsal and ventral positions amidships. Empty and loaded weights were 13,420 lb. and 20,636 lb. respectively. Performance included maximum and landing speeds of 261 m.p.h. and 68 m.p.h., a ceiling of 22,960 ft., and a range of 1242 miles. Dimensions were: span 70 ft. 4 in., length 51 ft. 7 in., height 15 ft. 11 in., and wing area 797.6 sq. ft.

RS.14
Probably the best-known C.M.A.S.A. product was the RS.14 all-metal, twin-engined, twin-

The prototype RS.14 reconnaissance floatplane.

float reconnaissance seaplane, flown for the first time in 1938. 840 h.p. FIAT A.74 R.C.38 radial engines were fitted. Initially, the prototype RS.14 was flown without provision for armament, but production models mounted one 12.7-mm. machine gun in a dorsal turret and three 7.7-mm. guns firing from two lateral hatches and from the nose position. Crew was 4-5 men. The RS.14B production models had ventral gondolas housing torpedoes or bombs, loads being two 352-lb. bombs, four 220-lb. bombs, or sixteen 33-lb. bombs. The RS.14C was an air-sea rescue version omitting the gondola.

Although placed in production, the RS.14 was not built in large quantities, the Cant Z.506B and Savoia-Marchetti SM.79 having already established themselves in the reconnaissance and torpedo-bombing roles. The RS.14 did not enter service until after Italy's entry into the war. By the time of the Italian surrender in September, 1943, some 39 RS.14's equipped various units of the Regia Marina; of these aircraft only 18 were serviceable. The RS.14

An RS.14 Serie III reconnaissance bomber floatplane. Armament was four machine guns. (MM 35653)

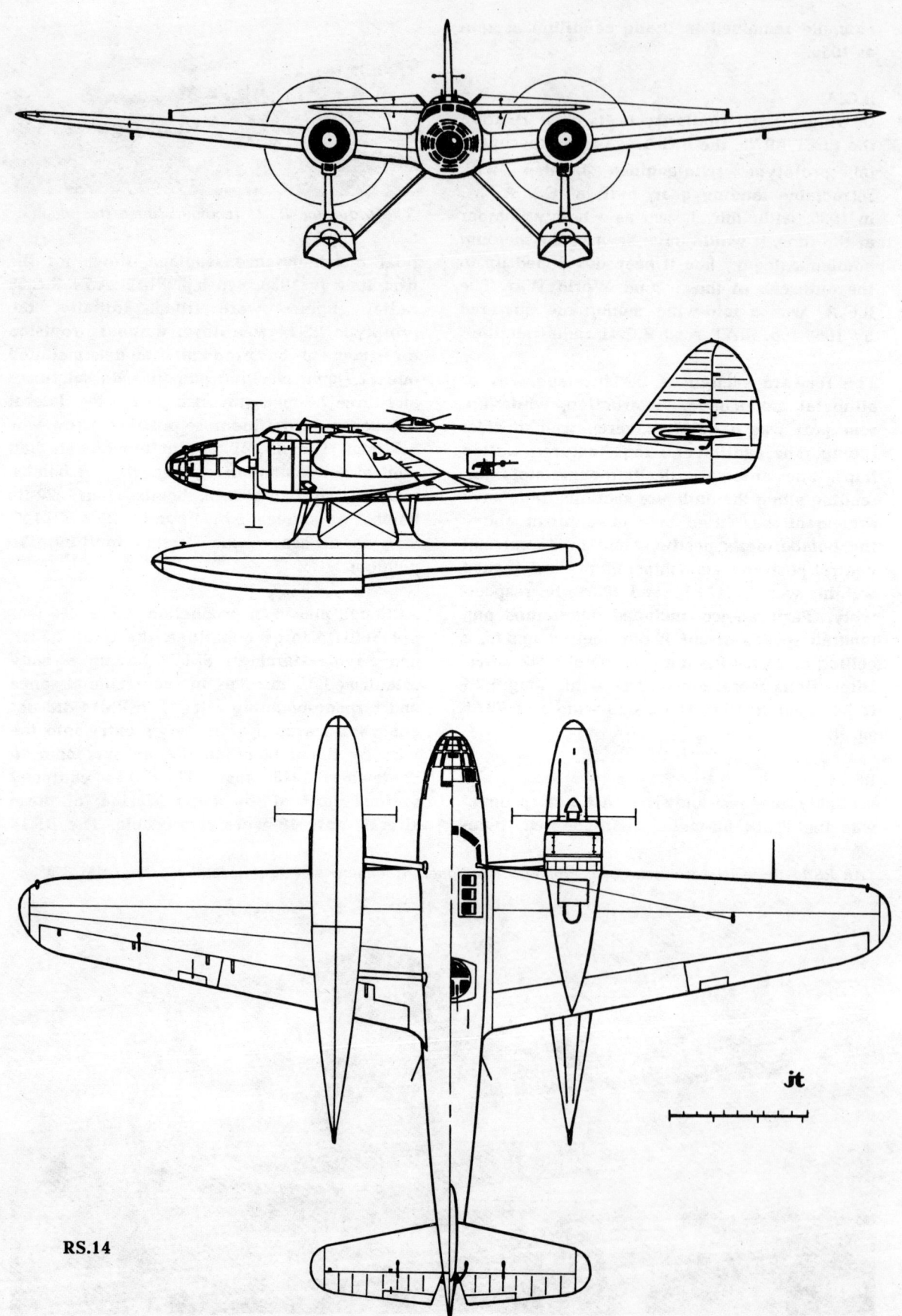

RS.14

Above, an RS.14. Below, an RS.14B with ventral gondola for torpedoes or bombs.

was operated by the Aviazione Alto Tirreno (upper Tyrrhenian Sea), Aviazione Alto Adriatico (upper Adriatic), Aviazione Basso Tirreno (lower Tyrrhenian), Aviazione Jonio e Basso Adriatico (Ionian islands and lower Adriatic), and Aviazione Sardegna (Sardinia).

The RS.14 weighed 12,100 lb. empty and 18,700 lb. fully loaded. Dimensions included a span of 63 ft. 11¾ in., a length of 44 ft. 11 in., a height of 17 ft. 9 in., and a wing area of 538 sq. ft. Maximum speed was 242 m.p.h. at 15,400

RS.14B

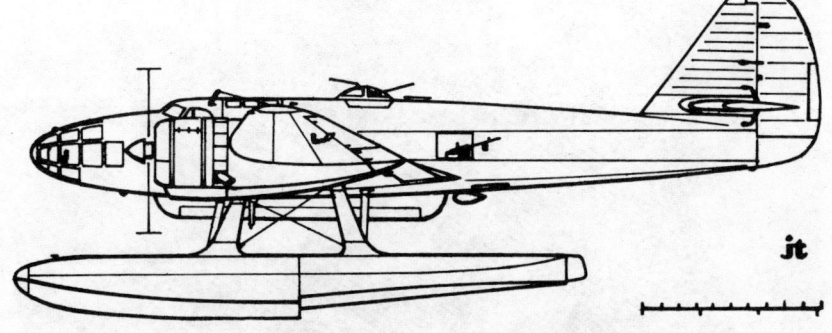

The AS.14 was a land-based development of the RS.14. The sole prototype was destroyed in 1943.

ft., ceiling 16,400 ft., and range 1553 miles.

AS.14

In 1942 a land-based attack version was built, designated AS.14. Employing the same engines and basic airframe, it had retractable landing gear in place of the twin floats.

The sole prototype, employing the same 840 h.p. A.74 R.C.38 engines, was a 3/4-seat model with a projected armament of one 45-mm. cannon, to be mounted in the nose, and two 12.7-mm. and two 7.7-mm. machine guns. Empty and loaded weights were 11,000 lb. and 17,930 lb. respectively. Maximum speed was 273 m.p.h., range 932 miles, and ceiling 24,600 ft. Dimensions were: span 63 ft. 11¾ in., length 43 ft. 9½ in., and wing area 538 sq. ft. The AS.14 was extensively tested at Guidonia, where it was finally destroyed at the time of the Armistice.

ICR.42

The ICR.42 was an experimental seaplane version of the FIAT CR.42 fighter. Except for the employment of twin metal floats, the ICR.42, constructed by C.M.A.S.A. and first flown in 1940, was identical to the well-known

This impression of the ICR.42 float fighter is actually a retouched photograph of the prototype CR.42.

The G.50B was a two-seat training version of the Freccia single-seat fighter. (MM 3615)

Falco biplane, described in a separate section of this book. Using the same 840 h.p. FIAT A.74 R.C.38 radial engine, the ICR.42 weighed 4070 lb. empty and 5335 lb. loaded, both figures being 286 lb. higher than those of the standard model. Maximum speed was 262 m.p.h., representing a 5 m.p.h. decrease. Range and ceiling of the ICR.42 were respectively 598 miles and 31,150 ft. Length was increased $9^{1}/_{4}$ in. by the fitting of floats, to 28 ft.

G.50B

Developed by C.M.A.S.A. from the standard FIAT G.50 Freccia single-seat fighter, the tandem two-seat G.50B was an unarmed training version which flew for the first time on April 30, 1940. The power unit was again the 840 h.p. A.74 R.C.38 radial. Empty and loaded weights were 4268 lb. and 5148 lb., representing decreases of 51 lb. and 136 lb. respectively, due to the omission of armament. Maximum speed was 283 m.p.h., range 310 miles, and ceiling 31,150 ft. One hundred G.50B's were built for Regia Aeronautica training squadrons.

G.50V

Another development of the Freccia by C.M.A.S.A. was the G.50V, incorporating a 1050 h.p. Daimler Benz DB 601A liquid-cooled engine in a standard G.50 airframe. The G.50V was essentially an experimental prototype for a production version to be designated G.52, which was later dropped in favor of the more advanced G.55. Flown for the first time on August 25, 1941, the G.50V reached 360 m.p.h. during tests. Empty and loaded weights were 5139 lb. and 6380 lb. respectively. Range was 777 miles, and ceiling 36,080 ft. Except for the increased length of 28 ft. $5^{1}/_{3}$ in., the dimensions of the G.50V matched those of the standard G.50 fighter. Armament was the same: two 12.7-mm. machine guns mounted in the cowl.

Below and right, two views of a G.50B trainer in wartime camouflage. Note non-standard white wing stripe. Just visible in background is FN.305.

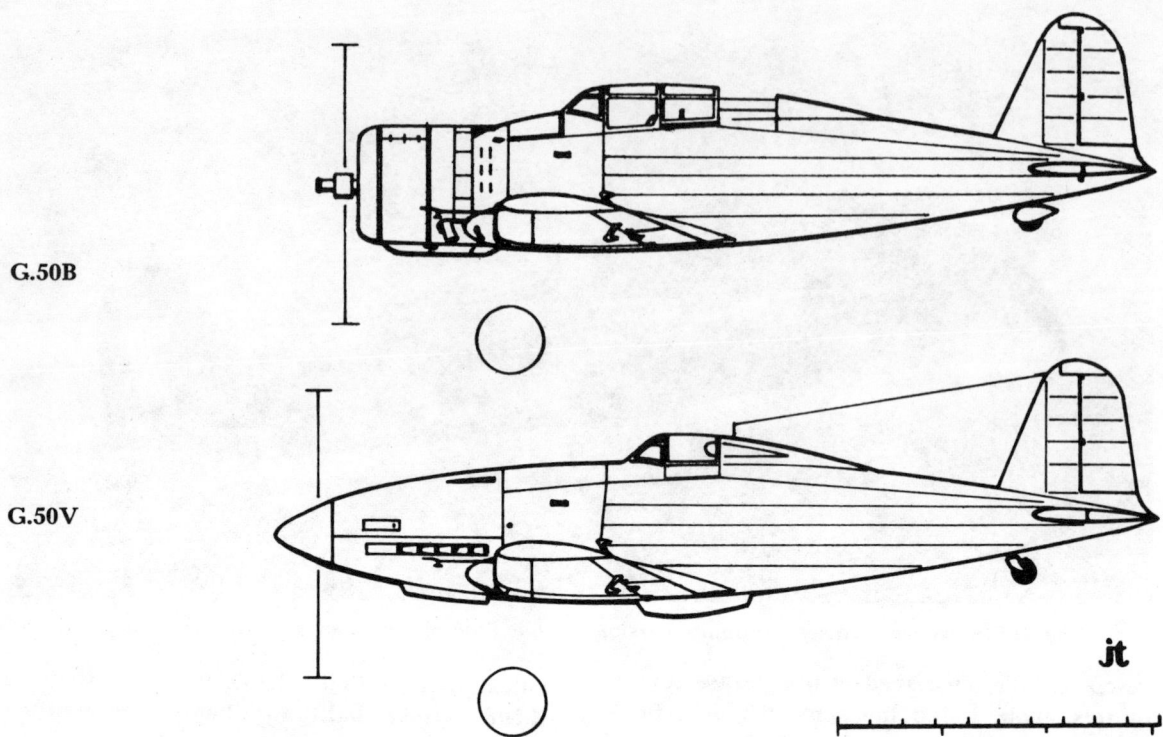

G.50B

G.50V

CS.15

The CS.15 high-speed monoplane, designed for an attempt on the World's Air Speed Record, was under construction in 1939 at C.M.A.S.A., but it finally had to be abandoned after Italy was firmly involved in the Second World War. To have been powered by the experimental 2250 h.p. FIAT AS.8 sixteen-cylinder vee engine (not actually completed until 1941), the CS.15 employed surface evaporation cooling and had an estimated maximum speed of 529 m.p.h., far in excess of any contemporary aircraft, including the record-holding Messerschmitt "Me 109R" (Me 209 V1).

Empty and loaded weights were 4213 lb. and 5060 lb. respectively. Span was 34 ft, $5^{1}/_{3}$ in. Endurance was expected to be approximately 30 minutes.

JS.54

The JS.54 was never more than a project. Under consideration during 1941-43, it was to have been a large six-engined civil flying boat. The plans were dropped altogether in September, 1943. No other information is available.

A photograph of a standard G.50 retouched to show the DB 601A installation of the experimental G.50V.

C.N.A.
Compagnia Nazionale Aeronautica (Caproni)

Founded in 1920 by Count Giovanni Bonmartini, the Compagnia Nazionale Aeronautica was originally composed of a group of ex-World War I airmen interested in contributing to the progress of Italian aviation. From 1921 until 1928 C.N.A. operated a flying school at the Cerveteri airfield in Rome, training 355 new pilots during this period. Under the aegis of C.N.A. was the Pegna-Bonmartini Costruzioni Navali Aeronautiche, a small factory which manufactured experimental aircraft for the Italian government. In 1923 the Pegna-Bonmartini interests were transferred to Piaggio & C. in accordance with a directive issued by the Commissario per l'Aeronautica, and Ing. Pegna became chief designer for the Piaggio firm.

When C.N.A. built the new Littorio civil airport in Rome in 1928, transferring its school facilities to the new field, it also established a factory to build aircraft designed by other companies, in addition to aero engines and experimental aircraft of original design. C.N.A. built 188 aircraft under license, in addition to its own products.

DELTA
Built in 1931, the C.N.A. Delta was a three-engined cabin monoplane with fixed landing gear, capable of carrying six passengers or a corresponding complement of mail. The engines were 90-140 h.p. FIAT A.50, A.53, or A.54 seven-cylinder radials. A later version of the Delta employed two 200 h.p. DeHavilland Gipsy-Six in-line engines.

BETA
A single-engined two-seat high-wing monoplane, the Beta appeared in 1932, powered by a C.N.A. C-7 seven-cylinder radial engine of 200 h.p. The Beta set several international records, piloted by Renato Donati and Furio Niclot.

ETA
Also powered by the centrifugally-supercharged C.N.A. C-7 radial engine, the C.N.A. Eta was a one or two-seat parasol-wing lightplane of disarming simplicity, built in 1933. Piloted by Niclot and Lanciani, it set two international lightplane records for altitude. Early in the year the pair gained the seaplane

The Eta parasol monoplane was a simple one or two-seat machine which captured several altitude records in both land and seaplane form. Shown below is the single-seat model with 170 h.p. C-7 radial engine.

Left, the Delta trimotor. Right, the C.N.A. 25 high-wing cabin monoplane.

record for Category II with an altitude of 24,148 ft., raising this to 27,588 ft. in November. The following month, Niclot set the landplane record for Category II at 32,826 ft. In 1936, Chiesi and Rossetti set a 100-km. closed-circuit speed record for seaplanes of Category I at 122.75 m.p.h. The engine was a 150 h.p. C.N.A. C.VI in-line.

Powered by the 170 h.p. C-7 engine, the tandem dual-control landplane weighed 904 lb. empty and 1100 lb. loaded. Maximum speed was 136 m.p.h., landing speed 40 m.p.h., and climb to 19,680 ft. in 25 min. Dimensions were: span 32 ft. $9^{1}/_{2}$ in., length 21 ft. 4 in., and height 8 ft. 2 in. The seaplane had a maximum speed of 130 m.p.h. and climbed to 19,680 ft. in 35 min.

TETA

The C.N.A. Teta (Theta), also produced in 1933, was a two-seat light trainer, unusual in that it could be flown as a biplane, sesquiplane, or monoplane, simply by fitting or detaching the different surfaces. In this way it was possible to acquaint the student progressively with the greater sensitivity of control required by reductions in wing area and corresponding stability. The power unit was a 220 h.p. Alfa Romeo-built Lynx radial engine. Further details of this interesting trainer are unfortunately unavailable.

MERAH

The Merah, produced in 1934, was a two-seat, low-wing monoplane which was not constructed in series. It was powered by a C.N.A. engine of undisclosed type.

C.N.A. 15

Powered by a 150 h.p. C.N.A. C.VI IRC.43 six-cylinder inverted in-line engine, the C.N.A. 15 was a four-seat low-wing cabin monoplane designed in 1935. It was probably intended for the Littorio Rally. Specifications were: span 38 ft. $5^{1}/_{3}$ in., length 26 ft. $6^{7}/_{8}$ in., height 6 ft. $10^{2}/_{3}$ in., useful load 735 lb., maximum speed 143 m.p.h., landing speed 53 m.p.h., and ceiling 20,664 ft.

C.N.A. 25

Employing the same C.N.A. C.VI IRC.43

Except for its landing gear, the PM.1 was similar to the postwar tricycle-gear Macchi MB.308. (MM 417)

engine, the C.N.A. 25 was a concurrent high-wing four-seat cabin monoplane. The wing featured leading-edge slots and split ailerons, and was braced only by I-struts extending up from the streamlined wheel pants. Specifications were as for the C.N.A. 15, except: height 7 ft. $2^5/_8$ in., useful load 814 lb., and maximum speed 152 m.p.h.

PM.1

One of the few C.N.A. aircraft for which full data are available, the PM.1 was a two-seat private plane intended for training and sport flying. Powered by a 60 h.p. C.N.A. D-4 four-cylinder horizontally-opposed engine, it featured a high-mounted, plywood-covered cantilever wooden wing. The fuselage was also of plywood-covered wooden construction. Movable control surfaces were fabric-covered. Although the PM.1 had a conventional fixed two-wheel landing gear with tailskid, it bore a remarkable resemblance to the postwar, tricycle-geared Macchi MB.308. The PM.1 was designed by students of the Instituto di Costru-

The designation PM.1 indicated the first design of the Regio Politecnico di Milano. (MM 417)

zioni Aeronautiche del Regio Politecnico di Milano (Milan Polytechnic Institute), hence its designation.

Performance included a maximum speed of 112 m.p.h., a cruising speed of 96 m.p.h., a landing speed of 42 m.p.h., a service ceiling of 13,120 ft., and a cruising range of 373 miles. The PM.1 climbed to 3280 ft. in 6 min. Dimensions were: span 34 ft. $9^1/_3$ in., length 23 ft. $2^1/_3$ in., height 6 ft. 8 in., and wing area 151 sq. ft. Empty and loaded weights were 792 lb. and 1276 lb.

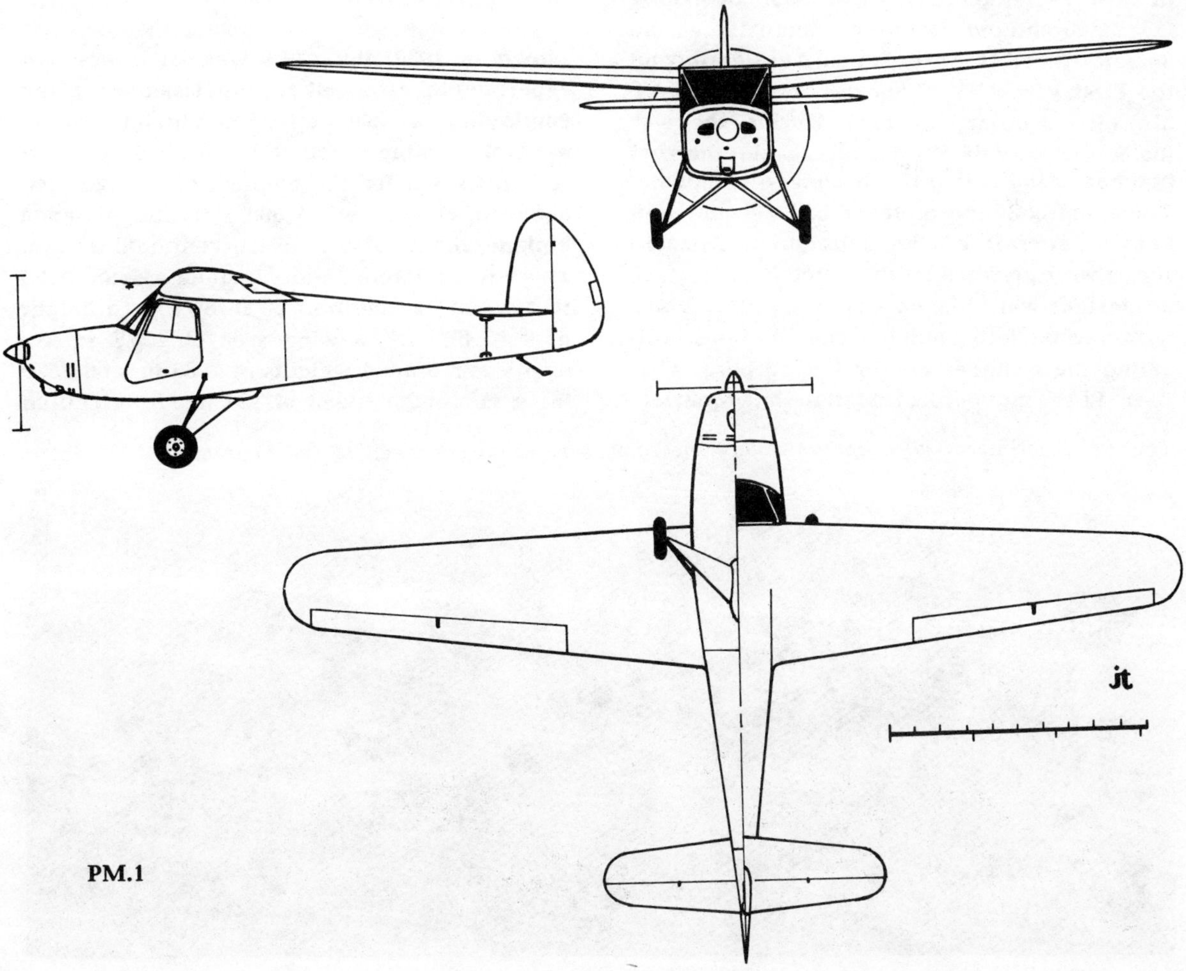

PM.1

FIAT
Società Anonima Aeronautica d'Italia

Originally founded at Turin in 1899 as the automobile manufacturing company, FIAT (Fabbrica Italiana Automobili Torino) soon branched out into all areas of transportation, becoming the strongest and most progressive industrial complex in Italy. It was one of the few airframe and aero engine manufacturers to survive the Second World War; today the motto Terra Mare Cielo (Land-Sea-Air) expresses the diverse interests of the firm.

FIAT began aero engine production in 1908 and, as the Società Italiana Aviazione, constructed its first aeroplane, a license-built Farman 5B biplane, in 1914. S.I.A. began building original designs, which included the S.P. (Savoia-Pomilio, after the designers) series, in 1916. The shipbuilding firm Gio. Ansaldo & C., which entered the aircraft industry as the Società Anonima Aeronautica Ansaldo during the First World War, became the main FIAT aircraft subsidiary in 1926. During the war the S.V.A. (Savoia Verduzio Ansaldo, the first two names indicating the designers) reconnaissance and bombing biplanes had become well known; aircraft of the subsequent Ansaldo series were prefixed by the letter A. After 1926 all designs were known simply as FIAT types with various letter-number combinations indicating the designer and/or the purpose. That year FIAT moved its aviation headquarters from the Mirafiori airport to the Ansaldo office, and the company became the Società Anonima Aeronautica d'Italia, which title prevailed during the period covered herein.

After the Second World War FIAT was quick to resume aircraft production (indeed the wartime G.55 fighter design was soon marketed to Argentina and Egypt with minor revisions), and although much of the output has been composed of license-built engines and airframes, the company has built a number of excellent Gabrielli-designed training aircraft as well as the first-rate G.91 close-support machine designed to NATO requirements. All of FIAT's present aircraft production is carried on under the name FIAT - Divisione Aviazione.

AN.1

Flown in 1930, the AN.1 was an interesting experimental two-seat reconnaissance biplane employing a 220 h.p. six-cylinder in-line naphtha-burning engine (also designated AN.1). Except for the engine, which had also been tried in an A.300/4 reconnaissance biplane, the AN.1 was of conventional design. The few available details include a span of 36 ft. $10^3/_8$ in., a length of 28 ft. $8^3/_8$ in., a height of 9 ft. $8^7/_8$ in., a wing area of 435.7 sq. ft., empty and loaded weights of 2886 lb. and 3520 lb., a maximum speed of 127 m.p.h., a ceiling

The APR.2 airliner was in approximately the same class as the Lockheed 12 and 14 transports. (I-VEGA)

of 17,040 ft., and an endurance of 3 hrs. 30 min.

APR.2

Derived from the design study by Celestino Rosatelli for the APR.1 (never built), the APR.2 eight-ten passenger transport was completed and first flown in 1935. Almost entirely of metal construction, with only the rear fuselage, tail surfaces, and ailerons of fabric covering, the APR.2 was originally powered by two 700 h.p. FIAT A.59R nine-cylinder radial engines driving controllable-pitch three-bladed airscrews, and featured retractable landing gear.

The very clean and attractive cantilever monoplane was built in a small series and served with the Avio Linee Italiane S.A. The main landing gear legs of the prototype had featured sheet metal fairings, omitted from production machines, while the A.59R engines were replaced by 840 h.p. A.74 R.C.38 fourteen-cylinder radials. The A.59-powered APR.2 weighed 8360 lb. empty and 14,740 lb. loaded, had a maximum speed of 242 m.p.h. at 6560 ft., and cruised at 217 m.p.h. Ceiling was 25,420 ft. and range 1242 miles. Dimensions were: span 63 ft. 11 in., length 46 ft. 11 in., height 11 ft. 7½ in., and wing area 621.1 sq. ft.

Powered by the A.74 R.C.38 engines, the transport had a maximum speed of 255 m.p.h. at 11,480 ft., a cruising speed of 217 m.p.h., and a landing speed of 71 m.p.h. using flaps. Service

A close-up of the APR.2 transport. (I-VEGA)

ceiling was 24,600 ft. and range 1242 miles. An altitude of 9840 ft. could be maintained on one engine. The APR.2 climbed to 6560 ft. in 5 min., to 13,120 ft. in 11 min. 30 sec., and to 19,680 ft. in 22 min. Empty weight was 10,450 lb. and loaded weight 14,740 lb. Dimensions were the same as for the original version except for a slightly lengthened fuselage (48 ft. 10½ in.) and an increased wing area of 634.8 sq. ft.

AS.1

The AS.1 two-seat high-wing monoplane, the first private touring plane built by FIAT, appeared in 1928, powered by an 85/100 h.p. FIAT A.50 seven-cylinder radial engine. Constructed of wood and metal, with fabric covering, in both open-cockpit and enclosed cabin forms, the AS.1 was produced in limited numbers but used extensively for record flights. During August 2-4, 1929, a squadron of

The first private plane built by FIAT was the two-seat AS.1 high-wing monoplane.

The AS.2 was similar to the AS.1. Note spinner, transparent side panels, and headrest. (I-AAVR)

eight AS.1 monoplanes won the Coupe Challenge International de Tourisme, flying a distance of 3905 miles.

On January 19, 1930, Donati and Capannini set lightplane records for endurance and closed-circuit distance with an AS.1 at 29 hrs. 4 min. 14 sec. and 1705.4 miles. On February 12-18 of the same year the famous pilot **Francis Lombardi** flew an AS.1 solo over the route Rome-Tripoli-Benghazi-Tobruk-Massawa-Bender Casim-Mogadiscio, a distance of over 5000 miles. The Tobruk-Massawa leg was flown non-stop without a mapped course solely by following the coastline. On February 21 Donati and Capannini set an altitude record of 22,245 ft. for Category I. Accompanied by Capannini, Lombardi left Vercelli July 13 on a famous flight across Russia and Siberia to Japan, arriving July 22 at Tachikawa, where the AS.1 (I-AAVE) was donated to the Students' Aviation League. In 1932 Donati and Lanciani raised the Category II altitude record successively to 28,976 ft. and 30,445 ft. For these two flights the AS.1 was fitted with a 200 h.p. C.N.A. C.7 radial engine.

In standard form, the AS.1 weighed 902 lb. empty and 1518 lb. loaded. Span was 34 ft., length 20 ft., height 8 ft. $7^{1}/_{2}$ in., and wing area 188.3 sq. ft. Ceiling was 22,300 ft., endurance 5 hrs. 30 min., and maximum speed 98 m.p.h. In 1930 the AS.1 was built as a seaplane and also with skis. The former (AS.1 idro) weighed 1034 lb. empty and 1650 lb. loaded. Maximum speed was 95 m.p.h. and endurance the same as standard. The latter (AS.1 sci) weighed 891 lb. empty and 1540 lb. loaded, and had a maximum speed of 96 m.p.h. With the C.N.A. C.7 engine, an AS.1 idro set an altitude record for its category of 24,180 ft. on December 28, 1932.

AS.2

Nearly identical to the AS.1, the AS.2 was built in small numbers in 1929. The nose was somewhat refined, featuring a pointed spinner, and the empty and loaded weights increased to 1012 lb. and 1628 lb. respectively. Provision for a greater fuel load improved the endurance to 7 hrs. 30 min., although the maximum speed (87 m.p.h.) and ceiling (20,990 ft.) were reduced. Three AS.2's, piloted by Francis Lombardi, Mario Rasini, and Franco Mazzotti, made a flight around Africa, a distance of nearly 18,000 miles, between October 29, 1930 and January 18, 1931. The AS.2 was 20 ft. $11^{1}/_{8}$ in. long and 8 ft. $3^{1}/_{4}$ in. high.

B.R.G.

The B.R.G., the first FIAT trimotor, was a very large bomber monoplane (the G standing for Gigante) of mixed construction, powered by two 750 h.p. FIAT A.24 twelve-cylinder vee engines below the wings and one 550 h.p. A.24R unit in the nose. With a crew of three, the B.R.G. featured a dorsal machine gun mounting in its slab-sided fuselage. General layout was not unlike that of the Caproni Ca 101. Empty and loaded weights were 14,520 lb. and 26,400 lb. Maximum speed was 149 m.p.h., ceiling 15,750 ft., and endurance 12 hrs. Span was 98 ft. $4^7/_8$ in., length 57 ft. $8^3/_4$ in., height 19 ft. $0^1/_4$ in., and wing area 1497.8 sq. ft. Only the prototype B.R.G. was built; except for the S.I.A. 1200 bomber of 1916, it was the largest aeroplane in the entire FIAT family.

The B.R.G. trimotor bomber prototype. (MM 116)

BR.3

The famous series of FIAT bombers designed by Ing. Celestino Rosatelli began in 1919 with the original BR (Bombardamento Rosatelli). The BR.3 two-seat day bomber biplane appeared in 1930, powered by a 1050 h.p. FIAT A.25 twelve-cylinder water-cooled vee engine. Featuring the Warren-type wing bracing that was first an Ansaldo and later a Rosatelli trademark, and providing for a ring-mounted machine gun in the rear cockpit, the BR.3, like its immediate predecessor the BR.2, became known for successful long-distance flights. In October, 1931, together with a FIAT A.120, a BR.3 won the Coppa Principe Bibescu (Prince Bibescu Cup) with a flight of 710 miles at an average speed of 156.6 m.p.h. Performance data included a maximum speed of 143 m.p.h. (with full military load), a ceiling of 20,500 ft., and an endurance of 3 hrs. 30 min. or a range of 466 miles. Empty and loaded weights were 6270 lb. and 9570 lb. Span was 56 ft. 8 in., length 34 ft. $7^1/_4$ in., height 9 ft. $6^1/_2$ in., and wing area 828.5 sq. ft. A few BR.3 bombers were supplied to China in 1935 after the establishment of an Italian Air Mission under Col.

The BR.4 of 1934 was a typical Rosatelli design.

Lordi, advisor to Generalissimo Chiang Kai-shek. Some BR.2's and BR.3's were still being used as trainers by the Regia Aeronautica as late as 1939.

BR.4

The last of the single-engined BR two-seat biplane series, the BR.4 was first flown in 1934. Although basically a modernized development of the BR.3 concept, using the same 1050 h.p. FIAT A.25 engine, the BR.4 was an entirely new design resembling an enlarged CR.30 or CR.32. In spite of being dated in comparison with the monoplane bombers then being designed, the BR.4 was an efficient machine featuring clean overall contours, a neat engine

Of interest in this view of the prototype BR.20 are the tail stripes, applied to both rudders and tailplane.

One of two BR.20A record planes built in 1937.

cowling, and such minor aerodynamic refinements as an airscrew spinner and streamlined wheel spats. Nevertheless, the BR.4 was still far too slow (maximum speed 173 m.p.h.) to compete with newer twin-engined types, and only the single prototype was built. Empty and loaded weights were 6831 lb. and 11,231 lb. Range was 807 miles and ceiling 18,860 ft. Span was 56 ft., length 35 ft. $4^{1}/_{3}$ in., height 12 ft. $5^{5}/_{8}$ in., and wing area 779.2 sq. ft.

BR.20

A complete departure from previous Rosatelli-designed aircraft, the BR.20 medium bomber became one of the best-known Italian bombers but did not actually play a very important role in Regia Aeronautica operations during the Second World War. Following the modern concept of twin-engined bombing monoplanes, the BR.20 embraced nearly every design advance current in 1936. In spite of a somewhat angular fuselage, the BR.20 possessed relatively clean lines, with low-mounted cantilever wing and retractable landing gear. Power was supplied by FIAT A.80 R.C.41 eighteen-cylinder radial engines of 1000 h.p. each. Armament of the original production model comprised three 12.7-mm. machine guns in nose and dorsal turrets and a ventral position. Empty and loaded weights were 14,300 lb. and 22,220 lb., the latter figure including a maximum bomb load of 2200 lb. within the fuselage. Maximum speed was 267 m.p.h., range 1863 miles, and ceiling 23,616 ft. Cruising and landing speeds were 217 m.p.h. and 66 m.p.h. (with flaps). The BR.20 climbed to 6560 ft. in 6 min. 30 sec., to 13,120 ft. in 14 min., and to 19,680 ft. in 22 min. 30 sec. Without bombs the ceiling was 36,080 ft., while fully loaded on one engine the figure was 9840 ft.

In 1937 the BR.20A civil record plane was flown for the first time, two entering in the Istres-Damascus-Paris air race later that year. Due to the lack of armament the empty weight was somewhat less at 14,080 lb., but an increased fuel load boosted the all-up figure to 28,149 lb. Maximum speed was 270 m.p.h., range 3850 miles, and ceiling 18,040 ft. In 1939 the Santo Francesco, another civil model officially designated BR.20L, was built for a record run from Guidonia to Addis Ababa, A.O.I. Piloted by Maner Lualdi, Giuseppe Mazzochi, and E. Valente, assisted by two crew members, the Santo Francesco flew the distance of 2773.7 miles non-stop on March 6-7, 1939, at an average speed of 242.9 m.p.h. Maximum speed of the BR.20L was 276 m.p.h.,

The BR.20L Santo Francesco, which flew to East Africa in 1939. Note often-used I-FIAT registration.

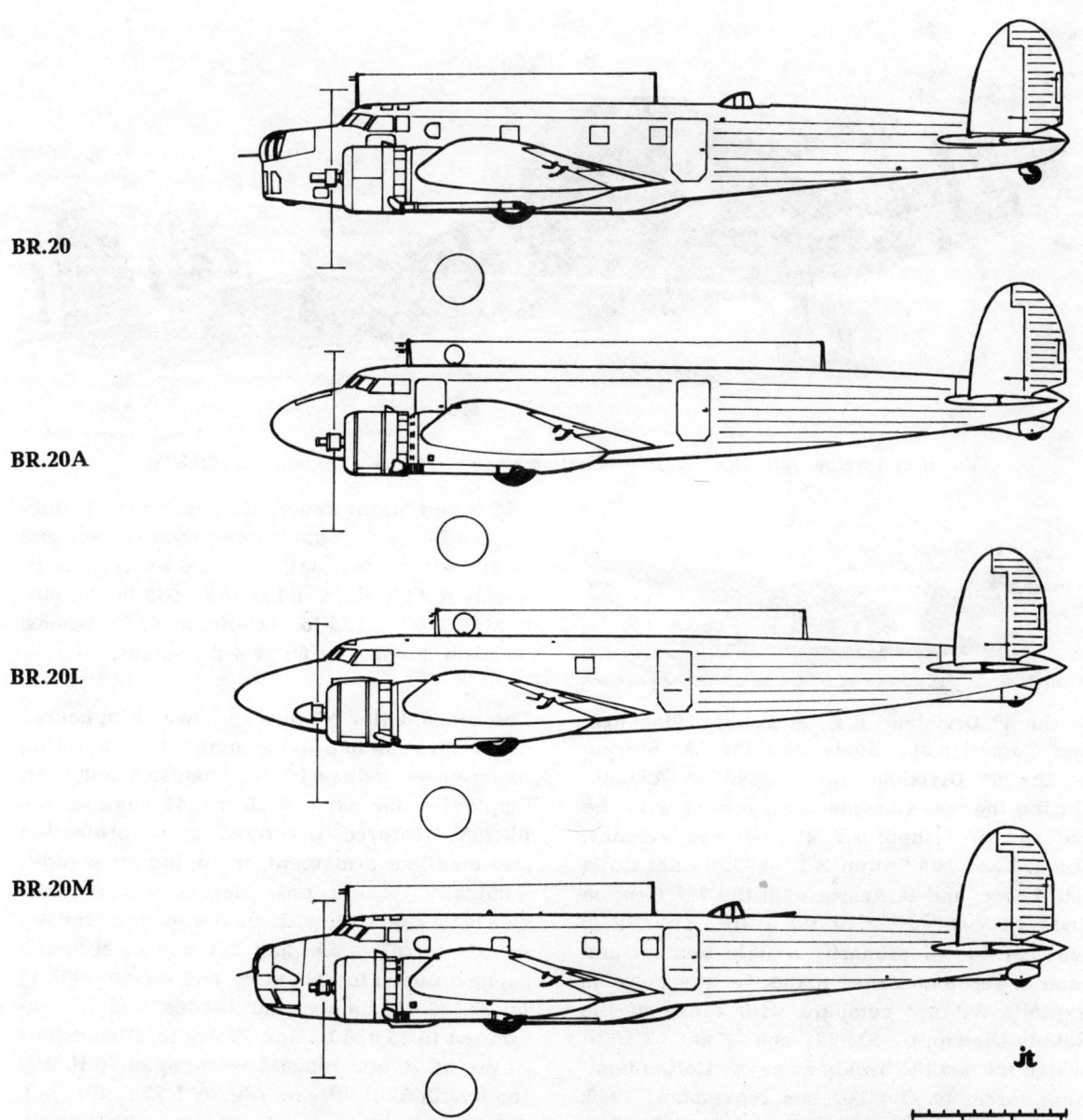

BR.20

BR.20A

BR.20L

BR.20M

ceiling being 21,320 ft. Empty and loaded weights were 13,706 lb. and 24,376 lb.

The first production examples were tested in Spain under operational conditions, serving with the 35° Gruppo Autonomo da Bombardamento of the Aviazione Legionaria. At the same time the Japanese government, after evaluating both the Caproni Ca 135 and the BR.20 for use with the JAAF in China, ordered 100 of the latter to supplant the aging Mitsubishi Ki-1 Type 93 heavy bombers. Designated Type I (Italy), Model 100 by the Japanese (the Allied code name Ruth was later applied, long after the BR.20 was withdrawn from Japanese service), about 75 of the FIAT bombers were supplied in early 1938 in exchange for Manchurian soy beans. In actual combat over China, the Type I bombers were considered unwieldy, poorly armed and easily susceptible to fire because of the fabric-covered wings. After generally unsuccessful operations, the FIATs were completely replaced by the new Mitsubishi Ki-21 Type 97 bombers in 1939. A few BR.20's were purchased by Venezuela in the late 1930's after the establishment of an Italian Air Mission in that country.

The production BR.20 bombers, named Cicogna (Stork), had gone into service with the Regia Aeronautica between 1936 and 1940, approximately 275 examples being delivered. On June 10, 1940, 219 BR.20's, of which 132 were serviceable, equipped the 7°, 13°, and 43° Stormi

Above and below left, the major production version of the Cicogna, the BR.20M.

of the 4ª Divisione B.T., at Lonate, Piacenza, and Cameri respectively, and the 18° Stormo of the 6ª Divisione B.T., based at Aviano. During the war Cicognas also served with the 25° and 99° Gruppi B.T. at Forli and Vicenza, the 37° and 38° Stormi B.T. at Gioia del Colle and Lecce, and in Russia with the 71° Gruppo Osservazione Aerea of the CSIR. The BR.20 was considered primarily a night bomber and later a reconnaissance plane; in any case its exploits did not compare with those of the Savoia-Marchetti SM.79 and Cant Z.1007, which formed the backbone of the Italian bombing force. In October and November, 1940, BR.20's of the 13° and 43° Stormi, based in Belgium as a part of the Corpo Aereo Italiano, participated to a limited extent in the Battle of Britain, making only two daylight attacks and a few night raids, all unsuccessful. Subsequently the Cicogna served over Greece and North Africa. Normal offensive loads comprised two 1100-lb. bombs, four 550-lb. bombs, twelve 220-lb., 154-lb., 110-lb., or 44-lb. bombs, 36 33-lb. bombs, or 60 26.4-lb. bombs.

The BR.20M (for Modificato), which appeared in 1939, was an improved bomber incorporating experienced gained in the Spanish Civil War. Employing the same A.80 R.C.41 engines, the BR.20M featured improved crew protection and modified armament, including an aerodynamically cleaner nose design. Performance was little changed, with maximum and cruising speeds of 267 m.p.h. and 211 m.p.h., although range dropped to 1242 miles and service ceiling to 22,140 ft. Empty and loaded weights increased to 15,070 lb. and 22,990 lb. Dimensions of the BR.20 and BR.20M were: span 70 ft. 8³/₄ in., length 52 ft. 9³/₄ in. (BR.20M 55 ft. 0³/₄ in.), height 14 ft. 1¹/₄ in., and wing area 796.5 sq. ft. The Agusta factory experimentally fitted one BR.20 with tricycle landing gear, the first Italian military aeroplane so equipped.

A group of BR.20M bombers being refuelled. Barely visible in this photograph are the small individual aircraft numbers applied on the noses, repeating those on the sides (240-8 and 240-4 in foreground).

FIAT

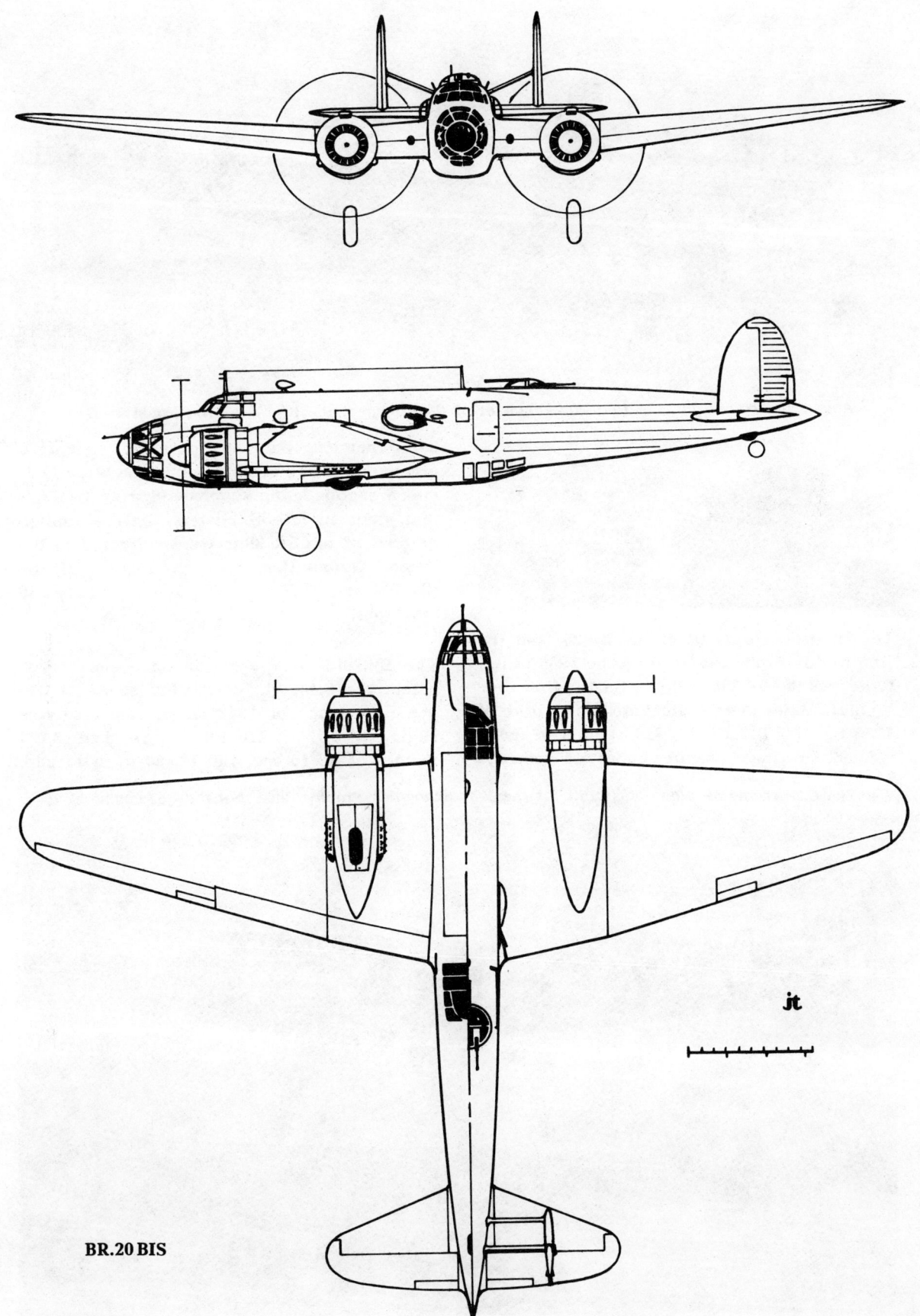

BR.20 BIS

Above and below left, the final development of the Cicogna, the BR.20bis, first flown in 1941.

The final development of the BR.20, and the first to differ extensively from the 1936 prototype, was the BR.20bis, flown for the first time in 1941. Major changes included the fitting of 1250 h.p. FIAT A.82 R.C.42S radials in much refined cowlings, greatly improved fuselage aerodynamics, and an increased defensive armament of five machine guns, the three 12.7-mm. weapons being supplemented by two 7.7-mm. guns in lateral blisters. Only a limited number of the BR.20bis were delivered to the Regia Aeronautica, total production of the BR.20M and BR.20bis being approximately 250 machines.

The BR.20bis had a maximum speed of 286 m.p.h. at 16,400 ft., a cruising speed of 230 m.p.h., a range of 1242 miles, and a service ceiling of 30,176 ft. The BR.20bis reached 13,120 ft. in 10 min. 10 sec. and 19,680 ft. in 15 min.

The C.29 racing seaplane was built for the 1931 Schneider Trophy Race, but did not compete.

Left, a CR.20 fighter. Right, the CR.20B two-seat trainer conversion; a few were built in 1927.

30 sec. Empty and loaded weights were 16,500 lb. and 25,300 lb. Dimensions included a span of 71 ft. 8¼ in., a length of 57 ft. 3 in., a height of 14 ft. 1¼ in., and a wing area of 807.3 sq. ft. By September, 1943, only 67 Cicognas of all variants remained in service, these machines equipping the 51ᵃ and 69ᵃ Squadriglie of the Aviazione Slovenia-Dalmazia, at Zara and Scutari, and the 38° Stormo B.T. of the Aeronautica Albania at Tirana-Schiak, plus the 21° Stormo O.A. (Slovenia-Dalmazia) and two Squadriglie in Greece belonging to the Aviazione per il Regio Esercito.

C.29

The FIAT C.29 was a twin-float racing seaplane flown for the first time in 1929 by Francesco Agello of the Scuola d'Alta Velocita (High Speed School), at Desenzano on Lake Garda, an organization which formed the basis for the Schneider Trophy teams. Built to compete in the 1931 Scheider contest, the sole C.29 was powered by the 1000 h.p. FIAT AS.5 twelve-cylinder water-cooled vee engine and had a maximum speed of 348 m.p.h., but it did not actually run in the race. Span was 21 ft. 8 in., length 17 ft. 10½ in., height 9 ft. 0¼ in., wing area 86.1 sq. ft., empty weight 1980 lb., loaded weight 2552 lb., and endurance 30 min.

CR.20

Paralleling the Rosatelli bombers was a famous series of fighter aircraft, mostly biplanes, by the same designer; these were designated by the letters CR (Caccia Rosatelli). Dating back to the CR prototype and CR. 1 production machines of 1923, the series included the CR.10 of 1924 and the CR.2 of 1928. The first really notable production machine was the CR.20, flown for the first time in 1926. Powered by 400 h.p. FIAT A.20 twelve-cylinder water-cooled vee engines, over 180 CR.20 single-seaters were built for the Regia Aeronautica, forming the basis of Italian fighter strength during the late 1920's and early 1930's. The CR.20 was of metal construction with fabric covering, except for the duralumin-sheet forward fuselage, and featured four machine guns, two Vickers guns in the cowl and two light Darne guns mounted in the fuselage sides. The upper wing was of greater span than the lower, reversing the arrangement of the original CR, and featured the customary Warren wing bracing.

Tested officially at Montecelio in late September, 1926, th CR.20 was flown by FIAT pilot Bottala with great verve, demonstrating loops, rolls, spins, and Immelmann turns easily, and recording maximum speeds of 174 m.p.h. at sea level, 169 m.p.h. at 6560 ft., and 149 m.p.h. at 19,680 ft. Landing speed was 56 m.p.h. The CR.20 climbed to 16,400 ft. in 13 min. 30 sec. and to 19,680 ft. in 18 min. 40 sec. Service ceiling was 26,200 ft. and endurance 2 hrs. 30 min. Empty and loaded weights were 2079 lb. and 3080 lb. Dimensions were: span 32 ft. 1¼ in., length 21 ft. 7¼ in., height 8 ft. 10¾ in., and wing area 278 sq. ft.

Several CR.20B (Biposto, or two-seater) fighter trainers were built in 1927, with a second cockpit immediately behind the regular one. Details differed little from the single-seat model, except for the empty and loaded weights of 2242 lb. and 3252 lb., the maximum speed of 155 m.p.h., and the ceiling of 24,600 ft.

A relatively large number of CR.20 idro fighter seaplanes were built by C.M.A.S.A., commencing in 1928. Specifications were similar to the standard model, except as follows: length 25 ft. 4¾ in, empty weight 2508 lb., loaded weight 3442 lb., maximum speed 158 m.p.h., ceiling

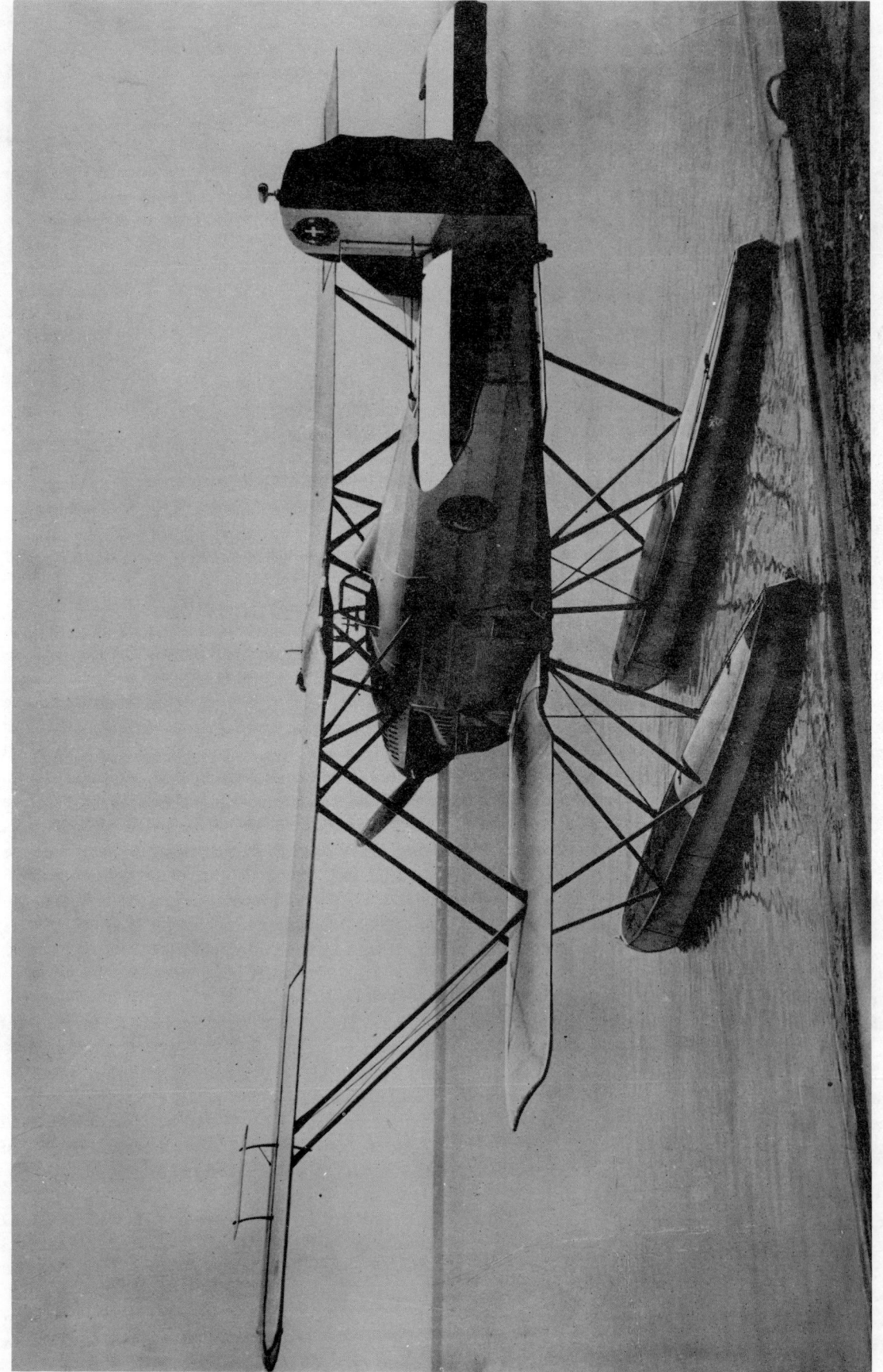

The CR.20 idro, the first FIAT floatplane fighter, was built in some numbers by C.M.A.S.A. It was not as successful as its land-based precursor.

On display at the Paris Salon, this CR.20 was left partially uncovered to reveal its metal construction.

24,600 ft., and endurance 2 hrs. 45 min. In contrast to the excellent handling of the landplane, the flying characteristics of the CR.20 idro were considered to be a bit vicious; particularly at the top of a loop, when the seaplane tended to drop inverted like a rock, giving the pilot no opportunity to bail out. The CR.20 idro was the first FIAT water-based fighter plane.

In 1929 the CR.20bis was flown for the first time. Featuring a slightly reduced wing area (274.3 sq. ft.) and minor refinements, it weighed 2134 lb. empty and 3058 lb. loaded. Ceiling was

An Austrian CR.20 in Luftwaffe markings following the German annexation in 1938.

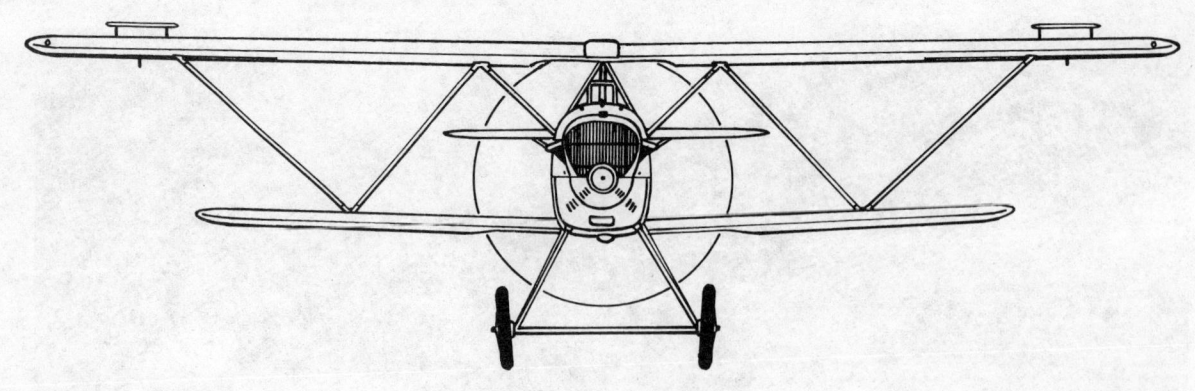
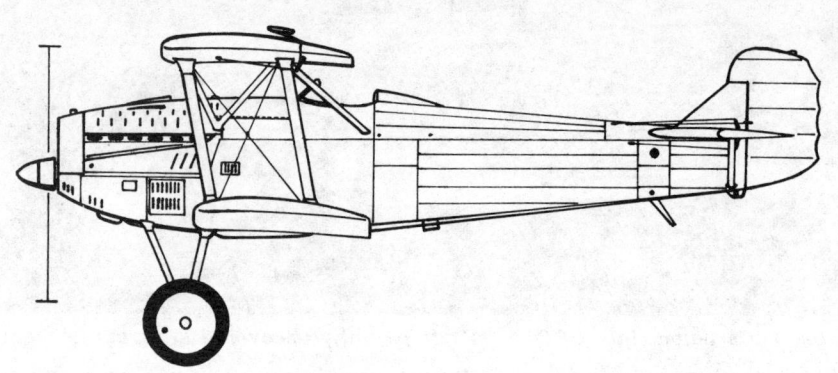
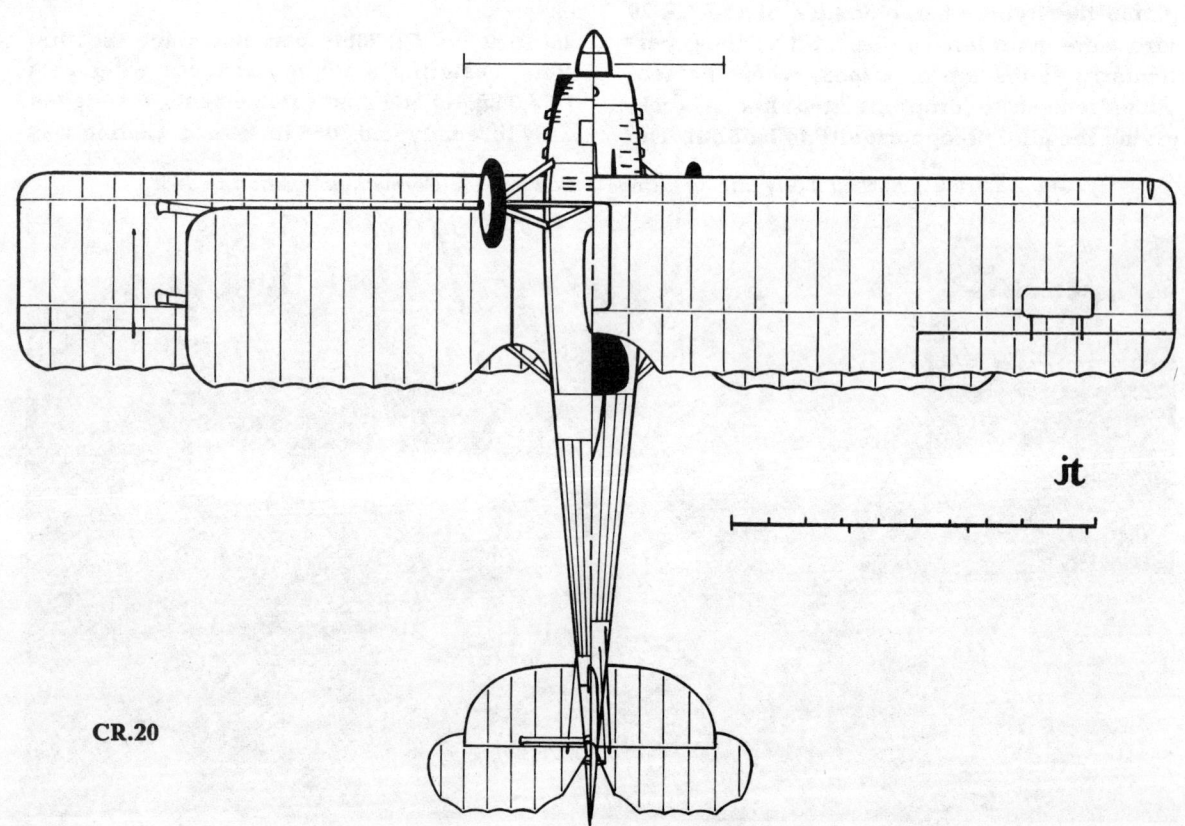

CR.20

Above, the prototype CR.30, built in 1932. Below, a production model; note differences in fin shape, windscreen, and headrest. Exhaust extension was not a standard fitting.

increased to 27,880 ft., although maximum speed was just 161 m.p.h. The CR.20bis was placed in series production, as was the final variant, the CR.20 A.Q., also built in 1929. The last model was identical to the CR.20bis except for the installation of a 425 h.p. FIAT A.25 A.Q. (Alta Quota, or high output) twelve-cylinder vee engine. Its performance matched that of the CR.20bis, although the A.Q. model was heavier at 2156 lb. empty and 3080 lb. loaded.

A number of FIAT CR.20 single-seat fighters were supplied to Austria in 1936. These aircraft became a part of the Luftwaffe on March 13, 1938, when Austria was absorbed by the Third Reich.

CR. ASSO

Built in series by C.M.A.S.A. in 1932, the CR. Asso was essentially a standard CR.20 fitted with a 450 h.p. Isotta-Fraschini Asso Caccia water-cooled engine. In spite of the increased power, the CR. Asso, which weighed 2347 lb. empty and 3271 lb. loaded, had a maximum speed of only 155 m.p.h. and a ceiling of only 16,400 ft.

CR.30

A completely redesigned biplane fighter appeared in 1932, designated CR.30 and powered by a 600 h.p. FIAT A.30 R.A. twelve-cylinder water-cooled vee engine. Spinner, wheel spats, fully cowled engine, and rounded wing tips and tail surfaces contributed to a greatly

modernized appearance, with performance to match. Maximum speed was 217 m.p.h., landing speed 65 m.p.h., ceiling 28,536 ft., and endurance 2 hrs. 30 min. The CR.30 climbed to 6560 ft. in 2 min. 40 sec., to 13,120 ft. in 6 min. 40 sec., and to 19,680 ft. in 12 min. 30 sec. Empty and loaded weights were 2959 lb. and 41.69 lb. Span was 34 ft. 5 in., length 21 ft. 11 in., height 9 ft. and wing area 291 sq. ft.

The CR.30 was placed in quantity production and became standard equipment of the Regia Aeronautica fighter units, along with the smaller, lighter, and faster CR.32 that appeared the following year. Armament was two 12.7-mm. Breda-SAFAT machine guns mounted in the cowl. Additional variants of the CR.30 were the CR.30B (Biposto) two-seat fighter trainer, of which several examples were built in 1932, and the CR.30 idro, of which a few were built in 1934. Piloted by Baldi and Buffa, a CR.30B won the Coppa Principe Bibescu of 1932. The trainer weighed 3025 lb. empty and 4345 lb. loaded, had a maximum speed of 214 m.p.h., a

Although smaller, the CR.32 was externally similar to the CR.30, and difficult to distinguish.

ceiling of 26,240 ft., and an endurance of 3 hrs. 15 min. The fighter seaplane weighed 3047 lb. empty and 4312 lb. loaded, had a maximum speed of 210 m.p.h., a ceiling of 27,860 ft., and an endurance of 2 hrs. 30 min.

Standard CR.30 fighters were supplied in limited numbers to Austria, China, and Paraguay during the period 1934—36. As in the case of the CR.20, those supplied to Austria were later taken over by the Luftwaffe.

CR.32

Probably the most successful fighter design of the 1930's was the FIAT CR.32. A refinement of the CR.30, the CR.32, employing the A.30 R.A. bis 600 h.p. engine, flew for the first time in 1933 and was still in limited service ten years later, having fought in both the Spanish Civil War and the Second World War. In addition, the CR.32 had been exported to the Air Forces of Austria, China, Hungary, Paraguay, and Venezuela. More compact than its predecessor, the CR.32 was difficult to distinguish visually, the major external changes being confined to a reduction in span, a more graceful fin, and a lengthened tailwheel fairing. In spite of the slight visible changes the newer fighter was faster and more maneuverable, due in part to the decreased empty and loaded weights, 2915 lb. and 4070 lb. respectively. The CR.32 was almost certainly the most maneuverable fighter ever built, becom-

Above, two views of a CR.32ter fighter. The CR.32quater, below, was the lightest production version.

Aviazione Legionaria CR.32bis fighters in Spanish markings. More than 300 CR.32bis were built.

ing the firm favorite of Italian pursuit pilots.

In September, 1937, a squadriglia of eleven CR.32's performed aerobatic displays in Argentina, Brazil, Chile, Peru, and Uruguay on the occasion of the International American Aviation Congress. This was just one of many impressive performances. As with the CR.30, armament consisted of two 12.7-mm. Breda-SAFAT machine guns mounted in the cowl. Maximum speed was 233 m.p.h., ceiling 28,864 ft., and endurance 2 hrs.

In 1935, after some 350 CR.32 fighters had been built, a modification designated CR.32bis appeared. The two 12.7-mm. machines guns were supplemented by two 7.7-mm. guns mounted in the lower wings, and one 220-lb. bomb or two 110-lb. bombs could be carried on a rack below the fuselage. Heavier and slower, the CR.32bis, with greater armament and an increased endurance, was nevertheless a more effective fighting machine. Empty and loaded weights were 3080 lb. and 4334 lb. Maximum speed was 217 m.p.h., ceiling 26,240 ft., and endurance 2 hrs. 30 min. More than 300 CR.32bis fighters were built. The type was sent to Spain in 1936 with the Squadriglia "La Cucaracha" of the Aviazione Legionaria, proving more than a match for the Republican biplanes it met in combat; although the newer Polikarpov 1-16 Type 6 and Type 10 monoplanes were faster by some 60 m.p.h. and had a superior rate of climb, the CR.32's usually overwhelmed the Russians in classic dogfighting combat. While this success no doubt elated the Italian pilots, it was in the long run to prove unfortunate for Italy, hindering the development of the faster, more heavily armed monoplane fighters that were to be required in the Second World War. This can be seen in the fact that by 1940 the CR.32 still comprised more than one quater of the fighter strength of the Regia Aeronautica, all the biplane types (CR.32, CR. 42, Ro 44) accounting for more than one half of the total strength and almost two thirds of the serviceable machines!

On June 10, 1940, the Regia Aeronautica possessed 294 CR.32's of all variants, of which 177 were serviceable. These equipped the 52° Stormo of the 8ª Brigata C.T., based at Pontedera, the 2° Gruppo C.T. at Grottaglie, the 1° Stormo of the 1ª Divisione C.T., at Palermo, the 9° Gruppo Autonomo C.T., at Monserrato, Sardinia, the 160° Gruppo C.T. at Tirana, Albania, the 13° Gruppo C.T. at Castelbenito, Tripoli, the 8° and 10° Gruppi C.T., with head-

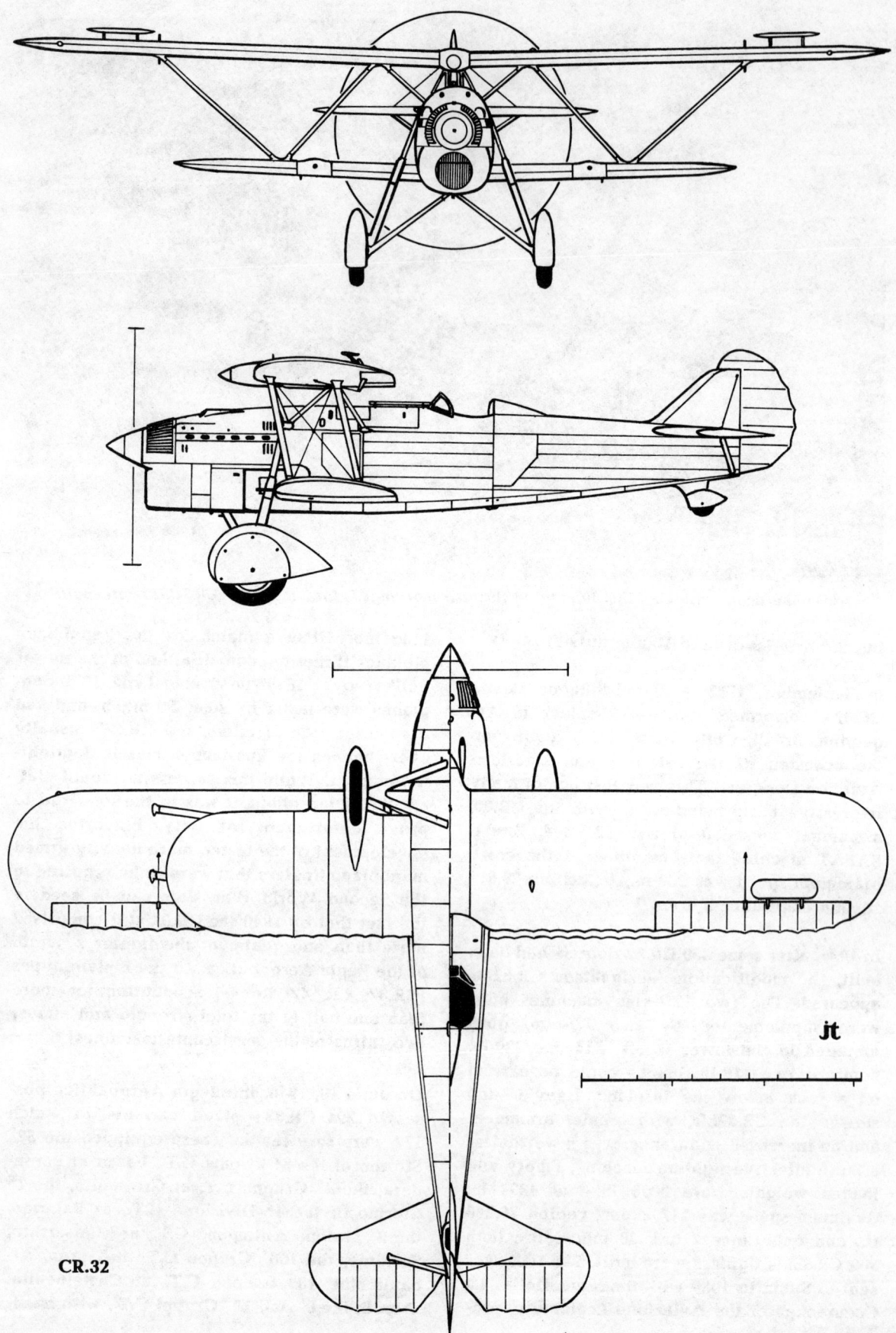

CR.32

Absorbed by the Luftwaffe in the late 1930's were a number of Austrian CR.32's like the one shown here.

quarters at Tobruk, and the 163ª Squadriglia C.T. on Rhodes in the Aegean Sea.

The CR.32ter and quater models which had been introduced in 1936 embodied minor modifications aimed at weight reduction, and featured a somewhat improved performance. The CR.32ter, of which some 100 machines were built, had a maximum speed of 218 m.p.h., a ceiling of 26,110 ft., and a range of 481 miles. Empty and loaded weights were 3058 lb. and 4213 lb. The CR.32quater reverted to the original two 12.7-mm. machine guns, and was the lightest model since the original, weighing 3036 lb. empty and 4191 lb. loaded. Maximum speed was 221 m.p.h. at 9840 ft., cruising speed 196 m.p.h., and landing speed 68 m.p.h. Range was 484 miles and service ceiling 24,764 ft. The CR.32quater climbed to 3280 ft. in 1 min. 30 sec., to 9840 ft. in 5 min. 10 sec., and to 16,400 ft. in 10 min. Dimensions of all models were: span 31 ft. 2 in. (upper) and 20 ft. $6^{1}/_{4}$ in. (lower), length 24 ft. $5^{3}/_{8}$ in., height 8 ft. 11 in., and wing area 237.8 sq. ft. About 450 CR.32-quater fighters were built.

In 1938 Hispano Aviacion obtained the Spanish manufacturing license for the CR.32quater, which was built in Spain as the HA-132-L Chirri. The type served as the standard fighter of the Ejercito del Aire, the Spanish air arm, during the 1940's, being designated C.1. Chirris were still active as aerobatic trainers as late as 1954, and one FIAT-built example was still flying in Italy two years later, being shown at the Fiumicino display of 1956.

CR.33

The CR.33, flown for the first time in 1937, was a further development of the CR.32 employing a 700 h. p. FIAT A.33 R.C.35 twelve-cylinder water-cooled vee engine driving a three-bladed metal airscrew. The CR.33 fitted the wing machine guns of the CR.32bis. Empty and loaded weights were 2992 lb. and 4202 lb. Maximum speed was considerably increased to 262 m.p.h.; ceiling and range were 34,440 ft. and 435 miles respectively. Span was 31 ft. and wing area 241 sq. ft.

By 1937, however, the G.50 fighter monoplane had already appeared; in addition, the radial-

The CR. 33 had A.33 engine, three-bladed airscrew.

Based on the CR.32, the CR.40 featured a revised upper wing and a 550 h.p. Bristol Mercury radial.

engined CR.40, CR.40bis, and CR.41 biplane prototypes had shown a higher performance potential that was to be fully realized two years later in the final FIAT biplane, the CR.42 Falco. Thus only a few examples of the CR.33 were built.

CR.40

The CR.40, powered by a 550 h.p. Bristol Mercury IV radial engine, was built in 1934. Although basically similar to the CR.32, the radial-engined fighter featured a number of refinements, including a modified landing gear and an upper wing joined directly to the fuselage by a gull center section, improving pilot visibility upward. Dimensions were: span 31 ft., length 23 ft. 4³/₄ in., height 8 ft. 8 in., and wing area 228.9 sq. ft. Empty and loaded weights were 2552 lb. and 3652 lb. This noticeable reduction permitted a maximum speed of 242 m.p.h. (a 9 m.p.h. increase over that of the CR.32), a ceiling of 37,720 ft., and an endurance of 1 hr. 50 min. Later the same year came the CR.40bis, powered by a 700 h.p. FIAT A.59R nine-cylinder radial engine. Slightly heavier (2640 lb. empty, 3740 lb. loaded), this model

The CR.41 fitted a Gnôme-Rhône radial, three-bladed airscrew, and taller tail surfaces. (I-ACLA)

The CR.41 in Regia Aeronautica markings. The design was dropped in favor of the more advanced CR.42.

had a maximum speed of 248 m.p.h. and a ceiling of 38,540 ft., endurance being the same. The wing area was reduced to 224.9 sq. ft.

CR.41
Essentially a modified version of the CR.40, the CR.41 of 1936 fitted a 900 h.p. Gnôme-Rhône 14 Kfs fourteen-cylinder radial engine, a three-bladed airscrew, larger vertical tail surfaces, and wing-mounted machine guns. Empty and loaded weights were 2882 lb. and 4147 lb. Wing area was increased to 243.5 sq. ft. Performance included a maximum speed of 264 m.p.h., a ceiling of 38,376 ft., and a range of 497 miles.

CR.42
The last biplane built by FIAT, and one of the last biplane fighters built anywhere in the world, the CR.42 Falco (Falcon), first flown in early 1939 and placed in production the same year, was an excellent machine, representing the definitive achievement in the biplane category and incorporating all the qualities that Italian pilots held dear. Unfortunately, the revised tactics of modern air warfare and the development of high-speed heavily-armed monoplanes caused the CR.42 to be badly

Above right, the prototype CR.42. Below, a rear view showing the clean lines of the biplane.

In spite of its technical obsolescence, the CR.42 was a good fighter which served in large numbers.

outclassed in combat; the only opponent which the Falco could meet on even terms was the British Gloster Gladiator, a biplane of even earlier vintage.

Incorporating the best lightweight metals, the CR.42 was of welded steel and alloy construction with fabric covering, except for the metal-panelled forward fuselage. The engine was an 840 h.p. FIAT A.74 R.C.38 fourteen-cylinder radial. The typical Warren wing bracing was employed along with fixed and spatted landing gear; the prototype had a retractable tailwheel. Armament was initially one 7.7-mm. machine gun and one 12.7-mm. gun mounted in the cowl. Maneuverability of the CR.42 was superb; this fact, allied to a maximum speed of 267 m.p.h. (only 25 m.p.h. slower than that of the FIAT G.50 monoplane), may have accounted for the export orders for the type placed with the FIAT company in 1939. Hungary received a number of Falcos late that year, while Belgium, which had ordered 34 aircraft in September, received 25 machines in May, 1940; most of the Belgian machines were soon destroyed during the rapid German invasion. Sweden took delivery of 72 CR.42bis fighters, fitted with two 12.7-mm. guns, between February, 1940, and September, 1941, these aircraft receiving the Swedish designation J 11. Compared to the Gladiators (J 8) also in Swedish service, the Italian fighter was initially considered superior on most counts, but the rate of wear and service problems of the CR.42 reversed this opinion. Nevertheless, CR.42's remained in first-line service until

Two views of a CR.42 shot down in England in 1940 and tested in British markings. The type makes interesting comparison with Britain's last fighter biplane, the Gloster Gladiator.

The CR.42 A.S. was an assault version for North African use. Modifications were revised air scoop and underwing fittings for two 220-lb. bombs or supplementary fuel tanks.

1945, when they were finally replaced by the Swedish-designed-and-built FFVS J 22 low-wing monoplanes.

In addition to the CR.42bis, further Falco variants were the CR.42ter with two additional 12.7-mm. machine guns in underwing fairings, the CR.42 A.S. (Africa Settentrionale, or North Africa) assault version with two 220-lb. bombs under the wings for use in 1942 desert warfare, the CR.42 C.N. (Caccia Notturna) night figther for defense of industrial centers in Northern Italy, cooperating with searchlight batteries, and the CR.42B, first flown in 1941, which employed a 1010 h.p. Daimler-Benz DB 601 liquid-cooled engine and had a maximum speed of no less than 323 m.p.h. A few CR.42's were experimentally fitted with underwing 20-mm. cannon. The ICR.42 floatplane version is described under C.M.A.S.A., the subsidiary which manufactured it.

In Regia Aeronautica service the standard Falco day fighters were used primarily for bomber escort. At the time of Italy's entry into the war the CR.42 was serving with the 3° Stormo (Novi Ligure) and 53° Stormo (Caselle) of the 2ª Divisione C.T., the 9° Gruppo C.T. at Gorizia, the 1° Stormo of the 1ª Divisione C.T. at Palermo, and the 13° Gruppo C.T. of the Aeronautica della Libia, based at Castelbenito.

At that time 300 CR.42's were available, 202 of these in serviceable condition. The CR.42 equipped a part of almost every fighter unit during the course of the war, serving honorably if not brilliantly on all fronts. CR.42's were among the aircraft employed with little success by the token Corpo Aereo Italiano in the Battle of Britain. Production of the Falco ended in 1942 with a total of 1781 machines. At least 113 still remained when Italy surrendered, although only 64 were serviceable. Of the latter, four were flown to Allied lines to join the anti-Fascist Co-Belligerent Air Force, the remainder serving with the Aviazione della RSI until the final defeat. A few of those CR.42's remaining were modified as two-seat dual-control trainers and used by the postwar Italian air arm, the Aeronautica Militare; one was still being used in 1950.

The CR.42 weighed 3784 lb. empty and 5049 lb. loaded. Performance included a maximum speed of 267 m.p.h. at 13,120 ft., a cruising speed of 214 m.p.h., a landing speed of 81 m.p.h., a service ceiling of 33,456 ft., and a range of 481-630 miles. Climbing times were: 3 min. 53 sec. to 9840 ft.; 5 min. 26 sec. to 13,120 ft.; and 8 min. 40 sec. to 19,680 ft. Dimensions included a span of 31 ft. 9¾ in., a length of 27 ft. 2¾ in., a height of 10 ft. 9⅞ in., and a wing area of 241 sq. ft. The CR.42B weighed 4290 lb.

Below left, a Hungarian CR.42. Right, the prototype retouched to depict the DB 601-powered CR.42B.

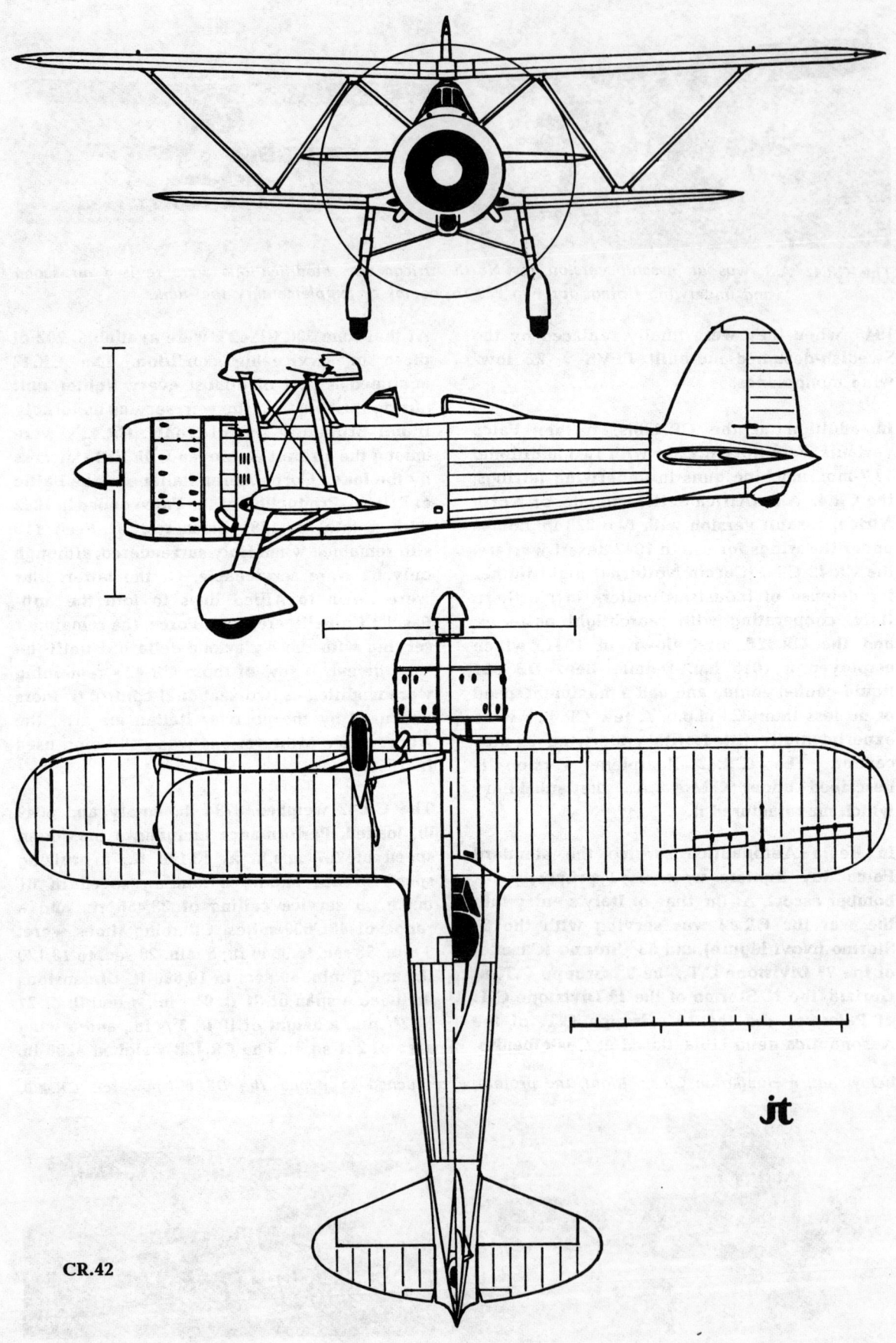

CR.42

Left, a CR.42 with postwar Italian markings. Right, the CR.42 biposto two-seat dual-control trainer conversion, several of which were employed by the Aeronautica Militare until 1950.

empty and 6017 lb. loaded. Ceiling and range were 34,768 ft. and 714 miles, respectively.

CR.25

The CR.25 did not follow the regular series of single-engined, single-seat biplane fighters, being a larger twin-engined, three-seat escort fighter and reconnaissance monoplane bearing a general similarity in layout to the same designer's BR.20. First flown in 1939, the CR.25 employed 840 h.p. FIAT A.74 R.C. 38 fourteen-cylinder radial engines. The original prototype was among the Italian aircraft displayed at Montecelio in 1939 for the first International Congress of Aeronautical Journalists, other military types being the Breda 88, Caproni Ca 310, Piaggio P.23R, Piaggio P.50-II, Savoia-Marchetti SM.75, and Savoia-Marchetti SM.85. Two prototypes were followed by ten pre-production machines, one of which was used as a transport by the Italian Air Attaché in Berlin, designated CR.25D.

ICR.42

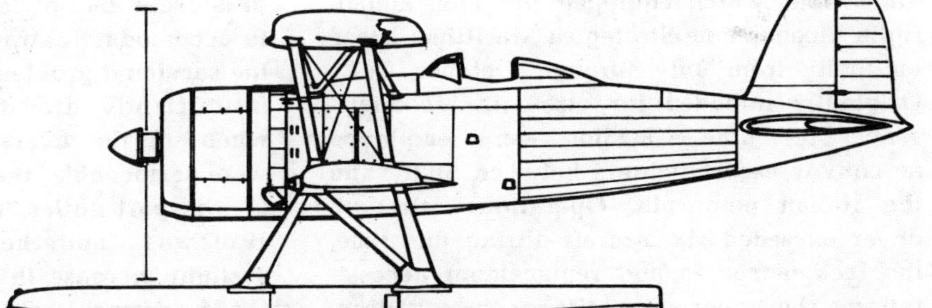

CR.42 BIPOSTO

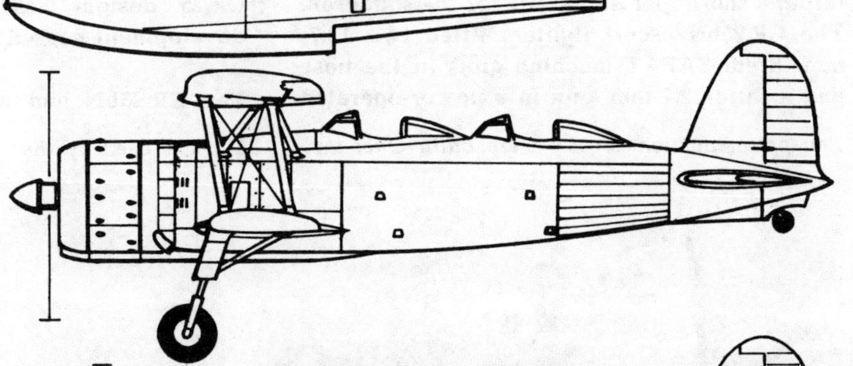

CR.42B

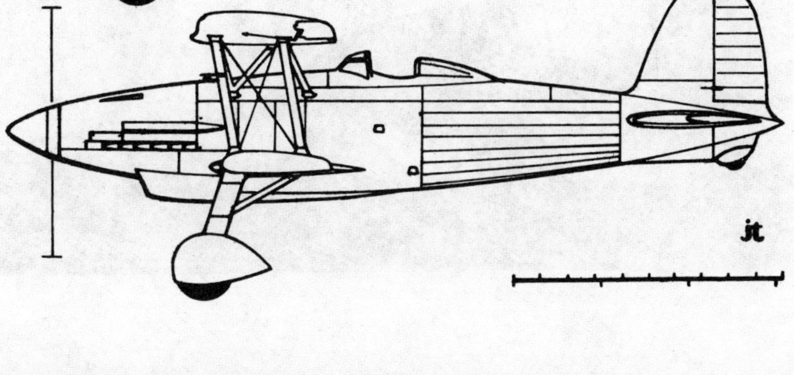

The CR.25 prototype, built in 1939, showed a strong family resemblance to the BR.20. (3651)

The designation CR.25bis was applied to the other nine, which equipped the 173ª Squadriglia Ricognizione Strategica Marittima based on Sicily from July through October, 1942. Originally intended for strategic reconnaissance, the nine CR.25bis were employed as convoy escort fighters between Sicily and the Italian peninsula. Operational strength never exceeded six aircraft during this time, the lack of spares and replacement necessitating a short operational life for the squadron. The CR.25bis escort fighters fitted two 12.7-mm. Breda-SAFAT machine guns in the nose and a third 12.7-mm. gun in a power-operated dorsal turret. The internal bomb bay, designed to house a load of 1550 lb., was normally used to accomodate extra fuel tanks. In addition to the servicing problems, the CR.25 proved to be insufficiently armed, and by October 1942, when on the average only three machines were serviceable, the type had been relegated to transport duties. The CR.25quater, flown in 1940, was a more heavily armed version with a slight increase in wing area, but the basic CR.25 design was abandoned and further development ceased.

The CR.25bis had a maximum speed of 286

Ten pre-production CR.25's were built. One, the CR.25D, was used by the Italian Air Attaché in Berlin.

FIAT

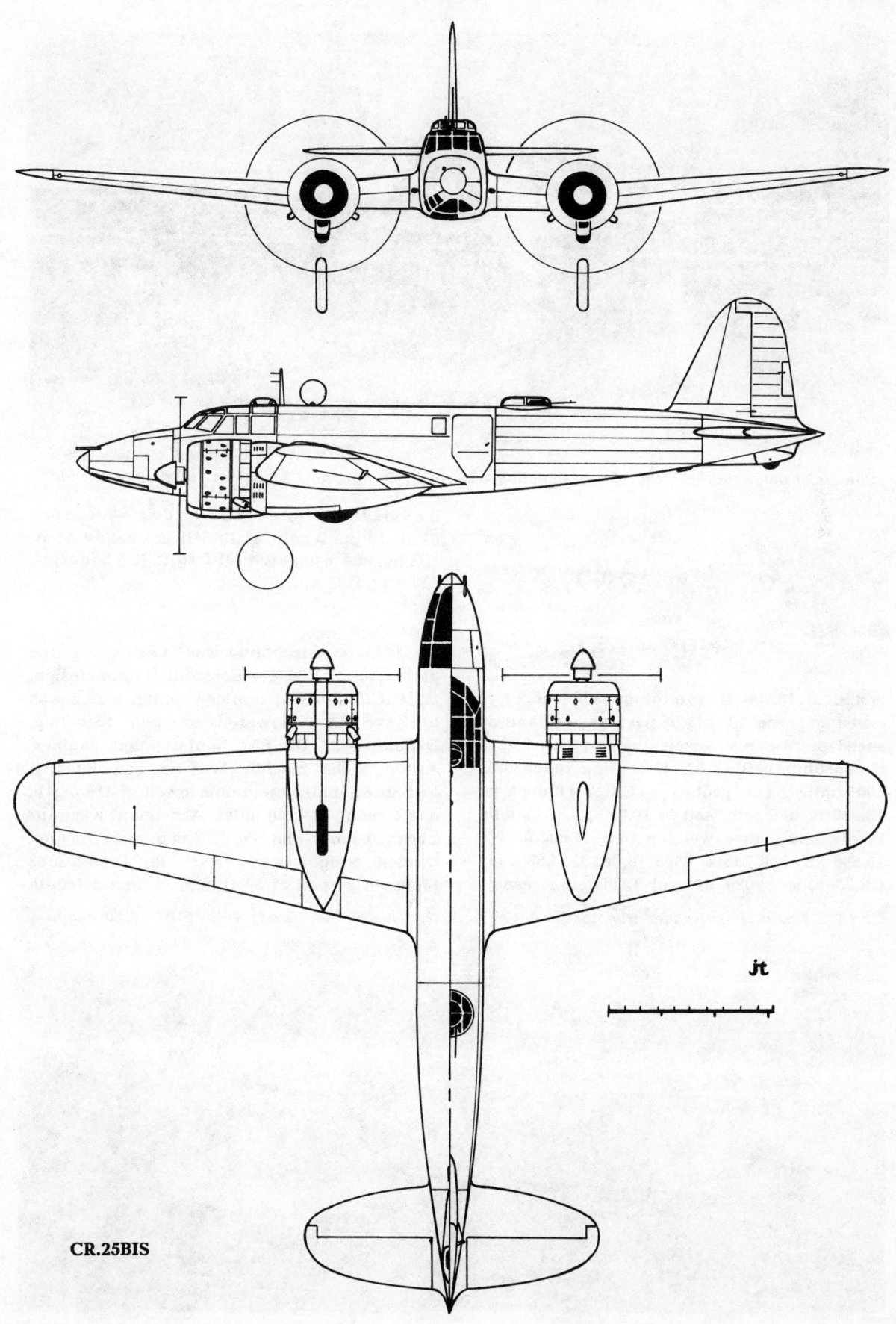

CR.25BIS

Above and below left, the CR.25bis designation was given to the nine machines used operationally.

m.p.h. at 18,200 ft. (prototype 304 m.p.h.), a cruising speed of 245 m.p.h., and a landing speed of 78 m.p.h. Service ceiling was 26,575 ft., absolute ceiling 32,140 ft., and range 972-1305 miles. The prototype CR.25 climbed to 13,120 ft. in 7 min. and to 19,680 ft. in 12 min. Empty and loaded weights were 8580 lb. and 13,596 lb. (CR.25bis, 9645 lb. and 14,385 lb.; CR.25quater, 9020 lb. and 14,080 lb., respectively). Dimensions of all models were: span 51 ft. 10 in., length 44 ft. 5^3/$_4$ in., height 11 ft. 1^3/$_4$ in., and wing area 421.8 sq. ft. (CR.25quater, 430.4 sq. ft.).

CR.23

In 1943 construction was begun on the prototype of the last Rosatelli fighter design, the CR.23 two-seat fighter-bomber, which was to have been powered by two 1510 h.p. Daimler-Benz DB 603 liquid-cooled engines. Although this machine was not completed, it had an estimated maximum speed of 416 m.p.h. and a range of 1180 miles. Armament was four 20-mm. cannon and one 12.7-mm. machine gun. Loaded weight was 21,826 lb. Dimensions included a span of 59 ft. 0^2/$_3$ in. and a length

The G.2 was a six-passenger trimotor produced in 1932. This is the G.2/1, with FIAT A.60 engines.

The G.2/4, with D.H. Gipsy-Queen III engines. The I-FIAT registration was 'applied' via the negative.

of 47 ft. 10¾ in.

G.2

Four prototypes of the FIAT G.2 three-engined six-passenger transport, designed by Ing. Giuseppe Gabrielli, were built in 1932, powered by different engines. They were the G.2/1-4, employing 135 h.p. FIAT A.60 four-cylinder inverted in-line, 135 h.p. FIAT A.54 seven-cylinder radial, 120 h.p. Alfa Romeo 110-I four-cylinder inverted in-line, and 120 h.p. DeHavilland Gipsy-Queen III inverted in-line engines, respectively. The G.2, largely of metal construction, was the first FIAT cantilever monoplane; none of the four models was placed in production. The G.2/1, weighing 3586 lb. empty and 5500 lb. loaded, had a maximum speed of 124 m.p.h., a ceiling of 13,776 ft., and a range of 497 miles. Dimensions were: span 53 ft. 3 in., length 39 ft., height 9 ft. 10 in., and wing area 419.6 sq. ft. Characteristics of the G.2/4 (D.H. Gipsy in-lines) were almost identical, except for a reduced wing area of 414.3 sq. ft.

The G.2/2 (FIAT A.54 radials) weighed 3960 lb. empty and 6160 lb. loaded, had a maximum speed of 150 m.p.h., a cruising speed of 130 m.p.h., a ceiling of 17,056 ft., and a range of 621 miles. Wing area was 412.1 sq. ft. The G.2/2 climbed to 6560 ft. in 9 min. 10 sec. (29 min. 30 sec. on two engines), to 13,120 ft. in 27 min. 30 sec., and to 16,400 ft. in 47 min. The Alfa Romeo-powered G.2/3 had similar characteristics to the G.2/2, except as follows: wing area 419.6 sq. ft., maximum speed 149 m.p.h., ceiling 19,352 ft., and range 838 miles.

The G.5 was a light two-seat aerobatic trainer designed by Ing. Gabrielli and built in 1933. (212)

Left and above, several G.5bis were used after the war, shown here fitted as single-seaters.

G.5

The G.5 was a light two/three-seat touring and aerobatic training monoplane powered by a 140 h.p. FIAT A.54 seven-cylinder radial engine. Built in 1933, it featured flaps and leading-edge slots, fixed spatted landing gear, and a Townend ring cowling. The G.5 weighed 1320 lb. empty and 1936 lb. loaded, and had maximum, cruising and landing speeds of 140 m.p.h., 121 m.p.h., and 50 m.p.h., respectively. Ceiling was 18,860 ft. and range 491 miles. Climbing to 3280 ft. required 3 min. 42 sec., to 6560 ft. 9 min. 22 sec., and to 9840 ft. 16 min. 25 sec. Dimensions were: span 34 ft. 4 in., length 25 ft. 11 in., height 8 ft., and wing area 184.9 sq. ft.

The G.5/2 was an almost identical model mounting a 142 h.p. FIAT A.60 four-cylinder inverted air-cooled engine. Except for the ceiling of 18,040 ft., characteristics and dimensions matched those of the G.5/1. Only one G.5/2 was built, although several of the first version were constructed.

The G.5bis, which appeared in 1934, featured the considerably more powerful 200 h.p. FIAT A.70 seven-cylinder radial engine; weights increased to 1386 lb. empty and 2002 lb. loaded. Maximum speed was 165 m.p.h., ceiling 22,960 ft., and range 394 miles. A small number of G.5bis trainers were built, at least one of them surviving the war and still flying in 1959.

G.12

The first G.12 trimotor transport was flown in October, 1940. Designated G.12C (Civile), the fourteen-passenger airliner was designed for high-altitude trans-Alpine routes. The power units were FIAT A.74 R.C.42 fourteen-cylinder radials of 770 h.p. each. Structure was of metal with mixed metal and fabric covering. Empty and loaded weights were 20,680 lb., and 34,100 lb. Maximum speed was 242 m.p.h. at 16,400 ft., cruising speed 192 m.p.h., ceiling 27,880 ft., and range 1962 miles. One civil airliner was placed in service with Avio Linee Italiane S.A. on the Milan-Venice-Vienna-Budapest route, but further wartime development was concentrated on military models.

The G.12T cargo and troop transport, which could carry 22 fully-equipped troops, flew in May, 1941; this version was placed in produc-

The original version of the G.12 trimotor transport was the G.12C fourteen-passenger civil airliner.

Above, the G.12 LGA was built for LATI in 1941, but received wartime camouflage. Below right, the G.12T military cargo and troop transport, which was placed in limited production earlier that year.

tion for the Regia Aeronautica and saw service in North Africa as well as in metropolitan Italy. The G.12T weighed 20,460 lb. empty and 33,000 lb. loaded and had a range of 1428 miles, other performance figures being similar to those of the G.12C. Dimensions common to most models of the G.12 were: span 93 ft. 10 in., length 65 ft. $11^{1}/_{3}$ in., height 16 ft. 1 in., and wing area 1215.9 sq. ft.

The G.12 Gondar (named after the base in A.O.I. which was one of the objectives during the Ethiopian war of 1935) was a further model of which several examples were built in 1941. Empty and loaded weights were 20,570 lb. and 37,059 lb., and range was no less than 3606 miles, a distance greater than that from the FIAT factory in Turin to Gondar. Maximum speed dropped slightly to 239 m.p.h. In 1942 one G.12A (Grande Autonomia, or long range) passenger airliner was built. In keeping with its designation, the G.12GA had an impressive range of 4350 miles. Maximum speed was 236 m.p.h. and ceiling 21,320 ft. Empty and loaded weights were 21,340 lb. and 39,600 lb.

Later the same year appeared the first G.12LGA passenger transport, of which a few were built for LATI (Linee Aeree Transcontinentale Italiane), the airline founded in September, 1938, to link Italy with South America. The G.12LGA was powered by 750 h.p. Alfa Romeo 126 R.C.34 nine-cylinder radials. Empty and loaded weights were 20,460 lb. and 34,100 lb. Performance included a maximum speed of 233 m.p.h., a ceiling of 19,680 ft., and a range of 2142 miles.

In late 1942 and early 1943 came the G.12RT and G.12RTbis prototypes, both extremely long-range transports powered by 895 h.p. Alfa Romeo 128 R.C.18 nine-cylinder radial engines. These two aircraft, although operating at lower altitudes at reduced speeds, were by far the heaviest and longest-ranged of the entire G.12 series. The G.12RT, weighing 21,197 lb. empty and 43,802 lb. loaded, had a ceiling of 15,580 ft. and a range of 4968 miles. The G.12RTbis carried an even greater fuel load, empty and loaded weights being 22,143 lb. and 46,640 lb., and had a ceiling of 14,100 ft. and a range of 5590 miles, exceeding that of all other wartime Italian aircraft and not greatly inferior to that of the Boeing XPBB-1 flying boat, which at that time was considered to have an exceptional endurance of seventy-two hours and a maximum range of 6300 miles.

Postwar versions of the G.12 built between 1945-50 included the G.12CA nineteen-passenger airliner (Alfa Romeo 128 R.C.18 radials), the G.12L 18-22-passenger airliner (FIAT A.74 R.C.42 radials) with lengthened fuselage and

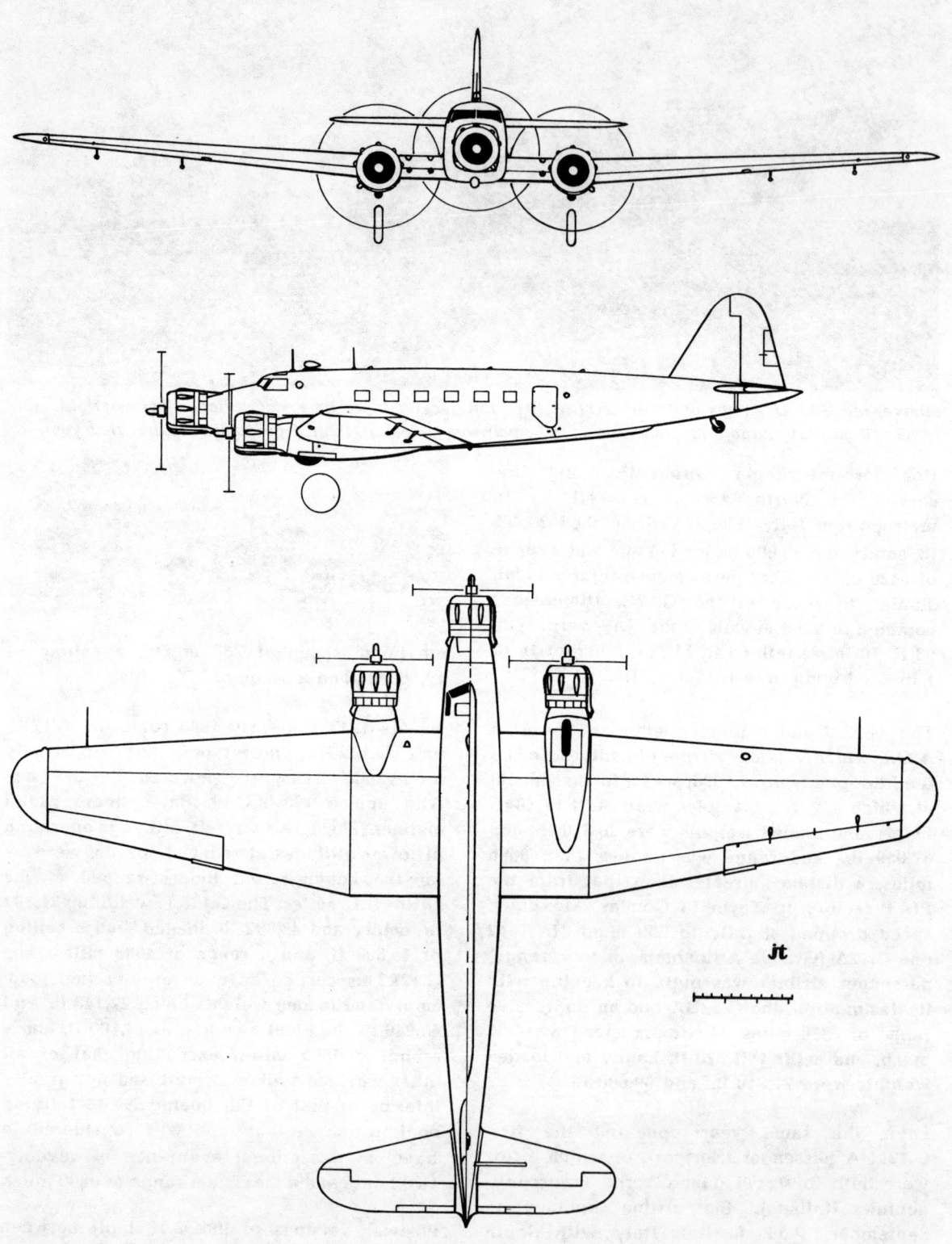

G.12

The G.12L was a postwar model for 18-22 passengers. Note longer fuselage, modified fin. (I-SASS)

modified fin, the G.12LB 16-22-passenger airliner (730 h.p. Bristol Pegasus 48 radials), the G.12LP 18-22-passenger airliner (1065 h.p. Pratt & Whitney R.1830 S1C3G radials), the G.12LA 16-22-passenger airliner (Alfa Romeo 128 R.C.18 radials) — all civil models — and the G.12 Aula Volante (Flying Classroom) military trainer (Alfa Romeo 128 R.C.18 radials). Commencing with the G.12L in 1947, the later models were of all-metal construction.

The G.212 was a larger, generally similar postwar development built in several versions, with accomodations for as many as 34 passengers. Wing span and area were increased to 96 ft. 3 in. and 1254.6 sq. ft. respectively. Performance was similar to the various models of the G.12.

G.18

Designed in 1935, the eighteen-passenger G.18 civil transport closely resembled the Douglas DC-2 in appearance and general layout. Powered by two 700 h.p. FIAT A.59R nine-cylinder radial engines and featuring a crew of three, the G.18 was produced in limited numbers for commercial operation by Avio Linee Italiane S.A. (along with the smaller Rosatelli-designed APR.2), and Ala Littoria. Empty and loaded weights were 12,980 lb. and 19,074 lb. Maximum speed was 211 m.p.h., ceiling 24,928 ft., and range 894 miles. Span was 82 ft., length 61 ft. 8 in., height 16 ft 5 in., and wing area 946.9 sq. ft.

In 1937 an improved model, the G.18V, made its first flight, powered by 1030 h.p. FIAT A.80 R.C.41 eighteen-cylinder radials. The wing area was increased to 949.7 sq. ft., but the only really noticeable external change was a modified fin and rudder. The G.18V weighed

Above right, the first G.18. Below, Avio Linee Italiane G.18V with FIAT A.80 R.C.41 radials. (I-ENEA)

This view of the G.18V stresses its resemblance to American DC-2 and DC-3 transports. (I-ENEA)

15,840 lb. empty and 23,760 lb. loaded. Maximum speed became 248 m.p.h. at 15,088 ft., cruising speed 211 m.p.h., and landing speed 68 m.p.h. The ceiling was 28,536 ft. (13,120 ft. on one engine) and the range 932-1025 miles. The G.18V could climb to 9840 ft. in 10 min. 25 sec. and to 16,400 ft. in 19 min. 10 sec.

In June, 1940, two G.18's serving with Ala Littoria on the Rome-Brindisi-Tirana route, and six serving with Avio Linee Italiane on the Rome-Milan and Milan-Venice-Zagreb-Belgrade-Bucharest routes, came under jurisdiction of the C.S.A.S. (Commando Servizi Aerei Speciali), which was responsible for maintaining airline service and communications during wartime.

G.50

The prototype G.50 fighter monoplane flew for the first time in February, 1937. Developed to meet the 1936 Air Ministry specification which also led to the Caproni-Vizzola F.5, the Macchi C.200, the Meridionali Ro 51, the Reggiane Re 2000, and the Aeronautica Umbra T.18, the FIAT fighter, named Freccia (Arrow), was the first all-metal Italian single-seat fighter.

Featuring a low-mounted three-piece cantilever wing and a monocoque fuselage, the G.50 was powered by an 840 h.p. FIAT A.74 R.C.38 fourteen-cylinder radial engine. Of forty-five pre-production G.50's, twelve were sent to Spain in 1938 with the Gruppo Caccia Sperimentale to gather operational experience. The veteran Italian pilots disliked the enclosed sliding cockpit canopy fitted to the pre-production machines; accordingly, after tests with various open arrangements, a pair of

The prototype G.50, the first all-metal Italian single-seat fighter, built in 1937. (MM 334)

Another view of the prototype G.50, showing a diagonal camouflage scheme. (MM 334)

folding transparent side flaps was substituted on later machines. The first type to incorporate the semi-open cockpit as standard was the G.50bis. In 1939 the Finnish government had ordered 35 G.50 fighters, but these did not arrive until after the end of fighting between Finland and Russia in 1940, having been detained in Germany. The Finnish G.50's served as first-line equipment until 1944, when they were shifted to training duties.

The G.50 was by no means a brilliant machine, being seriously deficient in both speed and firepower, but it had very good maneuverability and was the only reasonably modern fighter other than the MC.200 available to the Regia Aeronautica when Italy entered the war. On June 10, 1940, 118 Freccias were on strength, only 87 of these in serviceable condition. Units equipped with the type were the 51° and 52° Stormi of the 8ª Brigata C.T. at Ciampino Sud and Pontedera. In October, 1940, 48 G.50's of the 20° Gruppo C.T. were based in Belgium with the Corpo Aereo Italiano, but none were employed operationally over England. This unit was transferred to Libya in January, 1941. The fighters also served with the 2° and 154° Gruppi C.T. over Greece.

Empty and loaded weights of the G.50 were 4319 lb. and 5284 lb. Maximum, cruising, and

A production G.50. Note landing gear fairing panels, not fitted to the prototype. (MM 5388)

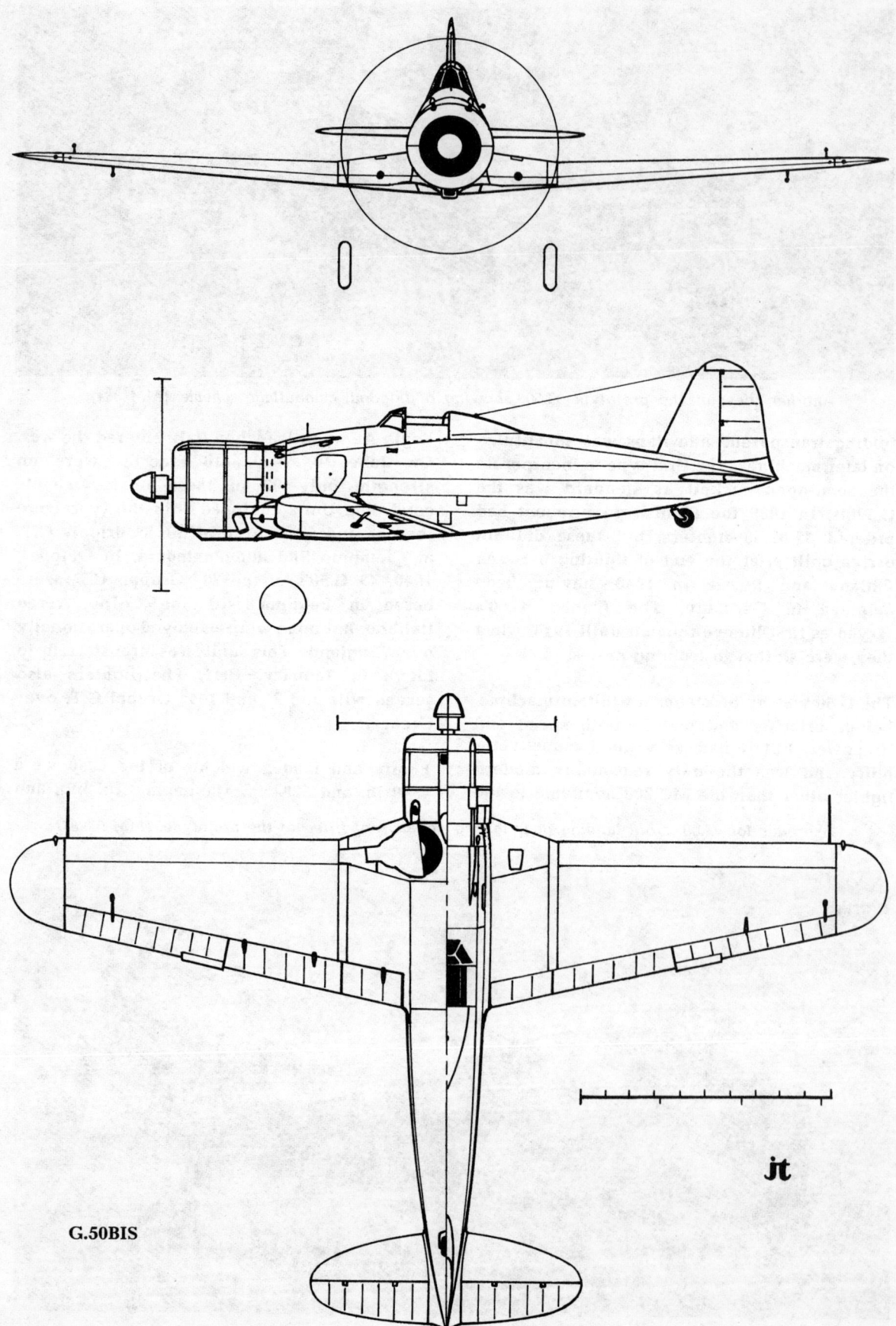

G.50BIS

This photograph of a production G.50 shows the semi-open cockpit to satisfy service pilots. (MM 5439)

landing speeds were 293 m.p.h., 250 m.p.h., and 71 m.p.h., respectively. Absolute ceiling was 35,430 ft. and range 261-416 miles. Dimensions were: span 36 ft. $0^3/_4$ in., length 26 ft. 4 in., height 9 ft. $8^1/_2$ in., and wing area 196.4 sq. ft. Armament was two 12.7-mm. Breda-SAFAT machines guns mounted in the cowl. An internal bay for small bombs was a feature.

The G.50bis, with the revised open cockpit, was flown in September, 1940. Other modifications included an increased fuel capacity, new landing gear, revised wing structure, and a lower fin and rudder of increased chord. Length became 27 ft. $2^1/_4$ in. Empty and loaded weights rose to 4631 lb. and 5505 lb. Performance was almost identical to that of the original G.50, except for an increased maximum range of 621 miles. Service ceiling was 32,480 ft. The G.50bis served in North Africa, principally with the 12° Gruppo C.T. at Castelbenito; in Sicily, the Aegean Islands, Albania, and Greece. Approximately 450 G.50bis fighters were built, of which ten were supplied to the Croatian Air Force in 1941, the rest to the Regia Aeronautica. No G.50's remained in service at the end of the war.

Further G.50 variants included the two-seat G.50B trainer and the Daimler-Benz-powered G.50V, both described under C.M.A.S.A.; the G.50ter, which achieved 329 m.p.h. in 1941 with a 1000 h.p. FIAT A.76 R.C.40 fourteen-cylinder radial engine (on which development had already been abandoned, however), and the G.50bis/A two-seat fighter-bomber which flew in October, 1942. This last machine featured additional 2 ft. $3^1/_3$-in. rectangular wings sections outboard of the landing gear, each section carrying a 12.7-mm. Breda-SAFAT machine gun and shackles for a 353-lb. bomb. Span increased to 40 ft. $7^1/_3$ in., empty and loaded weights rising to 5110 lb. and 7359 lb. respectively. Maximum speed was only 263

The G.50bis featured numerous revisions in wing and fuselage structure, including increased fuel tankage to boost range. (MM 5944)

Above left, a G.50bis keeping company with a Messerschmitt Bf 110. Right, a G.50 retouched as the G.50ter. Rocker arm fairings were necessary for the larger-diameter FIAT A.76 R.C.40 engine.

m.p.h., service ceiling 27,890 ft., and range 621 miles. The G.50bis/A also featured an arrestor hook to make it suitable for operation from the carriers Aquila and Sparviero, then under conversion from merchant ships.

G.51

The G.51 was a projected production version of the G.50V built by C.M.A.S.A. The G.51 project was abandoned in favor of the more advanced G.55.

G.52

The G.52 was another unrealized project, being essentially the G.50 design revised to take the experimental FIAT A.75 R.C.53 engine. The power unit was never built, and the G.52 was dropped.

PROTOTYPE G.50

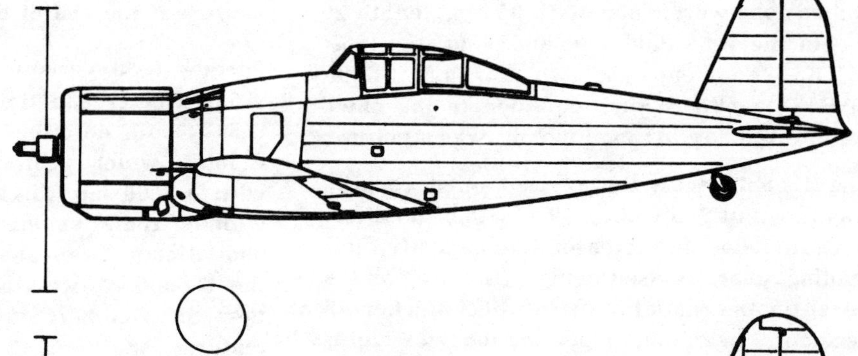

G.50TER

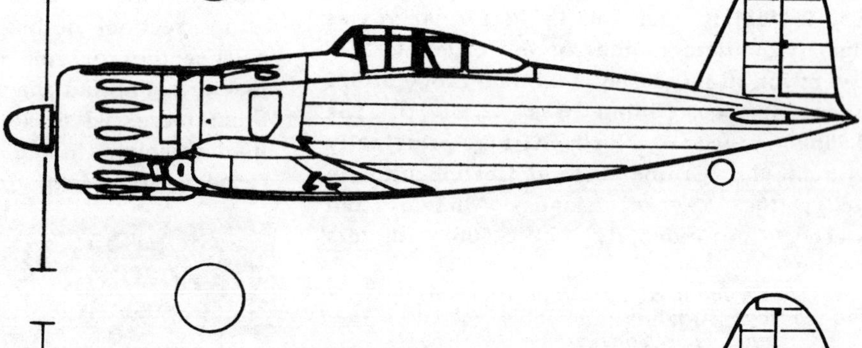

G.50BIS/A

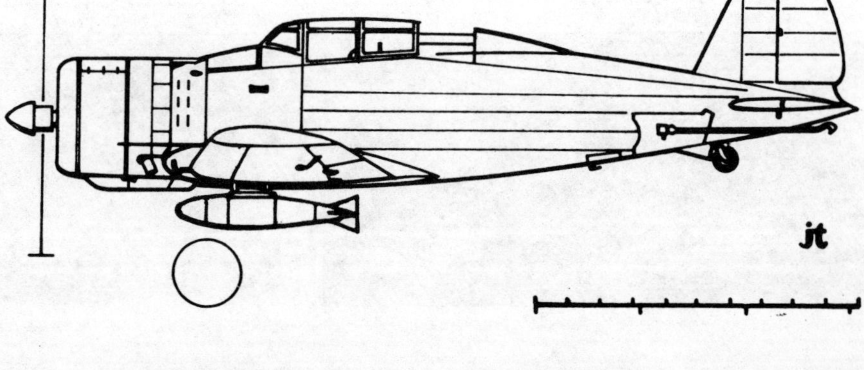

FIAT

Above and immediately below, a production G.55/0, one of Italy's best fighter designs.

G.55

Although based broadly on the G.50 and the DB 601A-powered G.50V, the G.55 Centauro (Centaur) incorporated so many improvements as to constitute an almost entirely new design. Employing a 1475 h.p. Daimler-Benz DB 605A-1 twelve-cylinder inverted vee engine (produced by FIAT as the R.A.1050 R.C.58 Tifone), the G.55 was first flown on April 30, 1942. Construction was all-metal, with fabric-covered movable control surfaces. The German engine permitted a fuselage of reduced frontal area and greatly improved aerodynamics; in addition, the redesigned wing was far more efficient, resulting in a maximum speed of 385 m.p.h. at 22,960 ft., an increase of nearly 100 m.p.h. over that of the G.50. Maneuverability was also excellent.

Production began in early 1943 with the G.55/0, with one 20-mm. Mauser MG 151 cannon and four 12.7-mm. machine guns, two in the fuselage and two in the wings. The G.55/I, which succeeded it shortly after, had two

Above right, a G.55 of the RSI. Right, a G.55 S with torpedo, twin radiators. Below left, a Luftwaffe G.55/I with wing cannon. Below right, the postwar development, the G.55A.

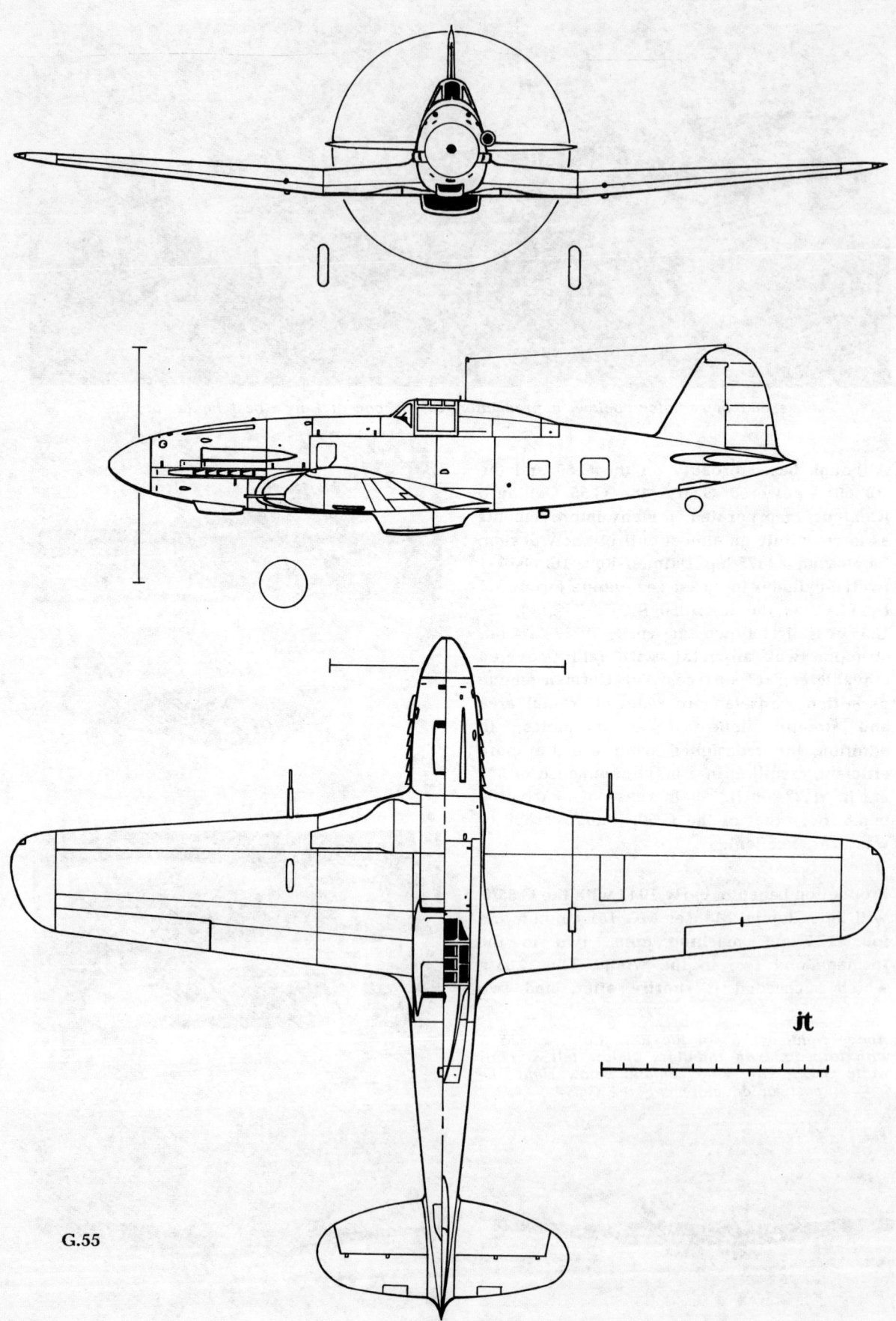

G.55

The G.56 prototype with DB 603A engine was the fastest Italian fighter, achieving 425 m.p.h.

additional MG 151 cannon in place of the wing guns. Unfortunately for the Regia Aeronautica, the fast, maneuverable, heavily armed Centauro was just beginning to equip operational units when Italy surrendered. At that time one example was in service with the 53° Stormo C.T. at Caselle Torinese, and twelve with the 353ª Squadriglia C.T. at Ciampino; of the latter, however, only two machines were operational. As a result of the surrender, German forces controlling Northern Italy took over the remaining Regia Aeronautica aircraft and ordered several thousand further examples for the Aviazione della RSI. However, few DB 605A-1 engines were delivered by Germany or by FIAT, and only 105 Centauros were completed by the end of the war. These included two 1944 developments, the G.55/II with no less than five MG 151 cannon, and the G.55S (Silurante, or torpedo fighter), which, in order to carry the 2167-lb. Whitehead Fiume torpedo beneath the fuselage, had two underwing radiators in place of the normal central one, and a lengthened tailwheel leg. The G.55S had a reduced maximum speed of 374 m.p.h.

The standard G.55 fighter had a cruising speed of 348 m.p.h., a ceiling of 42,640 ft., and a range of 745-1024 miles. It climbed to 19,680 ft. in 7 min. 12 sec. and to 26,240 ft. in 10 min. 11 sec. Empty and loaded weights were 5940 lb. and 8162 lb. (G.55S, 5954 lb. and 9702 lb., respectively). Dimensions were: span 38 ft. 10$^1/_2$ in., length 30 ft. 8$^7/_8$ in., height 10 ft. 3$^1/_4$ in., and wing area 227.1 sq. ft.

Immediately after the war FIAT resumed limited production for the Aeronautica Militare with the G.55A single-seat fighter and fighter-trainer and the G.55B two-seat trainer. From these were developed the various Rolls Royce Merlin-powered G.59 trainers; the smaller Alfa Romeo and DeHavilland Gipsy-powered G.46 sport and training aircraft were also based on the G.55 layout. One hundred G.55A's were sold to Argentina during 1946-47 and a number of G.55B's were sold to Egypt in 1949.

G.56

The most highly developed fighter produced in Italy during the war, the sole G.56 prototype was flown in March, 1944, under German authority. A G.55/I airframe was fitted with the improved DB 603A engine, which produced 1510 h.p. at 18,700 ft. and had a 1750 h.p. take-off and emergency rating. This engine was the only major change from G.55/I specification, yet it increased the length by 4$^3/_4$ in., the weight by 440 lb., and the maximum speed by 40 m.p.h. Retaining the excellent maneuverability that characterized almost all Italian fighter designs, the G.56 possessed sufficient speed and firepower (armament being that of

The TR.1 two-seat cabin monoplane was a contemporary of the basically similar AS.1 and AS.2 models. A seven-cylinder FIAT A.50 S radial engine provided 100 h.p. (I-AAVT)

the G.55/I) to match any Allied or German fighter on even terms, actually proving itself superior to the Bf 109G and Fw 190A in comparative tests. The shortage of engines which limited G.55 production was even more acute with respect to the DB 603 unit, with the result that no production of the G.56 was seriously contemplated.

The G.56 weighed 6380 lb. empty and 8479 lb. loaded. Maximum speed was 425 m.p.h. at 22,960 ft., cruising speed 334 m.p.h., range 795 miles, and service ceiling 43,952 ft. Dimensions were identical to the G.55/I except for the length of 31 ft. 1¼ in.

G.57

A projected experimental version of the G.55

The TR.1 was successful in competition. (I-AAVV)

with a radial engine, the G.57 was to have employed the 1250 h.p. FIAT A.83 R.C.24-52 eighteen-cylinder unit designed in 1943. However, no prototype was built due to the superiority of the German engines as well as to the critical stage of the war.

TR.1

Powered by a 100 h.p. FIAT A.50 S seven-cylinder radial engine, the TR.1 high-wing two-seat cabin monoplane was flown for the first time in 1930 by Renato Donati. Designed for training and touring, the TR.1 adopted the familiar duralumin tube structure with fabric covering, the forward fuselage being the only metal-covered section. The tandem seating featured dual controls, although only the rear position was provided with instruments. The TR.1 weighed 963 lb. empty and 1672 lb. fully loaded, had a maximum speed of 124 m.p.h., a range of 466-714 miles (or an endurance of approximately 4 hrs. 30 min.), and a ceiling of 17,284 ft. It climbed to 13,120 ft. in 36 min. Dimensions were: span 29 ft. 6⅓ in., length 21 ft. 6 in., height 8 ft. 5½ in., and wing area 145.3 sq. ft.

The TR.1 won several sporting events in 1931, being the first aeroplane to finish the Giro Aereo del Piemonte and comprising the first team to complete the Giro Aereo d'Italia.

MACCHI
Aeronautica Macchi S.p.A.

Founded in 1912 as the Società Anonima Nieuport Macchi, the Varese firm built its first plane, the Parasol, the following year. Since that time the company has produced a great number of different designs. Concentrating mainly on flying boats and seaplanes initially, including a succession of Schneider Trophy racing planes designed by Mario Castoldi, the firm turned to fighter design in the late 1930's, producing the best Italian fighter aircraft of the Second World War.

During the First World War Macchi built Nieuport fighters for the Italian Army as well as flying boats of original design, reaching a maximum output of 1375 machines in 1918, an average of over 114 per month. After the Armistice, although continuing to manufacture Nieuport designs, Macchi began its series of racing and record-breaking flying boats and seaplanes. While it is not within the scope of this book to present a complete picture of Macchi efforts during the 1920's, the high points are worthy of inclusion as background to the firm's later work.

Of the early racing machines, the M.7 pusher biplane flying boat, with a 250 h.p. Isotta-Fraschini twelve-cylinder vee engine, was the most successful, with a victory in the 1921 Schneider Trophy Race; it was piloted by Lt. Giovanni de Briganti to a record speed of 177.8 m.p.h. The M.20 was a small touring biplane powered by a 40 h.p. Anzani engine. As a landplane it won the 1924 Coppa d'Italia at Rome and placed second and third the following year. With floats, it won the 1925 Coppa del Mare at Naples. The experience gained in competition was incorporated in the large M.24 bomber flying boat (two 400 h.p. Lorraine-Dietrich engines) and the M.26 single-seat fighter flying boat (300 h.p. Hispano). The last of the Schneider flying boats, but the first of the Castoldi-designed contenders, was the M.33 monoplane powered by a 450 h.p. Curtiss D.12 engine. In the 1925 contest the most successful Italian pilot was again de Briganti, who brought the M.33 into third place at 168.4 m.p.h. As the wing of the M.33 was close to the waterline and the engine was mounted above the hull, it was difficult to get the flying boat on the step for take-off.

Consequently, the next Castoldi Schneider competitor, the M.39 of 1926, was a low-wing twin float monoplane of exceptional streamlining for that time. The three scarlet M.39's, powered by 850 h.p. FIAT AS.2 twelve-cylinder vee engines and piloted in the race by Maj. Mario de Bernardi, Capt. Arturo Ferrarin, and Lt. Adriano Bacula, were by far the fastest machines present. De Bernardi and Bacula finished first and third at 246.5 m.p.h. and 218 m.p.h. respectively. The M.39 was of plywood-covered wooden construction with metal-panelled forward fuselage. The mildly swept wing and the twin floats were externally braced. Dimensions were: span 30 ft. 4^1/$_2$ in., length 22 ft. 1^1/$_4$ in., height 10 ft. 0^1/$_2$ in., and wing area 156 sq. ft. Empty weight was 2866 lb., loaded weight 3542 lb. Maximum speed was 258.8 m.p.h., set on November 17, 1926, by Maj.

Below left, the 1926 Schneider-winning M.39 seaplane. Right, the M.52, which achieved 297.8 m.p.h. in 1927.

The M.67, powered by a 1400 h.p. Isotta-Fraschini W-type engine, had a maximum speed of 348 m.p.h.

de Bernardi over a 3-km. (1.863-mile) course.

In 1927 an improvement, the M.52, was built. Powered by a 1030 h.p. FIAT AS.3 twelve-cylinder vee engine, the M.52 had shorter, more sharply-swept wings, shorter floats, and a longer, better streamlined fuselage. Although all three M.52's retired with engine troubles from the 1927 Schneider contest, held at Venezia Lido, Maj. de Bernardi raised the seaplane speed record (actually, the absolute World Record) to 297.8 m.p.h. on November 4 of the same year. The speed exceeded that of the Schneider-winning Supermarine S.5 by 16 m.p.h. Span and wing area of the M.52 were reduced to 29 ft. 5$^{1}/_{4}$ in. and 143.1 sq. ft. respectively, while length was increased to 23 ft. 4$^{2}/_{3}$ in. Empty and loaded weights were 2618 lb. and 3133 lb., both substantial reductions.

The M.52bis was a revised version entered as a reserve machine in the 1929 Schneider event, backing up the new M.67's. The M.52bis differed from the M.52 only in a further reduction in wing span and area, to 25 ft. 9 in. and 118.4 sq. ft., and in the replacing of the streamlined spreader bars between the floats by streamline wires. On March 30, 1928, the Macchi M.52bis raised the World Speed Record to 318.6 m.p.h.; Maj. de Bernardi was again the pilot. In the 1929 Schneider race, held at Cowes, I.O.W., the M.52bis piloted by Dal Molin finished second (at 282.2 m.p.h.) to the winning Supermarine S.6, after the failure of the two M.67's.

The M.67, built in 1929, employed a 1400 h.p. Isotta-Fraschini Asso eighteen-cylinder W-type engine driving a three-bladed airscrew; due to the engine it was a considerably heavier machine at 3883 lb. empty and 4796 lb. loaded. Except for the different engine, the M.67 resembled the M.52bis closely, although the wings were of the same area as those of the original M.52. The two M.67's entered in the race were piloted by Remo Cadringheri and Monti, but both were forced to retire. The M.67 had a maximum speed of 348 m.p.h.

The 1929 event was the last in which Italian aircraft competed. However, the ultimate racing seaplane design was the MC.72, entered in the 1931 contest but not ready in time. The MC.72 is described separately below. Contrasting with the sleek racing aircraft was the M.53 twin-float light seaplane intended to be operated from submarines. Built in 1927, the angular low-wing monoplane was powered by an 80 h.p. Cirrus four-cylinder in-line engine and featured extremely thick wings. Empty and loaded weights were 1065 lb. and 1505 lb. Maximum speed was only 87 m.p.h. The M.53 climbed to 3280 ft. in 12 min., had an endurance

Below left, the M.53 submarine-borne reconnaissance seaplane. Right, the M.70 two-seat light biplane.

Left, the M.41 fighter flying boat. The M.71, right, differed only in the substitution of rigid bracing.

of 4 hrs., and alighted at 47 m.p.h. Span was 35 ft. 4 in., length 18 ft. 7 in., height 9 ft. 1 in., and wing area 172 sq. ft. Another relatively ordinary design was the M.70 two-seat light biplane built the same year. The power unit was a 75/80 h.p. Cirrus II four-cylinder air-cooled in-line engine. The M.73 was a more streamlined 1930 refinement of the same design featuring a 95 h.p. Colombo S.53 four-cylinder air-cooled in-line engine.

Today the Macchi company is still very active in aircraft design and production, working in cooperation with the American Lockheed firm. Well-known postwar products include the very successful MB.308 touring monoplane, the MB.320 twin-engined touring monoplane, the two-seat MB.323 trainer, the MB.326 jet trainer, and the Lockheed Macchi Santa Maria utility monoplane.

M.41

Although designed in 1927, the M.41 single-seat fighter flying boat was in service with the Regia Marina throughout the 1930's; a development, the M.41bis, was even listed as an operational fighter type in 1939, despite the fact that the eight machines so described had been relegated to training status. The biplane followed the lines of the earliest Macchi racers and was characterized by a very smooth and elegant hull. A 400 h.p. FIAT A.20 twelve-cylinder water-cooled vee engine was mounted on the upper wing, driving a pusher airscrew. In addition to the Italian M.41's, four were used by Spain's Aeronautica Naval and taken over by Franco's forces in 1936.

Empty and loaded weights were 2420 lb. and 3366 lb. Maximum and alighting speeds were 161 m.p.h. and 59 m.p.h., ceiling being 26,240 ft. and endurance 3 hrs. 30 min. The M.41 climbed to 6560 ft. in 4 min. 52 sec., to 9840 ft. in 13 min. 15 sec., and to 13,120 ft. in 21 min. Span was 35 ft. 6 in., length 28 ft. 8 in., height 10 ft. 3 in., and wing area 344 sq. ft.

The M.41bis, introduced in 1930, had a higher engine rating of 440 h.p.; maximum and alighting speeds were 163 m.p.h. and 50 m.p.h.

The MC.72 was the fastest racing seaplane ever built. It still holds the official seaplane mark of 440.6 m.p.h.

The MC.72 employed the 3100 h.p. twenty-four cylinder AS.6 engine and contra-rotating airscrews.

This model climbed to 9840 ft. in 8 min. and to 16,400 ft. in 20 min.

M.71
The M.71, built in 1932 for catapult operation from warships, was almost identical to the M.41bis except for the all-rigid wing bracing to facilitate dismantling. Maximum and alighting speeds were 159 m.p.h. and 50 m.p.h. Climbing performance, somewhat reduced, included times of 5 min. 39 sec. to 6560 ft., 9 min. 34 sec. to 9840 ft., 14 min. 8 sec. to 13,120 ft., and 20 min. 25 sec. to 16,400 ft. Ceiling was 19,680 ft. and range 435 miles. The M.71 was not built in series.

MC.72
The MC.72 (the letter C indicating Macchi's able designer Mario Castoldi for the first time) was the ultimate in racing seaplanes and the fastest aeroplane in the world in its day. Built in 1931 for what proved to be the final Schneider Trophy race, the MC.72 was powered by a FIAT AS.6 twenty-four-cylinder water-cooled vee engine (in effect two modified AS.5 twelve-cylinder units end to end) driving contra-rotating two-bladed tractor airscrews. The MC.72 was thus considerably larger and heavier than its predecessors, but with a considerably improved power to weight ratio. Weights were 5500 lb. empty and 6395 lb. fully loaded.

Trouble with the new engine prevented the MC.72's from competing in the race, won by a Supermarine S-6B flown by Flight Lt. J. H. Boothman. Later a more highly developed S-6B set a new speed record of 406.99 m.p.h. Had the Macchi C.72 been ready for the race, the series of contests might well have continued through the 1930's. After the last race Macchi concentrated on regaining the World Speed Record. This was accomplished handsomely on April 10, 1933, when Warrant Officer Francesco Agello reached 423.8 m.p.h. at Desenzano on Lake Garda with an MC.72 developing approximately 2600 h.p. On October 8 of the same year, with an improved output of 2800 h.p., an MC.72 flown by Lt. Col. Guglielmo Cassinelli averaged 390.8 m.p.h. over a 100-km. (62.1-mile) course. Two weeks later, on October 21, Lt. Col. Scapinelli became the first holder of the Coupe de Vitesse Louis Bleriot (the Bleriot Cup, donated to fill the gap left by the abandonment of the Schneider races), flying one-half hour at an average speed of 384.86 m.p.h.

By the following year the AS.6 engine had been developed further, producing 3100 h.p. On October 23, 1934, Lt. Francesco Agello set the all-time seaplane speed record at 440.68 m.p.h., a speed which remained the absolute record until March 30, 1939, when Capt. Hans Dieterle flew the Heinkel He 100V8 ("He 112U") landplane at a speed of 463.92 m.p.h.

Although faster seaplanes have been developed (one might note the 600 m.p.h.-plus Martin P6M Seamaster), the 1934 mark set by the MC.72 still stands as the official record for seaplanes. Preserved at Desenzano throughout the war, the record-holding machine still exists as an outstanding display item.

The MC.72 had a span of 31 ft. 1 in., a length of 27 ft. $3^2/_3$ in., a height of 10 ft. $9^7/_8$ in., and a wing area of 161.4 sq. ft.

MC.77
The MC.77 bombing and long-distance reconnaissance flying boat was a 1935 design powered by an 850/910 h.p. Isotta-Fraschini Asso 750R eighteen-cylinder W-type engine

MACCHI

MC. 72

Left, the MC.77 reconnaissance bomber. Right, an Ala Littoria MC.94 commercial flying boat. (I-LATO)

mounted above the hull on N-struts, and driving a three-bladed pusher airscrew. The four-man MC.77 was of all-wood construction, including the shoulder-mounted cantilever wing, in which were housed the bombs. Armament consisted of three machine guns, one each in nose and dorsal turrets and a third hand-held gun in a position behind the pilot. The MC.77 weighed 6600 lb. empty and 10,560 lb. loaded, had a maximum speed of 188 m.p.h., an alighting speed of 70 m.p.h., and a ceiling of 18,040 ft. Dimensions included a span of 58 ft. 4 in., a length of 41 ft. 5 in., a height of 12 ft. 11 in., and a wing area of 538 sq. ft. The MC.77 was not adopted by the Regia Marina.

MC.94

A twelve-passenger twin-engined flying boat, the MC.94, also appeared in 1935, and was built in limited numbers during 1936-38. The principal commercial operator was Ala Littoria, which was using six machines on the Rome-Cagliari-Palma route when the war broke out. Another customer was the Corporacion Sudamericana of Buenos Aires, Argentina. Powered by 750 h.p. Wright Cyclone SGR-1820F.52 radial engines, the original MC.94 anfibio (amphibian) version, flown by Giuseppe Burei and Enrico Rossaldi, set a number of international records in 1937. At Varese on April 15 the pair reached an altitude of 21,102 ft. carrying a payload of 2200 lb. On May 6, carrying the same load, the MC.94 achieved 154.7 m.p.h. over a 2000-km. (1242-mile) course. Three days later the 1000-km. (621-mile) record for the same load was set at 159.7 m.p.h.

The MC.94 also employed the Piaggio Stella radial of 670/700 h.p. Of predominantly wood construction, the flying boat had empty and loaded weights of 11,770 lb. and 18,040 lb., the latter figure including twelve passengers and the crew of three. Dimensions were: span 75

The MC.94 was built in limited numbers during 1936—38 to serve Italy's Mediterranean routes. (I-LIRI)

The addition of retractable wheel undercarriage, plus minor redesign, resulted in the MC.94 amphibian.

ft. 2½ in., length 53 ft. 0½ in., height 17 ft. 10½ in., and wing area 815.8 sq. ft. With 780/800 h.p. Alfa Romeo 126 R.C.10 nine-cylinder radial engines, the MC.94 had a maximum speed of 181 m.p.h. at 3280 ft. and a cruising speed of 152 m.p.h. Service ceiling was 19,680 ft.; on one engine the absolute ceiling was 3936 ft. Climbing times were: 7 min. 58 sec. to 6560 ft., 19 min. 30 sec. to 13,120 ft. Employing Wright Cyclone engines, the flying boat, weighing 16,610 lb. loaded, had maximum and cruising speeds of 180 m.p.h. and 155 m.p.h., a service ceiling of 17,210 ft., and an endurance of 5 hrs. 30 min. It climbed to 6560 ft. in 5 min. 29 sec. and to 13,120 ft. in 15 min. 50 sec.

The MC.94 anfibio, although heavier at 13,200 lb. empty and 18,150 lb. loaded, was of slightly smaller dimensions, span being 74 ft. 9⅛ in. and length 50 ft. 10⅞ in. Height with wheels extended was 20 ft. 6 in. In retracted position the wheels, mounted on the sides of the hull, seated in the leading edge of the wing, while the tailwheel swung up below the cut-out rudder. With the Wright Cyclone engines the MC.94 anfibio had a maximum speed of 175 m.p.h. and cruised at 149 m.p.h. Landing speed was 70 m.p.h., service ceiling 19,024 ft., and range 560 miles. Climb to 6560 ft. required 9

The twin-engined MC.99 reconnaissance bomber appeared in 1937 with two 836 h.p. Isotta-Fraschini Assos.

Above and below left, the MC.100 26-passenger commercial flying boat, built in 1938. (I-PLIO)

min. 24 sec.; to 13,120 ft. took 27 min. 42 sec.

MC.99

In 1937 Macchi built a twin-engined reconnaissance bomber flying boat designated MC.99 It was similar to the MC.94 but somewhat larger, employing 836 h.p. Isotta-Fraschini Asso XI R.C.15 twelve-cylinder water-cooled vee engines and twin fins and rudders. Armament comprised four machine guns, two in the nose, one amidships, and one in the tail, while the bomb load was 3300 lb., carried on racks below the wings on either side of the hull. Normal arrangement was twenty-four 110-lb. bombs, twelve 220-lb. bombs, or six 550-lb. bombs. Empty and loaded weights were 10,120 lb. and 25,520 lb. Maximum and alighting speeds were 169 m.p.h. and 62 m.p.h.; absolute ceiling was 17,220 ft. Dimensions included a span of 83 ft. 1 in., a length of 58 ft. 9 in., a height of 19 ft. 5 in., and a wing area of 1019.9 sq. ft. No production of the MC.99 was undertaken.

MC.100

Sharing the basic airframe of the MC.99, the MC.100 commercial passenger flying boat, built in 1938, differed in having three Alfa Romeo 126 R.C.10 nine-cylinder radial engines of 800 h.p. each, and modified interior accomodations for 26 passengers. As with the MC.94, the MC.100 went into service with Ala Littoria, four flying boats being employed on the Rome-Cagliari-Barcelona-Lisbon line in 1939-40. The MC.100 had a crew of four and weighed 18,810 lb. empty and 28,820 lb. fully loaded. Compared to the MC.99, the MC.100 had a wing of greater span and area, respectively 87 ft. $7^3/_8$ in. and 1076 sq. ft. Length and height were 58 ft. $0^1/_4$ in. and 20 ft. $0^7/_8$ in.

Performance included a maximum speed of 193 m.p.h. at 4592 ft., a cruising speed of 163 m.p.h., and an alighting speed of 65 m.p.h. Service ceiling was 20,000 ft.; the MC.100 could climb to 6560 ft. in 6 min. 57 sec., to 13,120 ft. in 17 min. 23 sec., and to 18,040 ft. in 33 min. 20 sec. On two engines it had a maximum speed of 155 m.p.h. and a ceiling of 7544 ft.

MC.200

Built to the single-seat interceptor requirement of Program "R" (for the modernization and expansion of the Regia Aeronautica), the MC.200, first flown in December, 1937, was the first Castoldi fighter design. Powered by an 870 h.p. FIAT A.74 R.C.38 fourteen-cylinder radial engine the MC.200 was a beautiful machine, outstanding in every respect except speed, limited by the low-powered radial, and fire-power, comprising only two 12.7-mm. Breda-SAFAT machine guns. Stability and maneuverability were superb, and diving performance was outstanding. In official trials at Guidonia in 1938, the MC.200 surpassed all its competitors, although closely followed by the Reggiane Re 2000. Ninety-nine MC.200 fighters, named Saetta (Thunderbolt), were ordered as a result, with deliveries to start in 1939. The Saetta was an all-metal low-wing monoplane with oval monocoque fuselage, two-spar three-section wing, retractable landing gear, and Magni-NACA engine cowling with its characteristic rocker arm fairings. In order to give the pilot a good view forward, the cockpit was placed high on the humpbacked fuselage, an arrangement with further limited the speed, only 314 m.p.h. at 15,744 ft.

The prototype and initial production machines featured an enclosed, transparent canopy and a retractable tailwheel; both features were dropped on later models, the former in deference to the wishes of veteran Italian pilots,

Above, the prototype MC.200 (MM 336), first flown in 1937, won 1938 fighter trials held at Guidonia.

Above right, two views of early series MC.200's with enclosed sliding canopies and airscrew spinners. The same version is shown below in uncamouflaged prewar form. Note retractable tailwheel. (MM 4496)

the latter as an aerodynamic luxury not justifying the weight increase. Anti-turnover pylons, fitted just behind the cockpit, protected the pilots of the open machines. Still later a compromise canopy arrangement of two transparent side flaps was fitted.

On June 10, 1940, 156 Saettas were in operation with the Regia Aeronautica (only 77 immediately serviceable). These equipped the 152° and 153° Gruppi of the 54° Stormo of the 2ª Divisione C.T. at Airasca, and the 6° Gruppo Autonomo of the 1ª Divisione C.T. at Catania. These units were followed as MC.200 exponents by the 1° Stormo, the 7°, 9°, 10°, 16°, 21°, 22°, 150°, and 157° Gruppi, and the 356ª, 370ª, 372ª, 373ª, and 374ª Squadriglie C.T. during 1940-42. The Saetta was qualitatively, if not quantitatively, the most important fighter in Italian service, performing well in the Mediterranean, Greek, North African, and Russian theaters.

Modifications included the MC.200 A.S. (Africa Settentrionale), with sand filters and other special equipment for North African desert use, and the MC.200 C.B. (Caccia Bombardiere) fighter bomber with racks for up to 700 lb. of bombs under the wings. On the last production series a wing similar to that of the MC.202 was

Top left, an initial series MC.200 with modified semi-open canopy. Center, a late series Saetta with side flaps. Bottom, an open model with Co-Belligerent roundels. Below, the definitive model. (MM 7705)

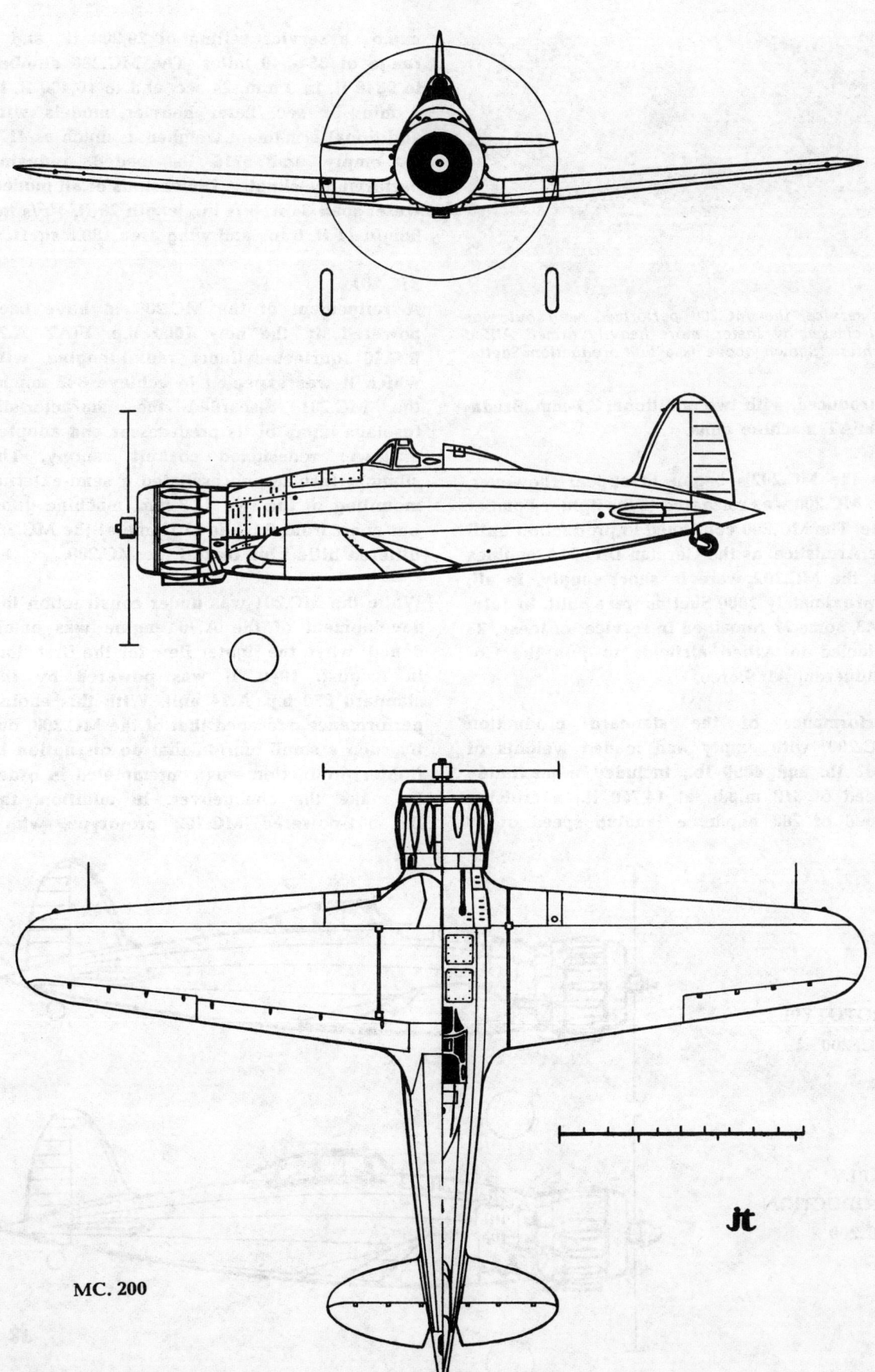

MC. 200

In service, the MC.200 performed well but was out-classed by faster, more heavily armed Allied fighters. Shown above is a late-production Saetta.

introduced, with two additional 7.7-mm. Breda-SAFAT machine guns.

As the MC.202's began to appear, however, the MC.200 was relegated to the fighter-bomber role. The MC.200 continued in production until the Armistice, as the German DB 601A engines for the MC.202 were in short supply. In all, approximately 1000 Saettas were built. In July, 1943, some 77 remained in service; of these, 23 defected to Allied airfields to join the Co-Belligerent Air Force.

Performance of the standard production MC.200, with empty and loaded weights of 3902 lb. and 4850 lb., included a maximum speed of 312 m.p.h. at 14,750 ft., a cruising speed of 283 m.p.h., a landing speed of 78 m.p.h., a service ceiling of 29,200 ft., and a range of 354-540 miles. The MC.200 climbed to 9840 ft. in 3 min. 24 sec. and to 16,400 ft. in 5 min. 52 sec. Later heavier models with additional armament weighed as much as 4175 lb. empty and 5715 lb. loaded, reducing performance slightly. Dimensions of all models were: span 34 ft. $8^1/_2$ in., length 26 ft. $10^5/_8$ in., height 11 ft. 6 in., and wing area 180.8 sq. ft.

MC.201

A refinement of the MC.200 to have been powered by the new 1000 h.p. FIAT A.76 R.C.40 fourteen-cylinder radial engine, with which it was expected to achieve 342 m.p.h., the MC.201 discarded the characteristic fuselage hump of its predecessor and adopted a lower redesigned cockpit canopy. The slimmer fuselage necessitated a semi-external mounting of the two 12.7-mm. machine guns, but apart from this the airframe of the MC.201 differed little from that of the MC.200.

While the MC.201 was under construction the development of the A.76 engine was abandoned; when the fighter flew for the first time in August, 1940, it was powered by the standard 870 h.p. A.74 unit. With this engine performance exceeded that of the MC.200, but by such a small margin that do disruption in fighter production was contemplated in order to make the changeover. In addition, the DB 601-powered MC.202 prototype, which

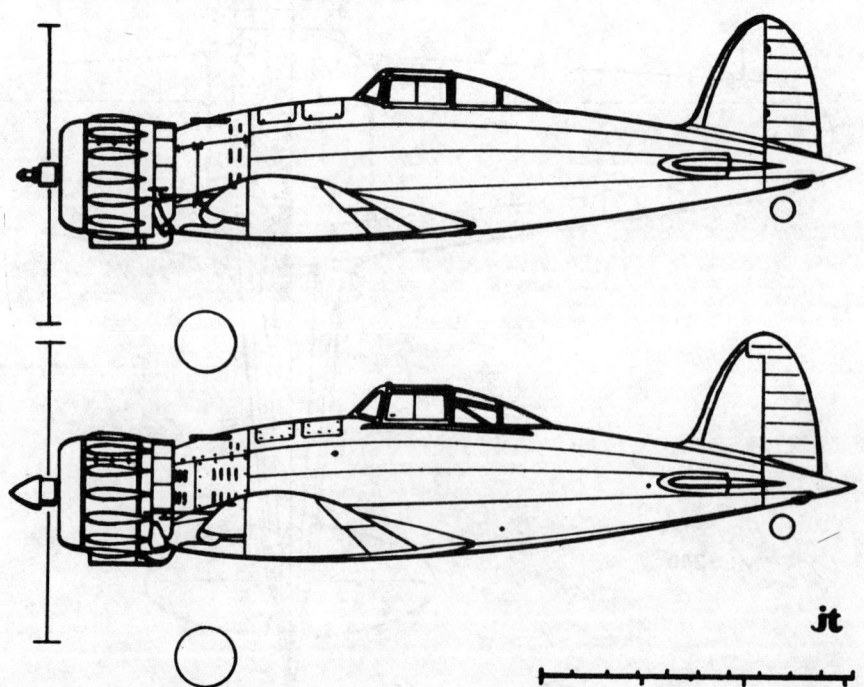

PROTOTYPE MC. 200

EARLY PRODUCTION MC.200

The MC.201 was characterized by a sleeker fuselage, enclosed cockpit, and prominent gun fairings.

made its first flight the same month, showed far greater promise. Accordingly, the MC.201 project was dropped.

Performance with the 870 h.p. engine included a maximum speed of 318 m.p.h., a cruising speed of 283 m.p.h., and a landing speed of 80 m.p.h. Cruising range was 354 miles and service ceiling 28,680 ft. Empty and loaded weights were 4297 lb. and 5258 lb. Dimensions were identical to those of the MC.200 except for the length of 26 ft. $10^{3}/_{8}$ in., a reduction of $1/_{4}$ in.

MC.202

The best Italian fighter to see combat in any numbers during the Second World War, the MC.202 combined the excellent maneuverability and handling of the Saetta airframe with the speed offered by an imported 1175 h.p. Daimler-Benz DB 601A-1 twelve-cylinder water-cooled vee engine, plus the added

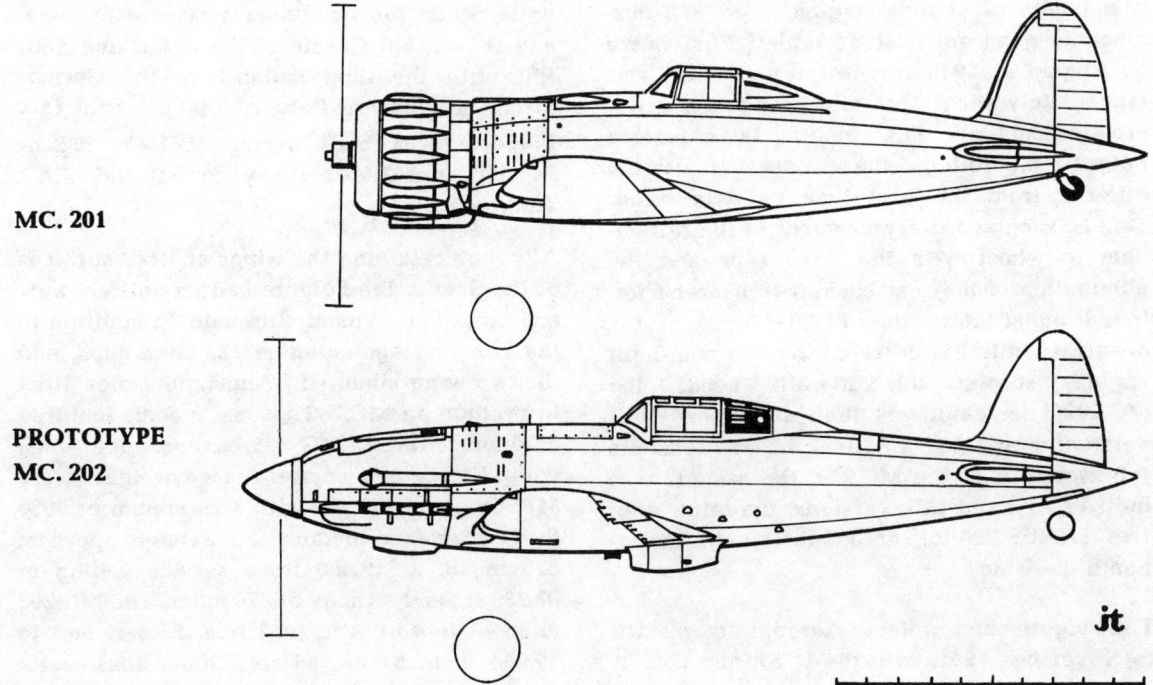

MC. 201

PROTOTYPE
MC. 202

Above and below left, the prototype MC.202 (MM 445), which flew on August 10, 1940.

armament of two wing-mounted 7.7-mm. machine guns on most examples. First flown on August 10, 1940, the prototype MC.202 was immediately successful, and production deliveries began only eight months later. Named Folgore (Lightning), the production version differed from the prototype only in minor details, such as the replacement of the retractable tailwheel with the fixed type and the elimination of the rear cockpit transparencies, found unnecessary due to the taper of the headrest. Initially powered by German-built engines surplus to Luftwaffe needs, the MC.202 later employed the Alfa Romeo-built version, designated R.A.1000 R.C.41 Monsonie (Monsoon). Like the MC.200, the MC.202 was built in A.S. and C.B. versions, the latter with two 110-lb., 220-lb., or 353-lb. bombs underneath the wings.

The Folgore entered Regia Aeronautica service in November, 1941, with the 1° Stormo C.T. in Libya, subsequently equipping the 3°, 6°, 8°, 13°, 17°, and 150° Gruppi C.T., and in 1942 the 3° and 4° Stormi. The Italian fighter was the equal of all its North African opponents, and superior to both the Hawker Hurricane and Curtiss P-40 by a substantial margin. A few MC.202's served with the 21° Gruppo in Russia. By September, 1943, 122 Folgores were still serving with the Regia Aeronautica, 53 of them in operational condition. Six of these later fought with the Allied Co-Belligerent units, while the remainder served with the I° and II° Gruppi Caccia of the Aviazione della RSI until the final collapse of the German forces in Northern Italy. A total of about 1500 Folgores was built during 1941-43, 392 by Macchi and the rest by Breda and S.A.I. Ambrosini.

Although retaining the wings and tail surfaces of the Saetta, the Folgore had an entirely new and more aerodynamic fuselage. In addition to the two fuselage-mounted 12.7-mm. guns, and the two wing-mounted 7.7-mm. guns later fitted to production MC.202's, some models featured a 20-mm. Mauser MG 151 cannon under each wing. Empty and normal loaded weights were 5181 lb. and 6459 lb., with a maximum of 6636 lb. Performance included a maximum speed of 370 m.p.h. at 16,400 ft., a service ceiling of 37,730 ft., and a range of 475 miles. The MC.202 climbed to 13,120 ft. in 3 min. 32 sec. and to 19,680 ft. in 5 min. 55 sec. Dimensions were:

Top, a standard Folgore in flight. Center an MC.202 A.S. (Africa Settentrionale) Serie III. (MM 7806) Bottom left, a late-production Folgore with wing-mounted 20-mm. Mauser MG 151 cannon supplementing the 7.7-mm. fuselage guns. (MM 91974) Bottom right, a late-production model with 7.7-mm. wing guns. In all, nearly 1500 MC.202 Folgores were built between 1941 and 1943 by Macchi, Breda, and S.A.I. Ambrosini. The Folgore was the most modern fighter available to the Regia Aeronautica during the Second World War. It was superior to the Hurricane and P-40, but no match for the Spitfire or P-51.

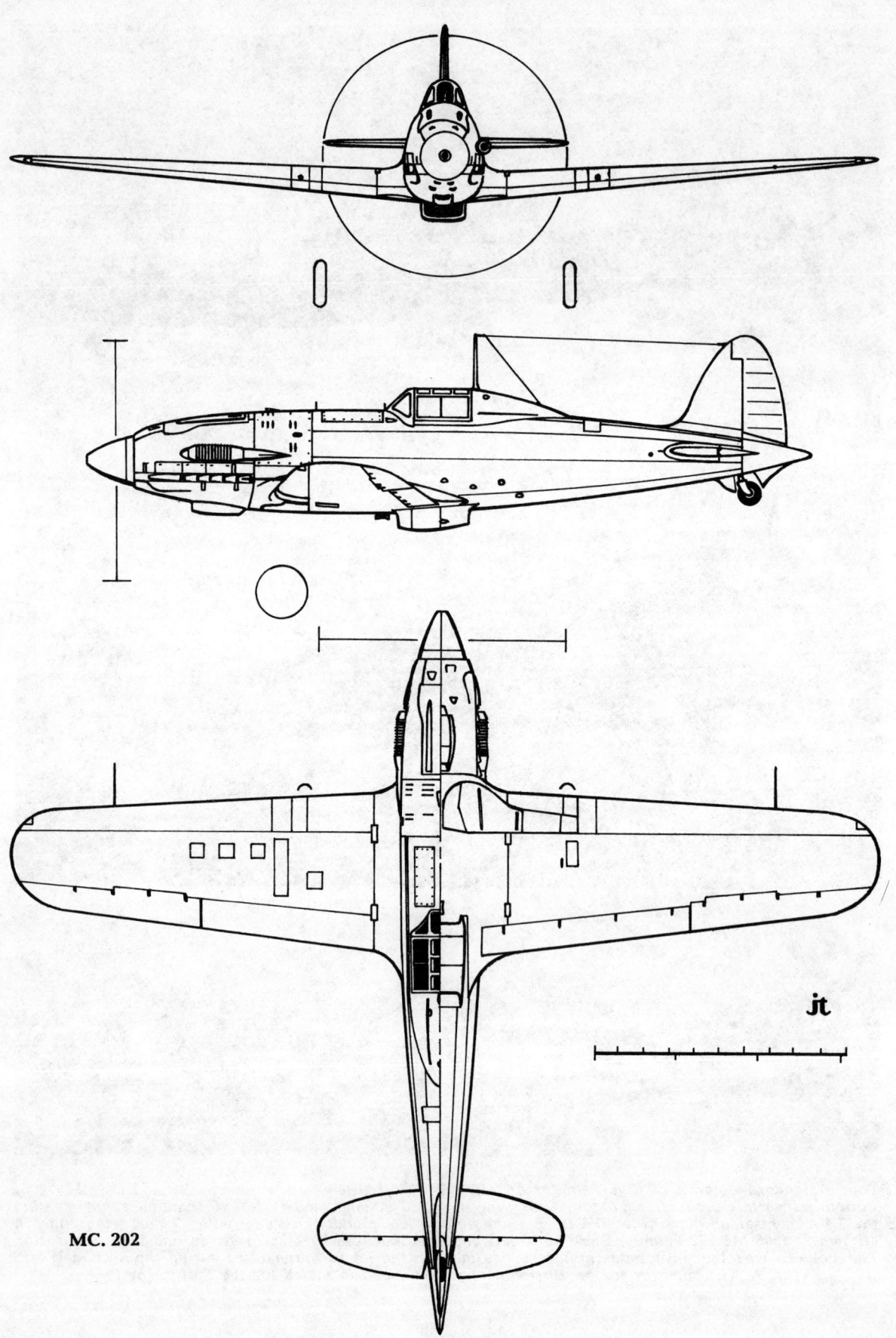

MC. 202

MACCHI

Above, two views of a captured MC.202 evaluated by the United States. Italian markings were later incorrectly re-applied as shown. USAAF insigne can still be seen below the starboard wing at right. Below right, another captured Folgore with 1942-style U.S. stars, Allied fin flash.

span 34 ft. 8½ in., length 29 ft. 0½ in., height 9 ft. 11½ in., and wing area 180.8 sq. ft.

MC.205

While the MC.202 represented a great improvement over the MC.200, Ing. Mario Castoldi produced an even further improved development powered by a 1465 h.p. FIAT R.A.1050 R.C.58 Tifone (license-built DB 605A) twelve-cylinder vee engine. Designated the MC.205V Veltro (Greyhound), the prototype employed an MC.202 airframe, flying for the first time on April 19, 1942. Other than in the type of engine, the Veltro differed only slightly from the Folgore, although the Serie III model replaced the two 7.7-mm. wing guns with 20-mm. Mauser MG 151 cannon. Bomb loads similar to those of the MC.202 could be carried. The Veltro weighed 5691 lb. empty and 7514 lb. loaded, attaining 399 m.p.h. at 23,620 ft. and cruising at 310 m.p.h. It could climb to 9840 ft. in 2 min. 40 sec. and to 22,960 ft. in 7 min. 6 sec. Service ceiling was 36,090 ft. and range

646 miles. Dimensions matched those of the Folgore exactly.

The MC.205V first saw action in July, 1943, over Pantelleria. At that time the Regia Aeronautica had received 30 MC.205 fighters. This number grew to 66 by the time Italy surrendered a month later. Six of these joined Allied Co-Belligerent units and the other 60 fought alongside the Luftwaffe. Further examples were built for the Aviazione della RSI, total production of the Veltro being 262 machines. The fighter was considered a match for the

Below, an MC.205V A.S. Serie III Veltro. Note the 20-mm. wing cannon. (MM 92215)

Above, an MC.205V Serie I at Guidonia in company with an MC.202, MC.200, and Ro 58. Below, a close-up showing twin oil coolers. (MM 9268)

P-51 Mustang by many experts. Although slower and less heavily armed than the famous American fighter, it was superior in handling and maneuverability, characteristics for which Italian aircraft have always been well known. In 1949 a few surviving Macchi C.205V fighters were purchased from Italy by the government of Egypt.

A further version with longer wings and a considerably refined fuselage flew in November, 1942, as the MC.205N-1 Orione (Orion). This prototype carried an engine-mounted 20-mm. cannon, two 12.7-mm. machine guns in the upper fuselage, and two 12.7-mm. guns above the wing roots. Empty and loaded weights were 5941 lb. and 7983 lb. Maximum speed was 390 m.p.h. at 22,960 ft., range 612 miles, and service ceiling 36,910 ft. The MC.205N-1 climbed to 9840 ft. in 2 min. 24 sec., to 16,400 ft. in 4 min. 46 sec., and to 26,240 ft. in 9 min. 48 sec.

A second Orione prototype, the MC.205N-2, flew in May, 1943. It was similar except that the 12.7-mm. machine guns mounted over the wing roots were replaced by wing-mounted 20-mm. cannon, bringing the total armament to three cannon and two machine guns. Slightly heavier at 6052 lb. empty and 8364 lb. loaded, the MC.205N-2 had a maximum speed of 389 m.p.h. at 22,960 ft. and a ceiling of 35,430 ft. Climbing times to 9840 ft., 16,400 ft., and 26,240 ft. were 3 min. 39 sec., 6 min. 14 sec., and 10 min. 47 sec. respectively.

MC.206

The MC.206 was a projected development of the MC.205N-2, with the same armament, employing a 1510 h.p. DB 603A engine and a longer wing of 39 ft. 9$^{7}/_{8}$ in. span. Loaded weight was expected to be 8030 lb. and maximum speed 398 m.p.h. A prototype was under construction in 1943 but never completed.

MC.207

Also a project for the 1510 h.p. DB 603A engine, the MC.207 was to have mounted four 20-mm.

Below, the MC.205N-1 Orione, with hub cannon and four 12.7-mm. machine guns. (MM 499)

Above, another view of the MC.205N-1, which was tested during the winter of 1942—43. (MM 499)

MG 151 cannon in the wings. Span was 39 ft. 9⁷/₈ in., length 31 ft. 11¼ in., loaded weight 9548 lb., and estimated maximum speed 435 m.p.h. As in the case of the MC.206, the prototype MC.207 was not completed.

C.3

The only non-fighter design produced by Macchi during the Second World War, the C.3 twin-engined trainer and light transport was a low-wing monoplane with twin fins and rudders. Power was supplied by two 155 h.p. Alfa Romeo 111 inverted in-line engines. First flown in 1943, the C.3 weighed 4312 lb. loaded and had a maximum speed of 197 m.p.h. Dimensions were: span 41 ft. 1 in., length 27 ft. 6½ in., height 8 ft. 1 in., and wing area 214 sq. ft. The design was considered for postwar production with Blackburn Cirrus Major III engines, but was not built in series.

Above, the MC.205N-2, incorporating wing cannon. Below, a postwar MC.205V for Egypt. (MM 92166)

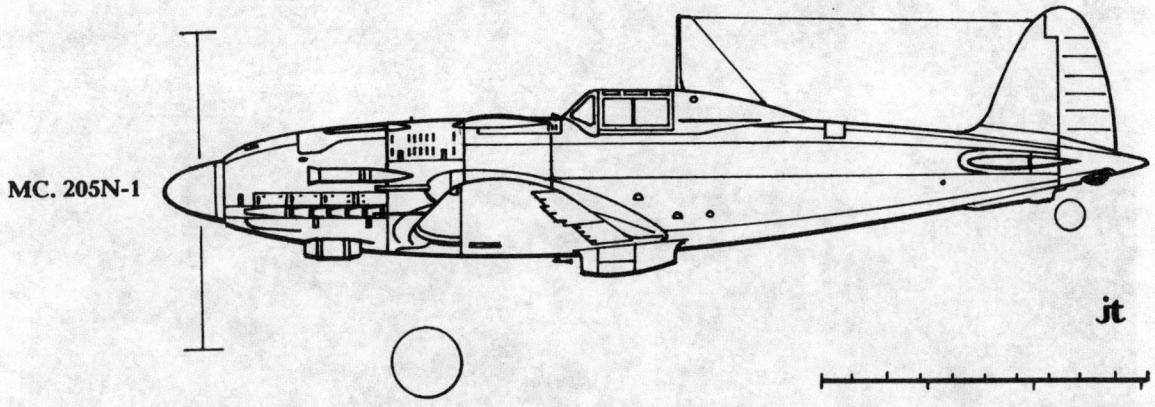

A beautiful salon shot of the Magni Vale 1937, polished to perfection. In the background, an Ro 41 and a Ca 135.

MAGNI
Piero Magni Aviazione S.A.I.

Founded in 1919 at Milan as the Laboratorio Costruzioni Aeronautiche Piero Magni, this small concern was involved principally with research, although several novel aircraft were built incorporating the various features and components developed by Signor Magni. Among these features were variable-incidence wings, lifting struts, air-brakes, and an enclosed radial engine housing which has been widely used to reduce drag on nearly every type of radial-engined aeroplane: the Magni-NACA cowling. The Magni Vittoria was a small single-seat parasol monoplane built in the 1920's and used to test most of the Magni experiments. Originally it had struts forming auxilliary variable-incidence wings, later replaced in 1925 with rigid lifting struts. In 1927 the two-seat Bi-Vittoria was built.

VALE
A small, single-seat high-wing touring and aerobatic monoplane of intriguing design, the Magni Vale was powered by a 130 h.p. Farina T.58 five-cylinder radial engine. The Vale featured swept wings of elliptical planform, constructed of wood with plywood covering, a very sleek plywood-covered fuselage, Magni engine cowling, spinner, and streamlined wheel pants, landing gear legs, and wing struts. Empty and loaded weights were 1188 lb. and 1683 lb. Maximum speed was 155 m.p.h., cruising speed 124 m.p.h., and landing speed 56 m.p.h. Service ceiling was 22,960 ft. and range 621 miles. Dimensions included a span of 29 ft. $2^{1}/_{4}$ in., a length of 18 ft. $0^{1}/_{2}$ in., a height of 6 ft. $7^{1}/_{2}$ in., and a wing area of 115 sq. ft.

PM.3-4 VALE 1937
A 1937 refinement of the Vale, the PM.3-4 differed very little, although empty and loaded weights rose to 1320 lb. and 1760 lb. respectively. Minor aerodynamic refinements, including a longer engine cowling, increased maximum speed to 162 m.p.h., while cruising speed became 131 m.p.h. In all other respects, except for the length of 18 ft. $4^{3}/_{8}$ in., the two aeroplanes were practically identical.

PM.4-1 SUPERVALE
Similar to its two predecessors, the PM.4-1 was built in 1937 for aerobatic and military training. A 140 h.p. FIAT A.54 seven-cylinder radial engine replaced the Farina unit.

JONA J.6
Designed by Ing. Alberto Jona and built by Magni in 1935, the J.6 was an experimental tandem two-seat cantilever sesquiplane, powered by a 140 h.p. FIAT A.54 seven-cylinder radial engine. The novel design featured a hinged, oscillating upper wing with automatic aileron control that rendered the machine spin-proof unless the wing was intentionally locked by the pilot. After completing many tests successfully, the J.6 was purchased by the Italian government

Empty and loaded weights were 1419 lb. and 2134 lb. Performance included a maximum speed of 124 m.p.h., a landing speed of 50 m.p.h., and a duration of 7 hrs. Dimensions were: span 33 ft. 6 in., length 24 ft. 4 in., height 8 ft. 4 in., and wing area 198 sq. ft.

The J.6/S was a military training version without the oscillating wing, powered by a 240 h.p. Alfa Romeo D2 C.30 nine-cylinder radial engine. Empty and loaded weights were 2010 lb. and 2552 lb. Dimensions were the same as those of the J.6 except for the length, reduced to 23 ft. 5 in. Performance was: maximum speed 158 m.p.h. at 9840 ft., landing speed 59 m.p.h., service ceiling 26,240 ft., and climb to 16,400 ft. in 18 min. No production of either Jona design was undertaken.

The Jona J.6 cantilever sesquiplane. (MM 313)

MERIDIONALI
S.A. Industrie Meccaniche e Aeronautiche Meridionali (I.M.A.M.)

In 1923 the Officine Ferroviarie Meridionali of Naples entered the aircraft industry. Two years later the firm obtained the Italian manufacturing rights for certain Fokker aircraft, including the C.V and F.VII/3m, built as the Ro 1 and Ro 10 respectively. Meridionali also buit forty FIAT CR pursuit biplanes during this period, twenty of these on a contract taken over from Montofano when that company (Officine e Cantieri Montofano, Napoli) closed down. Subsequent Meridionali aircraft were of original conception. In 1934 the Società Anonima Industrie Aeronautiche Romeo was formed to take over the aeronautical activities of Officine Ferroviarie Meridionali, and later all the industrial facilities; in 1936, changing the name to S.A. Industrie Meccaniche e Aeronautiche Meridionali, the reorganized company became a member of the Breda group.

The designation Ro, for Romeo, was applied to the entire series of aircraft from the original C.V (Ro 1) to the Ro 63, a light observation and liaison monoplane about to go into production at the time of the Italian surrender in 1943. During the war, Meridionali also built Breda 88, Cant Z.1007bis and Z.1018 bombers.

In 1955 Meridionali merged with the Officine di Pomigliano per Costruzioni Aeronautiche e Ferroviarie, which had been formed in 1949. Although retaining the I.M.A.M. title, the new company has adopted the name AERFER to designate its products, which include the Sagittario 2 (the Stefanutti-designed light jet fighter originally produced by Ambrosini) and the latest development, the Ariete.

RO 1

In 1925 Meridionali obtained the manufacturing license for the Fokker C.V single-engined, two-seat observation and training biplane. Produced in quantity at Naples as the Ro 1, the type was employed extensively in the Ethiopian war, having entered service with Regia

The Ro 1 bis, a development of the Fokker C.V, was a standard reconnaissance machine. (10489)

Aeronautica reconnaissance squadrons in the early 1930's. It was retained as late as 1939 for training duties. Power was furnished by an Alfa Romeo-built 500 h.p. Bristol Jupiter nine-cylinder radial engine. The Ro 1 bis was a modified version with a 550 h.p. Piaggio-built Jupiter VIII radial.

The Ro 1 weighed 2805 lb. empty and 4785 lb. loaded, had a span of 50 ft. 2$^1/_4$ in., a length of 31 ft. 0$^3/_8$ in., a height of 11 ft. 10$^3/_8$ in., and a wing area of 422.9 sq. ft. Performance included maximum, cruising, and landing speeds of 158 m.p.h., 112 m.p.h., and 53 m.p.h. respectively. Range was 745 miles and service ceiling 19,680 ft. The Ro 1 climbed to 3280 ft. in 2 min. 30 sec. and to 13,120 ft. in 18 min. 30 sec.

An Ro 1 reconnaissance biplane in Libya. This three-seat version was a field modification.

RO 5
A two-seat light monoplane powered by either an 85 h.p. FIAT A.50 seven-cylinder radial or an 85 h.p. Walter radial, the Ro 5 was built in a small series in 1929. It competed in various touring competitions, including the 1929 Round-Europe flight. The Ro 5 had a maximum speed of 112 m.p.h., cruised at 96 m.p.h., and landed at 37 m.p.h. Range was 621 miles and ceiling 16,400 ft. Empty and loaded weights were 882 lb. and 1499 lb. Dimensions were: span 36 ft. 11 in., length 23 ft. 3 in., height 7 ft. 1 in., and wing area 205 sq. ft.

RO 10
The Ro 10 was a license-built version of the F.VII/3m (three-motor) high-wing transport which was originally built by Fokker in 1925 as a conversion of the already successful single-engined F.VIIa. The Italian model fitted three 200 h.p. Alfa Romeo Lynx seven-cylinder radial engines.

RO 26
Also powered by the 200 h.p. Alfa Romeo Lynx radial, the Ro 26 was a Meridionali-designed single-engined two-seat aerobatic trainer built in both landplane and seaplane versions.

RO 30
The Ro 30 three-seat military reconnaissance and army cooperation biplane appeared in 1932, employing a 550 h.p. Piaggio-built Jupiter VII nine-cylinder radial engine, driving a four-bladed wooden airscrew. An alternate engine was the 530 h.p. Alfa Romeo Mercurius radial. The Ro 30 was used in limited numbers by the Regia Aeronautica during the 1930's, a few remaining aircraft being relegated to training functions by 1939. Armament was three machine guns and bomb load up to 976.8 lb., comprising twenty 26.4-lb. or 33-lb. bombs

The Ro 5 was a two-seat monoplane powered by an 85 h.p. FIAT A.50 seven-cylinder radial engine. (I-FIDO)

beneath the wings plus twelve 26.4-lb. bombs under the fuselage. Empty and loaded weights were 3498 lb. and 5808 lb. Maximum speed was 155 m.p.h. at 13,120 ft. and landing speed 59 m.p.h. Service ceiling was 24,600 ft. 18 min. were required to reach an altitude of 16,400 ft. Dimensions were: span 51 ft. 8 in., length 33 ft. 7 in., and height 11 ft. 5³/₄ in. The Ro 30 was a development of the Ro 1.

RO 37

The Ro 37 two-seat strategic reconnaissance plane was the first important original design by the Meridionali firm. Although still a biplane with fixed landing gear, the Ro 37 represented a great improvement over the earlier Ro 1 and Ro 30. Appearing in the mid-1930's, the Ro 37, which became the standard Regia Aeronautica land-based reconnaissance machine, was employed successfully in Spain with Nationalist units and exported to Afghanistan (where it was less successful), Ecuador, Hungary, and Uruguay during 1936-38.

The initial model, built in 1934, was powered by a 600 h.p. FIAT A.30 R.A. twelve-cylinder water-cooled vee engine. In appearance it was not unlike the FIAT BR. and CR. biplanes of the period, although lacking the characteristic Warren-strut arrangement of the FIAT types. Structure was all-metal with mixed metal and fabric covering. At the time of its introduction the Ro 37 was classified as a fighter-reconnaissance biplane, but it was never employed in the fighter role due to the advances in that field during the late 1930's. Approximately 200 FIAT-powered Ro 37's were built, this version comprising about half of the 283 Ro 37's available to the Regia Aeronautica in June, 1940. Probably less than 100 of the by then

Top left, the Ro 30 reconnaissance biplane. Immediately below, three air-to-air views of FIAT-powered Ro 37 reconnaissance biplanes. Bottom, a factory shot of the prototype Ro 37.

Above and below right, the Ro 37bis, which substituted a Piaggio radial engine for the FIAT unit.

extremely dated FIAT-powered type were in serviceable condition. Empty and loaded weights were 3432 lb. and 5269 lb. With 550 h.p. available at 13,120 ft., performance included a maximum speed of 199 m.p.h., a cruising speed of 161 m.p.h. (16,400 ft.), and a landing speed of 67 m.p.h. Ceiling was 21,976 ft. and range 726 miles. The Ro 37 climbed to 6560 ft. in 3 min. 45 sec., to 13,120 ft. in 9 min. 5 sec., and to 19,680 ft. in 17 min. 30 sec. Dimensions included a span of 36 ft. $4^{1}/_{8}$ in., a length of 28 ft. $3^{1}/_{4}$ in., a height of 9 ft. $8^{3}/_{4}$ in., and a wing area of 337.4 sq. ft.

A radial-engined version, the Ro 37bis, mounted either the 560 h.p. Piaggio P.IX R.C.40 or 700 h.p. P.XR nine-cylinder units. Dimensions were the same as for the original version, except for

Above right, an Ro 37bis in Spanish markings. Below, a standard Regia Aeronautica Ro 37bis. (MM 10907)

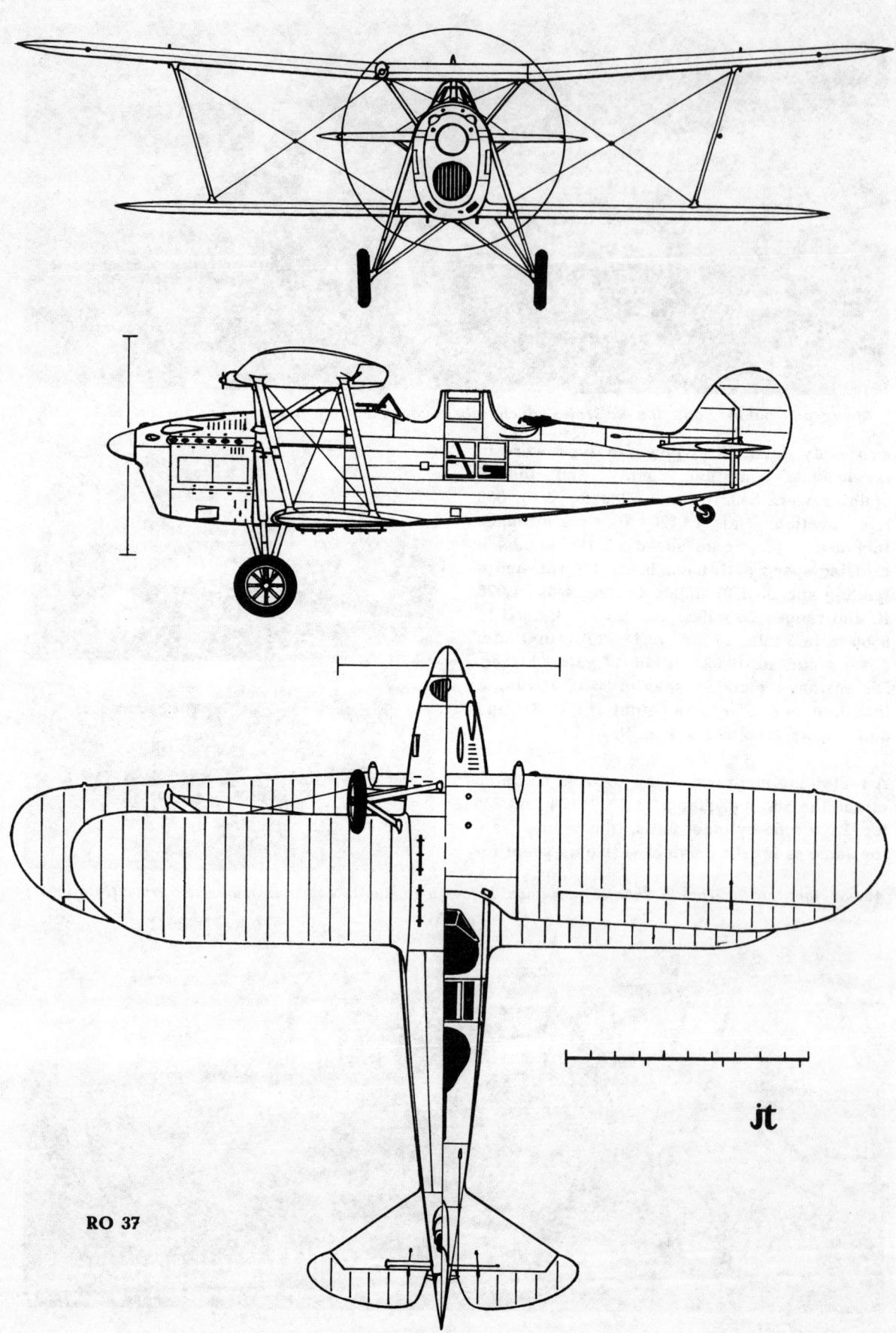

RO 37

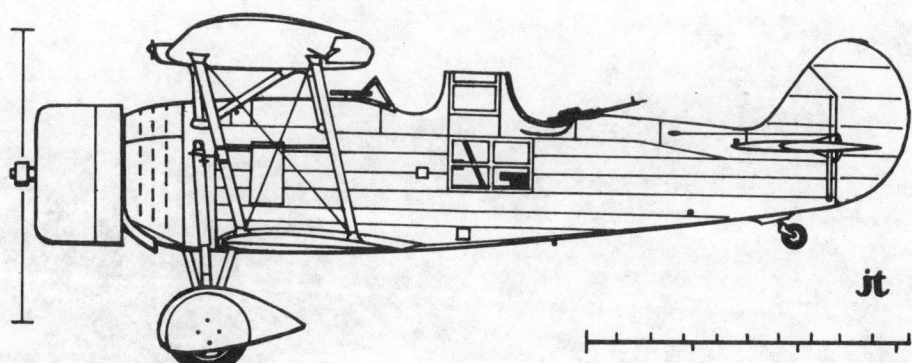

RO 37BIS

the length of 28 ft. 1¼ in. and the height of 10 ft. 3¾ in. Empty and loaded weights were respectively 3498 lb. and 5335 lb. (P.IX), or 3454 lb. and 5291 lb. (P.XR). With the P.IX engine, the Ro 37bis had maximum and cruising speeds of 205 m.p.h. and 155 m.p.h., both at 16,400 ft. Ceiling was 23,616 ft. and range 696 miles. Climb to 6560 ft. took 4 min. 10 sec., to 13,120 ft. 9 min. 20 sec., and to 19,680 ft. 16 min. 30 sec.

With the P.XR engine, rated at a lower altitude, the Ro 37bis had a maximum speed of 199 m.p.h. at 6560 ft. Ceiling was only 20,664 ft. Climb to 6560 ft. took 3 min. 40 sec., to 13,120 ft. 9 min. 30 sec., and to 19,680 ft. 20 min. In all, about 200 Ro 37bis were built.

Armament of all models comprised two forward-firing 12.7-mm. Breda-SAFAT machine guns and one hand-held 7.7-mm. gun in the observer's cockpit. A Breda turret was considered but never installed. Twelve 26.4-lb. or 33-lb. bombs could be carried on racks below the wings. Ro 37's were operated with and without streamlined wheel spats. During the Second World War the Ro 37 and Ro 37bis served on most fronts; Ro 37-equipped units included the 64°, 67°, and 73° Gruppi Osservazione Aerea in North Africa, the 5°, 63°, 70°, and 72° Gruppi O.A. in the Balkans, the 110[a] Squadriglia in A.O.I., and the 124[a] Squadriglia on Sardinia. During this period the Ro 37 was no longer in production; as a result of attrition, no Ro 37's remained in service by July, 1943, all of the type having been replaced by the several Caproni twin-engined machines.

RO 41

Similar in layout and appearance to the FIAT CR.40 and CR.41, the Meridionali Ro 41 single-seat fighter biplane appeared in 1935. The

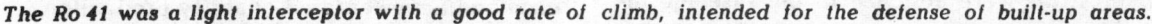

The Ro 41 was a light interceptor with a good rate of climb, intended for the defense of built-up areas.

Above, a two-seat Ro 41 fighter trainer. Below left, a single-seat Ro 41 in postwar service.

similarity was further served by a modified form of Warren wing bracing in which the inner struts were attached to the fuselage instead of to the upper wing, which had the same vee center section for forward visibility. However, the low output of the Piaggio P.VII C.45 seven-cylinder radial engine (390 h.p. at 14,760 ft.) considerably limited the performance of the Ro 41 in comparison to the FIAT fighter prototypes. The wing of the Ro 41 was of mixed wood and duralumin construction, covered partly with wood and partly with fabric, while the fuselage was of welded steel tubing with fabric and duralumin sheet covering. Landing gear was fixed, with spatted wheels. The airscrew was of the two-bladed, variable-pitch type. Armament comprised two 7.7-mm. machine guns firing through the airscrew disc. In addition to the single-seat fighter, a two-seat advanced training version with dual controls was built. The Ro 41 was not adopted by the Regia Aeronautica in either form and never entered quantity production.

While acceptable for a biplane of the Ro 41's weight (2178 lb. empty, 2728 lb. loaded) and power, the performance of the fighter was not outstanding, maximum speed being only 202

Below, the Ro 43, the standard Regia Marina shipboard reconnaissance floatplane.

Approximately 125 Ro 43 catapult floatplanes were built for the Regia Marina, but use was limited.

m.p.h. at 16,400 ft., cruising speed 180 m.p.h., landing speed 62 m.p.h., range 350 miles, and ceiling 25,580 ft. The Ro 41 climbed to 6560 ft. in 2 min. 50 sec., to 13,120 ft. in 6 min. 20 sec., and to 19,680 ft. in 10 min. 50 sec. Dimensions included a span of 28 ft. $10^{3}/_{4}$ in., a length of 21 ft. $6^{3}/_{8}$ in., a height of 8 ft. $8^{1}/_{4}$ in., and a wing area of 206.3 sq. ft. The two-seat model weighed 11 lb more empty and loaded, performance and dimensions being virtually identical, except for a reduced range.

RO 43

The Ro 43 two-seat reconnaissance and fighter floatplane and its single-seat fighter variant, the Ro 44, followed the same basic biplane formula established by the Ro 37 and Ro 41. Employing a single main float and two wingtip floats, the Ro 43 was powered by a 700 h.p. Piaggio P.XR nine-cylinder radial engine. The prototype had a two-bladed airscrew with spinner, replaced by a three-bladed airscrew without spinner on production machines. In addition, the streamlined rocker-arm fairings of the Magni-NACA cowling disappeared with the adoption of a smoother, larger-diameter cowling. Designed for catapult launching from warships, the Ro 43 was accepted by the Regia Marina as the standard machine of this type. Construction details followed the pattern of the earlier biplanes, with the addition of folding wings. Armament consisted of two 7.7-mm. Breda-SAFAT machine guns, one firing forward and the other mounted in the observer's cockpit. As with the Ro 37, a Breda turret was contemplated in place of the hand-held gun.

Approximately 125 Ro 43's were manufactured, 105 machines being available (42 in serviceable state) to the Navy when Italy entered the war. In addition to their use aboard ships, a few Ro 43's (average strength, four floatplanes) were employed by the 161[a] Squadriglia Caccia Marina of the Aeronautica dell'Egeo as fighter protection for the Italian-held islands in the Aegean Sea. Nevertheless, the Ro 43 was not used extensively during the war. In September, 1943, 48 machines still remained (only 22 serviceable) with the 2[a] and 3[a] Squadriglie Forze Navali aboard remaining Italian ships.

The Ro 43 weighed 3916 lb. empty and 5280 lb. loaded. Performance was: maximum speed 186 m.p.h. at 8200 ft., cruising speed 155 m.p.h., alighting speed 64 m.p.h., service ceiling 21,648 ft., endurance 4 hrs. 30 min. (corresponding range, approximately 497 miles) to 8 hrs. 30

An Ro 43 reconnaissance floatplane being hoisted aboard an Italian cruiser.

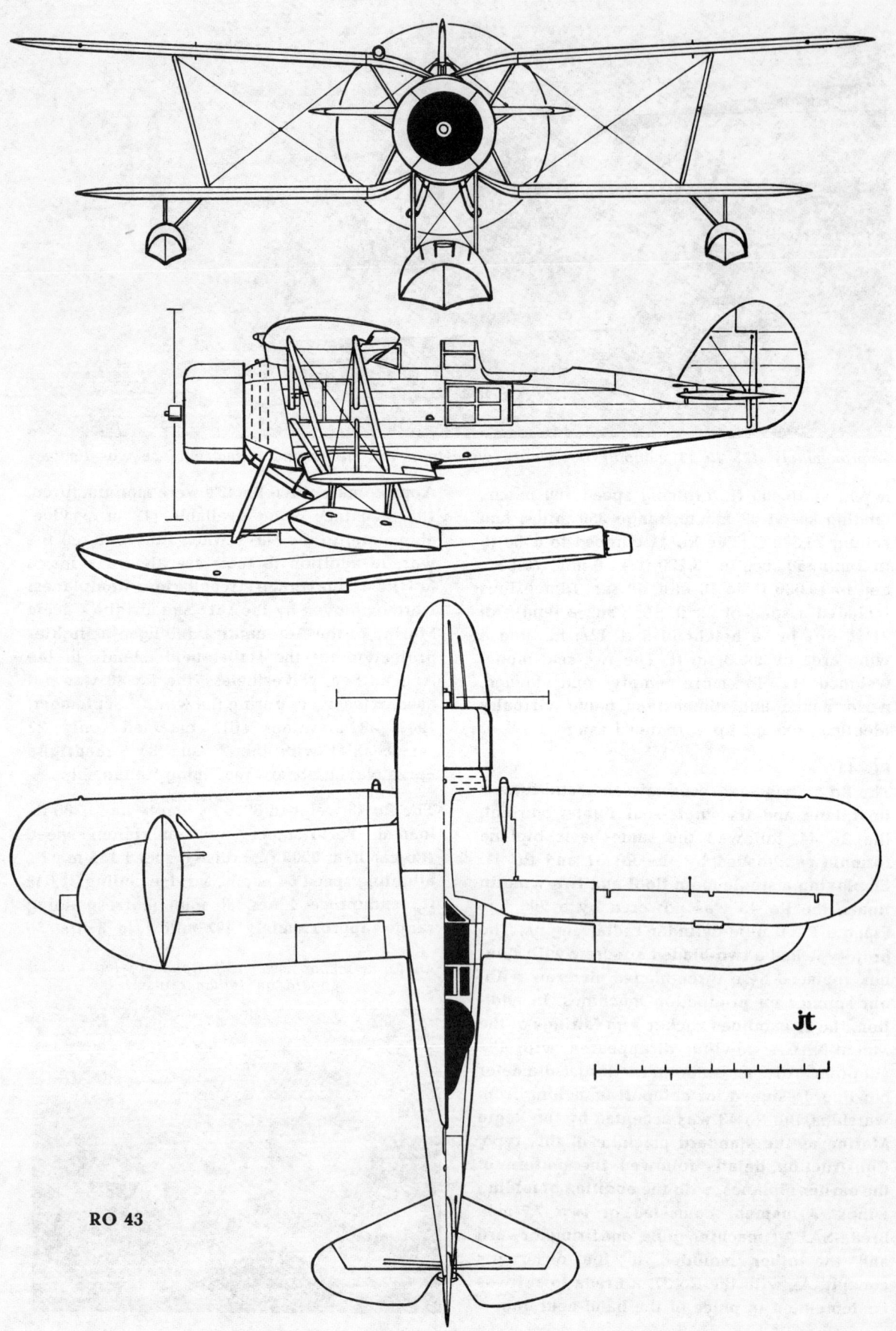

RO 43

Above and below right, the single-seat Ro 44 fighter floatplane, an Ro 43 development. (MM 3703)

min. (932 miles), climb to 6560 ft. in 4 min. 45 sec., to 13,120 ft. in 11 min., and to 16,400 ft. in 15 min. 50 sec. Dimensions included a span of 37 ft. $11\frac{1}{2}$ in., length 31 ft. $10\frac{3}{8}$ in., height 11 ft. $6\frac{1}{8}$ in., and wing area 358.9 sq. ft.

RO 44

Except for the modification to a single-seat fighter, with the fitting of two forward-firing 7.7-mm. Breda-SAFAT machine guns, the Ro 44 was almost identical to the Ro 43, employing the same engine and having the same dimensions. Weights decreased slightly to 3894 lb. empty and 4884 lb. loaded. With the omission of the observer's cockpit and canopy, a long faired headrest was built behind the pilot.

Although production figures are unavailable, probably no more than 50 Ro 44 fighter float-

planes were built, 31 machines being in service in 1939. As in the case of the Ro 43, the fighter served with the 161ª Squadriglia Caccia Marina at Lero, and aboard warships. By September, 1943, six Ro 44's remained, equipping the 2ª and 3ª Squadriglie Forze Navali.

Maximum speed was 189 m.p.h. at 8200 ft., cruising speed 173 m.p.h., and alighting speed 61 m.p.h. Service ceiling was 22,960 ft. and

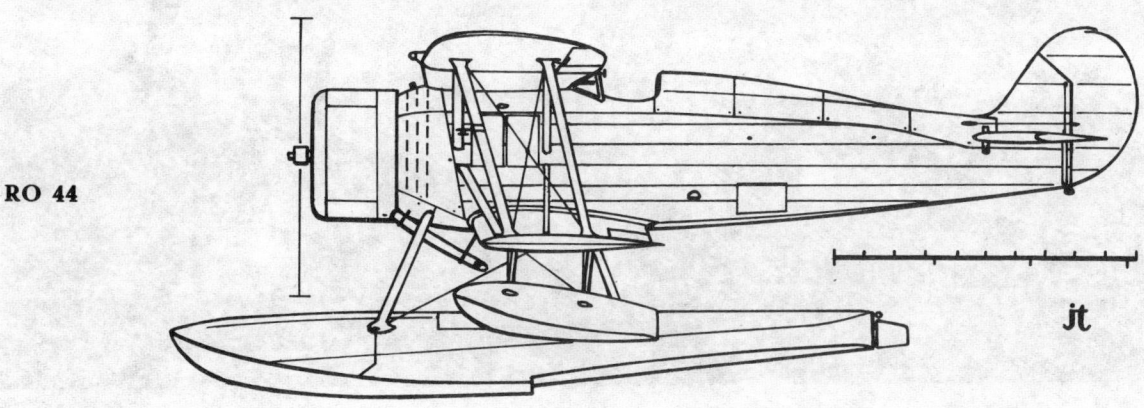
RO 44

The Ro 45 was an enlarged long-distance version of the Ro 37 reconnaissance biplane.

endurance 2-5 hrs. (298-745 miles). The Ro 44 climbed to 6560 ft. in 3 min. 30 sec., to 13,120 ft. in 8 min. 40 sec., and to 16,400 ft. in 12 min. 30 sec.

RO 45

The Ro 45 was a two-seat long-distance reconnaissance development of the Ro 37 mounting an 835 h.p. Isotta-Fraschini Asso XI R.C. twelve-cylinder water-cooled vee engine, initially driving a two-bladed airscrew. Other changes included a longer fuselage to increase the fuel capacity, revised landing gear and wing bracing, and later, as with the Ro 37bis, a three-bladed airscrew. No performance details are available.

RO 51

One of the immediate prewar generation of Italian fighter monoplanes, the Ro 51, employing the same 840 h.p. FIAT A.74 R.C.38 fourteen-cylinder radial engine that powered its competitors, was the first monoplane designed and built by Meridionali, appearing in 1938. Initially fitted with fixed spatted landing gear, the Ro 51, with a top speed of only 290 m.p.h. at 16,400 ft., was not successful in obtaining production orders, these being given to the FIAT G.50, the Macchi C.200, and later, the Re 2000 Serie II and III. The wing of the Ro 51 was all-wood with plywood covering, the fuselage was all-metal, and the tail surfaces were of fabric-covered welded-steel

The first prototype Ro 51 featured fixed landing gear and a very small fin-and-rudder assembly. (MM 338)

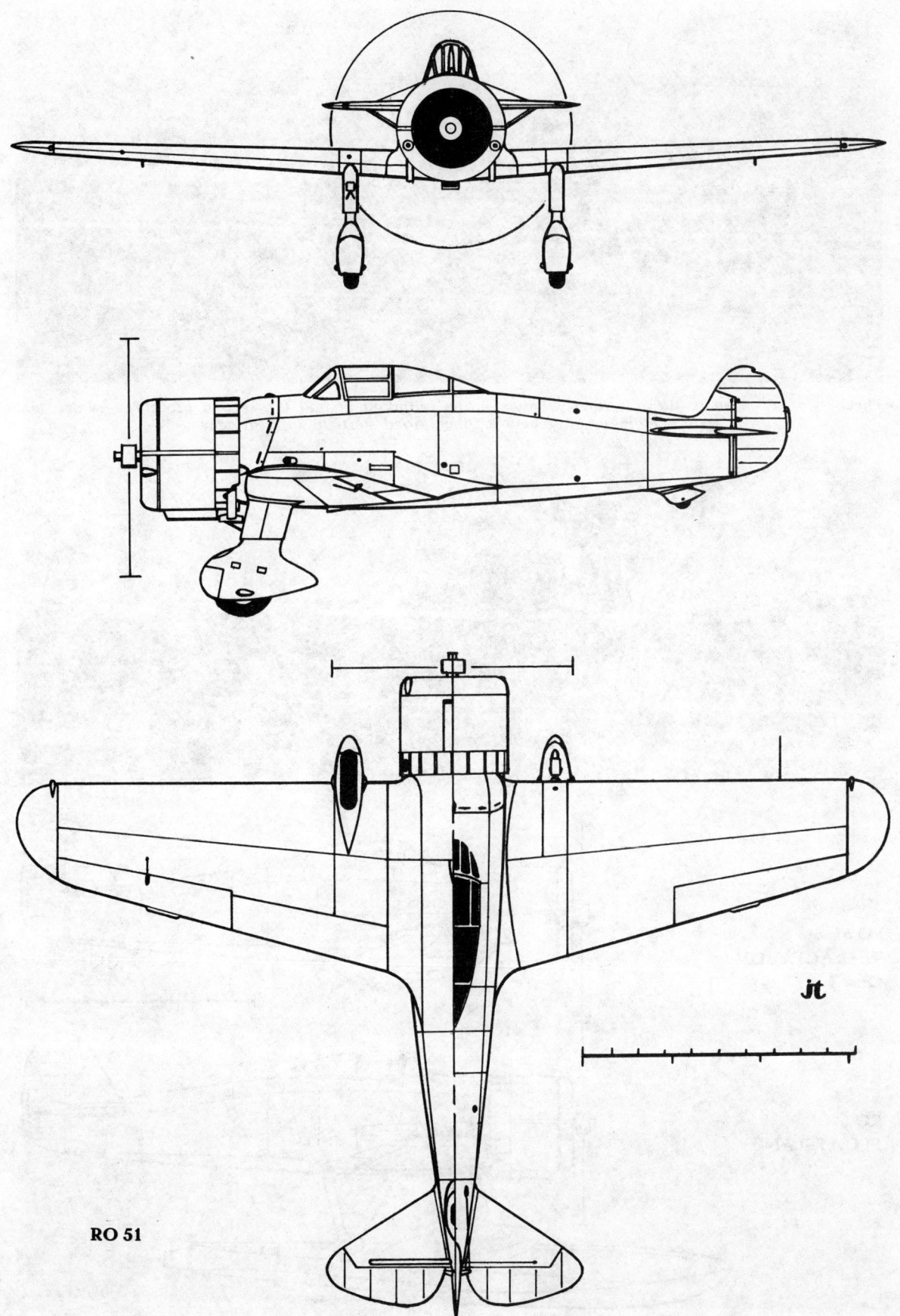

These two views show the differences between the initial Ro 51 and the second prototype, which had retractable landing gear and enlarged vertical tail surfaces.

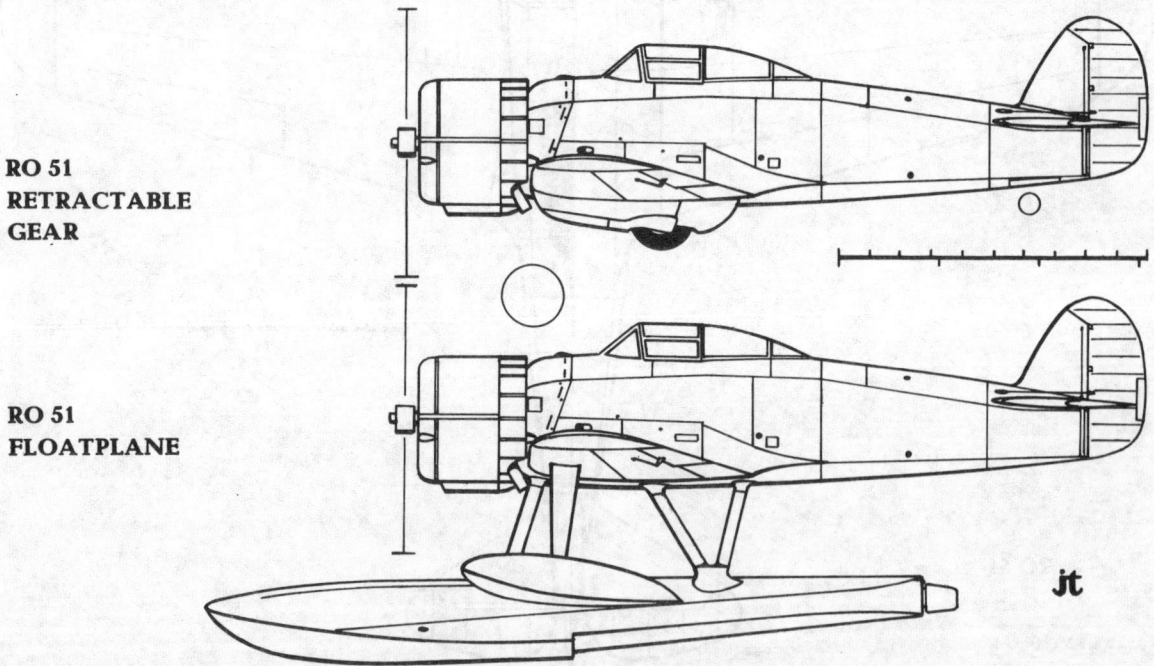

RO 51 RETRACTABLE GEAR

RO 51 FLOATPLANE

Above and below right, the twin-engined Ro 57 interceptor, used in small numbers during 1942—43.

tubing. Two 12.7-mm. Breda-SAFAT machine guns were mounted relatively low in the fuselage, firing through ports in the sides of the engine cowling.

On a second prototype rearward-retracting landing gear rather similar to that of the Seversky P-35 was fitted. A third prototype was built as a floatplane, intended as a replacement for the Ro 44. The main float was attached to the fuselage by a modified N-strut arrangement consisting of six members, while the wing floats were each attached by a single strut. Both the second and third machines featured larger vertical tail surfaces than the original. No Ro 51 variant went into production.

Performance of the second prototype, which weighed 3674 lb. empty and 4620 lb. loaded, included a maximum speed of 304 m.p.h. at 16,400 ft., a cruising speed of 255 m.p.h., and a landing speed of 78 m.p.h. Range was 745 miles and ceiling 29,530 ft. Climb to 19,680 ft. required 7 min. Dimensions were: span 32 ft. $0^1/_2$ in., length 24 ft. $5^2/_3$ in., and height 9 ft. $0^1/_4$ in.

RO 57

The Ro 57 made somewhat of a break with previous Meridionali practice, being a relatively advanced twin-engined single-seat interceptor with retractable landing gear. Designed in 1939 by Ing. Giovanni Galasso, the

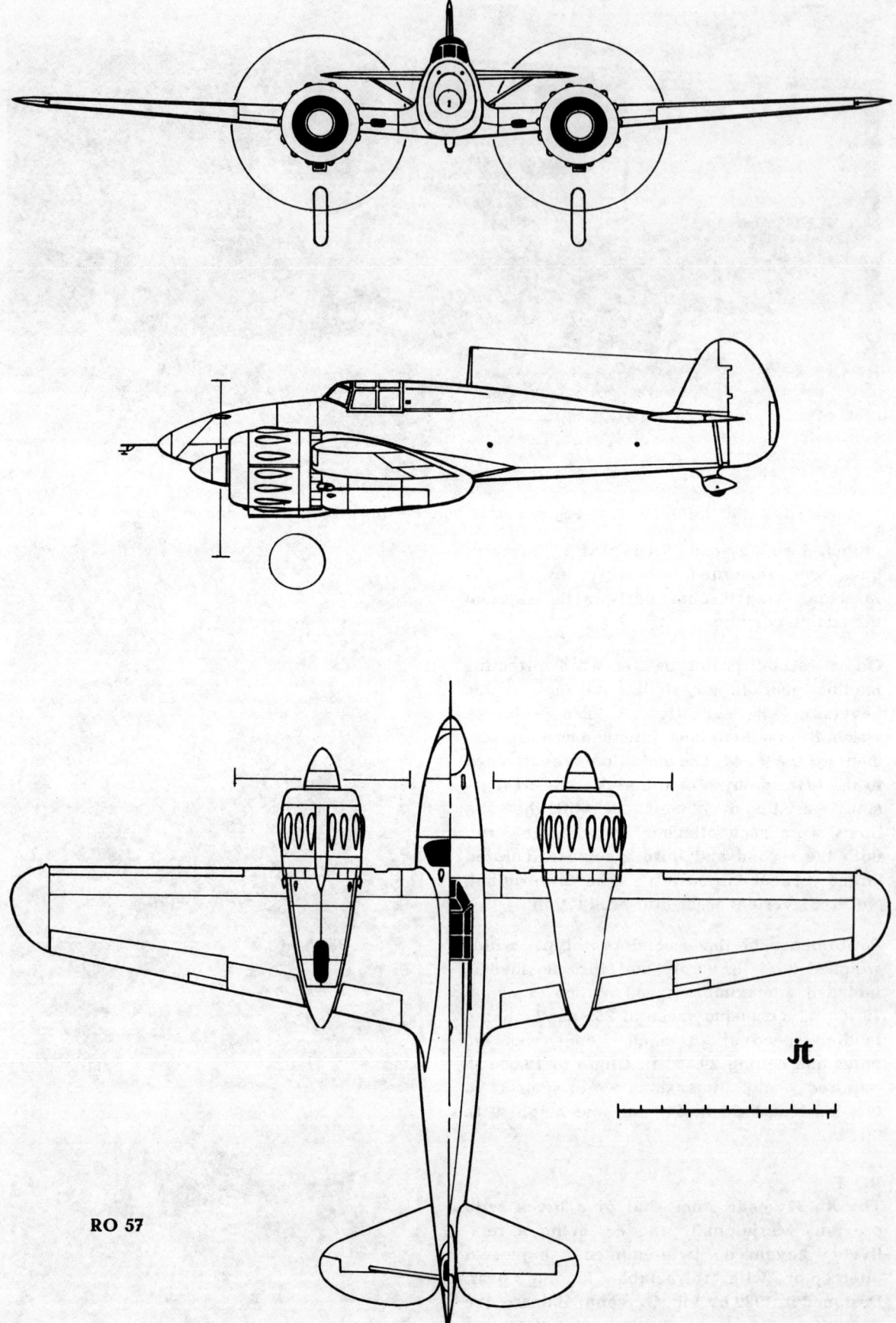

The Ro 57bis was a dive bomber modification with underwing air brakes and a crutch for an 1100-lb. bomb.

Ro 57 retained the mixed construction of the earlier machines with its wooden wings and duralumin-covered steel-tube fuselage, but the lines were considerably sleeker. The only anachronistic note was the braced tailplane, although the retractable tailwheel of the prototype was later discarded in favor of the fixed faired type, and armament was still only two 12.7-mm. Breda-SAFAT machine guns. The two 840 h.p. FIAT A.74 R.C.38 fourteen-cylinder radial engines were insufficient for the Ro 57's intended role of interceptor, maximum speed being only 311 m.p.h. at 16,400 ft. Maneuverability was only fair.

For these reasons, the small number of Ro 57's delivered to interceptor squadrons in 1942 were later withdrawn and adapted as fighter-bombers and dive bombers. In July, 1943, fifteen Ro 57's still equipped the 97° Gruppo Intercettori, of the 4ª Squadra Aerea, based at Crotone; a few were pressed into the defense of Sicily. The dive bombing variant, designated Ro 57bis, was fitted with dive brakes, two 20-mm. cannon in addition to the 12.7-mm. guns, and a crutch for bombs up to 1100 lb. under the fuselage.

The interceptor had a cruising speed of 242 m.p.h., a range of 745 miles, and a service ceiling of 25,590 ft. Climb to 19,680 ft. took 9 min. 30 sec. Empty and loaded weights were 7694 lb. and 11,000 lb. Dimensions were: span 41 ft. $0^{1}/_{8}$ in., length 28 ft. $10^{1}/_{2}$ in., height 9 ft. $6^{1}/_{8}$ in., and wing area 247.6 sq. ft.

RO 58

Powered by two 1175 h.p. Daimler-Benz DB 601A-1 twelve-cylinder inverted vee engines, the sole Ro 58 was tested at Guidonia in early

The Ro 58 was a two-seat heavy fighter powered by two Daimler-Benz DB 601A-1 liquid-cooled engines.

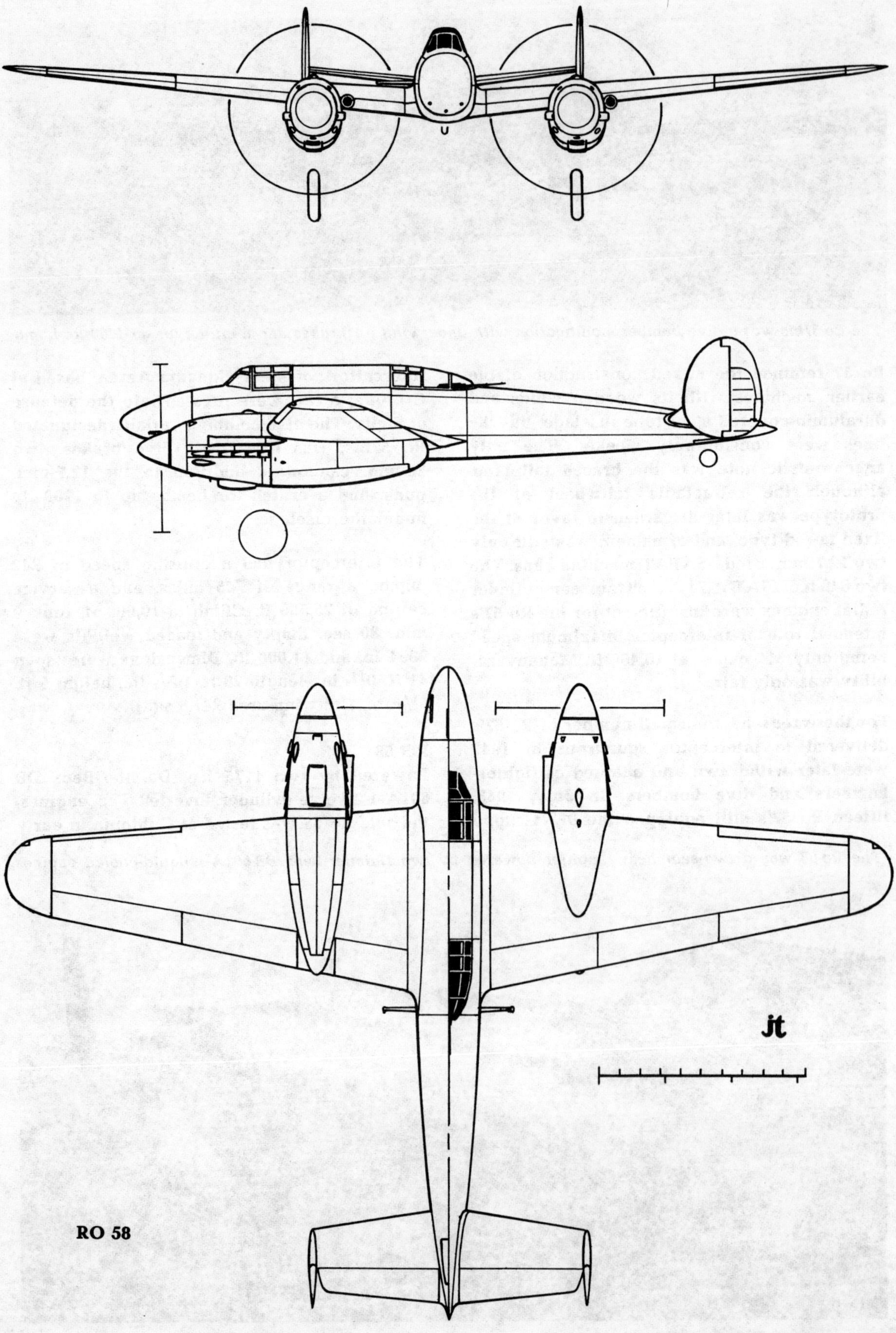

ITALIAN CIVIL AND MILITARY AIRCRAFT

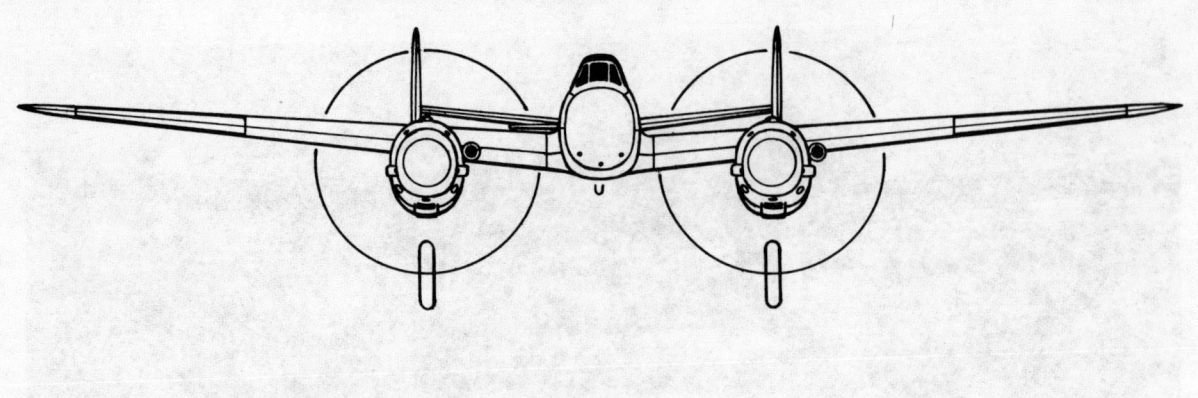

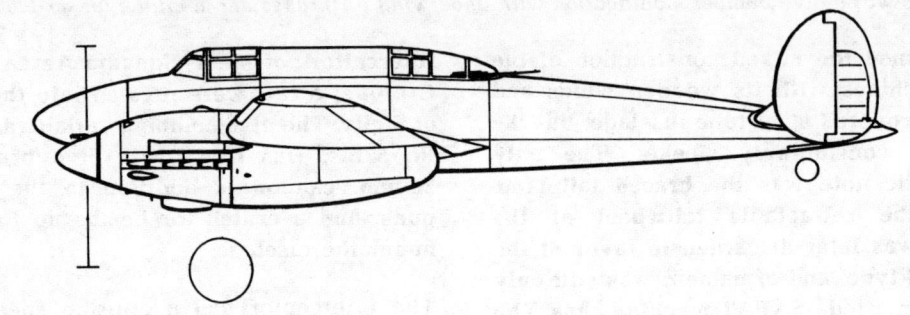

RO 58

The Ro 58 at Guidonia in company with an MC.200 Saetta.

1943 as a prototype two-seat long-range heavy fighter, corresponding to the German Zerstörer (Destroyer) class, exemplified by the Messerschmitt Bf 110. Maneuverability of the Ro 58 proved to be excellent for a twin-engined fighter, and quantity production was planned using the FIAT R.A.1050 R.C.58 Tifone engine, the license-built version of the Daimler-Benz unit. These plans were upset by the end of the war. The Ro 58 was an all-metal low-wing monoplane with twin fins and rudders. Armament consisted of five forward-firing Mauser MG 151 cannon, two of these in a ventral bulge which could be removed and replaced by a bomb rack, and one 12.7-mm. Breda-SAFAT defensive machine gun in the rear cockpit. Empty and loaded weights were 9590 lb. and 13,448 lb.

Performance included a maximum speed of 376 m.p.h. at 17,060 ft., a cruising speed of 314 m.p.h., a service ceiling of 31,170 ft., and a range of 932 miles. Time to reach 19,680 ft. was 9 min. Dimensions were: span 43 ft. $11^{1}/_{2}$ in., length 32 ft. $5^{3}/_{4}$ in., height 11 ft. $1^{7}/_{8}$ in., and wing area 282 sq. ft.

RO 63
The Ro 63 was a light, high-wing, two-three-seat artillery observation and liaison monoplane ordered into production just prior to the Italian Armistice. Powered by a 250 h.p. Hirth HM 508D eight-cylinder inverted vee air-cooled engine, the Ro 63 weighed 2332 lb. loaded. It could take off within 200 ft. and land in 180 ft., had a maximum speed of 126 m.p.h., and a range of 560 miles. No armament was fitted. Span was 44 ft. $3^{1}/_{2}$ in., length 31 ft. 6 in., and height 7 ft. $8^{2}/_{3}$ in. The Ro 63 was inspired by the Fieseler Fi 156 Storch, used in limited numbers by the Regia Aeronautica.

A.G.
In 1934 Meridionali built an experimental low wing monoplane, designed by Col. Aldo Guglielmetti, featuring an automatically-coordinated variable-incidence wing and tailplane. Designed simply the A.G., and powered by a 105 h.p. DeHavilland Gipsy II engine, it weighed 1156 lb. empty and 1706 lb. loaded. Maximum speed was 132 m.p.h., landing speed 50 m.p.h., and service ceiling 18,850 ft. (absolute ceiling 20,650 ft.). It climbed to 3280 ft. in 3 min. 26 sec., to 6560 ft. in 9 min. 13 sec., and to 13,120 ft. in 26 min. 55 sec. Dimensions included a span of 34 ft. $7^{1}/_{2}$ in., a length of 25 ft. 2 in., a height of 9 ft. 10 in., and a wing area of 177 sq. ft.

The Ro 63 liaison monoplane, inspired by the German Fieseler Fi 156 Storch, was built in early 1943.

NARDI
Ing. Fratelli Nardi

Founded in Milan in 1932 by the Nardi brothers, this very small company has developed and built a number of excellent aircraft and components, although facilities have never permitted large-scale manufacture. During the war the Piaggio firm produced the Nardi-designed FN.305 trainer in quantity. Since the war the company, now known as Nardi S.A. per Costruzioni Aeronautiche, has designed the novel FN.333 and FN.333-S all-metal three and four-seat amphibians, limited production of which was undertaken successively by FIAT and SIAI Savoia-Marchetti.

FN.305

Flown for the first time in February, 1935, by Arturo Ferrarin, the FN.305 two-seat light touring and training monoplane was an excellent aeroplane on all counts. Originally powered by a 185 h.p. Alfa Romeo 115-I six-cylinder inverted in-line engine, the FN.305 was one of the first Italian aircraft with retractable landing gear, the system employed being one of the simplest and most dependable produced anywhere up to that time. Ferrarin made a deliberate wheels-up landing at Guidonia in 1935; the ruggedness of the FN.305 was proved by the fact that only the airscrew was damaged.

The entire design was of extremely neat and efficient execution, structure being mixed metal and wood covered with plywood, aluminum, and fabric. The FN.305 was immediately successful both as a military trainer and as a private sport plane. In the latter capacity the 205 h.p. FIAT A.70 S seven-cylinder radial engine was used and the machine was designated FN.305D. The FN.305D was built with a variety of different fuselages, both single and two-seat, some with extremely long noses and aft-positioned cockpits to allow for increased fuel accomodation. On July 17, 1936, Capt. Giovanni Zappetta and Guido Stellingwerf set a light aircraft speed record of 193.1 m.p.h. over 621 miles of the Fiumicino-Ortobello-Livorno-Fiumicino course. In 1937 an FN.305D won the speed category of the Circuito Internazionale delle Oasi (International Circuit of the Oases, held at Cairo), piloted by Zappetta. The type also completed a record flight in March, 1939, from Rome to Addis Ababa, A.O.I., at an average speed of 149 m.p.h. (pilots Leonardo Bonzi and Giovanni Zappetta), gaining the distance record for two-seat light aircraft of Category I at 2773.7 miles. The same year the FN.305 won the endurance competition of the Raduno Internazionale del Littorio (Littorio International Air Rally).

A Piaggio-built FN.305 military trainer, powered by a 185 h.p. Alfa Romeo 115-I six-cylinder in-line engine.

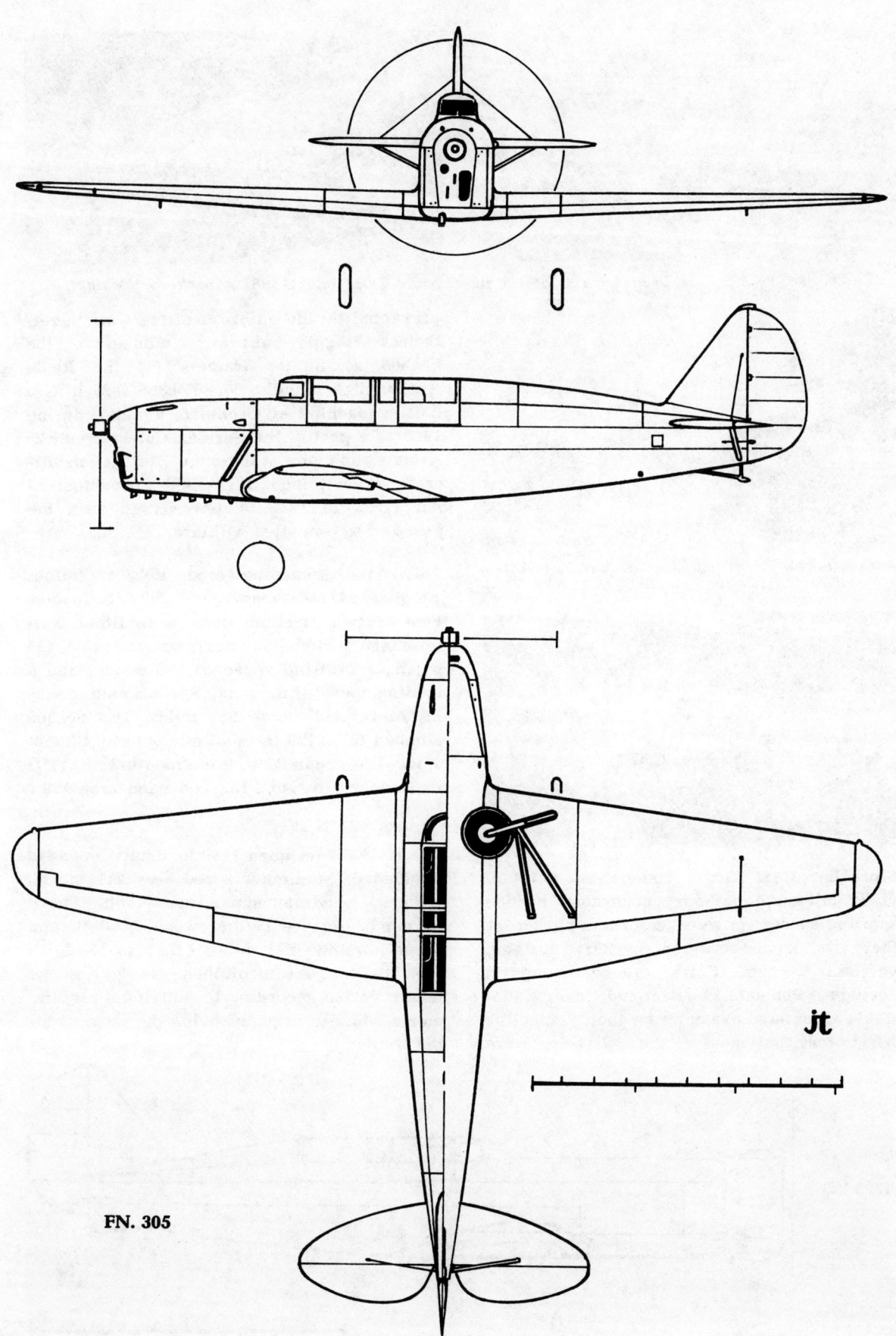

FN. 305

Above, the FN.305 was used as a fighter trainer. Note CR.32 and G.50B in background, right.

*Above, an FN.305 at Gorizia. (MM 52752, I-SUBA)
Below, a two-seat FN.305D. (I-TOMI)*

More important from a commercial point of view, (although perhaps encouraged by the sporting successes) were the orders placed for the Alfa Romeo-powered military training version. Belgium, Chile, France, Hungary, Portugal, Rumania, Switzerland, and Yugoslavia all ordered examples for their respective Air Forces, but most of the deliveries were prevented by the outbreak of the war. Nevertheless, Piaggio built large numbers of the FN.305 as fighter trainers for the Regia Aeronautica schools. One FN.305 served as a liaison machine at Grobnico, Croatia, during 1942 as a part of the Sezione Collegamenti 2ª Armata, and one was among the Italian aircraft which joined the Allied Co-Belligerent Air Force in 1943. A few served with the postwar Aeronautica Militare.

The Alfa Romeo-powered FN.305 trainer weighed 1474 lb. empty and 2090 lb. loaded. One or two machine guns were fitted. Performance included a maximum speed of 193 m.p.h., a cruising speed of 180 m.p.h., and a landing speed of 62 m.p.h. Service ceiling was 21,320 ft. and range 311 miles. The FN.305 climbed to 13,120 ft. in 13 min. 40 sec. Dimensions were: span 27 ft. 9 in., length 22 ft. $11^{1}/_{2}$ in., height 6 ft. $10^{2}/_{3}$ in., and wing area 129.1 sq. ft.

The FN.305D weighed 1188 lb. empty and 1848 lb. loaded. Maximum speed was 211 m.p.h., cruising speed 189 m.p.h., and landing speed 53 m.p.h. Service ceiling was 22,960 ft. and range normally 621 miles. Climb to 13,120 ft. took 13 min. As mentioned above, fuselage length varied according to individual requirements, other dimensions being the same as for the trainer.

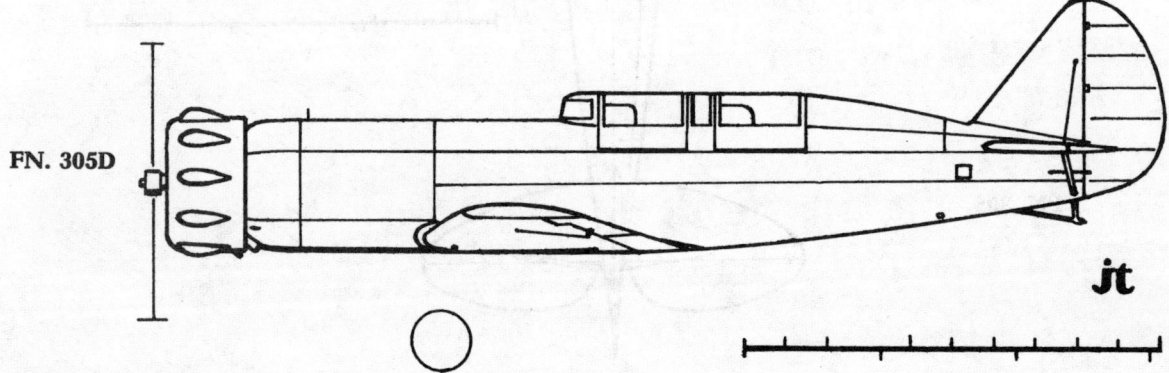

FN. 305D

Above and below right, the four-seat FN.310 cabin monoplane. (MM 381)

FN.310

Basically similar to the FN.305D in general layout, the FN.310, produced in 1938, was a larger four-seat cabin monoplane powered by the same 205 h.p. FIAT A.70 S seven-cylinder radial engine. Normally a touring machine, the FN.310 seated the passengers in two pairs with dual controls for the front seats, although it could be equipped as an ambulance with provision for stretcher and attendant. Weights were 1430 lb. empty and 2530 lb. loaded. In addition to the wider, higher, fuselage and increased weight, the FN.310 had a wing of increased span and area, 32 ft. $9\frac{1}{2}$ in. and 172.2 sq. ft. respectively. Length was 22 ft. $11\frac{1}{2}$ in. and height 7 ft. $2\frac{5}{8}$ in. Maximum speed was 186 m.p.h., landing speed 56 m.p.h., ceiling 19,680 ft., and range 870 miles.

FN.315

The FN.315 was almost identical to the FN.305 trainer except for the installation of a 280 h.p. Hirth HM 508D eight-cylinder inverted in-line air-cooled engine. It was built both as a trainer and as a two-seat touring plane, the latter featuring a cockpit canopy with extra transparent side panels to improve vision. Piaggio

A line-up of 11 Piaggio-built FN.315's for Hungary.

built a number of FN.315 military trainers for Hungary in 1939. Empty and loaded weights were 1562 lb. and 2255 lb. Performance was: maximum speed 239 m.p.h. at 8200 ft., cruising speed 220 m.p.h., landing speed 65 m.p.h., cruising range 590 miles, and climb to 13,120 ft. in 6 min. 40 sec.

An FN.315 with postwar registration and modified canopies, engine cowling, and landing gear. (I-VILD)

PIAGGIO
Società Anonima Piaggio & C.

Piaggio, a famous firm of railway car and ship builders, entered the aircraft industry during the First World War, building Caproni bombers in 1916. In August, 1923, following a government directive, Piaggio absorbed the Pegna-Bonmartini Costruzioni Navali-Aeronautiche, placing Ing. Pegna in charge of design. Early Piaggio-Pegna aircraft included the P.2 single-engined single-seat fighter monoplane, the P.3 four-engined bomber biplane described by the Italian Air Ministry in 1925 as "the best bomber ever built," the P.6, P.6bis, and P.6ter single-engined catapult observation biplanes, the P.8 single-seat submarine-borne light reconnaissance seaplane, and the P.9 single-engined two-seat cabin monoplane.

Piaggio had factories at Sestri Ponente (Genoa), Finale-Ligure, Pisa, and Pontedera. Bristol and Gnôme-Rhône engines were built under license at the latter plant until the firm established its own series of aero engines. In cooperation with C.M.A.S.A., Piaggio built a number of Dornier Wal flying boats under license. In 1930, to designs by Ing. Corradino d'Ascanio, the company produced the first D'Ascanio Elicottero (helicopter), which flew successfully on October 8 of that year. Further helicopter projects were undertaken during the following ten years, and the collaboration also resulted in the widely-used Piaggio-D'Ascanio variable-pitch airscrews. Piaggio also built an all-metal version of the Savoia-Marchetti SM.55 flying boat (SM.55 S), some Cant Z.506B seaplanes, and a number of Nardi FN.305 and FN.315 trainers during the 1930's. In 1936 Ing. Giovanni Casiraghi was placed in charge of the design office. He had formerly been with the Waco Aircraft Co. in the U.S.A.

Following the Second World War Piaggio began to rebuild, manufacturing Vespa (Wasp) motor-scooters and small automobiles. Aircraft design and production was resumed at Genoa, notable recent types being the P.136 twin-engine amphibian, the P.148 and P.149 single-engined trainers, and the P.166 twin-engined private and commercial transport; the latter was also adopted by the Aeronautica Militare in 1962. In cooperation with Douglas, Piaggio has produced the PD-808 Vespa-Jet seven/ten-passenger transport, also ordered by the Italian Air Force.

P.7
A really novel concept, some twenty years ahead of its time, was adopted for the P.7 Schneider Trophy racing seaplane, built in 1929. Designed by Ing. Pegna, the P.7 featured a pair of small hydrovanes in order to eliminate the drag imposed by floats; at first the machine rested in the water and was driven by a small two-bladed water-screw below the rudder, but as speed increased the vanes lifted the aeroplane out of the water to a point where the airscrew could be engaged. Tests were carried out by Warrant Officer Dal Molin. Insufficient knowledge of drive-shaft and clutch design caused the P.7 to be abandoned after Dal Molin experienced trouble with the drive to the

Left, a Piaggio-built Dornier Wal. (I-AZDZ)   Right, the D'Ascanio helicopter, flown in 1930.

Above left, a model of the novel P.7 racing seaplane. Right, the actual machine resting in the water.

water-screw due to clutch-slip. The power unit was an 850 h.p. Isotta-Fraschini twelve-cylinder water-cooled vee engine, with which a maximum speed of 373 m.p.h. was anticipated. This compared favorably with the maximum speed of 348 m.p.h. quoted for both the contemporary FIAT C.29 and Macchi M.67 racing seaplanes. The P.7 weighed 3093 lb. empty and 3709 lb. loaded. Dimensions were: span 22 ft. 2 in., length 29 ft. $0^3/_4$ in., height 8 ft. $0^1/_2$ in., and wing area 105.8 sq. ft.

P.10

Built in 1932, the P.10 single-engined three-seat reconnaissance seaplane was designed for catapult launching from warships, but this function was fulfilled by the later Meridionali Ro 43. The P.10 was a biplane with a single main float and auxilliary wing floats; it was powered by a 450 h.p. Piaggio-built Bristol Jupiter nine-cylinder radial engine. The pilot sat just ahead of the wings, while the observer had a separate cockpit near the tail. Between them, rather awkwardly placed just aft of the wings, was a Scarff ring-mounted machine gun.

Dimensions included a span of 45 ft. 3 in., a length of 33 ft. 8 in., a height of 14 ft., and a wing area of 500 sq. ft. Weights and performance data are unavailable. The P.10bis, built in 1933, was a land-based version.

P.11

The P.11 single-engined two-seat aerobatic and training biplane, built by Piaggio in 1932, was a license-built version of the Blackburn Lincock single-seat fighter of 1928.

P.12

Another Blackburn design produced under license in 1932, the P.12 was the Italian version of the Segrave twin-engined four-passenger touring monoplane.

The P.10 three-seat reconnaissance floatplane.

The P.11 aerobatic trainer (license-built Lincock).

The P.12 touring monoplane (license-built Segrave).

P.16

In 1934 the three-engined four-man P.16 bomber made its appearance, powered by 700 h.p. Piaggio Stella IX R.C. nine-cylinder radial engines in N.A.C.A. cowlings. The P.16 was the first of a series of highly original aircraft culminating in the P.108 bomber of the Second World War. An extremely unusual design in a number of ways, the P.16 featured a shoulder-

The P.16 was the first in a series of Piaggio bombers culminating in the four-engined P.108B.

mounted inverted gull wing braced to the lower part of the fuselage by four struts. The wing was fullest near the engine nacelles, tapering in chord and thickness toward the tips and in thickness toward the fuselage. Hydraullically-operated double-camber flaps extended over the entire span, the outer sections serving as ailerons. Construction was all-duralumin, while the fuselage and tail unit were fabric-covered welded steel tubing. Armament consisted of three machine guns, one in the leading edge of the wing, one in a retractable dorsal turret, and one in the rear fuselage below the high-positioned, overhanging tail. Landing gear was retractable except for the steerable tailwheel. Loaded weight was 18,590 lb., including up to 2200 lb. of bombs in the fuselage below the wings.

The P.16 had a maximum speed of 248 m.p.h. at 16,400 ft. and a landing speed of 65 m.p.h. Range was 1242 miles with an 1100-lb. bomb load, or 932 miles with 2200 lb. Climb to 19,680 ft. required 17 min. Dimensions were: span 72 ft. 2 in., length 43 ft. $9^{1}/_{2}$ in., height 11 ft. $5^{3}/_{4}$ in., and wing area 753.2 sq. ft.

P.23

Powered by four 900 h.p. Isotta-Fraschini Asso XI R twelve-cylinder vee engines mounted in tandem pairs and driving two tractor and two pusher airscrews, the P.23M commercial transport was to some extent a derivative of the P.16, incorporating the same semi-cantilever wing design (but of greater span, and braced by six struts). In addition to the four engines and the fuselage layout, the P.23M, which was built in 1935, differed in its all-metal construction and twin fins and rudders. A novel feature of the exceptional transport was the underside of the fuselage, which had a keel much like that of a flying boat, the aim being to facilitate

Above and below, the graceful P.23M, with fuselage "keel", tandem engines. Note missing gear fairing.

emergency landings at sea. Empty and loaded weights were 16,251 lb. and 40,566 lb., the useful load being 24,315 lb. or almost 150 per cent of the empty figure! Maximum speed was 248 m.p.h. and cruising range 3167 miles at 186 m.p.h. The P.23M climbed to 13,120 ft. in 14 min. Dimensions were: span 88 ft. $6^3/_4$ in., length 54 ft. $5^3/_8$ in., wing area 1049.1 sq. ft.

In spite of having the same type number, the P.23R three-engined record machine was almost a totally different design, the only common features being the twin fins and rudders and the camber-changing flaps. These flaps, plus leading-edge slots, were installed in an entirely new cantilever wing, placed low on the greatly elongated fuselage. The P.23R was one of the cleanest aircraft built up to that time. Initially the power plants were 900 h.p. Isotta-Fraschini Asso twelve-cylinder water-cooled units driving two-bladed variable-pitch airscrews, but these were replaced by three 1000 h.p. Piaggio P.XI R.C.40 fourteen-cylinder radials and three-bladed airscrews. In the latter form the P.23R established speed records over 621-mile and 1242-mile courses, carrying 11,000 lb. at 250.9 m.p.h. on December 30, 1938. Pilots were Angelo Tondi and G. Pontonutti, accompanied by two mechanics. For propaganda purposes the P.23R was referred to as the P.123 bomber.

Empty and loaded weights of the P.23R were 26,410 lb. and 41,857 lb. Maximum speed was 273 m.p.h., cruising speed 217 m.p.h., landing

The P.23R bore no direct resemblance to the P.23M. Below is the original Isotta-Fraschini powered version; the man standing in front of the machine makes its large size readily apparent.

The P.23R after the change to Piaggio P.XI R.C.40 radials. Enclosed cockpit was a further modification.

speed 93 m.p.h., service ceiling 23,871 ft., and range 2360 miles. Dimensions included a span of 96 ft. 6 in., a length of 77 ft. 10¾ in., a height of 16 ft. 2 in., and a wing area of 982.4 sq. ft. Only the one P.23R was built. The advanced features of the P.23M and P.23R were further developed in twin-engined bomber prototypes by Piaggio and Reggiane.

P.32

The Piaggio P.32 twin-engined bomber was a roundabout development of the two P.23 prototypes; the reactivated Reggiane firm also built experimental derivatives commencing in 1937. The Reggiane machines, the Ca 405 record plane and its bomber conversion, the P.32bis, featured the sleek contours associated with their P.23 predecessors, but the Piaggio development (also rather confusingly designated P.32) was a more practical all-wood military machine with a fuller fuselage of increased capacity. Built in 1936, the original model, the P.32-I, was powered by 820 h.p. Isotta-Fraschini Asso XI R.C. twelve-cylinder water-cooled vee engines and had retractable dorsal and ventral gun turrets just aft of the wings. In 1938 a revised version employing 1020 h.p. Piaggio P.XI R.C.40 fourteen-cylinder radial engines was built, designated P.32-II. Except for the engines and the supplementing of the two turrets amidships with a nose turret above the bombardier's position, there were few changes. Crew was five in both models. The internal bomb bay housed up to 3520 lb.,

The P.32-I medium bomber appeared in 1936 with 820 h.p. Isotta-Fraschini Asso XI R.C. water-cooled engines. Visible here are the semi-retractable dorsal and ventral machine gun turrets.

PIAGGIO

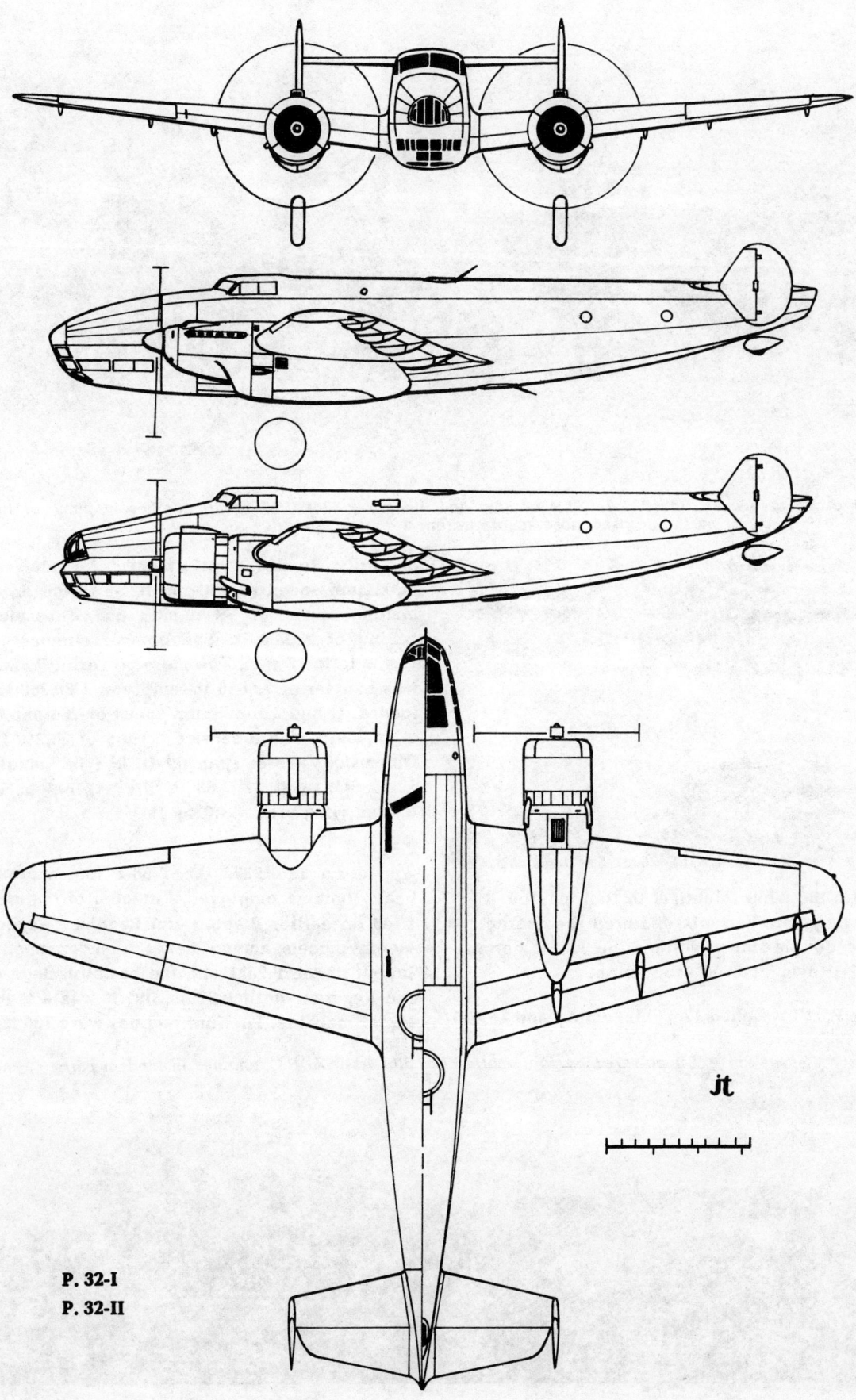

P. 32-I
P. 32-II

Above and below left, the P.32-II. This version had Piaggio P.XI R.C.40 radial engines in place of the Assos, plus a revised nose incorporating a gun turret above the bombardier.

while the wing (identical to that employed by the Reggiane variants) featured the characteristic double flaps. Neither the P.32-I nor the P.32-II ever entered production.

The P.32-I weighed 12,650 lb. empty and 16,170 lb. fully loaded. Performance included a maximum speed of 248 m.p.h. at 16,400 ft., a landing speed of 78 m.p.h., and a service ceiling of 22,960 ft. The bomber climbed to 13,120 ft. in 15 min. The more powerful P.32-II was heavier at 13,640 lb. empty and 20,350 lb. loaded. It had a maximum speed of 264 m.p.h. at 16,400 ft. and a service ceiling of 26,240 ft. Dimensions were: span 59 ft. $0^{1}/_{2}$ in., length 52 ft. $5^{3}/_{4}$ in. (P.32-I, 53 ft. $5^{1}/_{2}$ in.), height 17 ft., and wing area 634.8 sq. ft.

P.50

Appearing in 1937, the P.50-I four-engined heavy bomber employed a number of features tried on earlier Piaggio and Reggiane experimental models, among them the tandem engine layout of the P.23M and the basic fuselage of the Reggiane-built P.32bis, but it was a much larger machine. The four engines were 730 h.p.

Below, the P.50-I powered by four Isotta-Fraschini Asso XI R.C. engines in tandem pairs.

Isotta-Fraschini Asso XI R.C. twelve-cylinder vee units driving two tractor and two pusher three-bladed airscrews. The wing (mounted in shoulder position), the fuselage, and the tail surfaces were of welded steel construction, fabric-covered, while the movable control surfaces were wood. The tail was the normal single fin-and-rudder type similar to that of the P.108, of which the P.50-I and P.50-II were essentially prototypes. The P.50-II (1938) employed four 1000 h.p. Piaggio P.XI R.C.40 fourteen-cylinder radial engines mounted in normal fashion, this being the arrangement adopted for the P.108 (with, however, the higher-powered P.XII R.C.35 units). Dimensions of both versions of the P.50 were: span 84 ft. $7\frac{1}{2}$ in., length 64 ft. $11\frac{1}{3}$ in., height 15 ft. 7 in., and wing area 1076.4 sq. ft. The P.50-I, weighing 28,600 lb. empty and 44,000 lb. loaded, had a maximum speed of 270 m.p.h. and a range of 1863 miles. It climbed to 13,120 ft. in 22 min. Armament was three 12.7-mm.

Below, three photographs of the P.50-II, which was essentially similar to the P.50-I except for the four normally-mounted Piaggio P.XI R.C.40 radial engines replacing the tandem Assos.

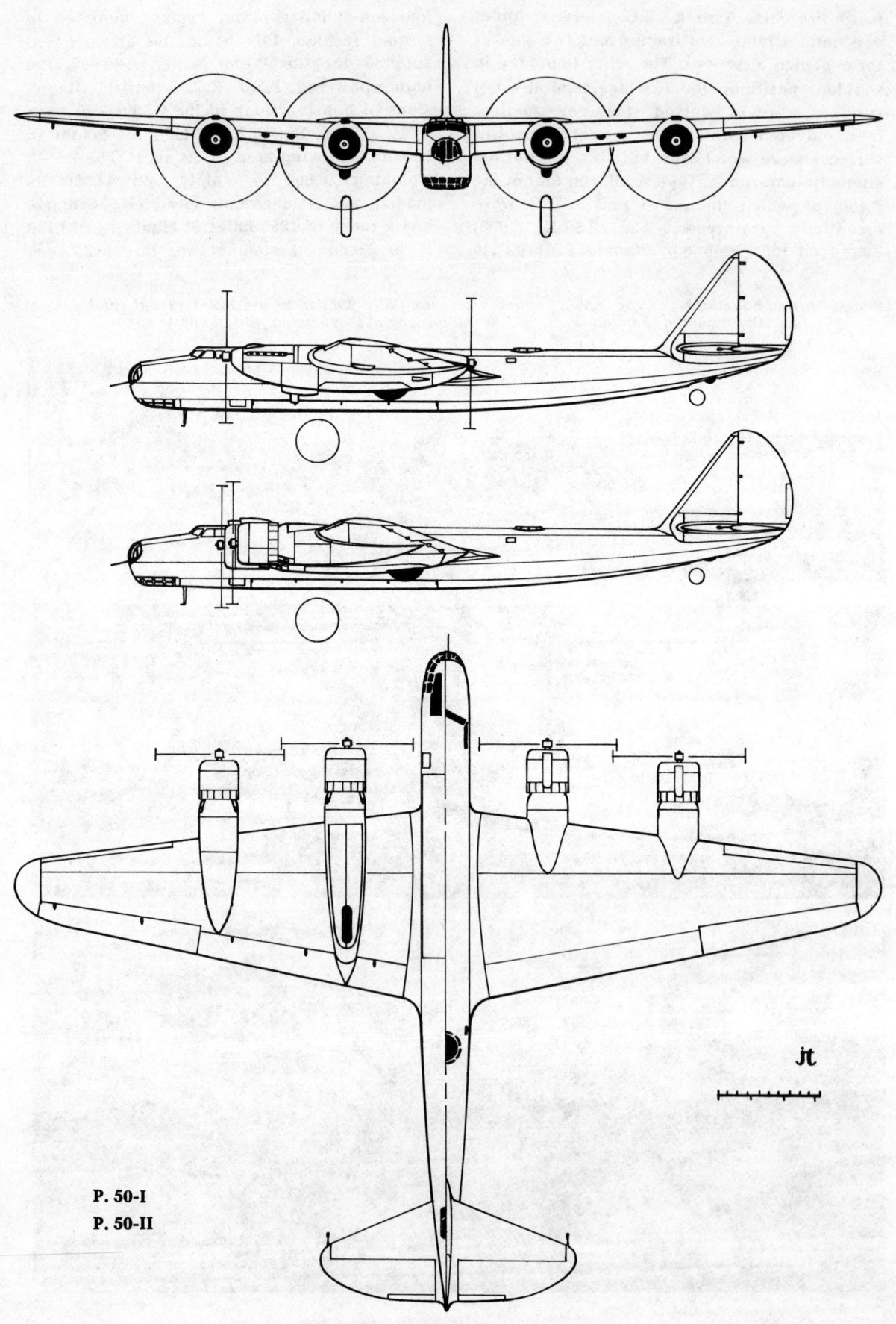

P. 50-I
P. 50-II

The P.108B was Italy's only four-engined heavy bomber. A total of 163 were delivered during WW II.

guns in nose, dorsal, and ventral positions.

The P.50-II weighed 29,040 lb. empty and 44,440 lb. loaded. It had a maximum speed of 279 m.p.h. at 13,120 ft., a cruising speed of 250 m.p.h., a landing speed of 87 m.p.h., a range of 2174 miles, a service ceiling of 25,290 ft., and could climb to 13,120 ft. in 15 min. A total armament of five defensive machine guns was proposed for the P.50-II.

P.108

As a result of the extremely original and advanced development work carried on by Piaggio under Ing. Casiraghi during the 1930's, the company had the distinction of building the only four-engined heavy bomber to be employed by the Regia Aeronautica during the Second World War. In fact, with the exception of the far-from-successful Heinkel He 177 Greif, the Piaggio P.108B was the only machine of the category to see service with any of the Air Forces of the Axis. Although production figures were insignificant compared to the number of heavy bombers built by Great Britain and the United States, the P.108B was an excellent machine bearing a strong similarity in appearance to the Boeing B-17, but differing greatly in detail.

The prototype P.108 flew in 1939, powered by 1500 h.p. Piaggio P.XII R.C.35 eighteen-cylinder radial engines. Although designed by Ing. Casiraghi in 1937, before the P.50-II had flown, the P.108B (Bombardiere) profited from the experience with the earlier bomber. An outstanding innovation of the P.108B was the use of two wing-mounted turrets, each with two 12.7-mm. machine guns, operated by remote control from sighting domes atop the fuselage; this arrangement preceded that of the B-29 Superfortress. Two additional 12.7-mm. guns were mounted in nose and semi-retractable ventral turrets, while two more guns were operated from lateral hatches, making a total defensive armament of eight weapons, extremely heavy by Italian standards. The maximum bomb load was 7720 lb.; alternatively, three 450-mm. Whitehead Fiume torpedoes could be carried.

So successful was the prototype that an initial batch of twelve pre-production machines was followed by substantial orders (by Regia

This front view of the P.108B emphasizes the bomber's resemblance to the American B-17 Flying Fortress.

Sighting domes for the P.108B's remote-controlled nacelle turrets can be seen here atop the fuselage.

Aeronautica standards), 163 aircraft eventually being produced. The first machines entered service in late 1942 with the 274ª Squadriglia Autonoma B.R.G. (Bombardamento a Grande Raggio, or long-range bombardment), which had tested the pre-production P.108B's, and took part in night raids on Gibraltar. Flame dampers for the exhausts and a less-extensively glazed nose without the turret were modifications made for the night raids. The surprise effect, due to the great range of the P.108B (hitherto unsuspected in any Italian bomber), had great psychological, if not truly destructive, results. The P.108B later served in the North African and Russia theaters, and in all operations over the Mediterranean Sea. The 274ª Squadriglia adopted Capt. Bruno Mussolini's name in tribute after the son of Il Duce was killed testing an early production P.108B near Pisa in 1942. At the end of the war only three P.108B's remained with the Mussolini Squadriglia, based at Foligno. Large numbers were lost during wartime operations, although it is open to question whether the majority were lost due to enemy action or to possible failures of the P.108 bombers themselves.

The P.108B had a crew of seven and weighed 38,104 lb. empty and 64,900 lb. loaded. Performance was: maximum speed 267 m.p.h. at 13,780 ft., cruising speed 198 m.p.h., landing speed 93 m.p.h., service ceiling 27,880 ft., maximum range 2484 miles, climb to 6560 ft. in 10 min., and climb to 16,400 ft. in 30 min. Dimensions were: span 104 ft. 11³/₄ in., length 75 ft. 2¹/₃ in., height 17 ft. 0³/₄ in., and wing area 1456.3 sq. ft. A late production P.108B, designated P.108M (Modificato) had a forward-firing armament of four 7.7-mm. machine guns and one 20.-mm. cannon.

The original prototype of the P.108B was rebuilt in 1943 with a new nose incorporating a 102-mm. cannon and redesignated P.108A

The P.108A (Artigliere) was a conversion of the prototype P.108B. A 102-mm. anti-shipping cannon replaced the bombardier's position in the nose. The P.108A was eventually destroyed by the Germans.

P.108B's of the 274a Squadriglia carried the name Mussolini in script over the white fuselage band, honoring Il Duce's son Bruno, killed while testing an early production P.108B near Pisa in 1942.

(Artigliere). This gun, with a range of six miles, was tested extensively beginning March 22, 1943. After successful completion of these tests (held at the Centro Sperimentale per l'Armamento, Furbara), the P.108A fired over 200 shells in flight at the Navy firing range at Viareggio. Subsequently, the anti-shipping machine was flown by the Luftwaffe to Rechlin, there to be ultimately destroyed. Dimensions and performance figures were similar to those of the standard P.108B.

Developed in parallel with the P.108B was the P.108C (Civile) 32-passenger transport, which, intended for use with LATI on the South Atlantic run, had an entirely new fuselage and longer wings. Incorporating the basic wing structure, engines, tail assembly, and landing gear of the P.108B, the prototype P.108C flew on July 16, 1942. Twenty-four were built, fifteen being pressed into service as military transports capable of carrying 56 fully-equipped troops. Empty and loaded weights

Above and below, the P.108C, originally conceived as a civil airliner for LATI.

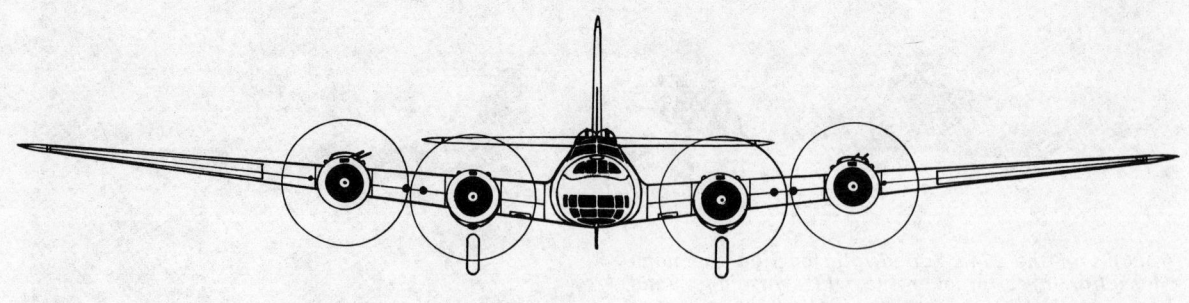
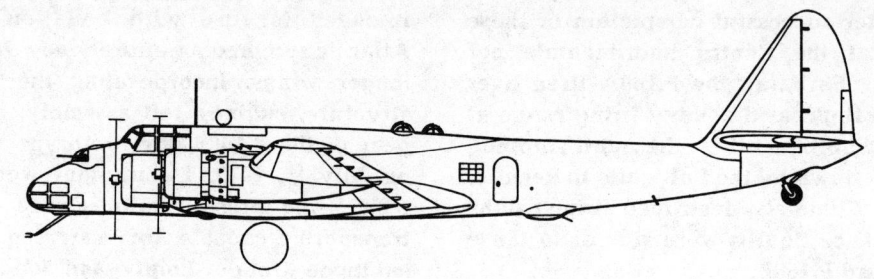

P. 108B

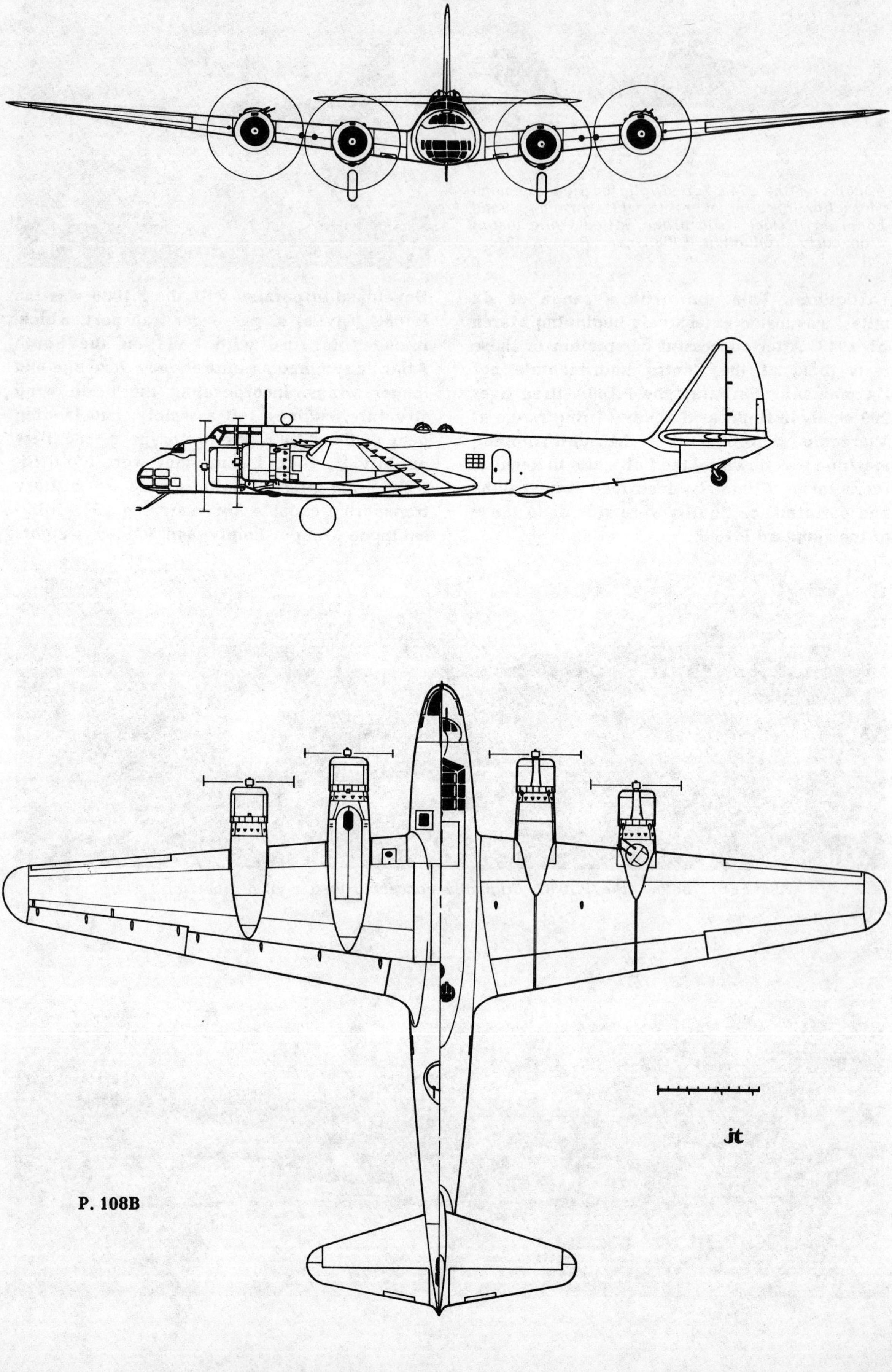

Above, a P.108C under construction. A list of P.23R records and a warning against sabotage, "To interrupt the work is a crime," are inscribed on the far wall. Below, the sole P.108T, designed especially as a military cargo transport to Luftwaffe requirements, had a 2741-cu. ft. interior.

were 37,840 lb. and 70,400 lb. respectively. Maximum speed was 273 m.p.h., ceiling 21,876 ft., and range 1553-2484 miles. Dimensions included a span of 108 ft. 4 in., a length of 84 ft. $6^1/_2$ in., a height of 18 ft. $8^7/_8$ in., and a wing area of 1537.1 sq. ft. P.108C transports and a few P.108B bombers were used by the Luftwaffe in evacuating the Crimea, carrying up to 125 men each!

Production of the P.108B and C was halted in accordance with a Luftwaffe request favoring a newer model, the P.108T (Trasporto) military freight transport, of which only the prototype was actually built in 1942. The P.108T could carry 80 fuel drums, eight large aero engines, or six torpedoes in its 2471-cu. ft. interior; loading was accomplished through two side

doors or a belly door (for vehicles). With the same dimensions as the P.108C, the P.108T weighed 35,266 lb. empty and 68,420 lb. loaded. Maximum speed was 273 m.p.h., cruising speed 239 m.p.h., ceiling 24,607 ft., and range 2237 miles. The P.108T climbed to 6560 ft. in 9 min. and to 16,400 ft. in 24 min. 50 sec. It was to have been fitted with four 12.7-mm. machine guns in dorsal, ventral, and two lateral positions. A postwar development, the P.108T2 48 to 60-passenger (or cargo) transport, was

P. 108T

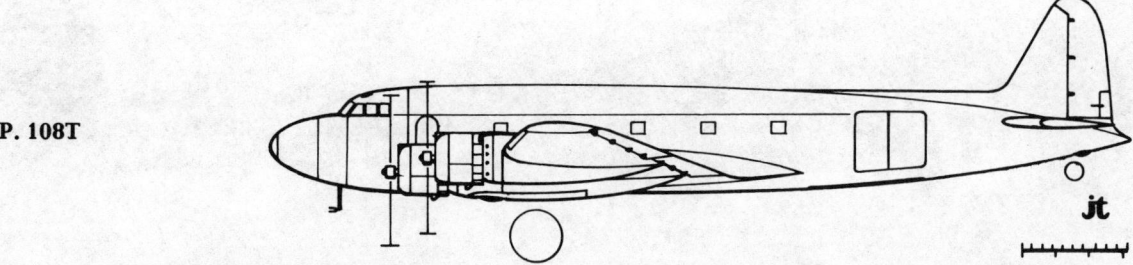

The P.111 was a high-altitude research plane built to test cabin pressurization techniques. (MM 465).

proposed with a variety of engines, including 1200/1450 h.p. Pratt & Whitney R-1830/2000 Twin Wasp radials, 2100 h.p. R-2800 Double Wasp radials, 1350/1900 h.p. Wright Cyclone R-1820/2000 radials, or 1690 h.p. Hercules 632 radials. Performance was expected to be similar to that of the wartime prototype, with a cruising speed of 260 m.p.h. and a range of 690-1950 miles (with 21,500-lb. or 11,000-lb. payload, respectively).

A greatly improved version of the P.108B, known as the P.133, was under construction in 1943, but abandoned at the time of the Armistice.

P.111

Purely a research aeroplane, the P.111 was designed in 1939 to investigate high-altitude cabin pressurization, in line with the development of the P.108C. Flown for the first time on April 9, 1941, the P.111 was a small monoplane powered by two 1000 h.p. Piaggio P.XII R.C. 100/2v eighteen-cylinder radial engines. A very thorough program of high-altitude research was carried out with the P.111, which had a ceiling of 39,360 ft. Empty and loaded weights were 11,550 lb. and 16,698 lb. Performance included a maximum speed of 357 m.p.h., a cruising speed of 279 m.p.h., and a range of 1031 miles. Dimensions were: span 56 ft. 9 in., length 40 ft. 8 1/8 in., height 12 ft. 10 in., and wing area 430 sq. ft.

P.119

The last wartime Piaggio design that actually

The P.111 flew on April 9, 1941, powered by two 1000 h.p. Piaggio P.XII R.C.100/2v radial engines. (MM 465)

Above and below right, the P.119 had an eighteen-cylinder P.XV R.C.60/2v radial buried in the fuselage.

flew was the P.119 single-seat fighter; like almost all Piaggio projects, it was of extremely original conception. Since 1938 Piaggio had been studying the possibility of installing a radial engine in the middle of the fuselage, driving the airscrew by an extension shaft. The design staff realized that this arrangement would result in good maneuverability due to the concentration of weight near the center of gravity, excellent aerodynamics and visibility due to a tapered nose and forward-placed cockpit, and a concentration of firepower by a close grouping of the guns. Construction of the prototype P.119 began in early 1941. The major problem had been in obtaining satisfactory engine cooling, but this was finally solved.

The all-metal fighter possessed very clean lines, broken only by the air intake for the buried Piaggio P.XV R.C.60/2v eighteen-cylinder engine, which developed 1650 h.p. at 5580 ft. The 1700 h.p. P.XXII eighteen-cylinder radial was the intended power unit, but none were available when the P.119 performed its first ground trials in November, 1942. The first flight was made on December 19. Considerable flight testing had been carried out by the time of the Armistice, but no production plans had been made, although the P.119 had proved itself to be an excellent machine free of vices.

Armament consisted of four 12.7-mm. machine

guns grouped together in the nose, plus one 20-mm. Breda CL 20 cannon firing through the airscrew hub. Provision was made for three bomb racks, one below the fuselage and two under the wings. Empty and loaded weights were 5374 lb. and 9020 lb. Maximum speed was 398 m.p.h. at 19,680 ft., cruising speed 340 m.p.h., landing speed 81 m.p.h., service ceiling 41,340 ft., and range 940 miles. Climbing performance included times of 3 min. 12 sec. to 9840 ft., 7 min. 10 sec. to 19,680 ft., and 12 min. 20 sec. to 29,520 ft. Dimensions were: span 42 ft. 7³/₄ in., length 31 ft. 10 in., height 9 ft. 10 in., and wing area 299.2 sq. ft.

P.127

The P.127 was a project begun in late 1941 for an extremely large, transoceanic, 40-passenger civil transport incorporating six 1575 h.p.

engines buried in the wing and driving contra-rotating airscrews through extension shafts. A pressurized cabin for high-altitude flight was included in the specification. Loaded weight was to have been 110,232 lb.; maximum speed was estimated at 355 m.p.h. Dimensions were: span 183 ft. 7 in., length 137 ft. 8 in., height 28 ft. 2 in., and wing area 2690 sq. ft.

The P.127 was never realized due to the war situation. Reconsidered for production in 1947, but never built, it compared favorably with many very successful postwar airliners. It would have been the largest Italian aeroplane ever built.

P.133

A larger, more powerful development of the P.108B, the P.133 was in the final stages of construction when Italy surrendered. Four 1650 h.p. Piaggio P.XV R.C.60/2v eighteen-cylinder radial engines were to propell the bomber, while defensive armament consisted of no less than six 20-mm. cannon and four 12.7-mm. machine guns in power-operated turrets. Empty and loaded weights were 38,500 lb. and 83,600 lb., the latter figure including a bomb load of 10,560 lb. Estimated performance was: maximum speed 304 m.p.h., cruising speed 248 m.p.h., maximum range 4037 miles, ceiling 26,240 ft., and climb to 6560 ft. in 8 min. 10 sec. Dimensions were: span 118 ft. 1 in., length 80 ft. $8^1/_4$ in., height 14 ft. $5^1/_4$ in., and wing area 1721.6 sq. ft.

In 1947, a 40-50-passenger airline version, the P.133C, was developed, although not completed. It had empty and loaded weights of 41,281 lb. and 70,597 lb., a length of 91 ft. 10 in., and a height of 19 ft. 3 in. Performance was expected to include a maximum speed of 300 m.p.h. at 29,600 ft., a cruising speed of 248 m.p.h., and a range of 1863 miles.

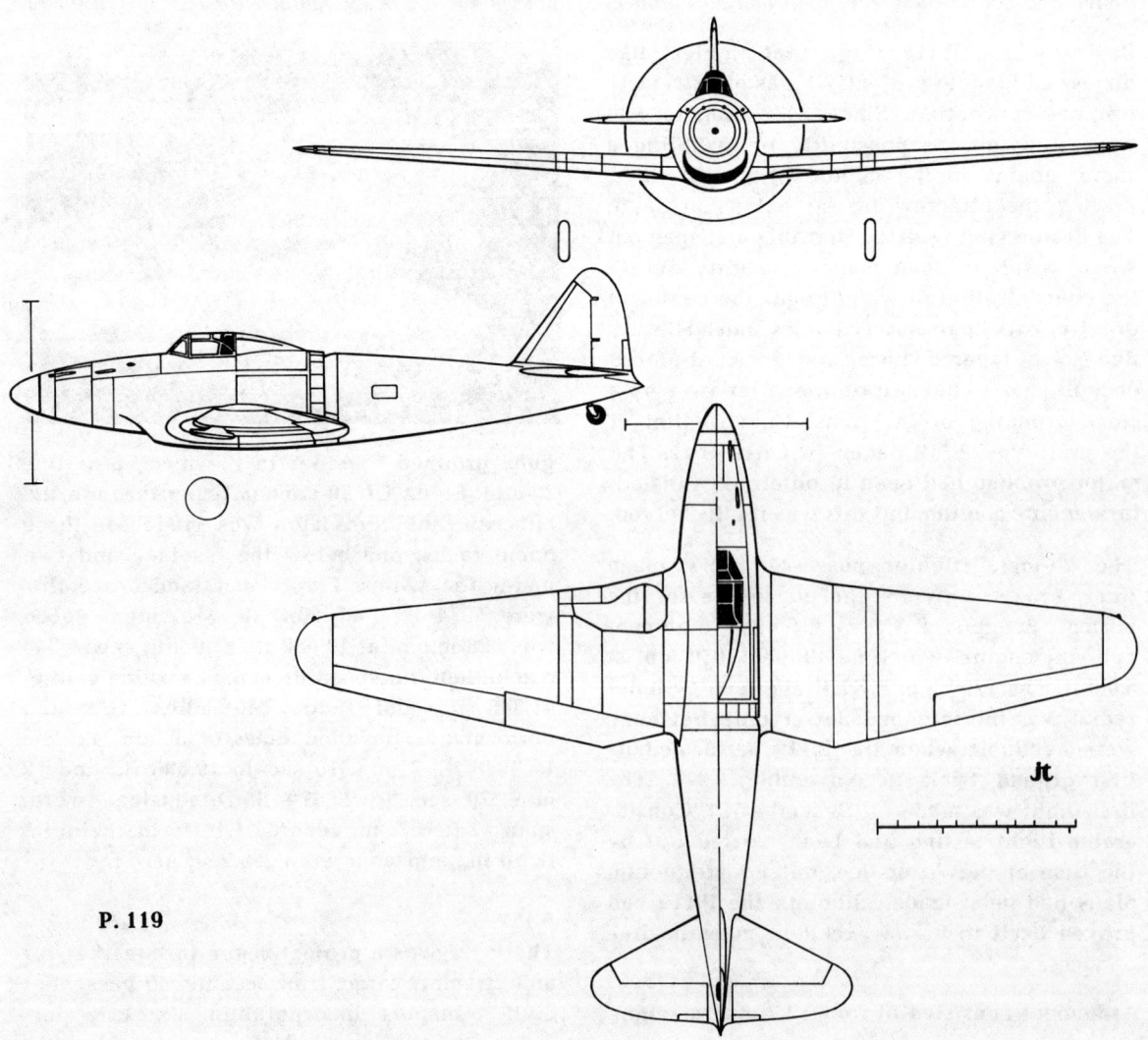

P. 119

REGGIANE
Officine Meccaniche "Reggiane" S.A. (Caproni)

As in the case of several other Italian companies, the Officine Meccaniche Italiane S.A., of Reggio Emilia, entered the aviation industry with contracts for the production of Caproni bombers during the First World War, fulfilled between 1915-18. No further aeronautical activity was undertaken until 1937, when the Caproni subsidiary was revived to develop the Ca 405 Procellaria and the subsequent P.32bis from Piaggio designs. At the same time, Reggiane began building the Savoia-Marchetti SM.79 under license, and the design office started work on a new series of single-seat fighters.

CA 405
The Ca 405, appropriately named Procellaria (after a family of long-winged, ocean-ranging birds that include the Petrel and Shearwater), was a 1937 Reggiane development of the Piaggio P.23, continuing the program of long-distance transoceanic aircraft. Designed as a record plane, the Ca 405 was an extremely graceful twin-engined monoplane inheriting the Piaggio double flaps and fuselage "keel" of the P.23M, but employing a constant-dihedral cantilever wing of all-wood construction, also used by the Reggiane P.32bis and the Piaggio P.32-I and P.32-II. The engines were 850 h.p. Isotta-Fraschini Asso XI R.C.40 twelve-cylinder vee units driving three-bladed variable-pitch airscrews. The forward section of the very slim oval fuselage was of steel tube construction covered with alloy panels, while the rear was a wooden monocoque. The tail unit was all-wood, consisting of twin fins and rudders, control surfaces being fabric-covered.

Two Ca 405's were entered in the International Istres-Damascus-Paris Race, held in August, 1937, but were not ready in time. The race was dominated by the three-engined Savoia-Marchetti SM.79C record planes; with 75 per cent greater power, the SM.79C was considerably faster than the Ca 405, although not as efficient aerodynamically. The success of the SM.79's strengthened the position of the three-engined formula in Italian bomber design.

The Ca 405 weighed 13,200 lb. empty and 24,200 lb. loaded. Maximum speed was 261 m.p.h. at 14,760 ft., landing speed 78 m.p.h., absolute ceiling 24,600 ft., and range 1553 miles. Dimensions were: span 59 ft. $0^1/_2$ in., length 50 ft. $10^1/_8$ in., height 10 ft. $9^7/_8$ in., and wing area 634.8 sq. ft.

P.32BIS
The P.32bis was a bomber modification of the Ca 405. Except for a revised fuselage featuring three power-operated machine gun turrets, an internal bomb bay (replacing the extra fuel tankage of the Procellaria), and a crew of five, the P.32bis was practically identical to the record machine. Performance was similar, only the landing speed (75 m.p.h.) and absolute ceiling (26,240 ft.) differing appreciably. The P.32bis was longer by 1 ft. $5^7/_8$ in. Later, the 850 h.p. Isotta-Fraschini water-cooled engines were replaced by two 1000 h.p. Piaggio P.XI R.C.40 fourteen-cylinder radial air-cooled units. These increased the maximum speed to 264 m.p.h. Neither the Piaggio P.32-II nor the Reggiane P.32bis was placed in production, Piaggio concentrating on the P.108B heavy

Below left, the Ca 405 Procellaria record plane, built for the Istres-Damascus-Paris Race. Right, the P.32bis medium bomber with Piaggio P.XI R.C.40 radials. Both types were developments of Piaggio aircraft.

Above left, the prototype Re 2000 in its original form. Right, the same machine after modifications to the carburetor air intake and the addition of a spinner (MM 408)

bomber and Reggiane on a series of fighters beginning with the Re 2000.

RE 2000

The first original product of the new Reggiane design office, the Re 2000 single-seat fighter, was projected in 1937 by engineers Alessio and Longhi, and bore a remarkable resemblance to the American Seversky Sev-7, 2-PA, and EP-1 (export P-35) monoplanes, which obviously provided a direct inspiration for the Italians. Nowhere was this similarity more evident than in Sweden, where EP-106 (J 9) and Re 2000 (J 20) fighters served together.

In spite of the close resemblance, which was especially evident in the all-metal construction, wing planform, tail surfaces, and fuselage proportions; the prototype Re 2000, first flown by Mario de Bernardi in 1938, differed in a number of important respects. Powered by a smoothly-cowled 986 h.p. Piaggio P.XI R.C.40 fourteen-cylinder radial engine, the Reggiane fighter was aerodynamically much superior to its American counterpart. In addition to the airscrew spinner (fitted after initial trials) and the lower, neater cockpit canopy, the Re 2000 possessed a better retraction mechanism for the main wheels, which rotated to lie horizontally below the wings, and a fully retractable tailwheel. At the same time that the spinner was fitted, aerodynamics were further improved by extending the carburettor air intake forward to the front edge of the cowling. In this form the Re 2000, unofficially named Falco I by the manufacturers (the FIAT CR.42 bore the name officially in Regia Aeronautica service), was demonstrated by Commandante De Bernardi in fighter trials held at Guidonia later in 1938. Due to the higher power of its Piaggio engine, the Re 2000 compared favorably with the FIAT-powered Macchi C.200, being some 6 m.p.h. faster (320 m.p.h.) at 16,400 ft. and at least as maneuverable as the Macchi. Later tests showed the Re 2000 to be far superior in close combat to the Messerschmitt Bf 109E. However, the positioning of the fuel tanks unprotected in the wing center section

The Re 2000 performed well in 1938 trials at Guidonia, proving faster than the Macchi C.200. (MM 408)

A front view of an Re 2000 Serie I Falco I fighter. Note horizontal stripes on elevator. Trimotor in hangar at right is an SM.75 transport, I-TIMO.

was a serious drawback. The redesign necessary to provide sufficient armor protection would have resulted in a new airframe with decreased performance. Therefore the Re 2000 was rejected initially by the Regia Aeronautica, and classified for export as the Re 2000 Serie I Intercettore (interceptor).

Customers included Sweden, which equipped the Flygvapnet with sixty Serie I machines under the designation J 20 in 1941 (these remaining in service until 1945), and Hungary, which secured a manufacturing license in addition to the Italian-built machines delivered in 1940. The Re 2000 was named Hejja in Hungarian use, the slightly modified Hungarian-built model entering service in 1943. This version had a Manfred Weiss-built 1000 h.p. Wright Cyclone GR-1280-G2 nine-cylinder radial engine driving a Hamilton Standard airscrew, the installation increasing length to 27 ft. $6^{1}/_{4}$ in. The original Re 2000 Serie I had an armament of two 12.7-mm. Breda-SAFAT machine guns and weighed 4576 lb. empty and

Above right, a Serie I Falco I with Hungarian insignia. Below, a similar Italian machine; in spite of the markings, this version was not ordered into production for the Regia Aeronautica. (MM 5066)

ITALIAN CIVIL AND MILITARY AIRCRAFT

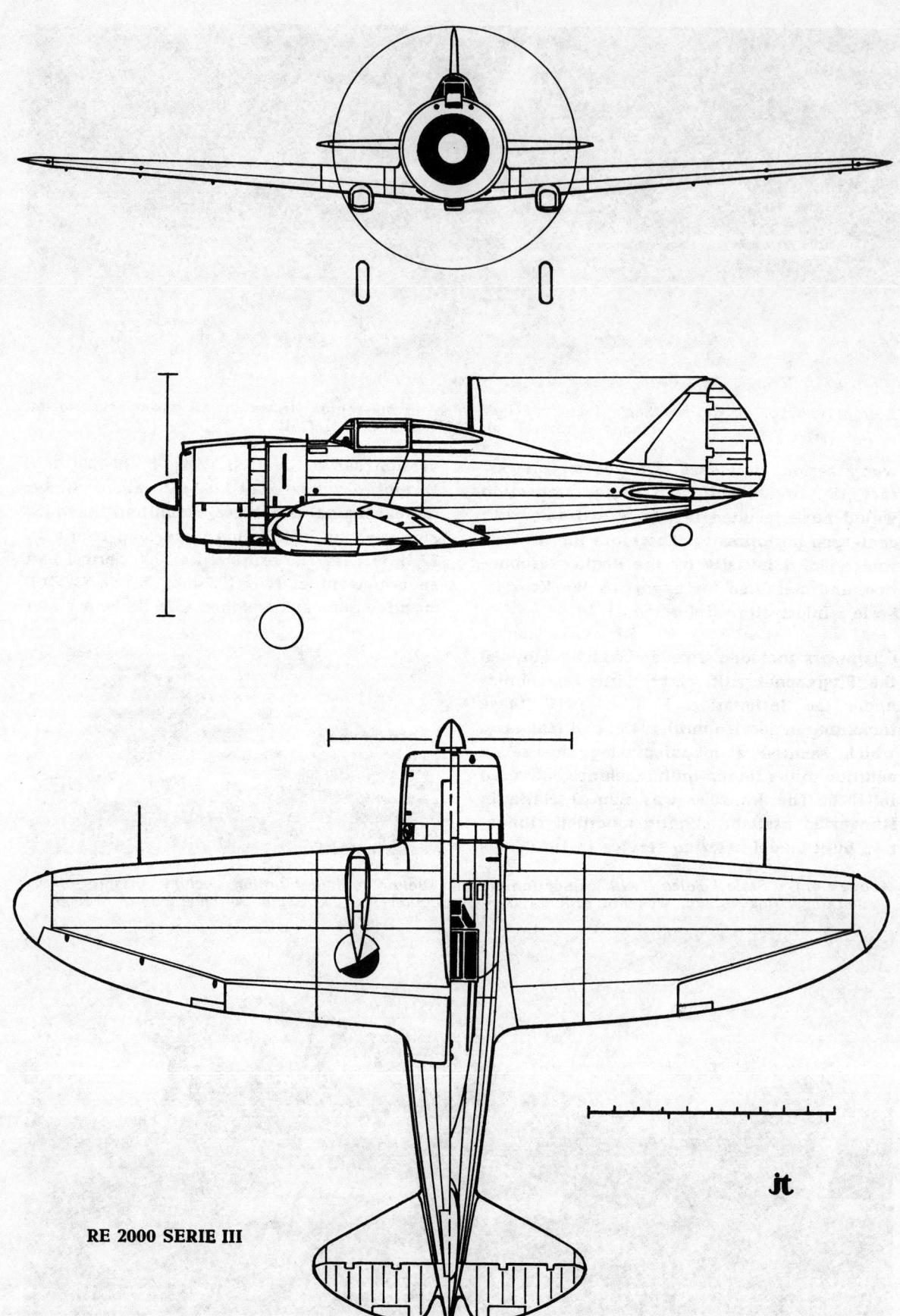

RE 2000 SERIE III

Above, an Re 2000 Serie III long range fighter. (MM 8288)   Below right, eight Serie II catapult fighters.

5610 lb. loaded. Performance included maximum, cruising, and landing speeds of 329 m.p.h., 267 m.p.h., and 68 m.p.h. respectively, a range of 522 miles, and a service ceiling of 36,736 ft. The fighter climbed to 19,680 ft. in 6 min. 10 sec. Dimensions were: span 36 ft. 1 in., length 26 ft. 2½ in., height 10 ft. 6 in., and wing area 219.5 sq. ft.

The Regia Marina began to take an interest in the Re 2000 as a catapult fighter during 1940; consequently twelve Re 2000 Serie II (Catapultabile) were ordered. These differed in being specially strengthened for catapult launching and in having a modified cockpit with rear transparencies omitted. The Piaggio P.XIbis R.C.40 radial of 1025 h.p. was fitted. The first launching trials were conducted on board a modified cargo ship in 1942, and later from the battleship Italia.

Twenty-four examples of a further variant, the Re 2000 Serie III Grande Autonomia (long

range) fighter, were also delivered in 1942 and attached to the Regia Marina, serving with the 377ᵃ Squadriglia Autonoma, based in Sicily, as escort fighters. Powered by the 1025 h.p. P.XIbis R.C.40, the Serie III fighters had an additional fuel tank and attachments for carrying a drop-tank or 440-lb. bomb. Empty and loaded weights were 4598 lb. and 6270 lb. Performance included a maximum speed of 326 m.p.h. at 16,400 ft., a range of 807 miles, a

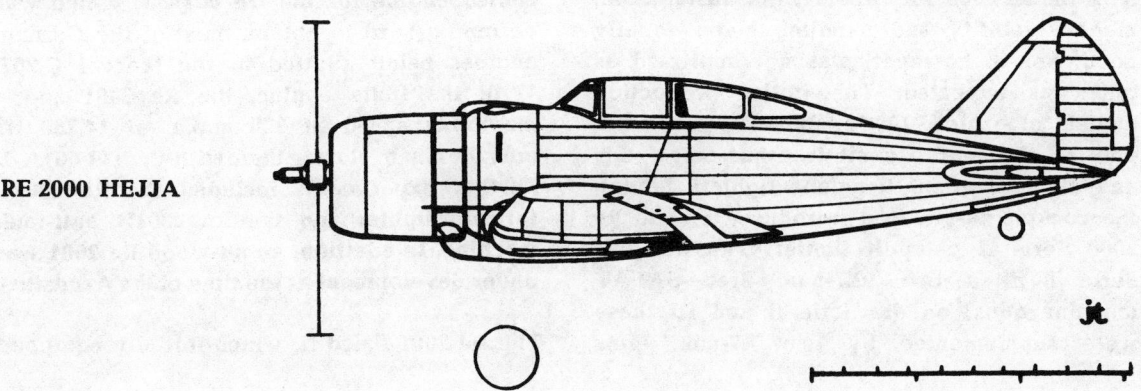

RE 2000 HEJJA

The prototype Re 2001 Falco II. Rear cockpit transparencies were omitted from production machines.

ceiling of 34,440 ft., and a time of 7 min. 45 sec. for a climb to 19,680 ft.

A total of 170 Re 2000 Falco I fighters were built by Reggiane; of these, only the 36 Serie II and III models were employed by Italy. In September, 1943, only two machines remained in service with the 1ª Squadriglia FF.NN. (Forze Navali), neither being serviceable..

RE 2001
As in the case of a great many other Italian aircraft, the Re 2000 was adapted for the higher-powered German Daimler-Benz liquid-cooled engines. First projected in 1940, the Re 2001 Falco II fitted an 1175 h.p. DB 601A-1 twelve-cylinder inverted vee engine (or the Alfa Romeo R.A.1000 R.C.41-Ia Monsonie, the license-built version). The prototype differed from the Re 2000 only in the engine installation, maneuverability and handling being equally good. Speed, however, was not improved as much as expected. The initial production model, of which 100 examples were built, omitted the rear cockpit transparencies, this and all subsequent Reggiane fighters having the cockpit design first introduced on the Re 2000 Serie II catapult fighter. The Re 2001 Serie I fitted two 12.7-mm. Breda-SAFAT machine guns; on the Serie II and III these were supplemented by two 7.7-mm. guns mounted in the wings. The Serie IV carried either a 1408-lb. bomb or a drop-tank beneath the fuselage. The Re 2001 CN (Caccia Notturna) night fighter, of which 150 machines were built, featured a 20-mm. Mauser MG 151 cannon under each wing. This variant entered service in 1943, defending industry in Northern Italy against night attacks by Allied bombers.

Experimental modifications included the employment of leading-edge radiators in place of the standard underwing type (this machine designated Re 2001bis); the fitting of deck arrestor hooks for trials to be held aboard the aircraft carriers Aquila and Sparviero, in the process of being converted from merchant ships; a revised tandem two-seat cockpit; and the substitution of an 840 h.p. Isotta-Fraschini Delta IV twelve-cylinder inverted vee air-cooled engine for the DB 601A-1, which was becoming hard to obtain, most of the German engines being allotted to the Macchi C.202. With the Delta engine, the Re 2001 had a maximum speed of 320 m.p.h. at 14,760 ft., only 17 m.p.h. slower than with the DB 601A-1. Further experiments included the Re 2001G torpedo fighter and the Re 2001H anti-tank machine. In addition, an all-wood Re 2001 was under development at the time of the Armistice.

The Re 2001 Falco II, which initially equipped

100 examples of the initial production Re 2001 were built, commencing in 1941. (MM 468)

the 2° Gruppo Caccia, based in Sicily in 1942, was still in service in September, 1943, with the 2° Gruppo, as well as with the 59° and 60° Gruppi Intercettori at Venegono and Lonate Pozzolo, the 22° Gruppo C.T. at Capodichino, and the 167° Gruppo Intercettori at Littoria. These units possessed 43 machines (21 serviceable). Eight joined the Allied Co-Belligerent Air Force, the remainder fighting on with the 2° Gruppo under the Aviazione della RSI.

Above, Re 2001 Falco II fighters being serviced in North Africa in 1942. Below, the Re 2001 Delta.

The Re 2001 Serie III interceptor weighed 5500 lb. empty and 7230 lb. loaded. Maximum speed was 337 m.p.h. at 16,400 ft., cruising speed 282 m.p.h., landing speed 75 m.p.h., range 646 miles, and service ceiling 39,200 ft. Climbing to 26,240 ft. required 12 min. 10 sec. Dimensions were: span 36 ft. 1 in., length 26 ft. $10^{3}/_{4}$ in., height 10 ft. $2^{3}/_{4}$ in., and wing area 219.5 sq. ft.

Below left, the Re 2001bis, an experimental version with leading-edge radiators. Right, an Re 2001 (foreground) with glide bomb below the fuselage. In the background is an Re 2002 Ariete with torpedo.

An early Re 2002 Ariete with small-diameter tapered engine cowling and small spinner.

RE 2002

Reverting to a radial engine, which was more suitable for the low-altitude attack role, Reggiane produced the Re 2002 Ariete (Ram) fighter-bomber in 1941 as a development of the Re 2000 Serie III. The engine was an 1175 h.p. Piaggio P.XIX R.C.45 Turbine B enclosed in an extremely efficient Messier-type cowling and driving a three-bladed airscrew with very large spinner. Except for these changes, and the fitting of two 7.7-mm. wing guns (as on the Re 2001), the Ariete was practically identical to the Serie III Falco I. A 440-lb. bomb could be carried beneath the fuselage; the fighter was also tested with a torpedo. The Re 2002bis was an experimental Ariete with the outward-retracting landing gear later employed by the Re 2005. The Re 2002S (Scorta) was an escort fighter with a drop-tank in place of the bomb.

The production Arietes, totalling about 50, entered service in late 1942 with the 5° Stormo Assalto over Sicily. In July, 1943, the Ariete began to equip the 101° and 102° Gruppi Assalto based at Lonate Pozzolo and Tarquinia. On September 8 thirty-four Arietes were in service, ten with the 50° Stormo and twenty-four with the 5° Stormo, then based at Mandur-

A production Re-2002 fighter-bomber with Co-Belligerent roundels. Note large spinner, revised cowling.

ia. Only sixteen were serviceable machines; these continued to fight with the Aviazione della RSI, and with the Allies, after the Italian Armistice.

Empty and loaded weights were 5225 lb. and 6878 lb. Performance included a maximum speed of 329 m.p.h. at 18,045 ft., a range of 683 miles, and a ceiling of 34,450 ft. The Re 2002 climbed to 6560 ft. in 2 min. 46 sec., to 13,120 ft. in 5 min. 52 sec., and to 19,680 ft. in 8 min. 48 sec. Dimensions were the same as for the Re 2000 except for the length of 26 ft. 9¼ in.

Above, an Re 2002 Ariete in Luftwaffe markings. (MM 97919) Below, the two-seat Re 2003 reconnaissance bomber, an experimental conversion of the Re 2000 Serie III single-seat fighter.

RE 2003

The Re 2003 was an experimental tandem two-seat reconnaissance bomber developed from the Re 2000 Serie III, and employing the same 1025 h.p. P.XIbis R.C.40 radial engine. In addition to the second cockpit with its angular canopy, further windows were provided on the sides of the fuselage. Two prototypes were

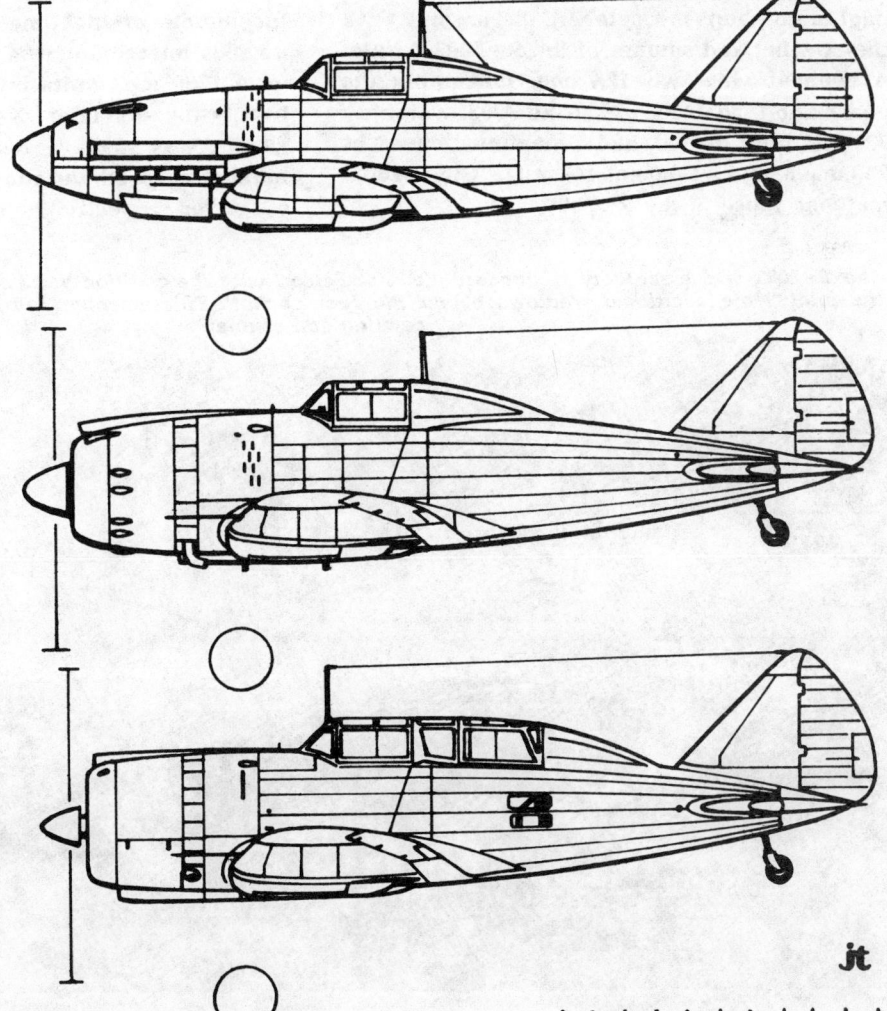

RE 2001

RE 2002

RE 2003

The Re 2003 two-seat reconnaissance bomber with the original Falco-type engine cowling and spinner.

built, the first with the regular Re 2000-type engine cowling and spinner, the second with the cowling and spinner of the Re 2002 Ariete. Armament was two 12.7-mm. machine guns and bomb load 1100 lb. The Re 2003, weighing 7209 lb. fully loaded, had a maximum speed of 293 m.p.h. and a range of 447 miles. Dimensions matched those of the Re 2000.

RE 2004
Incomplete at the time of the Armistice, the Re 2004 interceptor was to have been powered by a 1250 h.p. Isotta-Fraschini Zeta R.C.25/60 twenty-four-cylinder X-type engine. Loaded weight was to have been 7110 lb. Estimated maximum speed and range were 385 m.p.h. and 621 miles respectively. The Re 2004 was aban-

The Re 2003 was essentially a standard Re 2000 Falco I with the addition of an observer's cockpit behind the pilot. Note additional windows below the rear cockpit. This machine had a revised Ariete engine cowling and spinner.

The first prototype Re 2005 Sagittario. Outward-retracting main gear was a characteristic. (MM 494)

doned in favor of the superior Re 2005, which had already flown.

RE 2005

The last and best of the Reggiane fighters actually built was the Re 2005 Sagittario (Archer), the prototype of which flew in September, 1942. Powered by a 1475 h.p. Daimler-Benz DB 605A-1 twelve-cylinder vee engine, the Sagittario featured the outward-retracting main landing gear tested on the Re 2002bis, and extensive structural modifications. Production machines began to enter service in 1943, these having the FIAT-built version of the DB 605A known as the R.A.1050 R.C.58 Tifone. Armament consisted of two 12.7-mm. Breda-SAFAT machine guns in the fuselage, one 20-mm. Mauser MG 151 firing through the airscrew hub, and two similar wing-mounted cannon. In addition, the Re 2005 could carry up to 1390 lb. of bombs.

The 22° Gruppo C.T., based at Capodichino, Capua, and Littoria, had eight Sagittarios available in July, 1943, in addition to its MC.200, MC.202, Re 2001, and Dewoitine D.520 fighters. The Sagittarios formed the 262ª Squadriglia, used in the defense of Sicily. After the Armistice, production continued for the Aviazione della RSI, although it finally came to a halt as a result of intensive Allied bombing. The remaining Re 2005's were used as defensive interceptors in Rumania and Germany. In spite of their fine qualities, they were too few to be of consequence.

Weighing 5732 lb. empty and 7848 lb. loaded, the Re 2005 had a maximum speed of 390 m.p.h. at 22,800 ft., a cruising speed of 340 m.p.h., a ceiling of 39,360 ft., a range of 677-786 miles, and climbed to 6560 ft. in 1 min. 58 sec., to 13,120 ft. in 4 min. 4 sec., and to 19,680 ft. in 6 min. 33 sec. Dimensions were the same as for earlier Reggiane fighters except for the length of 28 ft. 7³/₄ in.

The Campini centrifugal compressor was considered for installation in the rear of the Re 2005, driven by an auxiliary 370 h.p. FIAT A.20 twelve-cylinder engine. Although never completed, this version of the Sagittario, designated Re 2005R (Reazione), had an estimated maximum speed of 454 m.p.h. The

The second prototype Sagittario could be distinguished by its larger, more bulbous spinner.

Above and below, the Re 2005 Sagittario was one of the best Italian fighters. Refined airframe and 1475 h.p. DB 605A-1 engine gave excellent performance. A few production machines began to enter service in mid-1943, too late to be effective. Some fought in Rumania and Germany. (MM 494)

project, initiated by Maj. Ferri, had reached the final drawing stage in July, 1943. Expected loaded weight was 8600 lb.

RE 2006

The Re 2006, a projected interceptor with a 1510 h.p. Daimler-Benz DB 603A engine, was on the drawing boards in 1943 when development was abandoned. Estimated performance included a maximum speed of 404 m.p.h. and a range of 897 miles. Armament was to have been the same as that of the Re 2005, but loaded weight was calculated to be no less than 13,640 lb. This showed that Italian designers had begun to accept the heavy fighter concept that proved so important during the latter stages of the Second World War, but this acceptance came too late, only a short time before the final Italian collapse.

REGGIANE

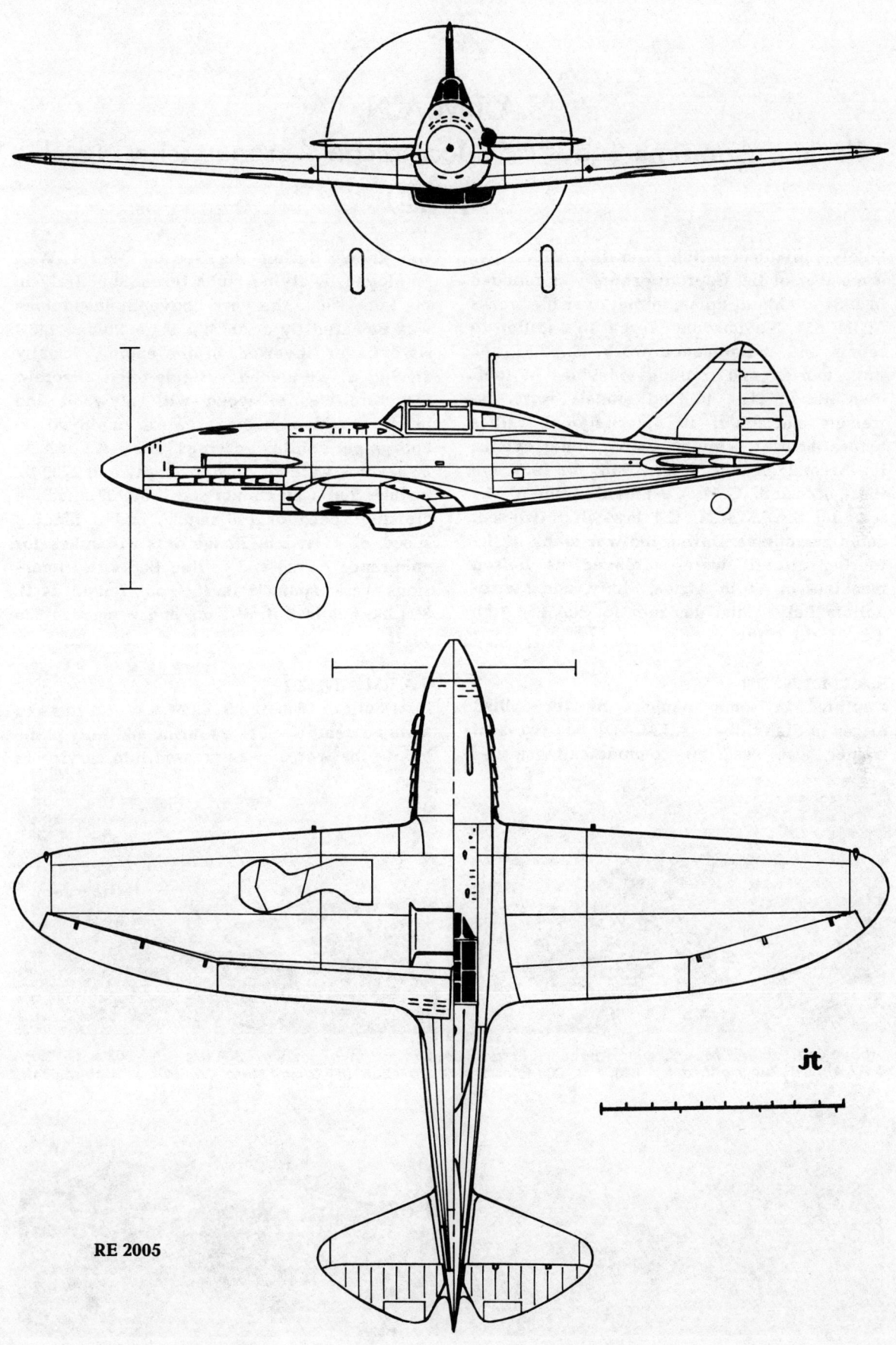

RE 2005

S.A.I.M.A.N.
Società Anonima Industrie Meccaniche Aeronautiche Navali
(Caproni)

Solely a producer of light aircraft, S.A.I.M.A.N., a member of the Caproni group, was founded in 1934 at Lido di Roma, taking over the works of the S.A. Navigazione Aerea. In addition to repair and maintenance work, S.A.I.M.A.N. built touring and training machines of their own design. The touring models were extremely successful in international rallies before the war, winning, among other events, the Second Annual Sahara Rally in 1937. On that occasion Gori Castellani piloted the winning S.A.I.M.A.N. C.4 low-wing two-seat cabin monoplane. During the war many of the touring aircraft were employed as liaison machines in North Africa, Sicily, and Metropolitan Italy. Chief designer for S.A.I.M.A.N. was Mario Bottini.

S.A.I.M.A.N. 200
Captured in some numbers by the Allied forces in Sicily, the S.A.I.M.A.N. 200 two-seat trainer, also used for communications, was well known during the Second World War. Employed by flying clubs throughout Italy in the late 1930's, the very conventional biplane was powered by a 200 h.p. Alfa Romeo 115-I six-cylinder inverted in-line engine, usually driving a two-bladed variable-pitch airscrew. Structure was of wood with plywood and fabric covering. Ailerons were employed on both upper and lower wings. The S.A.I.M.A.N. 200, which weighed 1606 lb. empty and 2209 lb. loaded, had a maximum speed of 137 m.p.h., a cruising speed of 116 m.p.h., and a landing speed of 43 m.p.h. Range was 310 miles (or endurance 2 hrs.) and ceiling 19,680 ft. Dimensions were: span 28 ft. 10$^{1}/_{2}$ in., length 24 ft. 3$^{1}/_{4}$ in., height 8 ft. 3$^{1}/_{2}$ in., and wing area 236 sq. ft.

S.A.I.M.A.N. 202
First built in 1936, the S.A.I.M.A.N. 202 has had a long career. Used as a touring and rally plane before the war, it was pressed into service as

Above left, a S.A.I.M.A.N. 200. Above right and below left, two postwar S.A.I.M.A.N. 202's. (I-ABPJ, I-ATAE) Below right, a S.A.I.M.A.N. 204 R of the Aero Club di Roma. Note Capitoline Wolf on tail.

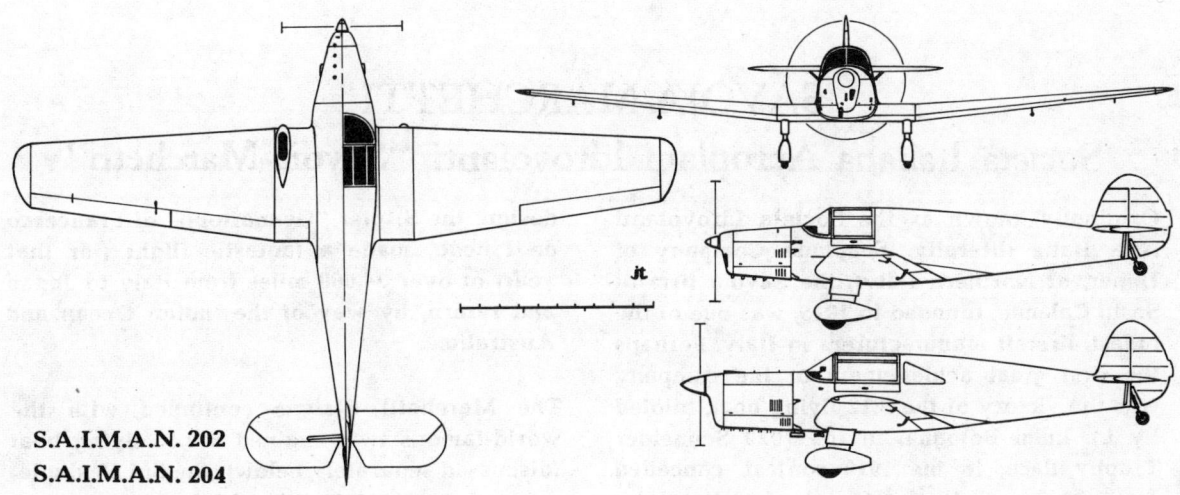

S.A.I.M.A.N. 202
S.A.I.M.A.N. 204

a liaison machine during the conflict, captured examples even equipping an R.A.F. communications squadron in 1943-44. Several remain in regular use today as private lightplanes. Just before the war, on January 29, 1939, Federigo Bazzi flew from Rome to Addis Ababa in 37 hrs. at an average speed of 119.25 m.p.h. After the war a small series of S.A.I.M.A.N. 202 trainers were built by the S.A. Costruzioni Aeronavali to fulfill a contract awarded by the Regia Aeronautica in 1943.

An all-wood two-seat low-wing monoplane, the S.A.I.M.A.N. 202 was characterized by clean, simple lines. The model 202/I was powered by a 120/130 h.p. Alfa Romeo 110 four-cylinder in-line engine. Usually fitted with wheel spats, it featured several different cabin arrangements, with and without rear quarter windows. Empty and loaded weights were 1386 lb. and 2046 lb. respectively. Performance included a maximum speed of 143 m.p.h., a cruising speed of 124 m.p.h., a landing speed of 51 m.p.h. (44 m.p.h. with flaps), a range of 434-683 miles, and a ceiling of 16,400 ft. The S.A.I.M.A.N. 202 climbed to 13,120 ft. in 24 min. Dimensions were: span 36 ft. 8 in., length 24 ft. 11 in., height 6 ft. 7 in., and wing area 193.6 sq. ft. The model 202bis, weighing 1364 lb. empty and 2068 lb. loaded, had a span of 35 ft. 7 in., a length of 25 ft. 3 in., and a wing area of 190 sq. ft. Performance was essentially the same.

S.A.I.M.A.N. 204

The S.A.I.M.A.N. 204 was a four-passenger version of the 202, powered by a 185 h.p. Alfa Romeo 115-I six-cylinder in-line engine. It was distinguished from the two-seat model by the longer canopy (with triangular rear quarter windows, used on a few two-seaters) and the longer cowling for the six-cylinder engine. Empty and loaded weights of the S.A.I.M.A.N. 204/R were 1650 lb. and 2860 lb. Performance was: maximum speed 183 m.p.h., cruising speed 155 m.p.h., landing speed 50 m.p.h. with flaps, range 683 miles, ceiling 16,400 ft., and climb to 13,120 ft. in 24 min. Dimensions were: span 32 ft. 9$^5/_8$ in., length 26 ft. 3 in., height 6 ft. 7 in., and wing area 172.2 sq. ft.

LB.2

Designed by Francis Lombardi and built under license by S.A.I.M.A.N., the LB.2 was a two-seat touring monoplane with twin booms, powered by a 110 h.p. Alfa Romeo 110-I four-cylinder in-line engine behind the cabin driving a pusher airscrew. Empty and loaded weights were 1364 lb. and 1980 lb. Speeds included a maximum of 130 m.p.h., cruising 118 m.p.h., and landing 44 m.p.h. Range was 310 miles and ceiling 18,040 ft. Spanning 38 ft. 4 in., the LB.2 was 22 ft. 8 in. long, 6 ft. high, and had a wing area of 163 sq. ft. The LB.2 was one of the earliest Italian aircraft with tricycle gear.

The LB.2 two-seat touring monoplane.

SAVOIA-MARCHETTI
Società Italiana Aeroplani Idrovolanti "Savoia-Marchetti"

Originally known as the Societa Idrovolanti Alta Italia (literally, Seaplane Company of Upper, or Northern Italy), the Savoia firm of Sesto Calende, founded in 1915, was one of the oldest aircraft manufacturers in Italy. Perhaps the first great achievement of the company was the victory of the S.12 flying boat, piloted by Lt. Luigi Bologna, in the 1920 Schneider Trophy Race; in the 1919 contest, cancelled due to poor weather, a Savoia S.13 flown by Janello distinguished itself by being the only entrant able to fly in the dense fog, although it did not complete the course. In 1922 Ing. Alessandro Marchetti, who had become known for his La Chimera sport biplane of 1910 and the M.V.T. (Marchetti-Vickers-Terni) scout biplane of 1917, became the chief designer and technical director of the firm. On December 28, 1922, his first design, the SM.51 single-seat racing seaplane, set a speed record of 173.9 m.p.h. at Sesto Calende, piloted by A. Passavala. In 1924 came the SM.52 all-metal pursuit biplane, a derivative of the M.V.T. powered by a 300 h.p. Hispano-Suiza engine and mounting two Vickers guns. In 1925, an earlier Savoia design, the S.16ter "Gennariello" of Francesco de Pinedo, made a fantastic flight (for that year) of over 34,000 miles from Italy to Japan and return, by way of the Indian Ocean and Australia.

The Marchetti designs continued with the world-famous twin-engined SM.55 flying boat (discussed separately below); the SM.56 single-engined two-seat training biplane amphibian, also built under license by the American Aeronautical Corporation of New York; the SM.57 two-seat fighter and reconnaissance flying boat, powered by a 300 h.p. Hispano-Suiza engine; the similar SM.58 single-seat fighter flying boat, which broke the World Altitude Record with 550-lb. load at 19,125 ft. in 1924, flown by Adriano Bacula; and the SM.59 three-seat reconnaissance flying boat, a development of the S.16 powered by a 400 h.p. Lorraine engine. The SM.59bis was used by the air arms of Argentina and Rumania in the late 1920's. The SM.62 three-seat bomber flying boat was a similar single-engined biplane produced in 1926; the Soviet Union purchased

Above left, an SM.56 flying boat. (I-AAQD) Right, a Canadian SM.56. (CF-AKL) Below left, an SM.57bis two-seat reconnaissance flying boat. Right, an SM.59 three-seat reconnaissance flying boat.

Two views of an SM.55P commercial flying boat of the Societá Aerea Mediterranea. (I-AABF)

24 examples, Spain bought 20 for the Aeronautica Naval, and one was imported by the Japanese Navy in 1932 for research purposes, later being sold to the Japan Air Transport Research Institute. Power unit was a 500 h.p. Isotta-Fraschini Asso. The SM.62bis replaced that engine with a 750 h.p. Asso. The SM.63 of 1927, a development of the twin-hull SM.55, featured a wider single hull and twin floats. Span and wing area were increased to 89 ft. $6^1/_2$ in. and 1140.5 sq. ft. The SM.63 was fitted either as a 10-passenger commercial transport or as a military flying boat, but was abandoned in favor of the later developments of the SM.55 and the still-larger three-engined SM.66.

In contrast to the Savoia-Marchetti aircraft of the 1920's, which were predominantly flying boats, most of the later designs were land-based aircraft, with emphasis on commercial transports and military bombers. These machines furthered the excellent reputation already gained by the impressive flights of the SM.55. The company, which changed its name (but not its initials) to Societa Italiana Aeroplani Idrovolanti in 1936, was one of the outstanding Italian aircraft manufacturers of the period, producing the best all-around Italian military aeroplane of the Second World War, the SM.79 medium bomber.

After the war Savoia-Marchetti produced the SM.95 four-engined transport, first built in 1942, the SM.101 single-engined touring monoplane, and the SM.102 eight-ten passenger twin-engined light transport, in addition to a few Nardi-designed FN.333 amphibians. Other design projects were the SM.103 two-seat fighter trainer, the SM.104 twin-engined military transport, and the SM.105 two or four-engined commercial transport with a separate detachable fuselage which could be loaded independently of the airframe. The last three designs were not built.

The designation SM has been applied here to all the Marchetti-designed aircraft in the interests of uniformity, although a number of the earlier designs were usually prefixed only by the letter S. Either form of designation is acceptable, however.

SM.55

One of the most highly-publicized aircraft in the world for its time was the Savoia-Marchetti SM.55 twin-engined twin-hull flying boat. Famous for a series of transatlantic flights in an era when any aerial crossing was considered extremely hazardous, the SM.55 rightly aroused great public interest. Understanding that most of these flights were made as propaganda demonstrations of the Fascist government does not alter the fact that the design was excellent and the accomplishments exceptional. Projected in 1923 as one of Ing. Marchetti's earliest designs for S.I.A.I., the SM.55 was conceived as a torpedo bomber and mine layer, for which roles the twin-hull arrangement adopted was ideal.

The highly original layout featured two hulls some 14 ft. 9 in. between centers, a thick cantilever three-section wing with pilots' cockpit in the leading edge, two engines mounted in tandem on pylons above the wing, driving tractor and pusher two-bladed airscrews, and a vertical tail assembly consisting of two fins and three rudders atop the tailplane, mounted on twin booms extending back from the hulls. The extremely sea-worthy structure was plywood-covered spruce, ash, and plywood throughout, with fabric-covered control surfaces.

The original military SM.55M of 1925, with two 400 h.p. Lorraine-Dietrich engines, featured observers' cockpits in the rear of each hull with Scarff ring mountings for 7.7-mm. machine guns. Torpedoes, bombs, or mines could be

The SM.55M military torpedo bombing and mine laying flying boat. Note uncowled engines, gun position, carried below the center section of the wing.

Nose gun positions were added later. In addition to the military model, ten to twelve-passenger (five-six in each hull) commercial models, the SM.55C and P, were built for Aero Espressa Italiana for the Brindisi-Constantinople line, and for the Società Aerea Mediterranea for the Rome-Cagliari run. The original SM.55 had a span of 78 ft. 9 in., a length of 52 ft. 6 in., a height of 16 ft. 5 in., and a wing area of 1000.7 sq. ft. Empty and loaded weights of the military model were 8140 lb. and 12,540 lb. Performance included a maximum speed of 131 m.p.h. and an alighting speed of 56 m.p.h. Hydrodynamic characteristics were excellent; in addition to the ruggedness and stability in heavy seas, the SM.55 was considered to be extremely graceful (for a six-ton machine!) when arising from or alighting on the water. Climbing, however, was not exceptional, 3280 ft. being reached in 3 min. 20 sec., 6560 ft. in 8 min. 21 sec., 9840 ft. in 16 min. 15 sec., and 16,400 ft. in one hour. The latter altitude represented for all practical purposes the service ceiling of the Lorraine-powered SM.55 Duration was 4-10 hrs.

In 1926 two 500 h.p. Isotta-Fraschini Asso twelve-cylinder vee engines replaced the Lorraines. Increased loaded weight limited maximum speed to 127 m.p.h., but additional fuel permitted a normal range of 750 miles or a maximum of 1350 miles. Cruising speed was 100 m.p.h. The same year the SM.55 captured fourteen world records for speed, altitude, load, and distance. With the same model, Col. Il Marchese de Pinedo made the first of the SM.55's many famous flights. In 1927, De Pinedo's flying boat, dubbed the Santa Maria, made a 28,000-mile flight around the Atlantic, starting from Elmas, Sardinia, on February 13. De Pinedo was on one stage towed 200 miles over the water to the Azores on his way back to Italy. In North America he landed on numerous lakes and rivers; on an artificial lake near Phoenix, Arizona, a carelessly discarded cigarette accidentally set fire to the plane and destroyed it. A second machine, the Santa Maria II[a], was sent by ship from Italy. With the replacement De Pinedo flew to the Eastern United States and Canada, and finally back to Italy by way of the Azores and Lisbon, completing the journey on June 16. Demonstrating the strength and dependability of the SM.55, De Pinedo's flight was a great boost for the possibilities of transatlantic commercial service, despite the fact that the Santa Maria was a military model. The following year the SM.55 of the Brazilians De Barros and Braga completed a more direct flight from Italy to their homeland.

The improved SM.55A, with two 700 h.p. FIAT A.24R twelve-cylinder vee or 800 h.p. Isotta-Fraschini Asso eighteen-cylinder W-type engines, appeared in 1930. Empty and loaded weights were 11,440 lb. and 16,940 lb. Maximum speed was 147 m.p.h., alighting speed 68 m.p.h., and range 1242-2174 miles. Climb to 3280 ft. required 4 min. 40 sec., to 6560 ft. 11 min. 40

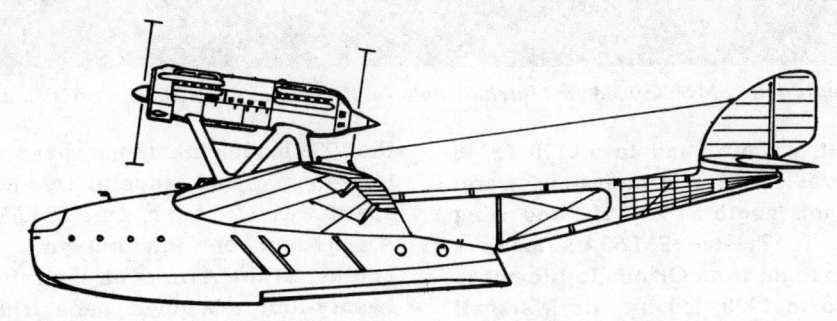

SM. 55

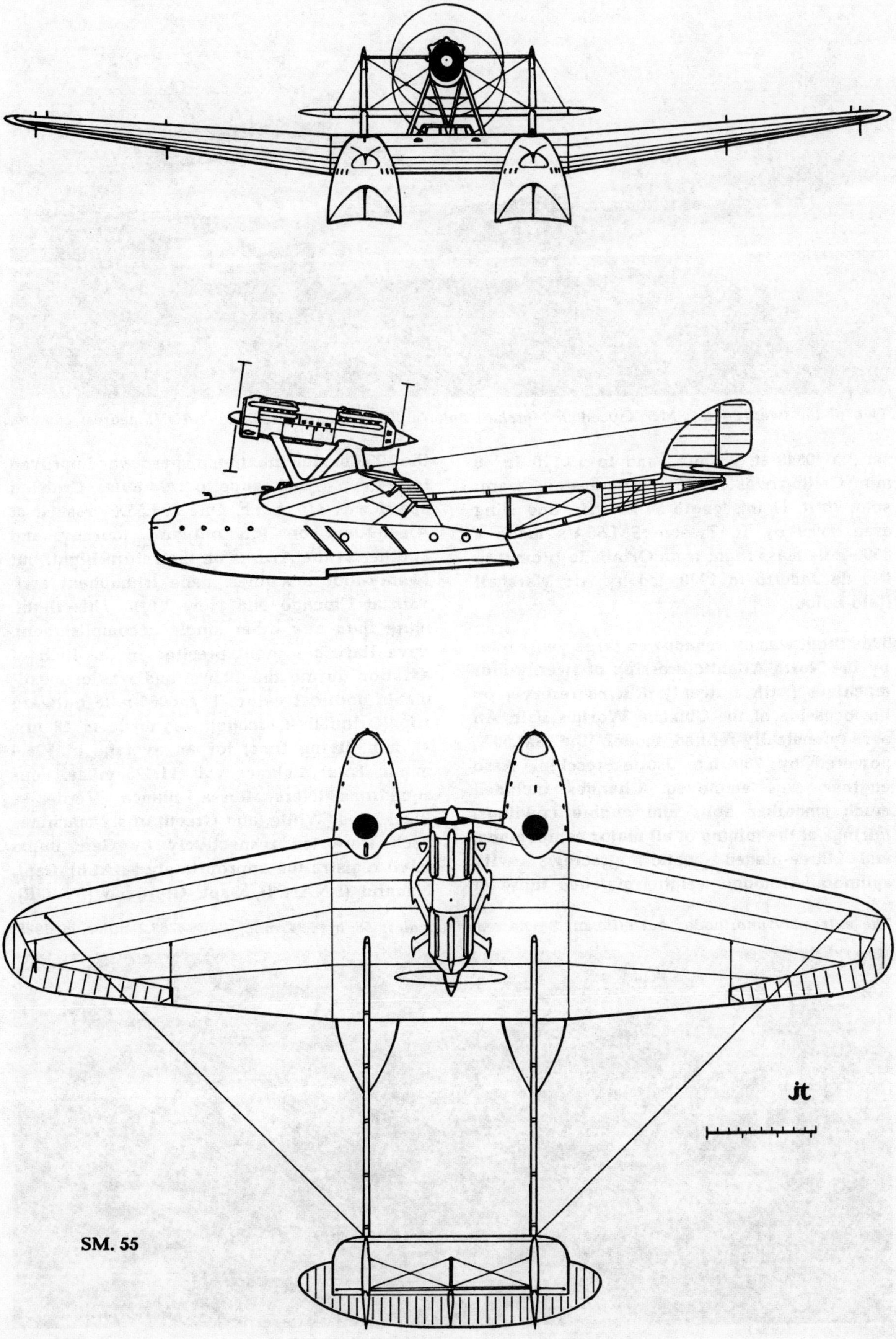

Two of the twenty-four SM.55X used in Marshall Balbo's 1933 Atlantic crossing. I-ROVI nearest camera.

sec., to 9840 ft. 23 min., and to 13,120 ft. 48 min. Ceiling was 13,776 ft. Dimensions were: span 79 ft. 11 in., length 54 ft. 2 in., and wing area 989.9 sq. ft. Twelve SM.55A's made a 6500-mile mass flight from Ortobello (Rome) to Rio de Janeiro in 1930, led by Air Marshall Italo Balbo.

This flight was overshadowed three years later by the North Atlantic crossing of twenty-four machines (with a twenty-fifth as reserve) on the occasion of the Chicago World's Fair. An aerodynamically-refined model, the SM.55X, powered by 750 h.p. Isotta-Fraschini Asso engines, was employed. Changes included much smoother hulls and engine cowlings, fairings at the joining of all major components, and three-bladed metal airscrews with spinners. Although weights matched those of the 1930 model, maximum speed was improved to 174 m.p.h. and range to 2794 miles. Cruising speed was 146 m.p.h. One SM.55X crashed at Amsterdam on the outward journey and another at the Azores on the return flight, but twenty-four machines made triumphant arrivals at Chicago and New York. This flight, more than any other single accomplishment, gave Italy her great prestige in the field of aviation during the 1930's, and was of inestimable political value. The 6065-mile outward trip (Ortobello-Chicago) was made in 48 hrs. 47 min. flying time, for an average of 124.6 m.p.h. Total distance was 11,495 miles. Four squadrons (Nera, Rossa, Bianca, Verde = Black, Red, White, and Green) of six machines each were led respectively by Gen. Balbo (civil registration appropriately I-BALB), Capt. Nannini (I-NANN), Capt. Giordano (I-GIOR),

The extremely unorthodox but efficient SM.64 remained aloft 58 hrs. 34 min., flew 4763.2 miles in 1928.

and Capt. Biani (I-BIAN). The registrations of the remaining 20 aircraft also indicated their captains (see Appendix).

A less well known flight of the SM.55 was that of Demcenko and Koukin from Sesto Calende to Petropavlovsk, approximately 14,000 miles across Siberia, in 1932. Besides the more spectacular long-distance flights, the SM.55 had a long career with the Regia Marina, serving for more than ten years. Although 13 machines were listed as available in 1939, the SM.55 had by that time reached the end of its service life, and was withdrawn. No machines of the type saw wartime service. The SM.60 was a landplane bomber version which was never built.

SM.64

Although considerably different from the SM.55 in concept, the SM.64 land-based record monoplane, powered by a 590 h.p. FIAT A.22T twelve-cylinder vee engine, was an equally efficient machine that brought additional fame to the house of Savoia. Designed four years later than the SM.55, in 1927, and first flown on April 10, 1928, the SM.64 made its initial impression during May 31-June 2 of that year with a World Closed-Circuit Distance Record of 4763.7 miles. Carrying 1717 gallons of gasoline, the SM.64, piloted by Capt. Arturo Ferrarin and Maj. Del Prete, took off from a specially-prepared 4265-ft. cement track at Montecelio (necessary because of the high take-off and landing speed of 93 m.p.h.) and remained aloft for 58 hrs. 34 min. Ferrarin and Del Prete shared the controls for the first 24 hrs., alternating with each other for the remainder of the flight.

One month later, between July 3 and 5, the pair captured the straight-line distance record with a transatlantic flight of 4466.5 miles from Montecelio to Touros, Brazil; flying time was 47 hrs. 55 min., for an average speed of 93.5 m.p.h. On May 31-June 2, 1930, after the closed-circuit record had been taken by France, it was regained for Italy by the SM.64bis, flown this time by Umberto Maddalena and Fausto Cecconi a distance of 5088.2 miles in 67 hrs. 13 min. The same Montecelio track was used. The SM.64 was a graceful design of predominantly wood construction. The cantilever wing, with an aspect ratio of 7:1, spanned 70 ft. 6¼ in. and had an area of 645.6 sq. ft. A small

A specially prepared 4265-ft. cement track was required for the SM.64's record flights. The SM.64 weighed 15,430 lb. loaded, lifted off at 93 m.p.h.

central nacelle accommodated the crew, while twin tail booms, each composed of two duralumin tubes, extended aft from the upper surface of the wing and from the landing gear fairings. A single fin and rudder was mounted in the center of the tailplane. The engine, which drove a two-bladed pusher airscrew, was housed in a streamlined nacelle on N-struts above the wing. It is worth noting that both the nacelles contributed a substantial amount of additional lift. So efficient was the SM.64 that the ratio of loaded weight to empty weight was almost 3:1, a great accomplishment considered almost ideal at that time and still excellent by today's standards. The figures were 5290 lb. empty and 15,430 lb. loaded. Length was 29 ft. 6 in. and height 12 ft. 1 in. Maximum speed at 50 per cent load was 146 m.p.h.; the theoretical maximum range was 7150 miles.

SM.65

A third very unorthodox twin-boom Marchetti design, the SM.65 twin-engined twin-float racing seaplane, did not achieve the success of the SM.55 and SM.64. Built in 1929 for the Schneider Trophy Race, the SM.65 fitted two 1000 h.p. Isotta-Fraschini twelve-cylinder water-cooled vee engines in a central nacelle, on ahead of and one behind the pilot, driving tractor and pusher airscrews. The twin booms were braced diagonally to the ends of the floats and, as in the case of the SM.64, a single

The SM.65 was a promising racing design. Unfortunately, a fatal accident ended its career.

The SM.66 was a larger three-engined eighteen-passenger commercial version of the SM.55. (I-REDI)

fin and rudder was located in the center of the tailplane. Two different tail units were tried: one with a one-piece elevator and notched rudder, another with split elevator and additional fin and rudder area below the tailplane. Construction was largely of wood.

In the closing months of 1929 the SM.65 was prepared for an assault on the seaplane and world speed records held by England at the time. Unfortunately, on January 18, 1930, while alighting on Lake Garda (at the Desenzano Scuola d'Alta Velocita) during tests, the SM.65 crashed and sank, the pilot Dal Molin losing his life. After this tragedy development of the seaplane was abandoned. Perhaps because of the ignominious finish, exact details and dimensions have never been made available, although maximum speed was probably on the order of 375-400 m.p.h.

SM.66
The SM.66 was generally similar to the SM.55, although it was considerably larger and employed three 550/610 h.p. FIAT A.22R twelve-cylinder vee engines, each driving four-bladed pusher airscrews. Built as a fourteen-passenger commercial flying boat, the SM.66 went into service in 1932 with Ala Littoria on the Rome-Cagliari-Tripoli and Rome-Athens-Alexandria routes. The A.22R-powered SM.66 weighed 15,532 lb. empty and 22,220 lb. loaded. It had a maximum speed of 152 m.p.h., a cruising speed of 129 m.p.h., an alighting speed of 71 m.p.h., a ceiling of 17,710 ft., and a range of 745 miles.

Later the flying boat was fitted with 700 h.p. FIAT A.24R twelve-cylinder vee engines, empty and loaded weights increasing to 16,390 lb. and 24,090 lb. respectively and passenger accommodation to eighteen. Maximum speed became 164 m.p.h., cruising speed 146 m.p.h., alighting speed 69 m.p.h., and ceiling 18,530 ft. The A.24R-powered SM.66 climbed to 6560 ft. in 7 min. 50 sec., to 9840 ft. in 13 min. 30 sec., to 13,120 ft. in 21 min. 50 sec., and to 16,400 ft. in 35 min. 25 sec. Dimensions were: span 108 ft. $2^7/_8$ in., length 54 ft. $5^3/_8$ in., height 16 ft. $0^7/_8$ in., and wing area 1363.3 sq. ft.

SM.67

Built in 1930, the SM.67 was a single-seat fighter flying boat for use aboard ships. The semi-cantilever wing was shoulder-mounted on a clean two-step hull, while a 400 h.p. FIAT A.20 twelve-cylinder vee engine, driving a pusher airscrew, was mounted above the fuselage on N-struts. Four additional struts braced the engine nacelle to the wing. Auxiliary floats were attached at approximately half span. Maximum speed was 140 m.p.h. Other details are unavailable.

The SM.67 was a water-based single-seat fighter.

Dimensions were: span 69 ft. $6^{3}/_{8}$ in., length 45 ft. 11 in., and wing area 645.6 sq. ft.

SM.71

Appearing in 1932, the SM.71 was a three-engined, high-wing, eight-ten-passenger commercial transport adopted by Ala Littoria on the Rome-Milan line. The engines were Walter Castor radials developing 240 h.p. each, later replaced by Piaggio P.VII C.45 radials of 390 h.p. each, driving two-bladed variable-pitch metal airscrews. The SM.71 weighed 7315 lb. empty and 11,352 lb. loaded. Maximum speed was 168 m.p.h., cruising speed 143 m.p.h., landing speed 62 m.p.h., and normal range 1211-1366 miles (maximum 2732 miles). Climbing performance included times of 2 min. 54 sec. to 3280 ft., 6 min. 38 sec. to 6560 ft., 11 min. 51 sec. to 9840 ft., 19 min. 30 sec. to 13,120 ft., and 42 min. 11 sec. to 18,040 ft.

Construction features included a cantilever wooden wing and a fabric-covered steel tube fuselage. The fixed landing gear were braced to the bottom of the fuselage and the undersides of the engine nacelles. A few models featured semi-enclosing wheel spats and streamlined steerable tailwheel fairing. Various cabin and window arrangements were used.

SM.72

Similar in appearance to the SM.71 from which it was developed, the SM.72 bomber was a larger machine powered by three 550 h.p. Bristol Pegasus II nine-cylinder radial engines. Flown for the first time as a transport in 1934, the SM.72 later featured a dorsal gun turret aft of the wing and another position in the bottom of the fuselage. Twenty production machines

Above, the prototype SM.72 heavy bomber.

Above right and below, two SM.71 transports. Note different landing gear. (I-ROMA, I-ALPI)

Left, the original SM.73 transport. Right, a later model used by the Czechoslovakian airline. (YR-BAB)

were built in 1935 for the Central (Nanking) Government Air Force of China. Prior to this, on June 15, 1934, Angelo Tivegna and Augusto Curumpai had set an altitude record of 20,992 ft. carrying a load of 11,000 lb. Empty and loaded weights were 14,960 lb. and 28,160 lb. Performance was: maximum speed 183 m.p.h. at 13,120 ft., cruising speed 152 m.p.h., landing speed 59 m.p.h. with flaps, range 1242-2174 miles, climb to 3280 ft. (with 12,100 lb. load) in 6 min. 15 sec., to 9840 ft. in 17 min. 15 sec., and to 16,400 ft. in 30 min. 49 sec. Dimensions included a span of 98 ft. $4^7/_8$ in., a length of 63 ft. $3^2/_3$ in., a height of 18 ft. $0^1/_2$ in., and a wing area of 1291.2 sq. ft.

SM.73

Forerunner of the SM.81 bomber that fought in Ethiopia, Spain, and in the Second World War, the SM.73 three-engined transport was produced in 1934. The prototype was powered by 600 h.p. Gnôme-Rhône 9 Kfs radial engines driving wooden airscrews (four-bladed on the nose engine, two-bladed on the outboard units), and featured the tall tail surfaces of the SM.71. The SM.73 went into production with a revised, longer fuselage, 700 h.p. Piaggio Stella IX R.C. nine-cylinder radials driving three-blade variable-pitch metal airscrews, and a lower, broader vertical tail assembly. As the SM.73P it entered service with Ala Littoria; as well as S.A.B.E.N.A., the Belgian airline; and C.S.A., the Czechoslovakian state airline.

The SM.73, weighing 12,760 lb. empty and 20,460 lb. loaded, had an all-wood cantilever wing and fabric-covered welded steel tube fuselage and tail group. Wheel spats were

A close-up of an SM.73 showing extractor exhausts, landing lights, oil coolers, optional spinners. (I-PISA)

Above and below right, two Ala Littoria SM.73 transports. (I-ASTI, I-ENNA)

fitted, open on early models, later fully-enclosing. Eighteen passengers and a crew of four were accommodated, plus up to 800 lb. of baggage in the bottom of the fuselage. Maximum speed was 205 m.p.h. at 13,120 ft., cruising speed 174 m.p.h., and landing speed 56 m.p.h. Service ceiling was 24,272 ft. and maximum range 994 miles. The SM.73 climbed to 6560 ft. in 10 min., to 13,120 ft. in 20 min., and to 19,680 ft. in 33 min. On two engines, maximum speed was 168 m.p.h. and service ceiling 14,432 ft. Dimensions were: span 78 ft. $8^2/_3$ in., length 57 ft. $2^3/_4$ in., height 15 ft. 1 in., and wing area 1000.7 sq. ft.

With Italy's entry into the war, the SM.73's of Ala Littoria came under the management of the Commando Servizi Aerei Speciali (C.S.A.S.) as military transports. Thirteen formed the 605a and 606a Squadriglie of the 148° Gruppo "T", based at Reggio Calabria. These were used for varied duties, including the supply of troops and equipment to North Africa. In many

One of three Ala Littoria SM.74's, the only four-engined Italian airliners of the prewar period. (I-URBE)

Above, an excellent view of the SM.74, I-ROMA. Below left, the same type in wartime camouflage. Three SM.74's served with the 616a Squadriglia "T", based at Littorio, during the hostilities.

ways the Italian counterpart of the German Junkers Ju 52/3m, the SM.73 was one of the earliest transports to serve efficiently on European air routes. A few were built by S.A.B.C.A. in Belgium.

SM.74

The first four-engined Savoia-Marchetti aeroplane was the SM.74 20-27-passenger commercial airliner, powered by 700 h.p. Piaggio Stella IX R.C. (later P.XR) radials. A development of the SM.72 bomber, utilizing the same basic wing and fuselage structure, the SM.74 appeared in 1934. Three machines went into service with Ala Littoria, later donning Regia Aeronautica camouflage and serving with the 616a Squadriglia "T" at Littorio. The high-wing transport weighed 17,160 lb. empty and 29,040 lb. loaded, the latter figure including 24 passengers and approximately 800 lb. of baggage and 1600 lb. of freight. Maximum speed was 205 m.p.h. (177 m.p.h. on three engines), cruising speed 186 m.p.h., and service ceiling 22,960 ft. The SM.74 climbed to 3280 ft. in 2 min. 48 sec., to 9840 ft. in 8 min. 55 sec., and to 16,400 ft. in 19 min. 43 sec. Span was 98 ft. $4^{7}/_{8}$ in., length 63 ft. $11^{1}/_{2}$ in., height 18 ft. $0^{1}/_{2}$ in., and wing area 1291.2 sq. ft.

SM.75

Considerably larger than its predecessors and the first Marchetti design with retractable landing gear, the SM.75 24-30-passenger commercial transport was designed in 1935 as a replacement for the SM.73P. Powered initially

The civil SM.75 entered commercial service in 1938. The later SM.82 was developed from it. (I-TESO)

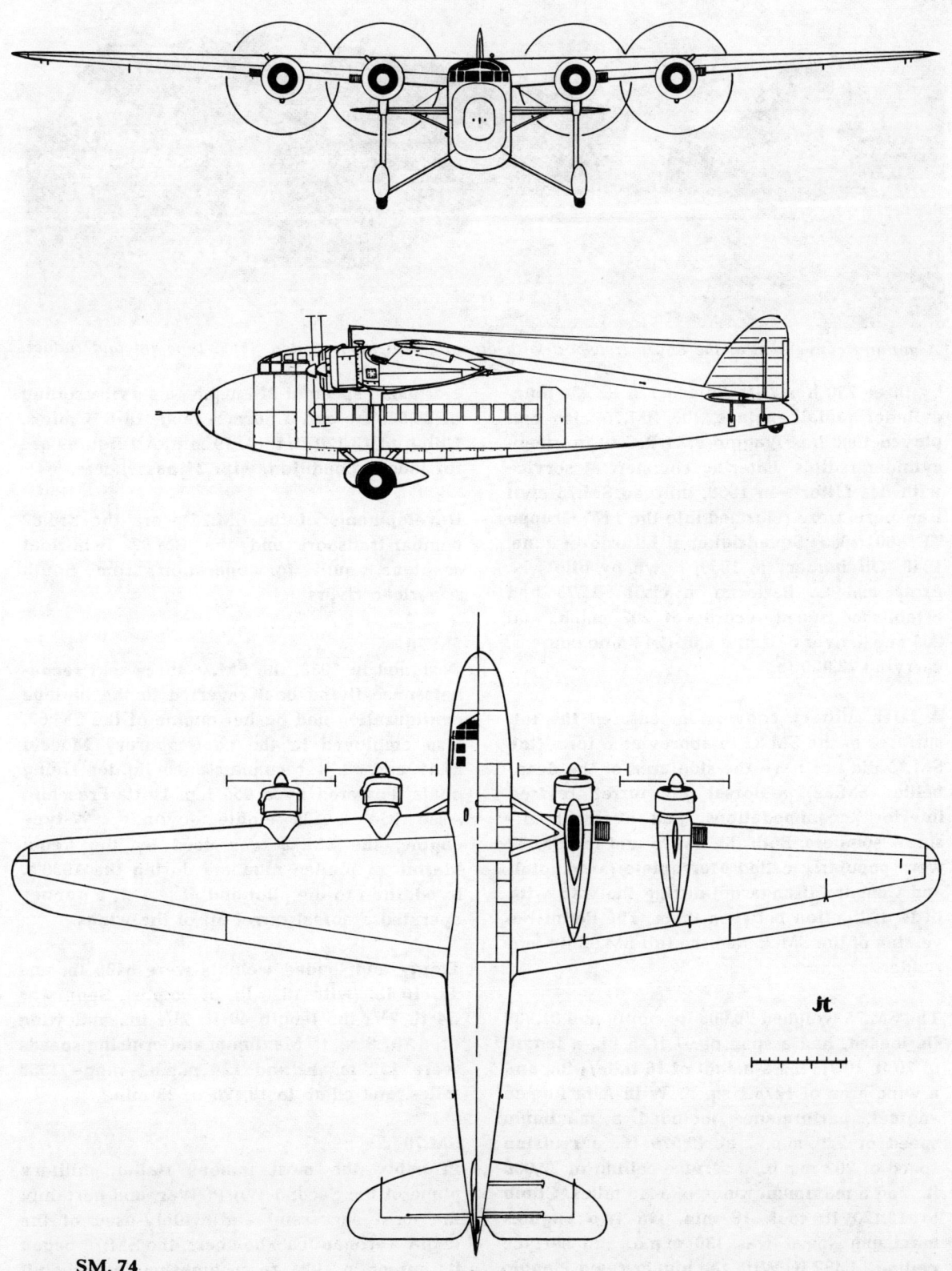

SM. 74

A military conversion of the SM.75 transport with dorsal turret, abbreviated SM.82-type fin and rudder.

by three 750 h.p. Alfa Romeo 126 R.C.34 nine-cylinder radial engines, the SM.75 also employed 1'000 h.p. Piaggio P.XI R.C.40 fourteen-cylinder radials. Entering commercial service with Ala Littoria in 1938, thirteen SM.75 civil transports were reformed into the 147° Gruppo "T" (601ª-603ª Squadriglie) at Littorio in June, 1940. On January 9, 1939, flown by pilots N. Prota and G. Bertocco, a civil SM.75 had established speed records of 207 m.p.h. and 205 m.p.h. over 621-mile and 1242-mile courses, carrying 22,000 lb.

A later military conversion featured the tail surfaces of the SM.82 in abbreviated form (the SM.75 did not have the side area of the deep-bellied SM.82), a dorsal gun turret, revised interior accommodations, and different airscrew spinners. Both the SM.75 and the SM.82 were popularly called Marsupiale (Marsupial) and Canguro (Kangaroo) during the war, with little distinction between them. The definitive version of the SM.75 had the full SM.82 fin and rudder.

The SM.75 weighed 20,900 lb. empty and 31,900 lb. loaded, had a span of 97 ft. 5 in., a length of 70 ft. $10^3/_{16}$ in., a height of 16 ft. $8^3/_4$ in., and a wing area of 1276.1 sq. ft. With Alfa Romeo engines, performance included a maximum speed of 229 m.p.h. at 10,070 ft., a cruising speed of 202 m.p.h., a service ceiling of 22,960 ft., and a maximum range of 1416 miles. Climb to 13,120 ft. took 18 min. On two engines maximum speed was 180 m.p.h. and service ceiling 14,432 ft. With the higher-rated Piaggio engines, which increased empty and loaded figures to 21,560 lb. and 32,560 lb. respectively, the SM.75 had a maximum speed of 245 m.p.h.,
a cruising speed of 214 m.p.h., a service ceiling of 29,520 ft., and a normal range of 621 miles. Climb to 13,120 ft. took 19 min. All figures are for loaded condition, with 24 passengers.

Developments of the SM.75 were the SM.82 bomber/transport and the SM.87 twin-float seaplane, built for operation from South American rivers.

SM.78
Designed in 1933, the SM.78 three-seat reconnaissance flying boat reverted to the biplane configuration and pusher engine of the SM.62, also employed in the contemporary Macchi M.41 and M.71 reconnaissance fighter flying boats. Powered by a 955 h.p. Isotta-Fraschini Asso 750 R.C.35 eighteen-cylinder W-type engine, the SM.78 was used by the Regia Marina in limited numbers during the 1930's. In addition to the pilot and observer, a gunner operated a dorsal turret aft of the wings.

Empty and loaded weights were 6490 lb. and 11,110 lb. (with 1320 lb. of bombs). Span was 54 ft. $7^3/_4$ in., length 40 ft. $2^1/_2$ in., and wing area 707.8 sq. ft. Maximum and cruising speeds were 152 m.p.h. and 124 m.p.h., range 1553 miles, and climb to 13,120 ft. 28 min.

SM.79
Probably the most famous Italian military plane of the Second World War, and certainly the most successful and widely-used of the Regia Aeronautica's bombers, the SM.79 began its career in 1934 as an eight-passenger civil machine intended for the MacRobertson London-Australia air race, but it was completed too late. Designated SM.79P, the civil version

Above, two views of the original SM.79P with Piaggio Stella engines. Below right, the same machine with Alfa Romeo 125 R.C.35 units. This "civil" prototype established several international records. (I-MAGO)

was initially powered by three 610 h.p. Piaggio Stella nine-cylinder radial engines. These were soon replaced by 750 h.p. Alfa Romeo 125 R.C.35 nine-cylinder radials (distinguished by larger, smoother, cowlings). Although the civil prototype established a number of international closed-circuit speed and load records (ultimately 266 m.p.h. for 621 miles with a 4400-lb. load, set in 1936 with 780 h.p. Alfa Romeo 126 R.C.34 engines), the military version, first built in 1935, pushed it into the background, to emerge in 1937 as the SM.83 civil transport. The SM.79P had a maximum speed of 267 m.p.h. (183 m.p.h. on two engines), a service ceiling of 25,912 ft., and a range of 932 miles. On one engine, ceiling was 7544 ft.

The bomber version entered production late in 1936 as the SM.79-I. Fitted with the Alfa Romeo 126 R.C.34 radials, it differed from the prototype principally in the addition of a gun fairing above the cockpit, a ventral bombardier's gondola, and the omission of the windows from the fuselage sides. Maximum bomb load was 2750 lb. (usually two 1100-lb.,

The SM.79 military prototype introduced the characteristic humped fuselage and ventral gondola.

Above, the SM.79 military prototype with landing gear extended. Production SM.79-I's differed very little. Below, the personal SM.79 of Italo Balbo. In spite of I-AGSB registration, machine sported camouflage.

five 550-lb., or twelve 220-lb. bombs, stored vertically within the fuselage) and defensive armament consisted of two rear-firing 12.7-mm. Breda-SAFAT maching guns (one dorsal, and one ventral, operated by the bombardier) and one 7.7-mm. Lewis gun firing from side windows. A forward-firing 12.7-mm. gun in the dorsal hump served both offensively and defensively. Performance was: maximum speed 267 m.p.h. at 13,120 ft., cruising speed 233 m.p.h., service ceiling 21,320 ft., range 1180-2050 miles, climb to 3280 ft. in 3 min. 28 sec., and climb to 16,400 ft. in 19 min. 45 sec.

The SM.79-I, named Sparviero (Sparrow Hawk) by the Regia Aeronautica and Gobbo Maledetto (Hunchback) unofficially, was successful from the outset. In Spain with the 8° and 11° Stormi Bombardamento Veloce of the Aviazione Legionaria the Sparviero established itself as a fast, efficient, and rugged bomber. A few SM.79-I bombers were fitted with 1350 h.p. Alfa Romeo 135 R.C.32 eighteen-cylinder radial engines. Sixteen machines were modified in 1937 for prestige flights; 1000 h.p. Piaggio P.XI R.C.40 fourteen-cylinder radials replaced the Alfa 126 R.C.34 units, and the dorsal and ventral housings were removed, along with all armament. Designated SM.79C (Corsa, or race), five modified Sparvieros (three competing, two reserve) were entered in the French Government-sponsored Istres-Damascus-Paris race, held in August, 1937. The Regia Aeronautica SM.79 team, nicknamed the Sorci Verde (Green Mice), completely overwhelmed the opposition, averaging 263 m.p.h. on the first leg, and completing the race at average speeds of 219 m.p.h. (Cupini-Paradisi, the winners) and 212 m.p.h. (Fiori-Lucchini and Biseo-Mussolini). Elapsed time of the winning SM.79 was just under 17 hrs. 33 min.

Using similar models with the Alfa 126 R.C.34 engines and increased fuel capacity, designated

The SM.79C and T record machines employed by the Sorci Verde were very successful. Three SM.79C's swept the Istres-Damascus-Paris Race in 1937; SM.79T's flew South Atlantic in 1938.

SM.79T (Transatlantico), the Sorci Verde made an impressive flight from Rome to Rio de Janeiro in two stages, stopping at Dakar, during the period January 24-25, 1938. Pilots were Col. Attilio Biseo/Maj. Amedeo Paradisi (I-BISE), Maj. Nino Moscatelli/Capt. Gori Castellani (I-MONI), and Lt. Bruno Mussolini/Lt. Renato Mancinelli (I-BRUN). Flying time for the 6116-mile flight was 24 hrs. 20 min. Average speed was 251 m.p.h., a rate of 266 m.p.h. having been maintained on the first leg (Rome-Dakar), suggesting that the maximum speed of the SM.79T was in excess of 280 m.p.h.

By the outbreak of the Second World War, the SM.79 had broken numerous other international records. The SM.79B, a twin-engined export version first flown in 1936, was demonstrated to air forces all over the world, eventually being purchased by those of Brazil, Iraq, and Rumania. Except for the revised transparent nose (similar to that tried on the twin-engined SM.81B), accomodating the bombardier and a 12.7-mm. Breda-SAFAT machine gun, and the employment of 1030 h.p. FIAT A.80 R.C.41 eighteen-cylinder radial engines, the SM.79B was very similar to the standard three-engined model. Maximum speed was 255 m.p.h., cruising speed 224 m.p.h., and range 995 miles (with 2640-lb. bomb load) to 1400 miles (with 1320-lb. bomb load). Four machines of this type were sold to Iraq in 1937, while Rumania bought 24 SM.79B's equipped with 1000 h.p. Gnôme-Rhône K.14 Mistral-Major radial engines. Three machines delivered to Brazil in 1939 employed 930 h.p. Alfa Romeo 128 R.C.18 radials. Rumania ordered a second batch of 24 machines, designated SM.79-JR, powered by 1220 h.p. Junkers Jumo 211Da twelve-cylinder liquid-cooled vee engines. Also built under license by I.A.R. (Industria Aeronautica Romana, Bucharest), the SM.79-JR weighed 15,840 lb. empty and 23,760 lb. loaded. Maximum speed was 276 m.p.h. at 16,400 ft., cruising speed 234 m.p.h., service ceiling 24,260 ft., and climb to 9840 ft. in 8 min. 36 sec. The SM.79-JR's were used on the Russian front. Forty-five SM.79-I three-engined bombers were purchased by the Royal Yugoslav Air Force, bringing the

The SM.79B was a twin-engined export version of the Sparviero purchased by Brazil, Iraq, and Rumania.

SM.79's warming up. The Sparviero was the most numerous and successful Italian warplane.

total number of export machines to 100.

On June 10, 1940, the Regia Aeronautica possessed 594 Sparvieros (403 in serviceable condition), which equipped the 9°, 11°; 12°, 41°, and 46° Stormi of the 3ª Divisione B.T., based at Viterbo, Comiso, Ciampino Nord, Catania, Gela, and Pisa; the 30° and 36° Stormi of 11ª Brigata B.T., at Sciacca and Castelvetrano; the 8° and 32° Stormi of the Aeronautica della Sardegna, at Villacidro and Decimomannu; and the 10°, 15°, and 33° Stormi of the Aeronautica della Libia, at Benina, Castelbenito, and Bir el Bhera. Thus the Sparvieros (both SM.79-I and SM.79-II) composed nearly two-thirds of the total Italian bombing force of 975 machines. The SM.79-II (of which some 200 were available in 1940) was a torpedo-bomber variant with 1000 h.p. Piaggio P.XI R.C.40 fourteen-cylinder radials, although a few employed 1030 h.p. FIAT A.80 R.C.41 radials. After extensive prewar tests, in which Italy developed the art of torpedo-bombing to a higher degree than that achieved by other

Three SM.79-II Sparvieros in formation over the Mediterranean. Note bombsights extended below gondolas.

SAVOIA-MARCHETTI

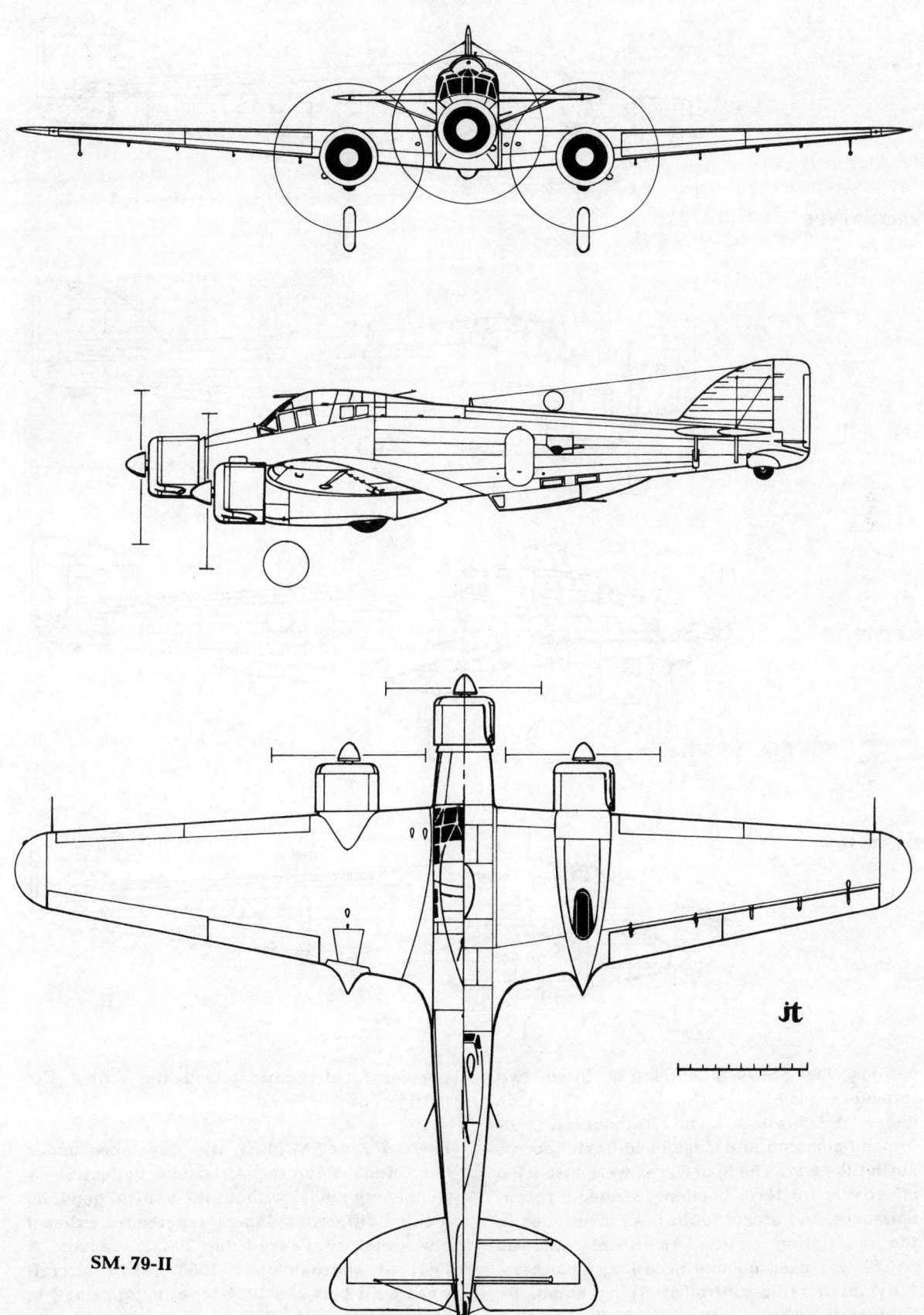

SM. 79-II

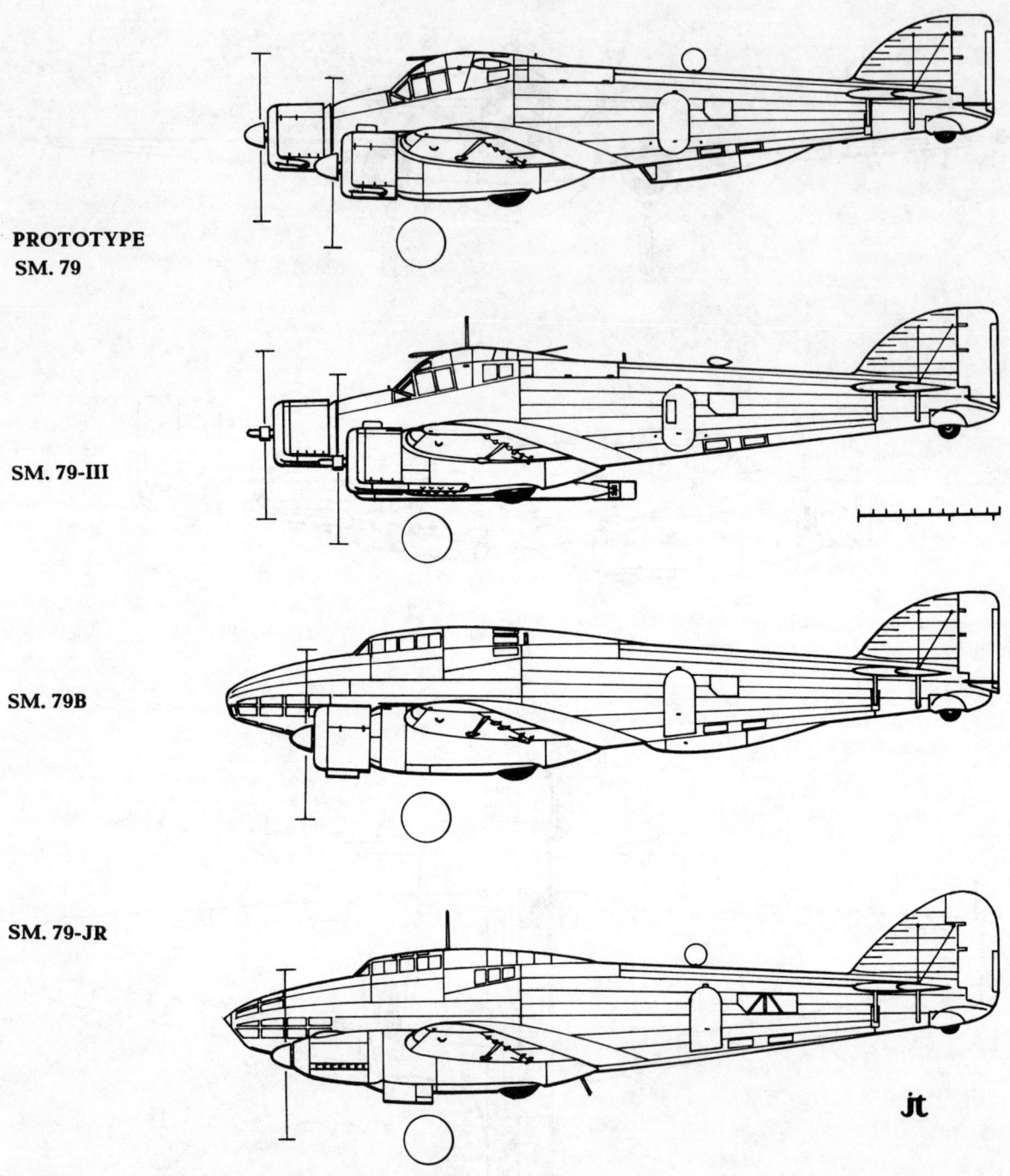

PROTOTYPE SM. 79

SM. 79-III

SM. 79B

SM. 79-JR

nations, the SM.79-II ultimately fitted two torpedoes (440-lb. warheads) side by side under the fuselage. The Aerosiluranti, or torpedo-bombing units, achieved great success during the war. The Sparvieros were also used effectively for level bombing, strategic reconnaissance, and assault duties. As mentioned in the description of the Ambrosini A.R., an SM.79 was used on one occasion, unsuccessfully, as a radio-controlled flying bomb. By September, 1943, only 61 SM.79 bombers remained in service, all of these as torpedo bombers. Thirty-four joined the Allied Co-Belligerent Air Force.

The S.579, or SM.79-III, was developed under the Germans for the Aviazione della RSI. A cleaned-up model without the ventral gondola, it fitted different spinners, lengthened exhaust pipes, and a forward-firing 20-mm. cannon. A total of approximately 1330 SM.79 aircraft were built between 1934-44; although small in comparison with Allied production figures, this number represented almost twenty per

Dorsal, lateral, and ventral machine guns are displayed by two SM.79-II bombers above. Below right, the S.579, or SM.79-III, was the final model, featuring 20-mm. cannon, revised spinners and exhausts.

cent of the total Ialian produciton of combat aircraft during the period under consideration. A number of SM.79's remained in service as transports with the postwar Italian Air Force, the Aeronautica Militare, three being sold to Lebanon in 1950. The trio was still in regular use as late as 1959.

The Savoia-Marchetti SM.79 Sparviero had a span of 69 ft. $6^{5}/_{8}$ in., a length of 53 ft. $1^{3}/_{4}$ in., a height of 13 ft. $5^{1}/_{2}$ in., and a wing area of 656.6 sq. ft. The SM.79-II weighed 16,750 lb. empty and 24,912 lb. loaded, had a maximum speed of 270 m.p.h. at 13,120 ft., a cruising speed of 255 m.p.h., a service ceiling of 22,960 ft., a range of 1242 miles, and climbed to 13,120 ft. in 10 min. 25 sec., and to 16,400 ft. in 14 min. 30 sec.

SM.80
In spite of a later type number, the SM.80 two-seat touring amphibian was designed in 1933. Powered by a 130 h.p. Colombo S.63 six-cylinder in-line engine mounted above the hull on N-struts and driving a two-bladed tractor

The SM.80 was a very appealing two-seat touring amphibian. Gear retraction was neat. (I-MORO)

The SM.80bis employed two 75 h.p. Pobjoy radials. Power matched that of the C.N.A. version, but increased drag limited performance appreciably.

airscrew, the shoulder-wing monoplane featured very clean contours, the hull and engine nacelle being particularly handsome. An alternate power unit was the 150 h.p. C.N.A. VI IRC.43 six-cylinder in-line engine. The landing gear retraction mechanism was noteworthy, the wheel nestling below the wing roots in neat streamlined fairings. Empty and loaded weights were 1540 lb. and 2200 lb. Maximum and landing speeds were respectively 141 m.p.h. and 55 m.p.h., while range was 621 miles. The SM.80 climbed to 3280 ft. in 4 min. 22 sec., to 6560 ft. in 11 min. 36 sec., to 9840 ft. in 20 min. 19 sec., and to 13,120 ft. in 33 min. 8 sec.; ceiling was 17,056 ft. Dimensions were: span 36 ft. 1 in., length 25 ft. 7 in., height 7 ft. $6^{1}/_{3}$ in., and wing area 193.7 sq. ft.

A twin-engined four-seat version, the SM.80bis, mounted two 75 h.p. Pobjoy R seven-cylinder radials driving pusher airscrews. The cabin was moved forward approximately two feet, but otherwise the basic structure was identical. Empty and loaded weights were 1716 lb. and 2596 lb. Maximum, cruising, and landing speeds were 125 m.p.h., 109 m.p.h., and 47 m.p.h. respectively. Climb to 3280 ft. required 4 min. 31 sec., to 6560 ft. 10 min. 46 sec., to 9840 ft. 19 min. 8 sec., and to 13,120 ft. 32 min. 2 sec.

SM.81

A military development of the SM.73 transport, the SM.81 bomber/transport appeared in 1934, seeing considerable use in the Ethiopian campaign of the following year. It fought in the Spanish Civil War and in the Second World War and was still in limited use as a transport in the immediate postwar period, in spite of the fact that it was already technically obsolete by 1936! Nevertheless, the SM.81 was the standard Italian bomber until the vastly superior SM.79 began to enter service in 1937.

The SM.81 was powered by three 750 h.p. Alfa Romeo 125 R.C.35 or 126 R.C.34 nine-cylinder radial engines, 900 h.p. Isotta-Fraschini (license-built Gnôme-Rhône K.14) fourteen-cylinder radials, or 900 h.p. Piaggio Stella IX R.C.40 nine-cylinder radials. Three distinct types of engine cowling were employed; the initial short-chord Townend ring was followed by a similar longer-chord type, finally replaced

The SM.81 was a bomber version of the SM.73. Note ventral turret, long-chord engine cowlings.

by the smoother Magni-N.A.C.A. tapered variety. A glazed bombardier's position was fitted below the fuselage just behind the engine nacelle, while two semi-retractable hydraulically-operated turrets, each with two 7.7-mm. machine guns, were located in dorsal and ventral positions. A fifth hand-held 7.7-mm. gun was fired from either of two lateral hatches. Crew was six. The normal bomb load was 2640 lb. (maximum 4400 lb.), stored vertically in the bottom of the fuselage. This method of bomb storage did not allow a predictable bomb trajectory, which partly explains the mediocre results often obtained by Italian bombing squadrons. Various loads were: four 1100-lb. or 550-lb. bombs, sixteen 220-lb. bombs, twenty-eight 110-lb. bombs, or fifty-six 44-lb. or 33-lb. bombs. The SM.81 was also tested in 1936 with two torpedoes mounted beneath the fuselage.

Operating both as a bomber and troop transport in the Ethiopian campaign of 1935, the SM.81 was an effective machine, although not used in as great numbers as the older Ca 133. In Spain it was satisfactory when given reasonable fighter cover (usually FIAT CR.32's), but by 1939 it was completely out-of-date. At that time 276 machines (130 effective) were in service in Metropolitan Italy, Albania, Libya, and the Aegean Islands, while a further 36 (16 effective) were stationed in Ethiopia (A.O.I.). In June, 1940, SM.81's still equipped the 37° Stormo B.T. at Lecce, the 38° Stormo of the Aeronautica dell'Albania at Tirana, the 14° and 15° Stormi B.T. of the Aeronautica della Libia at El Adem and Castelbenito, and the 39° Stormo B.T. of the Aeronautica dell'Egeo at Rhodes. During the war the bomber, receiving the name Pipistrello (Bat) because of its usual night bombing role, served in North

Above, the SM.81 was the standard Regia Aeronautica bomber of the mid-1930's. Large numbers were used in Italy, Ethiopia, and Spain to demonstrate Fascist airpower. The bottom photo shows camouflaged and uncamouflaged SM.81's in the same Squadriglia.

Below, an SM.81 in service with Nationalist forces during the Spanish Civil War. The encircled "M" designated the Mussolini unit. Performance was satisfactory against minimal Republican fighter opposition.

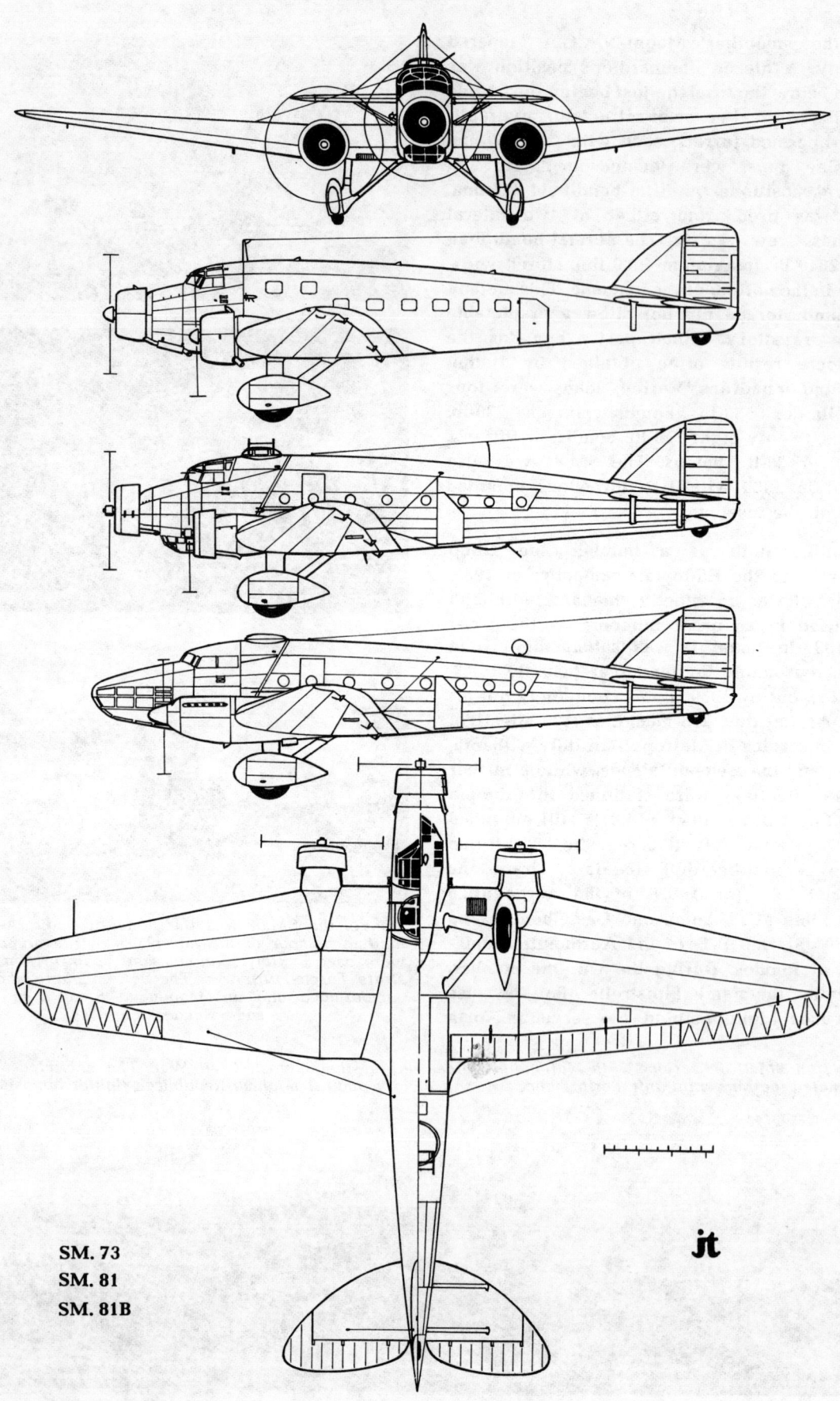

SM. 73
SM. 81
SM. 81B

Above, the twin-engined SM.81B, with 840 h.p. Isotta-Fraschini Asso XI R.C. engines. Below right, a standard SM.81 bomber over Greece. As a night bomber, the type earned the name Pipistrello (Bat).

Africa, Greece, and Russia, but it was increasingly employed for second-line duties such as paratroop and general-purpose transport. In this capacity 18 troops could be carried. When Italy surrendered five SM.81's joined the Allies, a few remaining machines being used by the Fascists.

The SM.81 weighed 14,300 lb. empty and 23,100 lb. loaded. Performance included a maximum speed of 196-214 m.p.h., depending on the type of engine fitted, a cruising speed of 180 m.p.h., a range of 932-1242 miles, and a service ceiling of 22,960 ft. Climb to 9840 ft. took 12 min. Dimensions were: span 78 ft. $8^{2}/_{3}$ in., length 60 ft. 1 in., height 15 ft. $11^{1}/_{4}$ in., and wing area 1000.7 sq. ft.

A twin-engined version, designated SM.81B, had 840 h.p. Isotta-Fraschini Asso XI R.C. twelve-cylinder vee engines and a glazed bombardier's position in the nose. Empty and loaded weights were 14,960 lb. and 22,880 lb. Length was 58 ft. $8^{1}/_{2}$ in. Performance included a maximum speed of 204 m.p.h., a cruising speed of 186 m.p.h., a service ceiling of 26,240 ft., and a range of 1366 miles. The SM.81B climbed to 3280 ft. in 4 min., to 6560 ft. in 7 min. 48 sec., to 13,120 ft. in 15 min. 30 sec., and to 19,680 ft. in 24 min. 30 sec.

SM.82

The SM.82 bomber/transport, basically an enlarged, more powerful military version of

The prototype SM.82 bomber with bombardier position extended. Also visible is dorsal turret.

As a troop transport, the SM.82 was especially valuable because of its great weight-carrying characteristics. Paratroops of the famed "Folgore" Division used the Canguro; 40 men were carried.

the SM.75, was one of the best aircraft Italy had at her disposal during the Second World War. First flown in 1938, the SM.82 operated successfully throughout the conflict and continued to serve as late as 1960 with the postwar Aeronautica Militare! Initially the SM.82 was powered by three 950 h.p. Alfa Romeo 128 R.C.21 radial engines, although surviving postwar examples fitted Pratt & Whitney radials. The main changes from the SM.75 were the deepened fuselage and taller fin and rudder. The SM.82 was designed as a heavy bomber and troop or freight transport; in the latter form it carried up to 8800 lb., typical loads being six aero engines, 40 fully-equipped troops, or 600 gallons of gasoline. As a result of the need for maintaining a rapid supply line to distant A.O.I., Lt. Col. Galante urged that the SM.82 also be able to accomodate dismantled fighters. Such were the interior dimensions that a complete CR.42 biplane could be housed, with wings and tail surfaces detached and stored longitudinally. At least 50 fighters were transported to A.O.I. this way. Appropriately, the SM.82 was called Canguro (Kangaroo) or Marsupiale (Marsupial), along with the SM.75

The fuselage of the SM.82 was of fabric-covered metal construction, while the wings and tail assembly were of wood. Loading was accomplished through doors in the bottom of the fuselage, an overhead runway being provided within the fuselage to facilitate the operation. As a heavy bomber, the SM.82 featured a semi-retractable bombardier's position, a dorsal turret with a 12.7-mm. machine gun, three 7.7-mm. machine guns in nose and lateral positions, and a bomb capacity of 8800 lb. (usually eight 1100-lb. bombs or twenty-seven 220-lb. or 110-lb. bombs). When

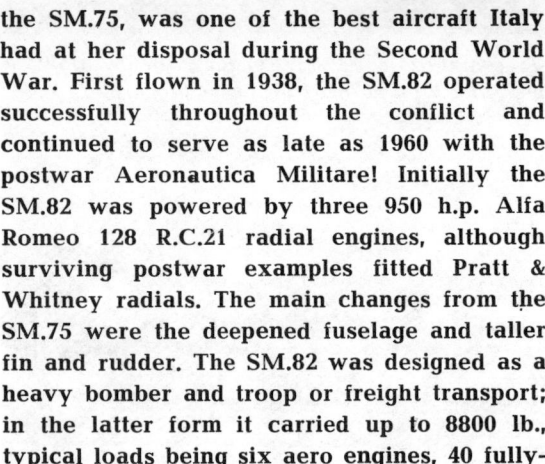

Above left and below, SM.82's continued to serve effectively as transports with the Aeronautica Militare after the war. The design was finally replaced by the Fairchild C-119G in the 1950's.

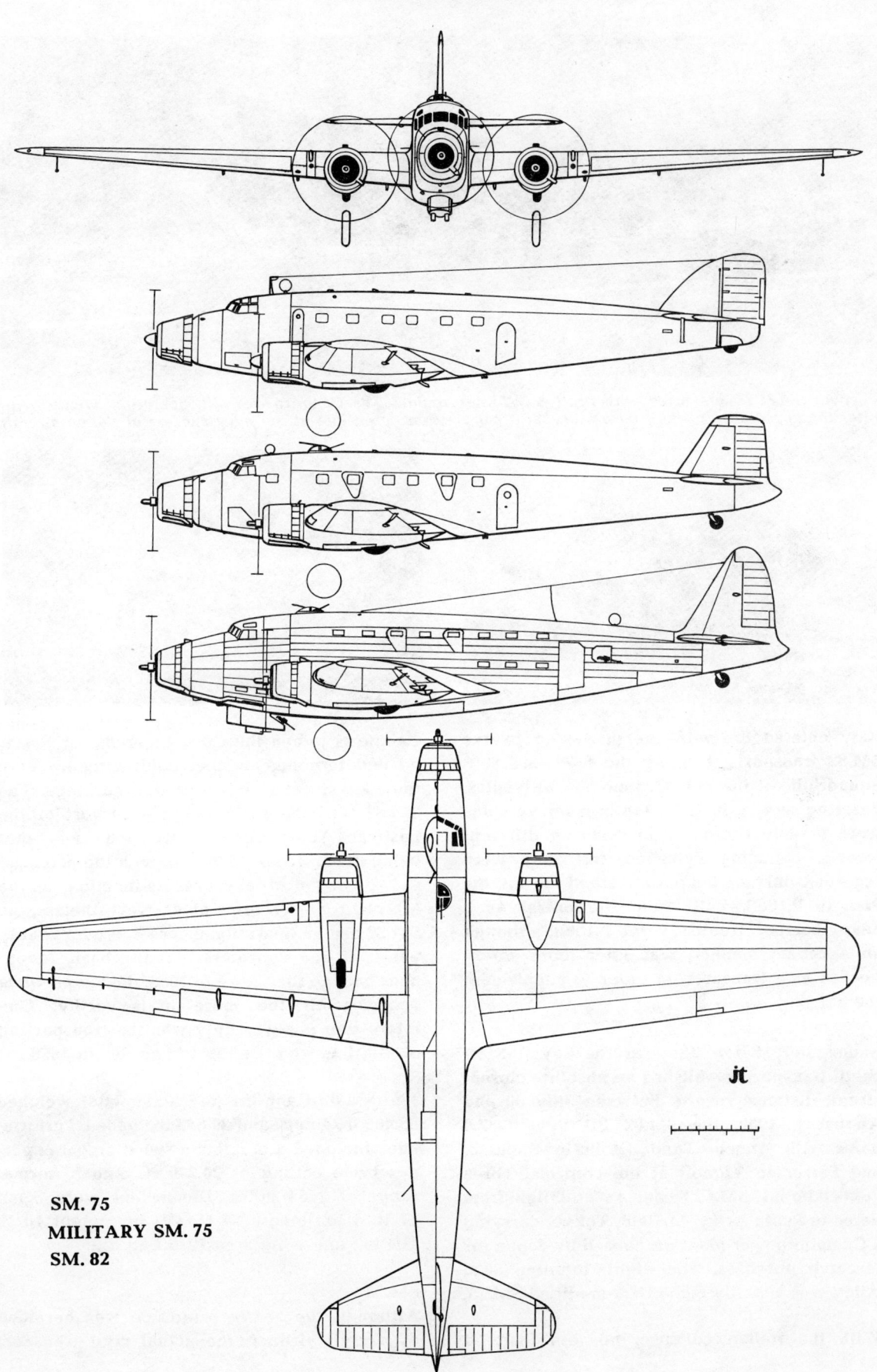

SM. 75
MILITARY SM. 75
SM. 82

Postwar SM.82's were fitted with Pratt & Whitney radials. The Canguro was still operating twenty years after the appearance of the first prototype; it can be considered one of the most successful Italian aircraft.

Italy entered the war, she possessed twelve SM.82 transports, forming the 607ª and 608ª Squadriglie of the 149° Gruppo "T" at Naples. Entering service in 1941, the bomber versions were used in a number of raids on different targets, including Palestine, but they were regarded only as temporary stand-ins for the Piaggio P.108B, built from the outset as a heavy bomber. Ironically, the P.108B, although an excellent bomber, was later more sorely needed as a transport, in order to supplement the SM.82!

Immediately before the war the Savoia-Marchetti transport established an absolute closed-circuit distance record. Between July 30 and August 1, 1939, the SM.82 PD flew 8037.9 miles with Angelo Tondi, Roberto Dagasso, and Ferruccio Vignoli at the controls. Three years later an "SM.82" made a secret flight from Rome to Fussa Army Airfield, Tokyo, carrying a Campini power plant purchased by Japan for research purposes. The flight, totalling 8023 miles, was actually made by a modified SM.75.

With the Italian collapse, no less than 30 Canguros joined the Co-Belligerent Air Force, an undetermined number continuing to serve the Fascist cause in Luftwaffe markings. The SM.82 was the main heavy transport of the postwar Aeronautica Militare, 31 machines being in service in 1948, although the Fairchild C-119G began to take over its functions as the Marchetti design grew older. Nevertheless, the SM.82 had an operational career of over twenty years; if one considers that the basic layout goes back to the SM.75 of 1935, the long service becomes all the more praiseworthy. One interesting postwar duty was the transporting of pilgrims from Dublin to Lourdes in 1958.

The SM.82 Canguro (or Marsupiale) weighed 26,400 lb. empty and 39,600 lb. loaded. Performance included a maximum speed of 200 m.p.h., a service ceiling of 20,230 ft., and a normal range of 2484 miles. Dimensions were: span 97 ft. 5 in., length 74 ft. $4^{1}/_{4}$ in., height 18 ft. $2^{1}/_{2}$ in., and wing area 1276.1 sq. ft.

SM.83

Although the SM.79 prototype was heralded as a civil airliner, the actual civil transport

The SM.83 was the civil version of the SM.79. It served with Ala Littoria and LATI. (I-LUCE)

version was the SM.83, produced in 1937. The SM.83 entered service with Ala Littoria S.A. Linee Atlantiche and L.A.T.I. (Linee Aeree Transcontinentali Italiane), the overseas line linking Italy and South America, during 1938-39. Except, of course, for the omission of all military equipment and the revised interior accomodations for ten passengers and a crew of three, the SM.83 differed little from the bomber. It weighed 14,960 lb. empty and 22,660 lb. loaded. Engines were three 750 h.p. Alfa Romeo 126 R.C.34 nine-cylinder radials, providing maximum and cruising speeds of 276 m.p.h. and 248 m.p.h. Service ceiling was 27,552 ft. (18,040 ft. on two engines) and range 932-1242 miles. The SM.83 climbed to 9840 ft. in 9 min. and to 13,120 ft. in 13 min. 30 sec. Dimensions were: span 69 ft. $6^{5}/_{8}$ in., length 53 ft. $1^{3}/_{4}$ in., height 13 ft. $5^{1}/_{2}$ in., and wing area 656.6 sq. ft.

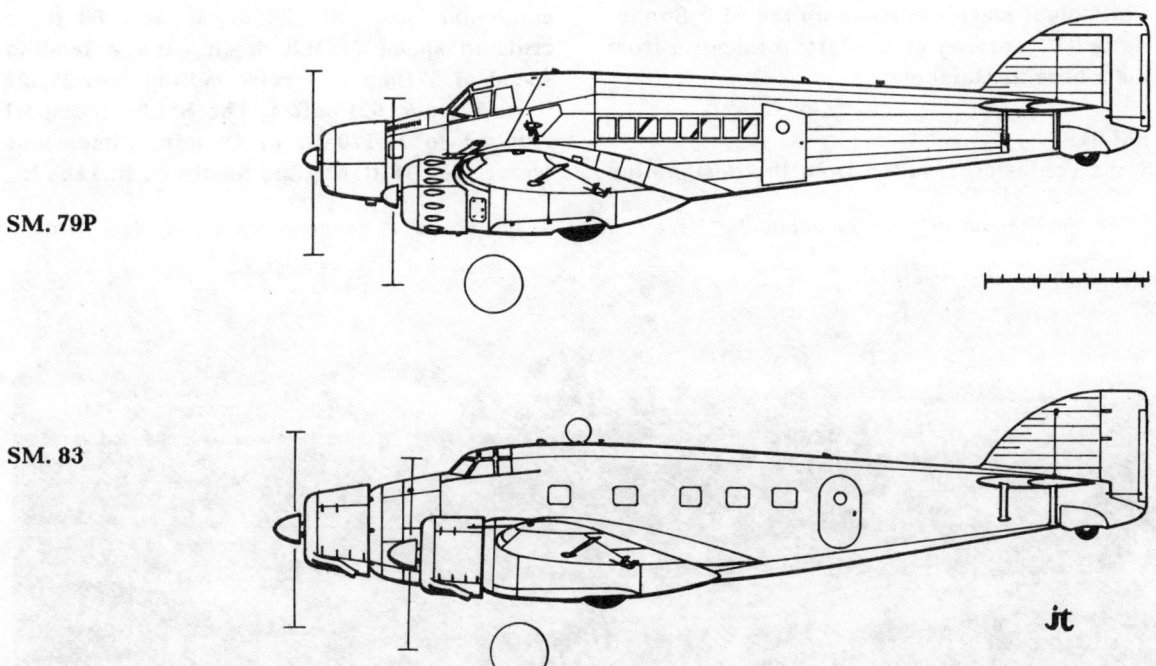

SM. 79P

SM. 83

The original SM.84 was a twin-engined airliner developed from the SM.73, resembling the DC-3. (I-SIAI)

Alternate versions were the SM.83A six-passenger transport (crew of four), which weighed 26,730 lb. loaded, including 5698 lb. of fuel and 2200 lb. of mail, and the SM.83T transoceanic mailplane, which, with a still further increase in fuel tankage to 8140 lb., weighed 26,763 lb. loaded, including an 1100-lb. payload. Both machines were built for Ala Littoria, the former for the Natal-Buenos Aires line, the latter for the Rome-Natal line. Ten SM.83's in service with L.A.T.I. in 1940 came under the Commando Servizi Aerei Speciali as communications transports with South America, Germany, and distant Italian colonies, while eight machines made up the 615ª Squadriglia "T", serving as military transports from their base at Guidonia.

SM.84

Some confusion resulted from the designation SM.84, originally applied in 1935 to a twin-engined transport. Later, during the war, the number was given to a three-engined bomber developed from the SM.79 Sparviero.

The civil transport, while bearing a general similarity to the Douglas DC-3 and no doubt influenced by it, was actually an eighteen-passenger twin-engined development of the SM.73. Powered by 900 h.p. Gnôme-Rhône 14 Krsd fourteen-cylinder radial engines, the SM.84 weighed 13,200 lb. empty and 20,900 lb. loaded, including 594 lb. of baggage and 1144 lb. of cargo and mail. Performance included a maximum speed of 220 m.p.h. at 6560 ft., a cruising speed of 196 m.p.h., and a landing speed of 57 m.p.h. Service ceiling was 25,584 ft. and range 621 miles. The SM.84 transport climbed to 13,120 ft. in 18 min. Dimensions were: span 78 ft. 8¾ in., length 64 ft. 11⅓ in.,

The SM.84 bomber was an unpopular development of the SM.79. It never matched the Sparviero.

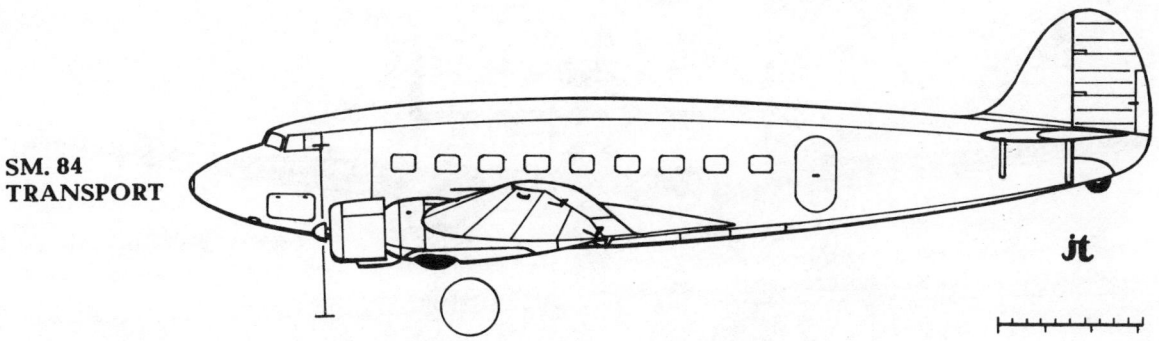

SM. 84
TRANSPORT

height 15 ft. 7 in., and wing area 1000.7 sq. ft. The airliner never went into production.

The SM.84 bomber, at first a special torpedo-carrying version of the Sparviero, was originally known as the SM.79bis, then SM.94, and finally SM.84 after the civil transport bearing the designation was abandoned. Featuring a longer fuselage than the SM.79, and lacking the characteristic humpback, the prototype SM.84 bomber (SM.79bis) had twin fins and rudders and three 850 h.p. Alfa Romeo 128 R.C.21 radial engines; it first flew in 1938. The production models replaced the Alfa units with 1000 h.p. Piaggio P.XI R.C.40 fourteen-cylinder radials. Defensive armament was six 12.7-mm. machine guns, one each in a dorsal turret and a ventral gondola, the remaining four firing from windows in the fuselage sides. Normal offensive load was two torpedoes carried below the fuselage, or 4400 lb. of bombs stored internally.

Although aerodynamically cleaner and better armed than the Sparviero, the SM.84 was not noticeably faster; in addition it suffered from inferior maneuverability and was generally

Above, three photos of SM.84 bombers in Regia Aeronautica service. Over 100 were built, but high rate of attrition during Mediterranean operations accounted for all but a few of these.

An SM.84 with bombardier's gondola extended. Cleaner than the SM.79, the SM.84 had poor maneuverability.

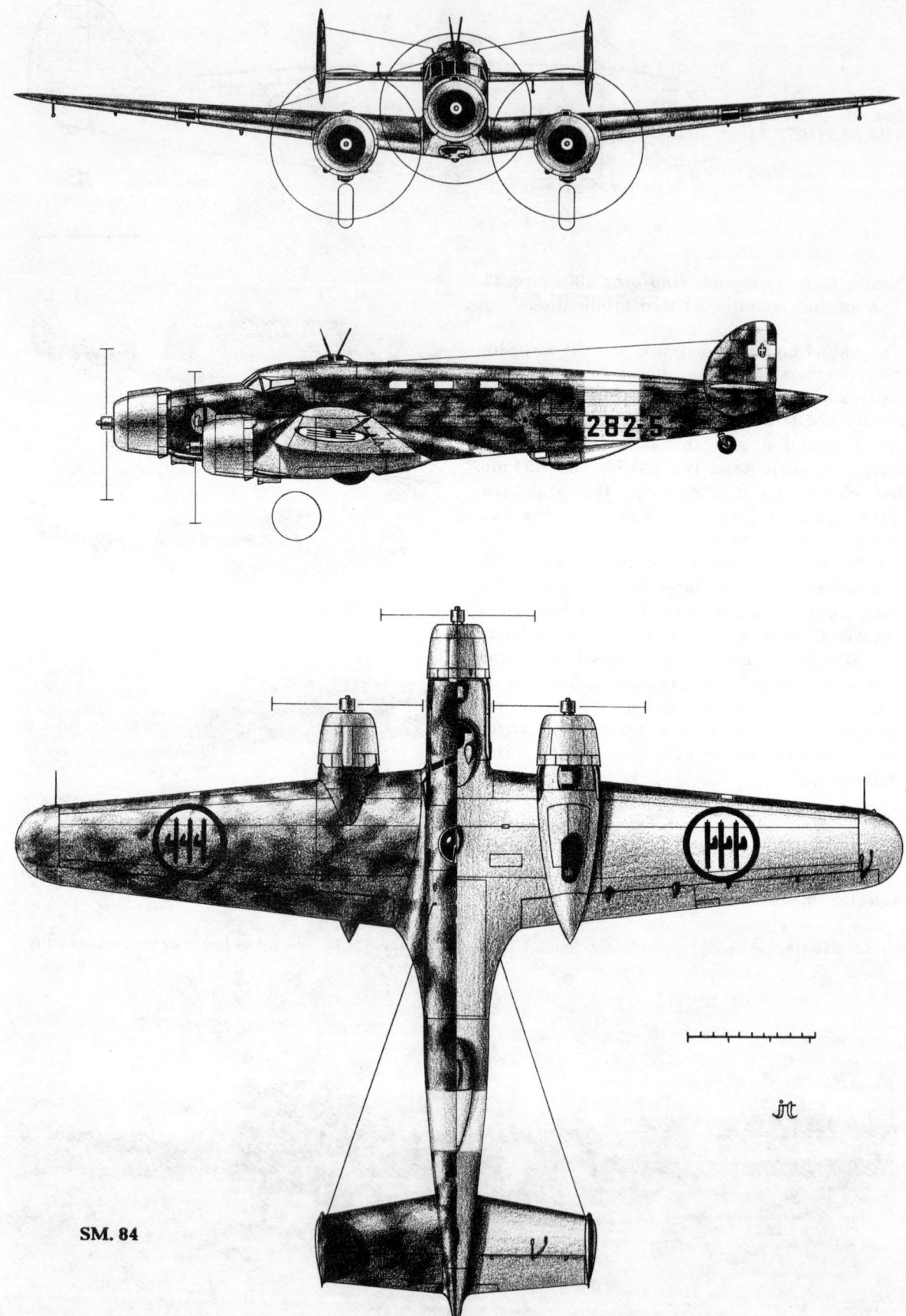

SM. 84

disliked by crews. Most of the more than 100 SM.84's built were active against Mediterranean convoys between November, 1941, and August, 1942. Based in Sicily, the 282ᵃ Squadriglia (torpedo bombers) participated in the operations against Malta; the 4° and 25° Gruppi B.T. also operated the type from Sicily. The SM.84 enjoyed some successes, including a direct torpedo hit on the battleship Nelson, but losses were heavy. By September, 1943, only the 48° Stormo B.T. (98° Gruppo at Gioia del Colle, and 99° Gruppo at Lonate Pozzolo) was still operating the bomber; of 30 machines remaining only 15 were serviceable. Those existing after the war were used by the Aeronautica Militare until broken up.

The SM.84 bomber weighed 19,465 lb. empty and 29,235 lb. loaded. Maximum speed was 266 m.p.h., cruising speed 247 m.p.h., ceiling 29,512 ft., and range 1130 miles. Dimensions were: span 69 ft. 6⅝ in., length 58 ft. 4⅝ in., height 14 ft. 9⅛ in., and wing area 656.6 sq. ft.

SM.85

Although widely publicized in the late 1930's, the SM.85 twin-engined single-seat dive bomber was an unsuccessful machine that never saw combat. Thirty-three pre-production SM.85's were issued to one unit, the 96° Gruppo B.T. at Pantelleria, in 1939-40, but these were soon withdrawn in favor of the Ju 87B. Designed in 1936, the SM.85 made its first flight in 1938. The engines were two 500 h.p. Piaggio

A few SM.84 bombers remained with the Aeronautica Militare after the war. This example was used for spares until finally broken up.

P.VII R.C.35 seven-cylinder radials. The offensive load consisted of one 550-lb. or 1100-lb. bomb; the pilot was provided with a window at his feet for observing targets, and one 12.7-mm. or two 7.7-mm. machine guns in the nose. Air brakes were fitted to the trailing edges of the wings. Construction was mixed metal and wood, with empty and loaded weights of 6504 lb. and 9237 lb.

Maximum speed was 228 m.p.h., cruising speed 193 m.p.h., and service ceiling 19,190 ft. Climb

Above right and below, the SM.85 was a twin-engined single-seat dive bomber. In spite of considerable publicity, it was not successful and served only briefly with one operational unit.

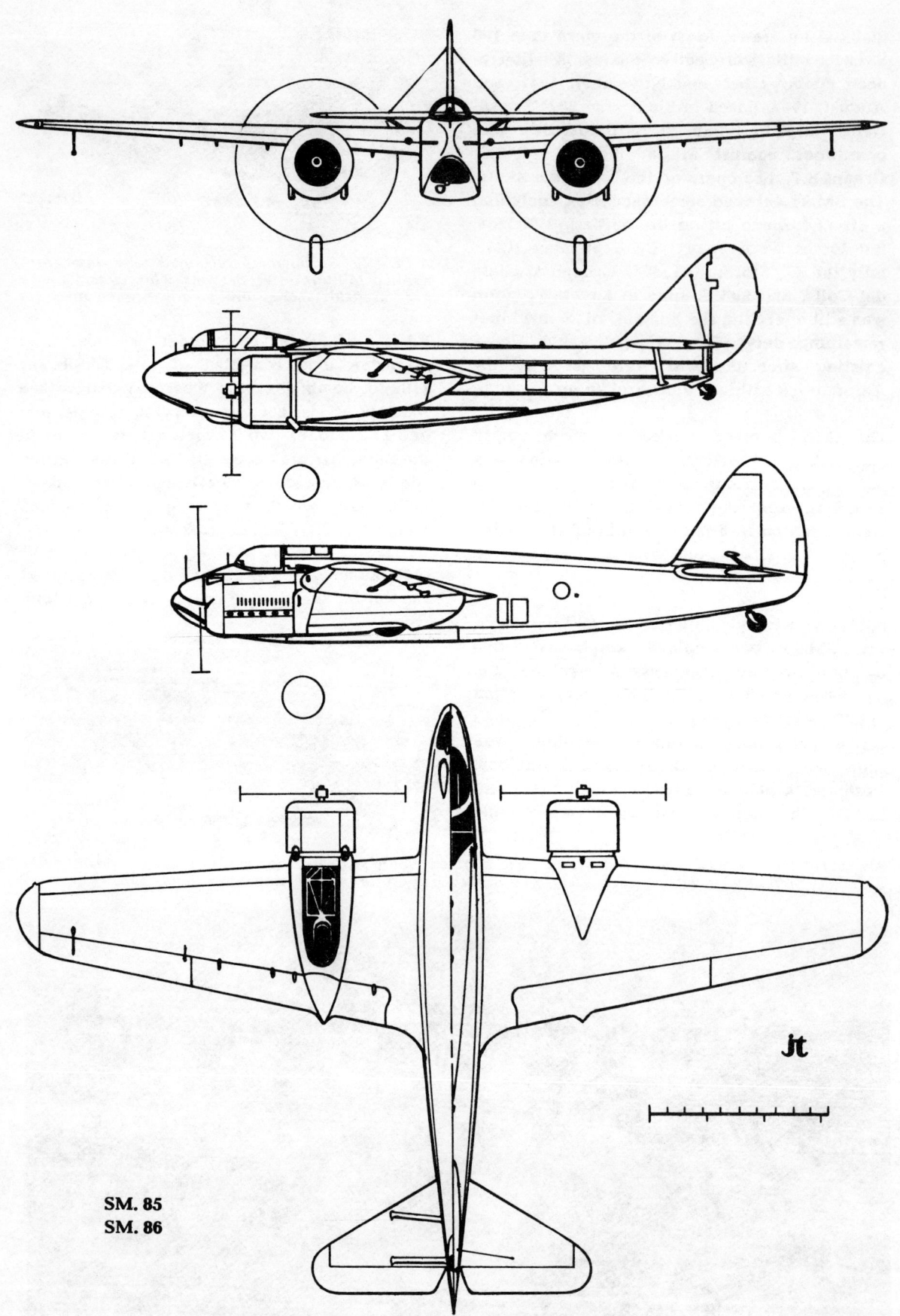

SM. 85
SM. 86

The SM.85 was powered by two 500 h.p. Piaggio P.VII R.C.35 seven-cylinder radial engines.

to 13,120 ft. required 13 min. 19 sec. A version with two 1000 h.p. Piaggio P.XI R.C.40 radials (giving twice the power of the P.VII R.C.35's) was projected, but never built, estimated maximum speed being 317 m.p.h. at 13,120 ft. Dimensions of the SM.85 were: span 48 ft. 11$^{1}/_{8}$ in., length 34 ft. 5$^{1}/_{3}$ in., height 10 ft. 9$^{7}/_{8}$ in., and wing area 277.7 sq. ft.

SM.86
The SM.86, an aerodynamically-refined version of the SM.85 with two 750 h.p. Isotta-Fraschini Delta R.C.40 twelve-cylinder inverted vee air-cooled engines, was built as a prototype only. 520 h.p. Walter Sagitta engines were originally specified. Except for the engines, a cleaner fuselage (length 35 ft. 9$^{1}/_{8}$ in.), and modified tail surfaces, the SM.86 was very similar to the SM.85. Loaded weight was 11,193 lb. and maximum speed 256 m.p.h.

SM.87
A twenty-four-passenger twin-float version of the SM.75, the SM.87 transport seaplane appeared in 1938 with 1350 h.p. Alfa Romeo 135 R.C.32 eighteen-cylinder radial engines. A version intended for operation from Argentine rivers employed 1050 h.p. Pratt & Whitney

Above right and below, the SM.86 was a development of the SM.85 incorporating Isotta-Fraschini Deltas.

The SM.87 was a twenty-four passenger float version of the SM.75. Only a few were built in 1938 (I-INNO)

SC3G fourteen-cylinder radials. The Alfa Romeo-powered model weighed 26,400 lb. empty, 37,400 lb. loaded, and had maximum and cruising speeds of 255 m.p.h. (11,480 ft.) and 224 m.p.h. respectively. Service ceiling was 23,945 ft. (or 15,745 ft. on two engines) and climb to 13,120 ft. required 20 min.

With the Pratt & Whitney units, weights were 23,100 lb. empty and 31,240 lb. loaded. Maximum speed was 227 m.p.h. at 12,465 ft., cruising speed 193 m.p.h., and service ceiling 19,680 ft. Climb to 13,120 ft. took 23 min. Dimensions of both models were the same as those of the SM.75, except for the height of 19 ft. $4^7/_8$ in. Probably the only remaining SM.87 was flown to Allied lines in September, 1943 to join the Co-Belligerent Air Force.

SM.89

A twin-engined development of the SM.84 bomber, the SM.89 was an assault plane powered by 1350 h.p. Piaggio P.XII R.C.35 radial engines. Designed in 1941, it was under evaluation at the time of the Armistice. Forward-firing armament, mounted in the nose, consisted of two 37-mm. or 54-mm. cannon and two 12.7-mm. machine guns, while a defensive armament of two further 12.7-mm. weapons was fitted in dorsal and ventral positions. Loaded weight was 27,888 lb. Performance included a maximum speed of 286 m.p.h. at 17,388 ft. and a range of 683 miles. Dimensions were: span 69 ft. $0^3/_8$ in., length 53 ft. $9^2/_3$ in., and wing area 656.6 sq. ft. Piaggio P.XV R.C.35 radials of 1500 h.p. each were planned for later prototypes.

The SM.89 twin-engined attack bomber had a forward-firing armament of two cannon and two machine guns.

Above and below right, the SM.91 long-range escort fighter, which made its first flight in March, 1943.

SM.90

The SM.90 was a three-engined commercial transport designed in 1941 but not developed due to the war situation. The power units were Alfa Romeo 135 R.C.32's of 1400 h.p. each.

SM.91

The SM.91 might be called the Italian P-38 as it was a twin-engined, twin-boom long-range escort fighter, but it differed from its American counterpart in having a crew of two. Designed in 1941 and competing with the Caproni Ca 380 Corsaro (also a twin-boom design) for production orders, the SM.91 flew for the first time on March 10, 1943, powered by 1475 h.p. Daimler-Benz DB 605A-1 twelve-cylinder inverted vee engines. Only one prototype was finished. One of the few all-metal Savoia-Marchetti aircraft, it mounted three forward-firing 20-mm. Mauser MG 151 cannon in the central nacelle and two similar weapons in the wing roots. Four 220-lb. or 353-lb. bombs or a single 1100-lb. bomb (or 218-gal. drop-tank) could be carried externally on racks below the wings and central nacelle. Empty and loaded weights

were 14,110 lb. and 19,600 lb. Maximum speed was 363 m.p.h. at 22,960 ft., cruising speed 320 m.p.h., service ceiling 36,090 ft., and range 994 miles. Climb to 19,680 ft. required 8 min. 30 sec. Dimensions were: span 64 ft. 7$\frac{1}{2}$ in., length 43 ft. 5$\frac{3}{4}$ in., height 12 ft. 7$\frac{1}{2}$ in., and wing area 449.5 sq. ft.

SM.92

Retaining the same engines, wing, and tail surfaces of the SM.91, the SM.92 was a refined

The SM.92, developed from the SM.91, placed the crew in the port boom, omitting the central nacelle.

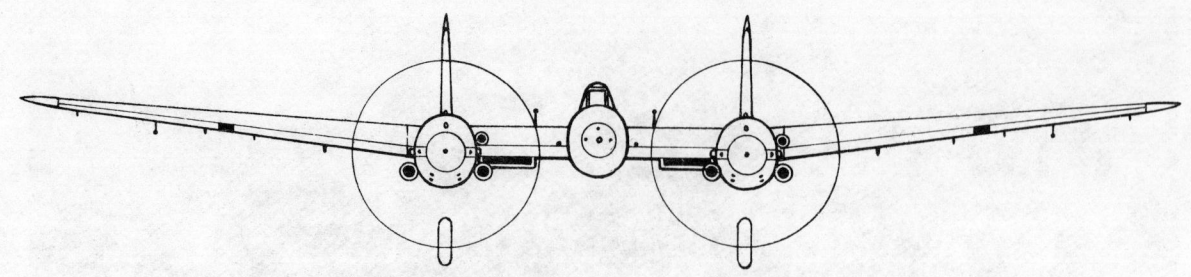
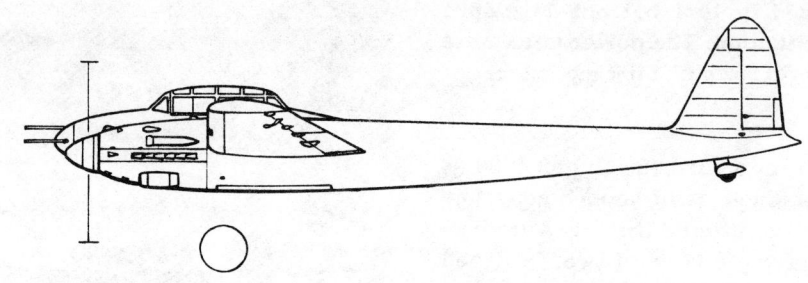
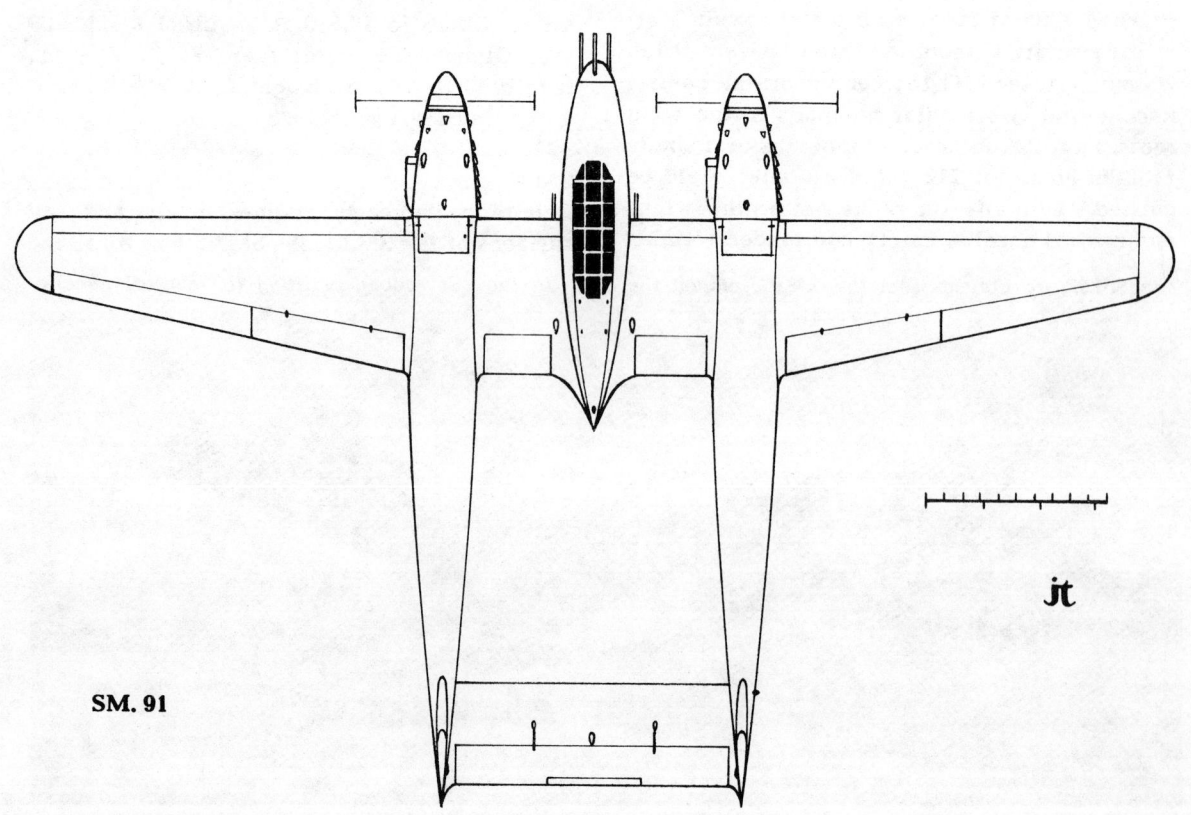

SM. 91

SAVOIA-MARCHETTI

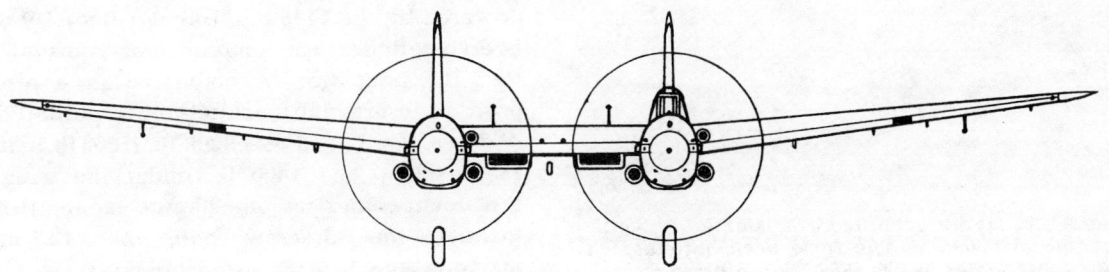

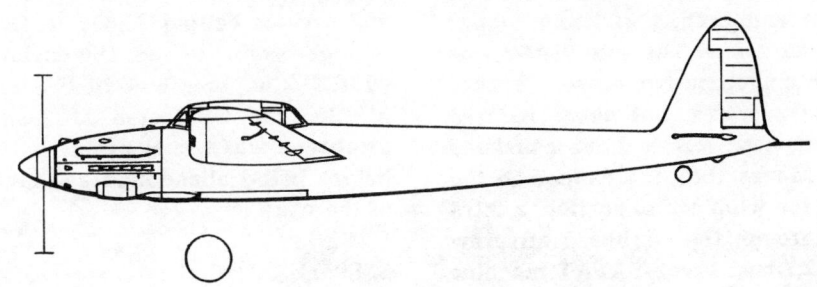

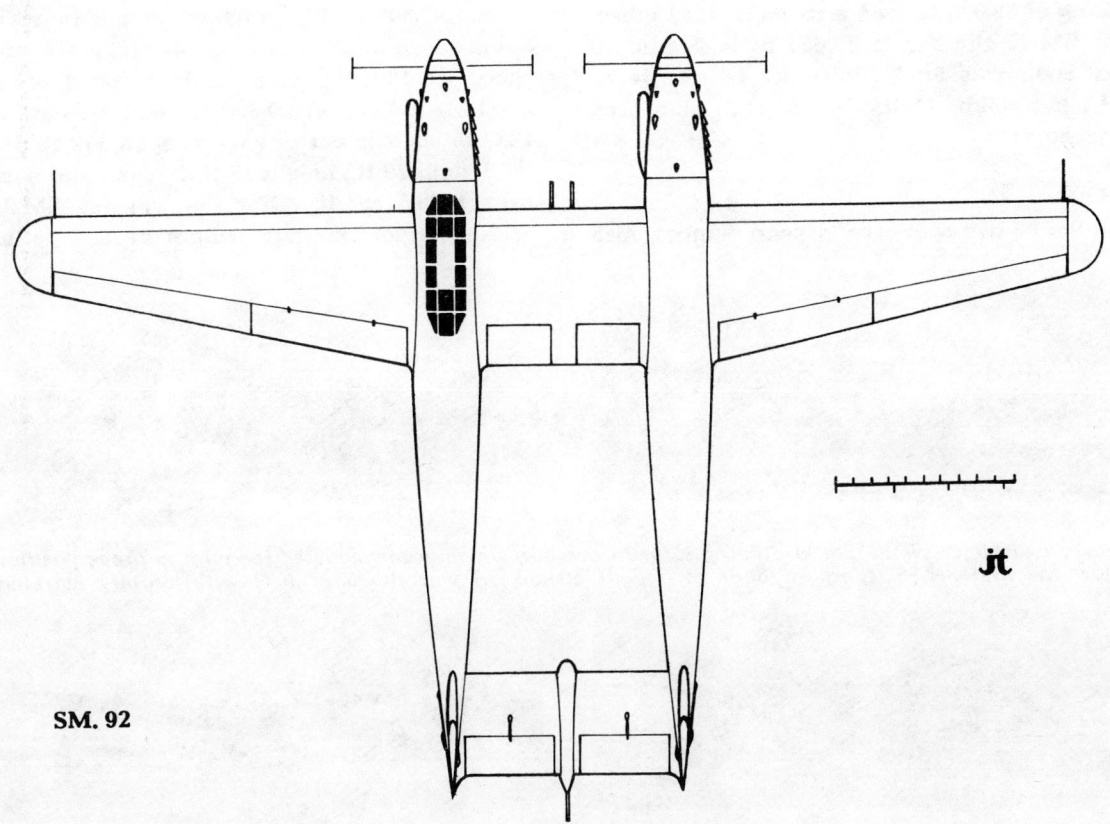

SM. 92

The SM.92 layout permitted a substantial reduction in drag and weight. The same basic formula was used later by the P-82 Twin Mustang.

version omitting the central nacelle and placing the crew in the port boom, balanced by fuel tanks in the starboard boom. The omission of the nacelle saved considerable airframe weight and drag, permitting higher speeds and longer range. The sole SM.92 was flown for the first time on November 12, 1943 under Luftwaffe auspices, but never entered production. Armament was to have consisted of two 20-mm. Mauser MG 151 cannon in the leading edge of the wing center section, a third cannon firing through the starboard airscrew hub, and five 12.7-mm. Breda-SAFAT machine guns, two beneath each engine and one rear-firing remote-controlled gun in a barbette under the tailplane. Empty and loaded weights were 13,779 lb. and 19,290 lb. Performance included maximum and cruising speeds of 382 m.p.h. (29,935 ft.) and 335 m.p.h., a service ceiling of 39,370 ft., and a range of 1242 miles. The SM.92 climbed to 19,680 ft. in 7 min. 10 sec. Span was 60 ft. $10^{1}/_{3}$ in., length 44 ft. $11^{1}/_{3}$ in., height 13 ft. $7^{1}/_{3}$ in., and wing area 414.6 sq. ft.

SM.93

The SM.93 two-seat dive/torpedo bomber, also powered by the 1475 h.p. Daimler-Benz DB 605 twelve-cylinder vee engine, was unusual in that the pilot was accomodated in a prone position to prevent blacking-out in pulling out of dives. Bomb load was 3200 lb. (1800 lb. below the fuselage and 1400 lb. under the wings); armament comprised one 20-mm. cannon firing through the airscrew hub, one 12.7-mm. machine gun in each wing, and a third 12.7-mm. gun fired by the observer. Loaded weight was 12,125 lb. Performance included a maximum speed of 360 m.p.h. at 22,960 ft., a cruising speed of 314 m.p.h., and a maximum diving speed of 590 m.p.h. Range was 994 miles and service ceiling 32,800 ft. Climb to 13,120 ft. took 5 min. 10 sec. Dimensions were: span 45 ft. $7^{1}/_{4}$ in., length 36 ft. $1^{3}/_{4}$ in., height 12 ft. $5^{1}/_{2}$ in., and wing area 334.7 sq. ft. The sole prototype was tested by the Luftwaffe in 1943 before being abandoned at that critical stage of the war.

SM.95

A four-engined eighteen-passenger transatlantic airliner designed in 1942 and built by S.A.I. Ambrosini during the war (three examples), the SM.95 was powered initially by 850/930 h.p. Alfa Romeo 128 R.C.18 nine-cylinder radial engines. Empty and loaded weights were 29,700 lb. and 47,300 lb. Performance included a maximum speed of 224 m.p.h. at 9840 ft., a cruising speed of 196 m.p.h., a landing speed of 81 m.p.h., a ceiling of 20,830 ft., and a range of 1242 miles. Dimensions were: span 112 ft. $5^{1}/_{4}$ in., length 73 ft., height 17 ft. $2^{2}/_{3}$ in., and wing area 1380.5 sq. ft. After the war the SM.95, with a larger fuselage (length 81 ft. $2^{7}/_{8}$ in.)

Above, two views of the SM.93 dive or torpedo bomber, which accommodated the pilot in prone position. Below the first SM.95 transport. Built as a civil airliner, it was flown in 1942 with military markings.

SAVOIA-MARCHETTI

and accomodations for 30-50-passengers, was built in limited numbers for short-range continental routes. This version could be powered by 1000 h.p. Bristol Pegasus 48 nine-cylinder radials. The Italian Air Ministry purchased two Alfa-powered SM.95's, while Alitalia received five machines with both engine types.

An SM.95 used by the postwar Italian Air Ministry.

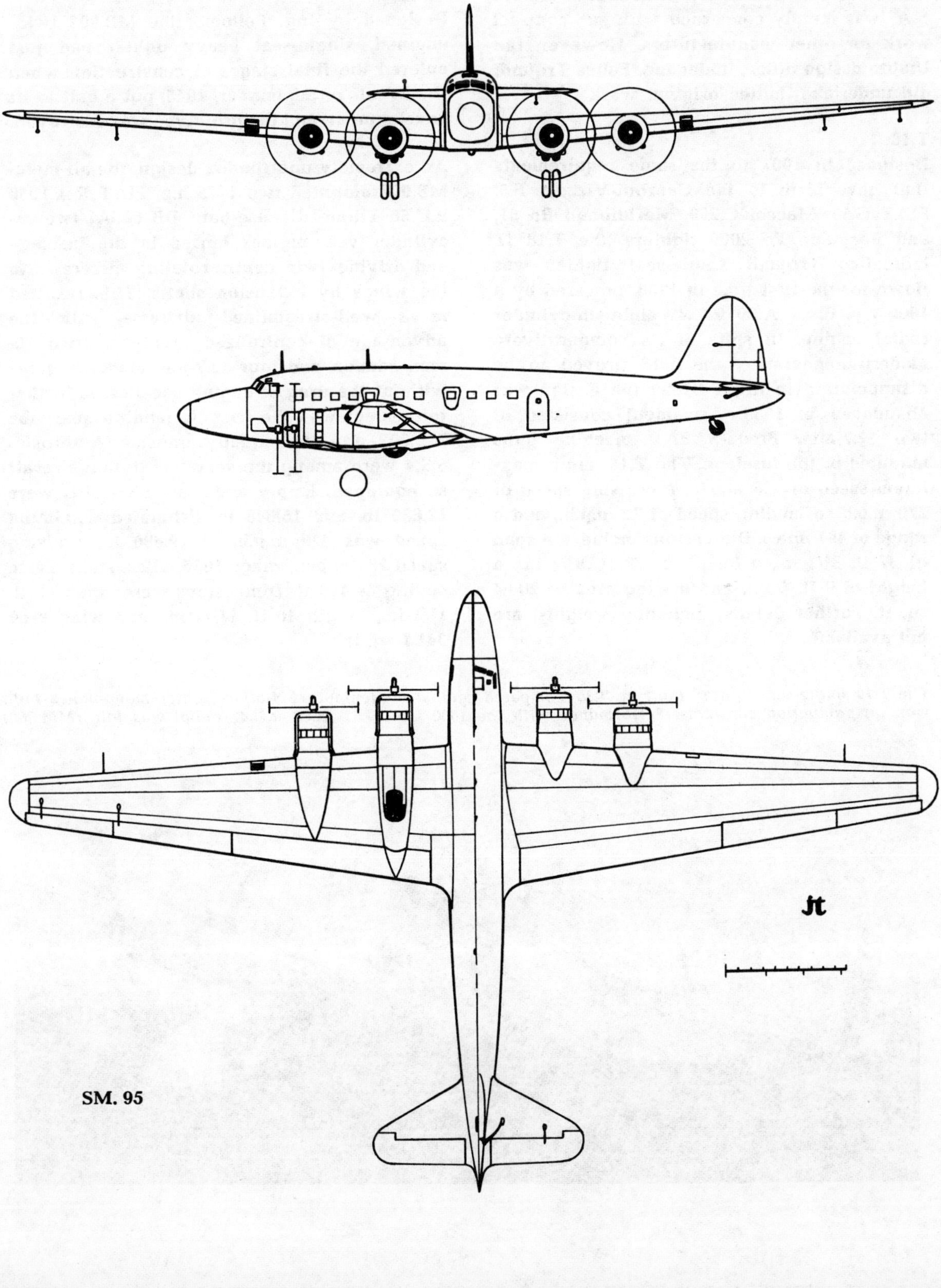

SM. 95

UMBRA
Aeronautica Umbra S.A. Costruzioni Aeronautiche e Meccaniche

Formed in 1935 at Foligno, Aeronautica Umbra S.A. was mainly concerned with sub-contract work for other manufacturers. However, the Umbra design office, under Ing. Felice Trojani, did undertake limited original work.

T.18

Designed in 1937 to the same requirements that gave birth to the Caproni-Vizzola F.5, FIAT G.50, Macchi C.200, Meridionali Ro 51, and Reggiane Re 2000 fighters, the T.18 (T indicating Trojani) single-seat fighter was flown for the first time in 1938, powered by a 1000 h.p. FIAT A.80 R.C.41 eighteen-cylinder radial engine. In spite of its comparatively modern appearance, the T.18 proved to be disappointing in flight trials; the design was abandoned in 1939. Armament consisted of two 12.7-mm. Breda-SAFAT machine guns mounted in the fuselage. The T.18 had a maximum speed of 335 m.p.h., a cruising speed of 278 m.p.h., a landing speed of 72 m.p.h., and a range of 497 miles. Dimensions included a span of 37 ft. 8³/₄ in., a length of 28 ft. 8³/₄ in., a height of 9 ft. 5 in., and a wing area of 204.4 sq. ft. Further details, including weights, are not available.

MB.902

Designed by Ing. Bellomo, the MB.902 twin-engined, single-seat heavy fighter had just entered the final stages of construction when the events of September, 1943, put a halt to its development, and the prototype was destroyed.

An extremely unorthodox design, the all-metal MB.902 mounted two 1475 h.p. FIAT R.A.1050 R.C.58 Tifone (license-built DB 605A) twelve-cylinder vee engines buried in the fuselage and driving twin contra-rotating airscrews in the wings by extension shafts. This resulted in a well-streamlined airframe with the advantage of centralized firepower (two 20-mm. cannon and four 12.7-mm machine guns) without the drag of engine nacelles. A further refinement was the tricycle landing gear; the MB.902 and the equally unusual Ambrosini S.S.4 were among the very few Italian aircraft so equipped. Empty and loaded weights were 12,650 lb. and 15,840 lb. Estimated maximum speed was 429 m.p.h. at 19,680 ft., cruising speed 261 m.p.h., range 1056 miles, and service ceiling 34,440 ft. Dimensions were: span 47 ft. 1¹/₄ in., length 46 ft. 11³/₄ in., and wing area 341.1 sq. ft.

The T.18 single-seat fighter, built in 1938, competed against contemporary Italian fighter monoplanes but won no production contracts. Performance with the 1000 h.p. FIAT A.80 R.C.41 radial was fair. (MM 363)

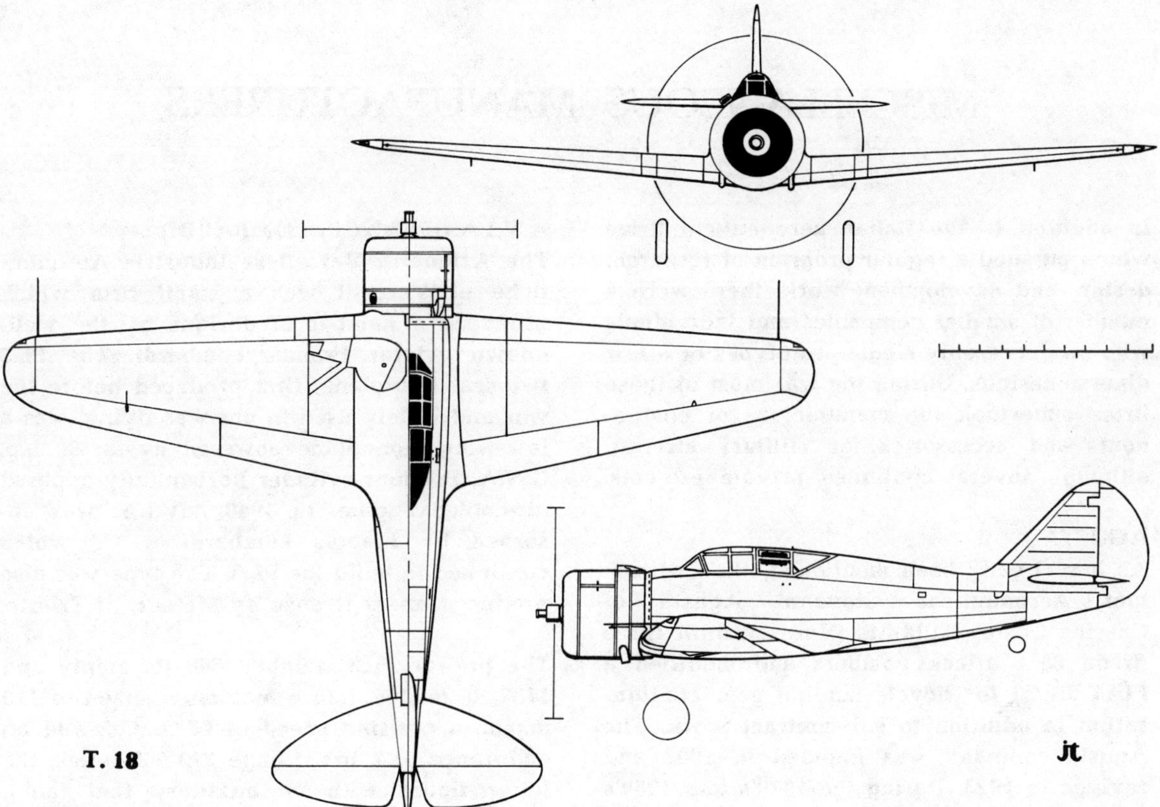

UMBRA

T. 18

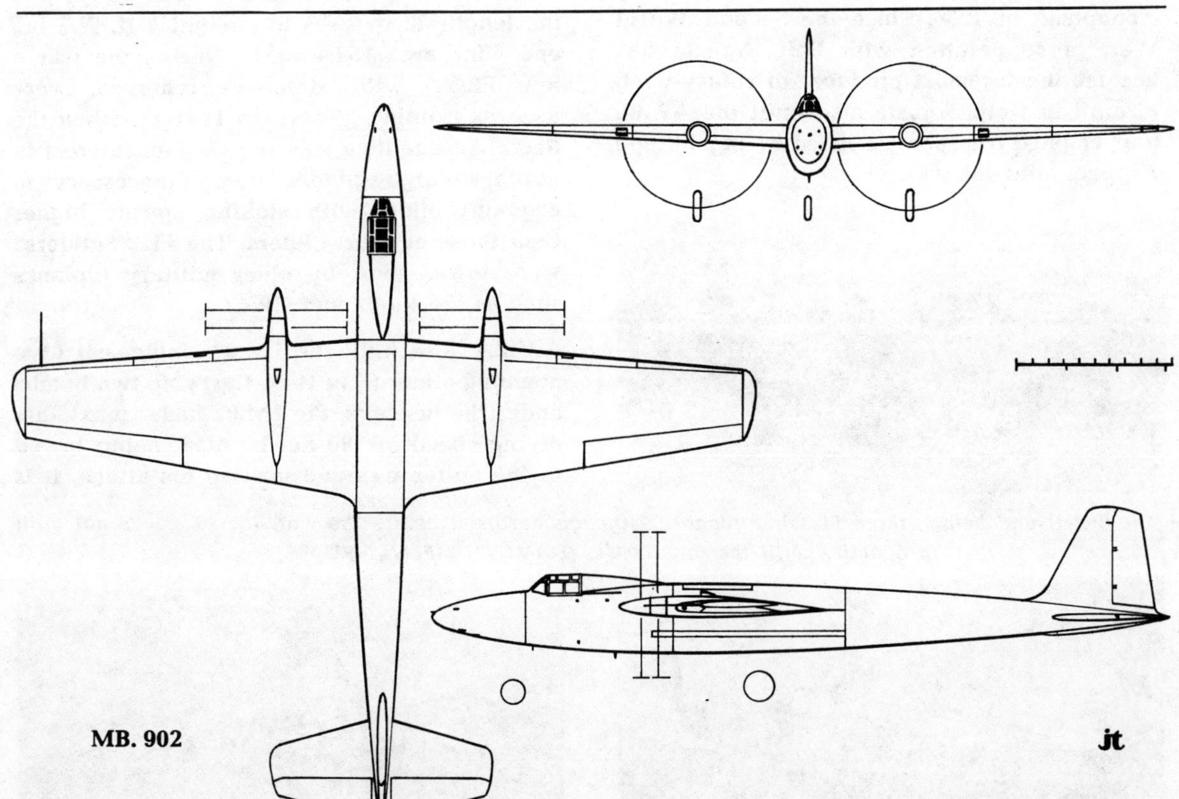

MB. 902

MISCELLANEOUS MANUFACTURERS

In addition to the Italian aeronautical firms which pursued a regular program of research, design, and development work, there were a number of smaller companies and individuals who produced only single prototypes or a few diverse designs. During the war most of these firms undertook the manufacture of components and accessories for military aircraft, although several continued private projects.

AGUSTA

As has already been mentioned, the Costruzioni Aeronautiche Giovanni Agusta of Cascina Costa, Gallarate (Varese), built three Breda 88M attack bombers and modified a FIAT BR.20 to tricycle landing gear configuration in addition to sub-contract work. The Agusta company was founded in 1908 and revived in 1923. During the 1920's and 1930's Agusta concentrated on sailplanes and light aircraft, producing the Agusta 6 touring monoplane in 1936. Since the Second World War, in cooperation with Bell, Agusta has become the foremost producer of rotary-wing aircraft in Italy. Agusta also built the AZ 8L four-engined transport designed by Ing. Filippo Zappata after the war.

A.V.I.A.-(FRANCIS LOMBARDI)

The Azionaria Vercellese Industrie Aeronautiche of Vercelli was a small firm which produced a number of designs by the well-known aviator Francis Lombardi. The FL.3 two-seat lightplane, first produced before the war and widely used in postwar flying, was a low-wing monoplane powered by an 80 h.p. C.N.A. D.4 four-cylinder horizontally-opposed air-cooled engine. In 1948 A.V.I.A. was absorbed by Francis Lombardi & C., which continued to build the FL.3. The type was also produced under license by Meteor, of Trieste.

The prewar FL.3 weighed 660 lb. empty and 1133 lb. loaded, had a maximum speed of 110 m.p.h., a cruising speed of 93 m.p.h., and an endurance of 4 hrs. (range 373-509 miles, the latter figure with an auxiliary fuel tank). Ceiling was 16,400 ft. and initial rate of climb 10 ft./sec. Dimensions were: span 32 ft. $3^{3}/_{4}$ in., length 20 ft. $10^{3}/_{4}$ in., height 5 ft. $7^{1}/_{3}$ in., and wing area 154.4 sq. ft. During the war a few FL.3's, with airscrews removed, were used as training gliders. In 1941-42, when the Regia Aeronautica was showing an interest in military cargo gliders, it was necessary to acquaint pilots with sinking speeds higher than those of sport gliders. The FL.3 "gliders" were towed aloft by older military biplanes such as the Ro 37 and CR.42.

A.V.I.A. also built the LM.02 single-seat dive bombing glider (!) in 1942. Carrying two bombs under the fuselage, the LM.02 had a maximum diving speed of 280 m.p.h. After being towed to the battle area and making his attack, it is

Above left and below, three FL.3 lightplanes. Although designed before the war, the FL.3 was not built in quantity until the late 1940's. (I-AVIG, I-MFLN, I-NUMA)

presumed that the pilot would attempt to glide back to his own lines. Of all-wood construction, the LM.02 had Junkers-type dive brakes and jettisonable landing gear. Empty and loaded weights were 2467 lb. and 6283 lb. Span was 52 ft. 6 in. and length 35 ft. 3$^{1}/_{4}$ in.

BELTRAME

In 1937 Ing. Quinto Beltrame built a novel single-seat ultra-light canard called the Colibri (Hummingbird). It was powered by an 18 h.p. Beltrame one-cylinder two-stroke air-cooled engine. Described as "La Motocicletta dell'-Aria" (the Motorcycle of the Air), the all-wood fabric-covered Colibri was claimed to be the smallest, lightest, and most economical aeroplane in the world. The variable-incidence forward aerofoil served as elevator, ailerons, and rudder. Empty and loaded weights were only 154 lb. and 352 lb. Span was 19 ft. 10$^{7}/_{8}$ in., length 10 ft. 11$^{7}/_{8}$ in., height 3 ft. 3 in., and wing area 48.4 sq. ft. Performance included maximum, cruising, and landing speeds of 99 m.p.h., 87 m.p.h., and 37 m.p.h. respectively, and a range of 310 miles. Take-off and landing runs were 405 ft. and 165 ft. respectively.

BONOMI (LOMBARDA)

Established in 1931, the Aeronautica Vittorio Bonomi of Milan built several two-seat cabin monoplanes before turning to sailplanes and gliders. Among the better-known of the latter were the gullwing BS.2 (span 59 ft. 0$^{1}/_{2}$ in., empty weight 301 lb., sinking speed 2.03 ft./sec.), the simple parasol BS.7 (span 36 ft. 6 in., empty weight 198 lb.), the BS.8 (span 43 ft. 11$^{3}/_{8}$ in., empty weight 220 lb., sinking speed 2.46 ft./sec.), the BS.24 Roma, and the BS.28 Alcione (Kingfisher). The Alcione had a span of 47 ft. 6$^{3}/_{4}$ in., a length of 21 ft. 7$^{3}/_{4}$ in., a height of 3 ft. 8$^{7}/_{8}$ in., and a 187 lb. useful load.

The most interesting Bonomi product, however, was the pedal-driven Bossi-Bonomi sailplane. Basically a normal sailplane with two chain-driven tractor airscrews in the leading edges of the wings, the Pedaliante B.B. had a span of 55 ft. 9$^{1}/_{8}$ in. and carried 172 lb. It flew a distance of approximately 1000 yards, but did not achieve true man-powered flight, having been catapult-launched.

The Bonomi firm was taken over by Aeronautica Lombarda S.A. in 1937. Lombarda designed the AL 12P cargo and troop glider built by S.A.I. Ambrosini.

The postwar Alaparma AM.75 was a development of the series begun in 1942 by Mantelli. (I-DONI)

MANTELLI

Ing. Adriano Mantelli, a fighter ace in the Spanish Civil War and a Colonel in the Regia Aeronautica during the Second World War, designed a series of light twin-boom pusher monoplanes, commencing with the AM.6 (the designation indicating the wing area in square meters) in 1942. Powered by a 17 h.p. Aubier & Dunne two-cylinder in-line motorcycle engine mounted low in the central nacelle behind the pilot and driving the airscrew by a chain, the AM.6 was of wood construction with mixed plywood and fabric covering. Landing gear consisted of a small main wheel below the center of gravity and a skid on the nose, with small stabilizing wheels at the wingtips. A single fin-and-rudder was mounted in the center of the tailplane. Loaded weight was 440 lb. Maximum, cruising, and landing speeds were respectively 93 m.p.h., 81 m.p.h., and 31 m.p.h., the latter with flaps. Range was 404 miles and initial rate of climb 11.5 ft./sec. Dimensions were: span 20 ft. 7$^{1}/_{4}$ in., length 13 ft. 5$^{3}/_{8}$ in., and wing area 64.5 sq. ft. After the war Mantelli built further models, the AM.65, 75, 8, 9, 10, 11, and 12, with correspondingly greater wing areas. Several were produced in series by Alaparma.

NUVOLI

Under the direction of Ing. Prospero Nuvoli, the Laboratorio Artigiano Aeronautico designed the series of "N" light aircraft. The first was the N.3 low-wing two-seat sportplane designed in 1931 and built by FIAT in 1932. Weighing 616 lb. empty and 946 lb. loaded, it was powered by a 40 h.p. Salmson nine-cylinder radial engine and had a wing area of 192.9 sq. ft. Performance was: maximum speed 102 m.p.h., cruising speed 90 m.p.h., landing speed 43 m.p.h., and ceiling 18,040 ft. With a 90 h.p. engine and designated N.3/S, it weighed 803 lb. empty and achieved a maximum speed of 121 m.p.h., a cruising speed of

Left, the Nuvoli N.3 sport plane, built in 1932. Right, the O.S.A.135 two seat cabin monoplane. (I-FERT)

109 m.p.h., a landing speed of 36 m.p.h., and a ceiling of 24,600 ft.

In 1932 the N.5R, with a 75 h.p. Pobjoy R seven-cylinder radial engine, was designed. At Montecelio on December 2, 1933, piloted by Giovanni Zappetta and Francesco Ragusa, it set an altitude record of 22,799 ft. for light aircraft of Category III. Empty and loaded weights were 594 lb. and 1144 lb., and wing area was 134.5 sq. ft. The N.5R had a maximum speed of 127 m.p.h. and a landing speed of 65 m.p.h. The normal touring model of the N.5 also appeared in 1933. Powered by the same engine, it weighed 616 lb. empty and 1166 lb. loaded, and had a greater wing area of 166.8 sq. ft. Performance included a maximum speed of 124 m.p.h., a landing speed of 65 m.p.h., and a ceiling of 19,680 ft.

A further record model with a great reduction in wing area was designed in 1934 to gain the speed record for Category III. Designated N.5RR, it achieved 138 m.p.h. over a 62-mile close course at Littoria on February 17, 1935. Pilots were Sebastiano Bebendo and Rinaldo Stenico. Empty and loaded weights of the N.5RR were 594 lb. and 1144 lb., wing area 96.8 sq. ft., landing speed 71 m.p.h., and ceiling 19,680 ft.

The N.5Cab, designed in 1935, was a higher-powered two-seat Gran Turismo cabin model. The engine was a 180 h.p. FIAT A.70 seven-cylinder radial. The N.5Cab weighed 1012 lb. empty, 1672 lb. loaded, and had a wing area of 156 sq. ft. Performance was: maximum speed 140 m.p.h., landing speed 65 m.p.h., and ceiling 22,960 ft. Similar was the N.5AQ (Alta Quota, or high altitude) monoplane designed in 1936 as a trainer for high-altitude flight on relatively low power outputs. Wing area was increased marginally to 157.1 sq. ft., while loaded weight was slightly less at 1496 lb. Maximum speed was 137 m.p.h., landing speed 59 m.p.h., and ceiling 29,520 ft. Both the N.5Cab and the N.5AQ featured two-bladed wooden airscrews, Magni engine cowlings, and fixed landing gear with wheel spats.

O.S.A.

Officine Sommese Aeronautica of Somme Lombardo, Varese, built a two-seat cabin monoplane in 1937 for the Littorio Rally. Designated the O.S.A.135, it was powered by a 130 h.p. Alfa Romeo 110-I four-cylinder inverted air-cooled engine. Construction was all-wood, featuring split flaps and slotted ailerons. Loaded weight was 2420 lb. The O.S.A.135 had a maximum speed of 143 m.p.h., a cruising speed of 124 m.p.h., a landing speed of 48 m.p.h., a range of 621 miles, and a ceiling of 17,712 ft. It climbed to 3280 ft. in 5 min. 22 sec. Dimensions were: span 37 ft. 5½ in., length 24 ft. 8¾ in., height 7 ft. 4½ in., and wing area 196.9 sq. ft. The O.S.A.200 was a projected higher-powered version with a 185 h.p. Alfa Romeo 115 six-cylinder engine.

S.C.A.

The Stabilimento Costruzioni Aeronautiche was a small firm at Guidonia. In addition to other projects it built the Stefanutti-designed SS.2 single-seat and SS.3 two-seat tail-first lightplanes, the forerunners of the SS.4 fighter, discussed under Ambrosini.

The SS.2 single-seat and SS.3 two-seat tail-first lightplanes were forerunners of the SS.4 canard fighter.

APPENDICES

I—Notes on Conversion Factors

Most of the data drawn upon for this book were gathered directly from Italian sources, and converted from their original metric form. Weights and dimensions have been converted to the nearest pound or fraction of an inch; wing areas have been carried to one decimal place. Performance details, however, have not been so finely denoted. The reader will appreciate that the original figures in most cases were not precise and absolute, but rather round figures indicating the aeroplane's basic capabilities. Individual examples of a particular type differed considerably from one another in performance, which depended on equipment, trim, true engine output, age, and condition. It would be illogical, for example, to convert a service ceiling given as a round figure of 5500 meters to 18,044.565 ft., or even to 18,045 ft. The figure 18,040 ft. expresses the service ceiling with approximately the same degree of accuracy of the original metric figure. Likewise, distances and speeds given in kilometers (km) and kilometers per hour (km/h) have been converted only to the nearest mile or m.p.h. For example, a speed of 225 km/h has been expressed as 140 m.p.h. rather than 139.725 m.p.h. In cases of international records, however, when precise measurement was made, the official metric figures have been converted as exactly as possible.

The following conversion factors have been used:
1 meter (m) = 3.28 ft. or 39.37 in.
1 square meter (m²) = 10.76 sq. ft.
1 kilometer (km) = 0.621 mile (1 km/h = 0.621 m.p.h.)
1 kilogram (kg) = 2.2 lb.
1 liter (L) = 0.265 (U.S.) gal.

The 7.7-mm and 12.7-mm machine guns referred to throughout this book correspond to 0.303-in. and 0.5-in. weapons, respectively.

II—Aircraft Designations

Unlike other major air forces, the Regia Aeronautica did not adopt a standardized designation system for military aircraft, relying instead on the original manufacturers' nomenclature. In the late 1930's, however, some attempt was made to avoid the duplication of numbers, as in the German system. Up to that time there had been frequent duplication (e.g. Macchi C.72 and Savoia-Marchetti SM.72; Breda 32 and FIAT CR.32), but little confusion is likely to have existed. As with other manufacturers throughout the world, Italian builders used a variety of individual designation systems; their meanings are explained, where known, in the descriptions of the particular aircraft. The letters usually indicated the manufacturer (e.g. S.A.I. 7, for the Società Aeronautica Italiana), the designer (Z.506, for Ing. Zappata), or purpose (BR.20, for Bombardamento Rosatelli, indicating a bomber designed by Ing. Rosatelli).

Suffix letters often stood for the purpose or modification involved (e.g. C.6B for Biposto, or two-seat; Ca 311M for Modificato, or modified; Re 2001 CN for Caccia Notturna, or night fighter), although they sometimes merely indicated a series (A,B,C, etc.) as in German and American practice. The most common series suffixes, however, were bis, ter, and quater, denoting the second, third, and fourth variants of a design. The letter S was frequently used to indicate a sporting version of a civil machine. The word idro, of course, designated a seaplane conversion.

III—Aircraft Engines

As an aid to the reader, all of the engines powering the aircraft described in this book are presented below in tabular form, giving the designation, number of cylinders, type, cooling system, and power range.

In Italian engine designations, the letter R (Riduttori) indicated reduction gearing, and the letter C (Compressore) indicated supercharging.

Key: I = in-line O = opposed R = radial V = vee-type W = W-type X = X-type inv. = inverted
A = air-cooled L = liquid-cooled

ALFA ROMEO				
110-I, -II	4	I inv.	A	110/130
111	4	I inv.	A	155
115-I	6	I inv.	A	150/200
125 R.C. 35	9	R	A	750
126 R.C. 10, R.C. 34	9	R	A	650/800
127 R.C. 55	9	R	A	750
128 R.C. 18, R.C. 21	9	R	A	850/950
135 R.C. 32 Tornado	18	R	A	1350/1400
D. 2, D. 2 C. 30	9	R	A	240
Dux	9	R	A	270
Jupiter	9	R	A	500
Lynx	7	R	A	220/220
Mercury	9	R	A	420
Mercury (Mercurius) IV	9	R	A	550
Pegasus, -II	9	R	A	530/700
R.A. 1000 R.C. 41, -la, R.C. 44-la Monsonie	12	V inv.	L	1175
BELTRAME				
(motorcycle)	1	—	A	18
C.A.N.S.A. (FIAT)				
C. 80			A	80/90
C.N.A.				
C. II bis	2	O	A	38
D-4	4	O	A	60/80
C. VI, -IRC. 43	6	I inv.	A	150/160
C-7	9	R	A	170/180
COLOMBO (ALFA ROMEO)				
S. 53	4	I	A	95
S. 63	6	I	A	115/155
FARINA				
T. 58	5	R	A	130
FIAT				
A. 20, -A.Q.	12	V	L	400/440
A. 22R, -T	12	V	L	550/610
A. 24R	12	V	L	700/750
A. 25	12	V	L	1050
A. 30 R.A.	12	V	L	600
A. 33 R.C. 35	12	V	L	700

A. 50, -S	7	R	A	85/100
A. 53	7	R	A	100
A. 54	7	R	A	135/140
A. 59 R, R.C.	9	R	A	700
A. 60	4	I inv.	A	135
A. 70 S	7	R	A	180/205
A. 74 R.C. 38, R.C. 42	14	R	A	770/870
A. 76 R.C. 40	14	R	A	1000
A. 80 R.C. 41	18	R	A	1000/1050
A. 82 R.C. 42 S	18	R	A	1250
A. 83 R.C. 24/52	18	R	A	1250
AN. 1 (naphtha)	6	I		220
AS. 2	12	V	L	850
AS. 3	12	V	L	1030
AS. 5	12	V	L	1000
AS. 6	24	V	L	2800/3100
AS. 8	16	V	L	2250
R.A. 1000	12	V inv.	L	1250
R.A. 1050 R.C.58 Tifone	12	V inv.	L	1475

ISOTTA-FRASCHINI

Asso	12	V	L	250
Asso	12	V	L	500
Asso Caccia	12	V	L	440/480
Asso IX R.C. 45	12	V	L	815
Asso L. 121 R.C. 40	12	V	L	900/960
Asso XI R, R.C., R.C. 15, R.C. 40, R2C. 15	12	V	L	730/960
Asso 750 R. R.C., R.C. 35	18	W	L	750/955
Asso 1000	18	W	L	900/1000
Asso (racing)	18	W	L	1400
Asso L. 180 IRCC. 45	18	R	A	1430
Beta R.C. 10	12	V inv.	A	280
Gamma R.C. 35 IS	12	V inv.	A	540
Delta R.C. 21/60, R.C. 35, R.C. 40	12	V inv.	A	700/770
Delta IV	12	V inv.	A	840/850
Zeta R.C. 25/60, R.C. 35, R.C. 42	24	X	L	1150/1250
K. 14	14	R	A	800/900
80 T	6	I		

PIAGGIO

P. VII C.16, C.35, C.45	7	R	A	370/460
P. VII R.C., R.C.35	7	R	A	460/500
P. IX R, R.C., R.C.40	9	R	A	560/700
P. X R, R.C.	9	R	A	610/700
P. XI R.C.40, -bis R.C.40, R.C.100	14	R	A	700/1025
P. XII R.C.35, R.C.100/2v	18	R	A	1000/1500
P. XV R.C.60/2v	18	R	A	1450/1650
P. XVI R.C.35	9	R	A	650/700
P. XIX R.C.45 Turbine	14	R	A	1100/1175
P. XXII	18	R	A	1700
Jupiter VI, VII	9	R	A	450/575

ARGUS (German)

As. 8	4	I	A	95

AUBIER & DUNNE (French)

	2	I	A	17

BLACKBURN (English)

Cirrus II, -III	4	I	A	75/85
Cirrus Minor	4	I	A	82/90
Cirrus Major III	4	I	A	138/150

BRAMO (German)

Sh 14 A 4	7	R	A	150/160

BRISTOL (English)

Mercury IV	9	R	A	550
Pegasus 48	9	R	A	730/1000
Hercules 632	14	R	A	1690

DAIMLER-BENZ (German)

DB 601, -A, -A-1	12	V inv.	L	1050/1250
DB 605, -A-1	12	V inv.	L	1250/1475
DB 603, -A	12	V inv.	L	1510/1550

DE HAVILLAND (English)

Gipsy-Minor I, II, III	4	I	A	85/120
Gipsy-Major I	4	I	A	120/130
Gipsy-Six	6	I	A	185/200

GNÔME-RHÔNE (French)

9 Kf 2	9	R	A	600
14 Kfs, Kfrs Mistral Major	14	R	A	900/1025

HIRTH (German)

HM. 508D	8	I inv.	A	280

HISPANO-SUIZA (French)

12 Ycrs	12	V	L	860/900
12 Y-21	12	V	L	910

JUNKERS (German)

Jumo 211 Da	12	V inv.	L	1050/1220

LORRAINE (French)

5 Pc	5	R	A	130
—	12	V	L	400

POBJOY (English)

R	7	R	A	75

PRATT & WHITNEY (U.S.)

Wasp-Junior	9	R	A	320
Twin-Wasp SC3G, S1C3G	14	R	A	1050/1200
Double-Wasp R-2800	18	R	A	2100

WALTER (Czechoslovakian)

Castor	7	R	A	240
Major-Six	6	I inv.	A	185/200
Sagitta I-MR	12	V inv.	A	500/600
Venus		R	A	85

WRIGHT (U.S.)

Cyclone SGR-1820	9	R	A	750
Cyclone R-1820	14	R	A	1350
Cyclone R-2600	14	R	A	1900

Key: I = in-line O = opposed R = radial V = vee-type W = W-type X = X-type inv. = inverted A = air-cooled L = liquid-cooled

APPENDICES

IV—Civil Registrations

In the early 1920's a civil registration system, using the letter I (Italia) followed by a dash and four individual identifying letters, was instituted. Originally the first letter after the dash indicated the district in which the aeroplane was registered, as follows:

- I-A = Torino (Turin)
- B = Milano (Milan)
- C = Bologna
- D = Pisa
- E = Roma (Rome)
- F = Napoli (Naples)
- G = Brindisi
- H = Catania
- I-I = Cagliari
- L = Venezia (Venice)
- M = Ancona
- N = Udine
- O = Trieste
- P = Genova (Genoa)
- V = Verona

However, all registrations did not strictly adhere to this system, particularly when it became popular (and very good propaganda) to use letters spelling out names or parts of names associated with Italy or Italian cities, districts, manufacturers, and personalities. Registrations such as I-TALY, I-ROMA, I-CANT, I-FIAT, and I-SIAI are obvious, while combinations like I-BALB (for Air Marshall Italo Balbo), I-BRUN (for Bruno Mussolini), and I-ZAPP (for Cant engineer Filippo Zappata) honored pilots and designers. In fact, the registrations of all twenty-four SM.55X flying boats which crossed the Atlantic in the mass flight of 1933 indicated the commanders of the respective machines. The company registrations such as I-FIAT were used over and over again on prototypes.

Readers with a knowledge of Italian will find other interesting associations in many of the registrations, including a few English coincidences. After the Second World War some English words were intentionally formed in certain registrations, such as I-GULL (Piaggio P.136L) and I-HAWK (Pasotti F.9 Sparviero, or Hawk). Again, the manufacturers were indicated in such postwar designations as I-BREZ (Breda-Zappata BZ.308), I-MACH (Macchi MB.320), and I-PIAG (Piaggio P.136L).

The following list is merely representative, and includes only aircraft built or registered in Italy during the years 1930—45. However, it does provide a good indication of the major civil types in regular use during the period.

Registration	Aircraft
I-AAAP	Breda 15
AAAQ	Breda 15
AAAR	Breda 15
AAAS	Breda 15
AABF	Savoia-Marchetti SM.55P
AABU	Macchi M.18
AACJ	Cant 10
AACK	Cant 22 R1
AACN	Cant 21
AADE	Breda 15
AALF	Caproni Ca 97
AANQ	Bonomi monoplane
AANR	FIAT AS 1 sci
AANT	Macchi M.70
AAPO	Cant 26
AAQD	Savoia-Marchetti SM.56
AAQI	Macchi M.73
AAQR	Caproni Ca 101
AARB	Macchi M.18
AASW	Caproni Ca 102
AAUI	Breda 15S
AAUJ	Breda 15S
AAVA	FIAT AS.1
AAVE	FIAT AS.1
AAVJ	Breda 15S
AAVN	Bonomi 2S
AAVQ	FIAT AS.2
AAVR	FIAT AS.2
AAVS	FIAT AS.2
AAVT	FIAT TR.1
AAVU	FIAT TR.1
AAVV	FIAT TR.1
AAWQ	Breda 15
AAWU	Breda 25
AAXY	Meridionali Ro 10
AAYP	Savoia-Marchetti SM.71
AAYU	Cant 26
AAZA	Caproni Ca 101
ABBR	Savoia-Marchetti SM.55
ABCB	Caproni Ca 101
ABCE	Caproni Ca 105
ABCM	Caproni Ca 100
ABEK	Caproni Ca 97
ABFG	Breda 25 idro
ABFQ	Breda 28
ABFT	Breda 79S
ABFU	Breda 79S
ABFZ	Breda 79S
ABIL	Meridionali Ro 26
ABIV	Savoia-Marchetti SM.71
ABJR	A.V.I.A. FL.3
I- ABLB	Cant Z.1010
ABMA	Caproni Ca 101
ABMO	Savoia-Marchetti SM.71
ABMT	Caproni Ca 100
ABNO	Caproni Ca 310
ABOR	Savoia-Marchetti SM.55
ABOV	S.A.I.M.A.N. 204
ABPJ	S.A.I.M.A.N. 202
ABRA	Savoia Marchetti SM.66
ACCA	Caproni Ca 113
ACIE	Breda 39
ACLA	FIAT CR.41
ADDA	S.A.I. 2S
ADUA	Meridionali Ro 10
AECI	Caproni Ca 148
AFUA	Nardi FN.305
AGIL	Cant Z.501
AGSB	Savoia-Marchetti SM.79
AICA	Nardi FN.305
ALAL	Cant Z.506
ALCE	Savoia-Marchetti SM.83
ALPE	Savoia-Marchetti SM.74
ALPI	Savoia Marchetti SM.71
ALTE	Savoia-Marchetti SM.66
AMBH	S.A.I. 7
AMBI	S.A.I. 7
AMBY	S.A.I. 3
AMER	Savoia-Marchetti SM.83
AMIR	S.A.I. 2
ARAM	Savoia-Marchetti SM.55
AREM	Savoia-Marchetti SM.83
ARNO	Ansaldo A.300/T; Macchi C.94
ASTI	Savoia-Marchetti SM.73
ATAE	S.A.I.M.A.N. 202
ATAG	S.A.I.M.A.N. 202
ATLA	Cant Z.509/4
AVIC	A.V.I.A. FL.3
AVIE	A.V.I.A. FL.3
AVIG	A.V.I.A. FL.3
AVIH	A.V.I.A. FL.3
AVIM	A.V.I.A. FL.3
AVIO	A.V.I.A. FL.3
AVIP	A.V.I.A. FL.3
AWIG	A.V.I.A. FL.3
AXUM	Caproni Ca 133
AYLA	Gabardini G.4
AYLZ	Gabardini G.7
AZDZ	Piaggio-built Dornier Wal
AZIR	S.A.I. 1
BACC	Macchi M.16
BADG	Macchi M.14

I- BAFV	Macchi M.7	I- LONG	Savoia-Marchetti SM.55
BAHG	Macchi M.17	LUAL	Caproni Ca 310
BALB	Savoia-Marchetti SM.55	LUCE	Savoia-Marchetti SM.83
BALC	Breda SG.4	LUDO	Breda 39S
BARS	Caproni Ca 82C	LUPA	Caproni Ca 310
BAUP	Caproni Ca 73	MAGO	Savoia-Marchetti SM.79P
BBBY	Savoia-Marchetti SM.62P	MANU	Caproni Ca 310
BFBB	Caproni Ca 310	MARR	A.V.I.A. FL.3
BFFI	FIAT G.5bis	MELO	Caproni PS.1
BIAN	Savoia-Marchetti SM.55	MERA	Caproni Borea
BIBI	Breda 33	MFLN	A.V.I.A. FL.3
BIOB	S.A.I.M.A.N. 202	MIGI	Nardi FN.305
BIOL	S.A.I.M.A.N. 202	MONI	Savoia-Marchetti SM.79
BIOZ	S.A.I.M.A.N. 202	MORO	Savoia-Marchetti SM.80
BISE	Savoia-Marchetti SM.55; SM.79	NANN	Savoia-Marchetti SM.55
BONZ	Jona J.6	NAPO	Savoia-Marchetti SM.55
BORG	Savoia-Marchetti SM.55	NEPI	Macchi C.94 anfibio
BRUN	Savoia-Marchetti SM.79	NINO	Savoia-Marchetti SM.79
CALO	Savoia-Marchetti SM.55	NUMA	A.V.I.A. FL.3
CANN	Savoia-Marchetti SM.55	OLTE	Cant 10 ter
CANT	Cant Z.506	OMBO	Breda 42
CIDO	S.A.I.M.A.N. 202	ONEA	Cant 7
COME	Caproni Ca 164	ONIO	Cant 6 ter
CORE	Breda 33	ONNO	Breda 15
DACN	Savoia-Marchetti SM.95	ONTO	Cant 6 ter
DALL	Savoia-Marchetti SM.95	OZIR	S.A.I. 2S
DALO	Savoia-Marchetti SM.95	OZZO	A.V.I.A. FL.3
DEVI	Cant Z.506	PELL	Savoia-Marchetti SM.55
DINB	S.A.I. 7	PIER	S.A.I. 3S
DINI	Savoia-Marchetti SM.55	PISA	Savoia-Marchetti SM.73
DOAV	Bonomi BS.24 Roma	PLIO	Macchi C.100
DOMI	Cant Z.506	PURE	Nardi FN.315
DUDA	Nardi FN.305	QUES	Savoia-Marchetti SM.55
DUNA	Cant Z.506	RANA	Breda 42
EAME	FIAT G.18V	RANI	Savoia-Marchetti SM.55
EION	FIAT G.18V	RATO	Breda 33
ELCE	FIAT G.18V	RECA	Savoia-Marchetti SM.55
ELIS	S.A.I. 2S	REDI	Savoia-Marchetti SM.66
ENEA	FIAT G.18V; G.212 CP	RIZI	A.V.I.A. FL.3
ESTE	FIAT G.212 AL	ROMA	Savoia-Marchetti SM.71; SM.74
ETIS	Ansaldo A.1 Balilla	ROVI	Savoia-Marchetti SM.55
FACE	Meridionali Ro 5	SASS	FIAT G.12L
FANO	Cant Z.506	SAUL	Savoia-Marchetti SM.73
FBAA	Savoia-Marchetti SM.66	SEBM	Breda 32
FEDE	FIAT G.8	SELE	S.A.I. 2S
FERT	O.S.A. 135	SEPI	S.A.I.M.A.N. 202
FIAT	FIAT G.2; BR.20L; etc.	SETI	Savoia-Marchetti SM73
FIDO	Meridionali Ro 5	SIAI	Savoia-Marchetti SM.84, etc.
FOFO	Meridionali Ro 5	SILE	Macchi C.94
FRAN	Caproni PS.1	SIRO	S.A.I. 2S
GAGG	A.V.I.A. FL.3	SITA	Savoia-Marchetti SM.73
GALL	Savoia-Marchetti SM.55	SOLE	S.A.I. 2S
GARD	Breda 39	STAR	Savoia-Marchetti SM.73
GELA	Savoia-Marchetti SM.73	SUBA	Nardi FN.305
GEPI	S.A.I.M.A.N. C.4	TACO	Savoia-Marchetti SM.75
GIOR	Savoia-Marchetti SM.55	TALY	Caproni Bergamaschi PL.3, etc.
GIRO	FIAT AS.1	TAMO	Savoia-Marchetti SM.83
GORO	Cant Z.506	TATI	Savoia-Marchetti SM.80bis
GTAB	Caproni Ca 100	TESO	Savoia-Marchetti SM.75
HOMS	Caproni Ca 100	TEUC	Savoia-Marchetti SM.55
INGL	Savoia-Marchetti SM.55	TICI	Breda 15
INNO	Savoia-Marchetti SM.87	TIMO	Savoia-Marchetti SM.75
LAMA	Cant Z.506B	TITO	Savoia-Marchetti SM.75
LARE	Breda 33	TOCE	Macchi C.94
LATI	Savoia-Marchetti SM.95	TOMI	Nardi FN.305
LATO	Macchi C.94	TUFF	C.A.N.S.A. FC.12
LEON	Savoia-Marchetti SM.55	UEBI	Nardi FN.305
LERO	Cant Z.506A	URBE	Savoia-Marchetti SM.74
LIAN	Savoia-Marchetti SM.75	VECC	Cant Z.508
LIBS	Caproni Ca 309	VEGA	FIAT APR.2
LIPP	Savoia-Marchetti SM.55	VERC	Savoia-Marchetti SM.55
LIRA	Caproni Ca 310	VICE	Breda 39S
LIRI	Macchi C.94	VILD	Nardi FN.315
LITT	Savoia-Marchetti SM.75	VONN	A.V.I.A. FL.3
LOGO	S.A.I. 3	ZAPP	Cant Z.505

APPENDICES

V—Organization of the Regia Aeronautica

During the First World War, the Italian flying forces were known as the Corpo Aeronautico Militare. After that conflict military aviation in Italy dwindled rapidly, but with the advent of Benito Mussolini (himself an enthusiastic amateur aviator) a Commissariat for Aviation was established, and an autonomous air force, the Regia Aeronautica (literally Royal Aviation, or Royal Air Force), was formed in March, 1923. Aviation flourished in Italy during the late 1920's and 1930's, many propaganda and record flights enhancing Italian and (supposedly) Fascist prestige. The one-sided Ethiopian conquest and the successes of the Aviazione Legionaria in Spain added to an awesome display of power.

Because of Italy's limited industrial capacity, however, the Regia Aeronautica never possessed the large numbers of aircraft credited to it by many sources to the Second World War. Claims as high as 8530 aircraft had been made in 1939, but in actual fact Regia Aeronautica strength in Metropolitan Italy on June 10, 1940, the date of the Italian entry into the war, was only 3345 machines (1332 bombers, 1160 fighters and fighter-bombers, 497 reconnaissance and observation aircraft, and 49 military transports), plus 38 communications transports and about 2450 training aircraft. Equipment in A.O.I. (Africa Orientale Italiana) totalled about 325 aircraft, mostly obsolete Ca 111, Ca 133, and SM.81 bombers, CR.32 fighters, and Ro 37 reconnaissance biplanes.

Italy was divided into three Squadre Aeree, with headquarters at Milan, Rome, and Palermo. A fourth unit was the 4a Zona Territoriale at Bari. Italian territories were served by the Aeronautiche delle Sardegna (Sardinia), Albania, Libia (Libya), and Egeo (Aegean Islands). The Squadra Aerea comprised two or three Divisioni (Divisions) or Brigate (Brigades), usually two of bombers and one of fighters. The Divisione usually comprised three Stormi (Groups). Organization of the smaller units was as follows:

Stormo = 2 Gruppi (Wings)
Gruppo = 2—3 Squadriglie (Squadrons)
Squadriglia = 3 Sezioni (Flights)
Sezione = 3 aircraft.

The Italian Army and Navy were further served by the Aviazione per il Regio Esercito and the Aviazione per la Regia Marina, respectively.

On June 10, 1940, operational strength of the Regia Aeronautica was 32 Stormi, plus an additional 13 Gruppi, 60 Squadriglie, and 4 Sezioni. The Italian aircraft industry was never able to keep up with wartime attrition; by September, 1943, only 1306 aircraft remained, little more than one-third of these in serviceable condition. The aircraft and crews which joined the Allied cause in the south were formed into the Co-Belligerent Air Force. In addition to 203 Italian aircraft, this force employed a number of Allied types. The remainder of the Regia Aeronautica came under the control of the German-dominated Republica Sociale Italiana, as the Aviazione della RSI. After the war, the new Italian Air Force was known as the Aeronautica Militare Italiana.

VI—Color Schemes, Camouflage, and Markings

A description of all the color schemes and markings employed on Italian aircraft is naturally impossible within reasonable limits, and a thorough understanding of this aspect of Italian aviation can be gained only through a close study of many individual aircraft depicted in photographs and drawings in this book and other sources. However, an explanation of the general practices will be helpful to the aviation student and modeller.

Civil Aircraft —

All Italian civil aircraft other than prototypes and export machines bore the registration letters mentioned in Appendix IV above. These letters were applied to both sides of the fuselage and to the upper lower surfaces of the wings. For example, the Macchi C.94 flying boat I-LATO carried the letters I-L on the upper port and lower starboard wing surfaces, and ATO on the upper starboard and lower port surfaces, with the complete registration on the rear fuselage and the single national letter I on the rudder. Lettering was usually black over natural metal or doped aluminum, white, or cream finishes. As most Italian aircraft were wood or fabric-covered, natural metal surfaces were limited to engine cowlings, wheel pants, etc. On dark or brilliantly colored aircraft the registration letters were white or outlined in white; rudders were also white to contrast with the black letter I. Competing rally aircraft carried numbers (or letter-number combinations) within contrasting or outlined squares on the wings and fuselage. On postwar civil aircraft the national letter was usually omitted from the rudder, although the entire registration often appeared across the fin and rudder in smaller letters.

The small national insigne, the fasces (a Roman symbol consisting of a bundle of rods and an axe with the blade projecting), occasionally appeared on the sides of civil machines, as did the green, white, and red tail stripes usually associated with the Regia Aeronautica. It should be emphasized that many "civil" aircraft were in fact thinly-disguised government-owned military or V.I.P. machines. The tail stripes often extended over the horizontal as well as vertical tail surfaces. Occasionally in lieu of the stripes, the Italian flag was painted on the fin, always with the hoist (green) toward the front. On transports the name of the operating airline was painted in small Roman letters on the sides of the fuselage, usually above the windows. Variations among individual aircraft preclude a more exact verbal description; the photographs and drawings show the color schemes and disposition of markings.

Military Aircraft —

Three types of national insignia were applied to Regia Aeronautica machines prior to 1939. These consisted of the large fasces insigne applied to the upper and lower surfaces of the wings, the smaller, more detailed fuselage device, and the vertical green, white, and red tail stripes. The wing insigne was composed of three stylized black fasces (the blades always facing toward the wing tips) on a white disc outlined in black. The insigne was positioned at approximately 70 to 80 per cent of the distance from the center of the aeroplane to the wing tip; the diameter of the disc was 60 per cent of the chord at that point, never overlapping the aileron. Wing insignia were not applied to all Regia Aeronautica aircraft during the pre-1939 period.

The fuselage device (also applied to most civil aircraft) consisted of a much smaller blue or grey disc with a single gold or brown fasces symbol, usually painted in some detail. The silver axe blade always faced toward the front. Sometimes a capital A and Roman numeral were lettered on the background opposite the blade; the A stood for Anno (year) and the numeral indicated the current year of the Mussolini government, starting with 1923. For example, $\dfrac{A}{XIII}$ denoted the thirteenth year of Italian Fascism, or 1935. The size, style, and placement of the fasces insigne varied considerably; sometimes no background disc was used, sometimes the disc was a gradation of light to dark grey, sometimes it was outlined in black, sometimes white, etc. Just as no strict rules can be made regarding the fuselage insigne, the tail stripes also varied in width and placement, covering the rudder or the entire fin and rudder. The usual practice was to paint the forward green stripe (corresponding to the hoist of the national flag) just ahead of the rudder post, with the white and red stripes on the rudder proper. The arms of Savoy, painted on the white center band, varied in style.

Few military machines during this period were camouflaged, "natural" aluminum or white finishes being applied to most aircraft. For East African and maritime use, in fact, an "anti-camouflage" was adopted to make the aircraft instantly visible against vast expanses of desert or sea. This consisted of radiating bands of red on the upper surfaces of the wings. The principle was the same as that used today in day-glo paint schemes and brightly colored parachutes. In the late 1930's a number of aircraft began to appear with an experimental wavy dual-pattern camouflage of sand and dark olive green over the upper surfaces; the lower surfaces were left "natural" aluminum or painted light grey or sky blue. This was the scheme used predominantly in Spain. Squadriglia and individual numbers were often applied to the sides of the fuselage. For example, a camouflaged SM.81, the fourth machine of the 211a Squadriglia, carried the numerals 211-4; 211-6 was an uncamouflaged SM.81 of the same Squadriglia.

Just before Italy's entry into the war the markings and camouflage were modified. The wing and fuselage fasces insignia remained essentially unchanged, although the underwing device was often reversed (i.e. white fasces on a black disc outlined in white) to contrast with the pale lower surfaces. On the upper surfaces the white disc was often omitted, allowing the camouflage to show within the black outer ring. A large white tail cross (usually painted on the rudder only) replaced the green, white, and red vertical stripes, with the crest of Savoy placed at or just above the intersection of the horizontal and vertical bands. When a light overall color scheme (aluminum or white) was used, a black background distinguished the white rudder cross. A white recognition band was usually painted around the rear portion of the fuselage. The width of this band was approximately 6 to 7 per cent of the fuselage length, or about 2 ft. on fighters and 4 ft. on larger aircraft, such as bombers or transports. When used, Squadriglia and individual numbers usually overlapped a part of the band.

The wavy dual-pattern camouflage gave way to a mottled sand and dark olive green scheme with light grey (or unpainted aluminum) lower surfaces, or alternatively, overall dark olive green upper surfaces with sky blue below. The mottled pattern was left more or less to the discretion of the sprayer, resulting in numerous subtle variations reflecting the operational needs of various theatres. Some schemes consisted of spots or patches, others of thin, wavy lines or even rings. Desert camouflage employed a sand background with olive green patches sprayed over, while in more densely vegetated theatres this was reversed, with green the background color. Over dry and barren country a sand and terracotta combination was used. Spinners and engine cowlings were often painted in white or distinctive colors; in addition, some units employed their own identifying insignia. Some of these markings are shown in the photographs and drawings.

In 1943, aircraft of the Co-Belligerent Air Force re-adopted the World War I wing and fuselage roundels, consisting of a red outer ring, white inner ring, and green center, in place of the Fascist insignia. The fuselage roundel was applied in the normal Allied position, rather than over the fasces device, which was painted out. The roundels were officially reinstated by the postwar Aeronautica Militare. Aircraft of the Aviazione della RSI adopted a revised Fascist device for the wings, consisting of two fasces symbols, one inverted, within a square. This was painted in white on the upper surfaces and in black below. Small Italian tricolors were painted on the sides of the fuselage and on the fin. German markings (wing and fuselage crosses and tail swastika) were applied to some Italian aircraft after September, 1943, whether they were experimental machines or aircraft actually in use with the Luftwaffe.

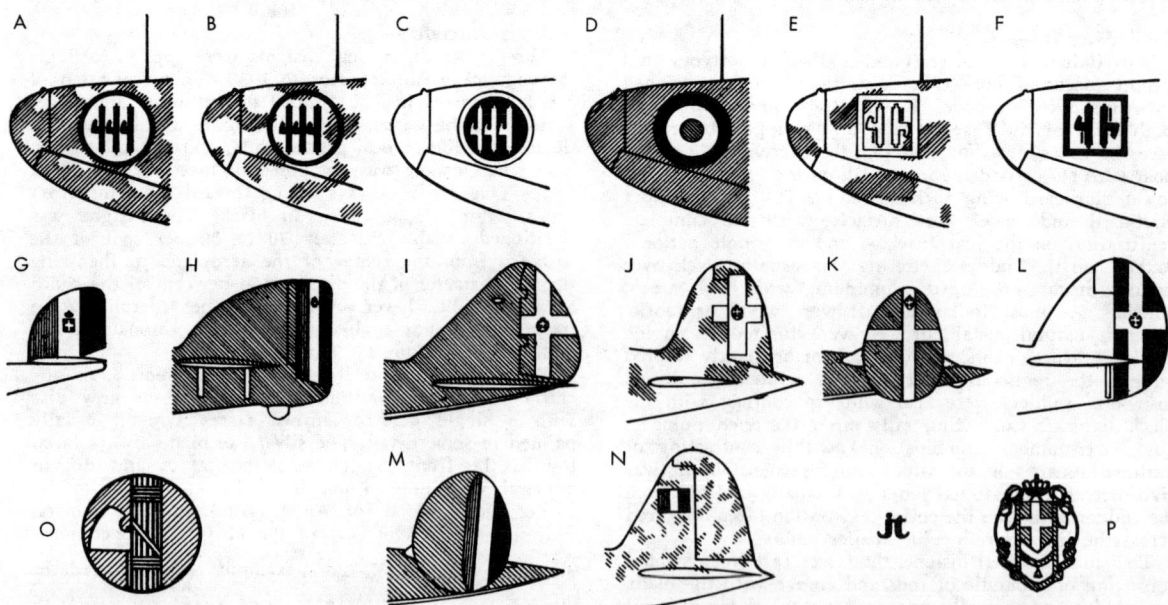

A - wing insigne: black fasces on white disc encircled in black. B - variation with white area omitted. C - underwing variation, reversed to contrast with lighter background. D - Co-Belligerent roundel (also applied to fuselage sides): red outer ring, white inner ring, green center. E & F - RSI wing device (reversed underwing). G & H - variations of pre-war tail stripes: green, white and red bands, green always forward (S.64, SM.79). I, J, K, & L - variations of wartime white tail cross (Re2005, MC.200, FC.20bis, Ro 43). M - tail stripes readopted on a few Co-Belligerent aircraft: crest of Savoy omitted (Z.1007bis). N - RSI tail flag (G.55). O - fuselage fasces device. P - crest of Savoy: note variation in placement on all forms of tail insignia. Note: drawings not to constant scale.

APPENDICES

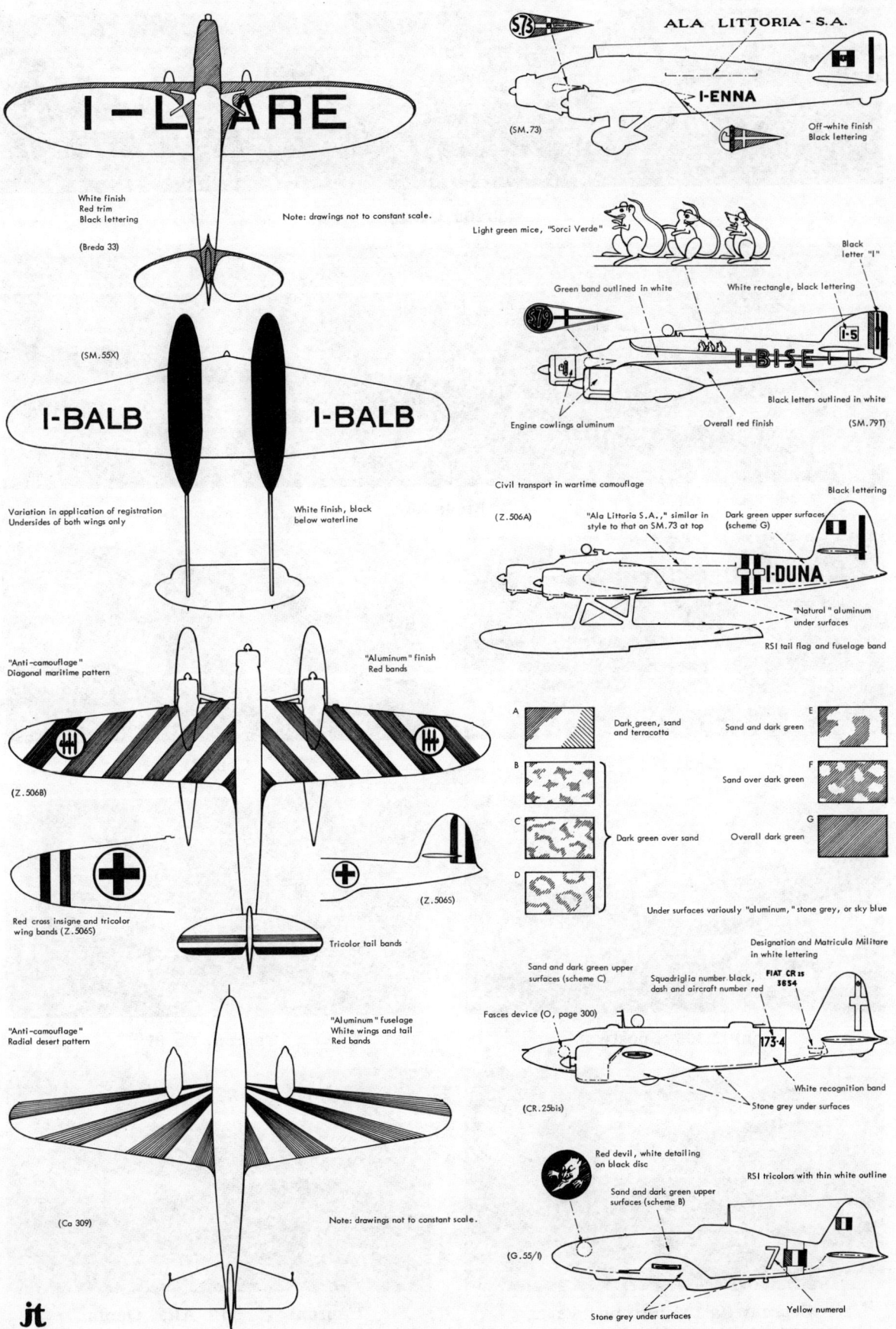

ITALIAN CIVIL AND MILITARY AIRCRAFT

Breda CC.20

Breda 46

Cant 22

Cant 23

Cant Z.506 S postwar

Caproni Ca 87

Caproni Ca 100 Idro postwar

Caproni Ca 113 Alta Quota

APPENDICES

Caproni Ca 123 prototype

Caproni Ca 123

Caproni Bergamaschi Ca 310 idro

C.M.A.S.A. G.8 postwar

FIAT G.212

Romeo Ro 10

Romeo Ro 26

Piaggio P.2

Piaggio P.3

Piaggio P.6

BIBLIOGRAPHY

Books:

Aerosphere (New York: Aerosphere, Inc., 1939-1943)

Aircraft Identification — Italian Fighters Bombers and Seaplanes (London: Temple Press Ltd., 1941)

Air News Yearbook (New York: Duell, Sloan & Pearce, 1943, 1944)

American Heritage History of Flight (New York: American Heritage Publishing Co., Inc., 1962)

Bignozzi, G., and Catalanotto, B., **Storia degli Aerei d'Italia dal 1911 al 1961** (Roma: Editrice Cielo, 1962)

Cooke, David C., **War Planes of the Axis** (New York: Robert M. McBride and Company, 1942)

Fifty Years of Japanese Aviation (Tokyo: Kantosha Co., Ltd., 1961)

Green, William, **Famous Bombers of the Second World War** (London: Macdonald, 1959)

—— **Famous Fighters of the Second World War, Second Series** (London, Macdonald, 1962)

—— **War Planes of the Second World War — Fighters Volume Two** (London: Macdonald, 1961)

—— **War Planes of the Second World War — Flying Boats Volume Five** (London: Macdonald, 1962)

—— **War Planes of the Second World War — Floatplanes Volume Six** (London: Macdonald, 1962)

Green, William, and Cross, Roy, **The Jet Aircraft of the World** (New York: Hanover House, 1955)

Green, William, and Fricker, John, **The Air Forces of the World** (New York: Hanover House, 1958)

Jane's All the World's Aircraft (New York: The MacMillan Company, and London: Sampson Low, Marston & Co., Ltd., 1925-1948)

Mattioli, Guido, **Mussolini Aviatore** (Roma: L'Aviazione, 1935)

Modern Italian Aircraft (Roma: Consorzio Italiano Esportazioni Aeronautiche, 1940)

Munson, Kenneth G., **Enemy Aircraft (German and Italian) of World War II** (London: Ian Allan Ltd., 1960)

Santoro, Giuseppe, **L'Aeronautica Italiana nella Seconda Guerra Mondiale** (Milano: Edizioni Esse, Two Volumes, 1957)

Taylor, John W. R., **A Picture History of Flight** (New York: Pitman Publishing Corporation, 1956)

Die Wichtigsten Italienischen Kriegsflugzeuge (Luftwaffe, 8 Anlagen, 1940)

Periodicals:

Aero Modeller *
The Aeroplane Spotter
Air Pictorial
Air Progress
Ala d'Italia
Alata
Ali di Guerra
European Aviation News **

Interconair — Aviazione e Marina
Lightplane Review
Model Airplane News
The National Geographic Magazine ***
Rassegna di Modellismo ****
Rivista Aeronautica
Royal Air Force Flying Review

* Italian Schneider Trophy Racers, by Franco Bugada
** Italians in Sweden, by Olov Sundgren
*** By Seaplane to Six Continents, by Comm. Francesco de Pinedo
**** Macchi M.52R, by Silvio Taberna